12A

# Evaluating the Welfare State

*Social and Political Perspectives*

# Evaluating the Welfare State

## Social and Political Perspectives

Edited by

## SHIMON E. SPIRO

School of Social Work and
Department of Sociology and Anthropology
Tel Aviv University
Ramat Aviv, Tel Aviv, Israel

## EPHRAIM YUCHTMAN-YAAR

Department of Sociology and Anthropology
Tel Aviv University
Ramat Aviv, Tel Aviv, Israel

1983

### ACADEMIC PRESS

*A Subsidiary of Harcourt Brace Jovanovich, Publishers*
New York London
Paris San Diego San Francisco São Paulo Sydney Tokyo Toronto

ACADEMIC PRESS, INC.
111 Fifth Avenue, New York, New York 10003

*United Kingdom Edition published by*
ACADEMIC PRESS, INC. (LONDON) LTD.
24/28 Oval Road, London NW1 7DX

Library of Congress Cataloging in Publication Data

Main entry under title:

Evaluating the welfare state.

"Outgrowth of an international and interdisciplinary
conference on policy evaluation held at Tel Aviv University
in December 1980, under the auspices of the Pinhas Sapir
Center for Development"–Pref.
  1. Welfare state–Congresses.  2. Social policy–Congresses
I. Spiro, Shimon E.  II. Yuchtman-Yaar, Ephraim.
III. Merkaz le-fituaḥ 'al-shem P. Sapir.
HN28.E9    1982      361.6'5      82-22596
ISBN 0-12-657980-6

PRINTED IN THE UNITED STATES OF AMERICA

83 84 85 86      9 8 7 6 5 4 3 2 1

# Contents

# 2

## Class Politics and the Western Welfare State

27

MICHAEL SHALEV

# 3

## Political Legitimacy and Consensus:
## Missing Variables in the Assessment of Social Policy

51

HAROLD L. WILENSKY

# 4

## Social Policy Evaluation
## and the Psychology of Stagnation

75

BURKHARD STRÜMPEL

# 5

## Expectancies, Entitlements, and Subjective Welfare

89

EPHRAIM YUCHTMAN-YAAR

# II
## Boundaries of the Welfare State and the Foci of Policy Evaluation

# 6
## The Growing Complexity of Economic Claims in Welfare Societies — 111
LEE RAINWATER AND MARTIN REIN

# 7
## Systematic Confusions in the Evaluation of Implementing Decisions — 131
MURRAY EDELMAN

# 8
## The Welfare State: Issues of Rationing and Allocation of Resources — 149
ABRAHAM DORON

# 9

Charting the Iceberg:
Visible and Invisible Aspects of Government                    161
YAIR AHARONI

# III

Evaluation Research: Concepts and Issues

# 10

The Scope of Evaluation Activities in the United States        179
PETER H. ROSSI AND RICHARD A. BERK

# 11

Equity Criteria for the Evaluation of
Social Welfare Programs: Mothers' Summer Recreation           205
SHIMON E. SPIRO AND RUTH LIRON

# 12
## Community Mental Health in Israel: An Interim Policy Assessment 217
URI AVIRAM

# 13
## Reward Structures and the Organizational Design of Institutions for the Elderly 233
SEYMOUR SPILERMAN AND EUGENE LITWAK

# 14
## Evaluating Slack in Public Programs by the Experience Curves Method 255
GIDEON DORON AND URI ON

# IV
## Policy Evaluation in Selected Fields

# V
## Debate, Choices, and
## the Impact of Evaluation

# 21
## Hardness of Choice                                        387
ERIK COHEN

# 22
## The Political Culture of Social Welfare Policy           397
WILLIAM A. GAMSON AND KATHRYN E. LASCH

# Contributors

*Numbers in parentheses indicate the pages on which the authors' contributions begin.*

**Yair Aharoni** (161), Faculty of Management, The Leon Recanati School of Business Administration, Ramat Aviv, Israel 69978

**Uri Aviram** (217), School of Social Work, Tel Aviv University, Ramat Aviv, Tel Aviv, Israel 69978

**Richard A. Berk** (179), Department of Sociology, University of California, Santa Barbara, Santa Barbara, California 93106

**Erik Cohen** (387), Department of Sociology and Social Anthropology, The Hebrew University of Jerusalem, Jerusalem, Israel 91905

**James S. Coleman** (273), Department of Sociology, University of Chicago, Chicago, Illinois 60637

**Abraham Doron** (149), Paul Baerwald School of Social Work, The Hebrew University of Jerusalem, Mt. Scopus, Jerusalem, Israel 91905

**Gideon Doron** (255), Department of Political Science, Tel Aviv University, Ramat Aviv, Tel Aviv, Israel 69978

**Murray Edelman** (131), Department of Political Science, University of Wisconsin–Madison, Madison, Wisconsin 53706

**William A. Gamson**[1] (397), Department of Sociology, University of Michigan, Ann Arbor, Michigan 48109

**Anthony King** (7), Department of Government, University of Essex, Wivenhoe Park, Colchester, Essex CO4 3SQ, England

[1]PRESENT ADDRESS: Department of Sociology, Boston College, Chestnut Hill, Massachusetts 02167.

**Stephen Kulis** (337), School of Social Work, Columbia University, New York, New York 10027

**Kathryn E. Lasch** (397), Department of Sociology, University of Michigan, Ann Arbor, Michigan 48109

**Gaea Leinhardt** (295), School of Urban and Public Affairs, Carnegie-Mellon University, Pittsburgh, Pennsylvania 15213

**Samuel Leinhardt** (295), School of Urban and Public Affairs, Carnegie-Mellon University, Pittsburgh, Pennsylvania 15213

**Ruth Liron** (205), School of Social Work, Haifa University, Haifa, Israel

**Eugene Litwak** (233, 337), Department of Sociology and Social Work, Columbia University, New York, New York 10027

**Stanley Masters**[1] (319), Institute for Research on Poverty, University of Wisconsin–Madison, Madison, Wisconsin 53706

**Uri On** (255). Department of Political Science, Tel Aviv University, Ramat Aviv, Tel Aviv, Israel 69978

**Irving Piliavin** (319), School of Social Work, University of Wisconsin–Madison, Wisconsin 53706

**Lee Rainwater** (111), Department of Sociology, Harvard University, Cambridge, Massachusetts 02138

**Martin Rein** (111), Department of Sociology, Harvard University, Cambridge, Massachusetts 02138

**Peter H. Rossi** (179), Department of Sociology, University of Massachusetts, Amherst, Massachusetts 01003

**Michael Shalev**[2] (27), Department of Labor Studies, Tel Aviv University, Ramat Aviv, Tel Aviv, Israel 69978

**Seymour Spilerman** (233), Department of Sociology, Columbia University, New York, New York 10027

**Shimon E. Spiro** (205), School of Social Work, Tel Aviv University, Ramat Aviv, Tel Aviv, Israel 69978

**Burkhard Strümpel** (75), Department of Economics, Free University of Berlin, Berlin, West Germany

**Daniel Tarschys** (375), Institute for Political Science, University of Stockholm, Stockholm, Sweden

**Carol H. Weiss** (361), Graduate School of Education, Harvard University, Cambridge, Massachusetts 02138

**Harold L. Wilensky** (51), Department of Political Science, University of California, Berkeley, Berkeley, California 94720

**Ephraim Yuchtman-Yaar** (89), Department of Sociology and Anthropology, Tel Aviv University, Ramat Aviv, Tel Aviv, Israel 69978

[1]PRESENT ADDRESS: Department of Economics, State University of New York at Binghamton, Binghamton, New York 13901.

[2]PRESENT ADDRESS: Departments of Sociology and Political Science, The Hebrew University of Jerusalem, Jerusalem, Israel 91905.

# Preface

This volume, together with its companion *Social Policy Evaluation: An Economic Perspective* (edited by Elhanan Helpman, Assaf Razin, and Efraim Sadka) is the outgrowth of an international and interdisciplinary conference on policy evaluation held at Tel Aviv University in December 1980, under the auspices of the Pinhas Sapir Center for Development. The conference brought together scholars from the fields of economics, sociology, political science, social work, and administration. The papers presented at this conference approached the welfare state and social policy evaluation from a number of different theoretical and methodological perspectives. A selection of these papers has been included in this volume.

The Sapir Center, which hosted the conference, also supported the preparation of this book. Professor Asher Arian, who was dean of the Faculty of Social Sciences at the time of the conference, played a major role in the planning of the program and the selection of the papers. Later he served, along with Professor Anthony King of the University of Essex and Professor Peter H. Rossi of the University of Massachusetts, on an editorial advisory panel.

This volume would not have materialized were it not for the insight, initiative, and persistence of Ruth Bokstein, who acted as editorial assistant. Connie Wilsack and Tamar Berkowitz, who alternated as copy editors, very ably dealt with the problems arising from the varying styles and traditions of the contributors.

Our thanks are given to all those mentioned.

# Introduction

In the decades following World War II, the welfare state as a system of government "organized to ensure the well-being of citizens and to use their resource to this end [Bruce 1961, p. 293]" has reached a state of relative maturity. All western industrialized democracies have devised policies of income security and are providing their citizens with free or subsidized services in diverse areas such as education, health, housing, counseling, employment, and recreation. The proportion of national products devoted to these programs has increased steadily over the last three decades.

The growth of the welfare state is not seen by all as a cause for celebration. On the contrary, throughout the West there have been many expressions of disenchantment with the idea that the state could (or should) assure the well-being of citizens through taxing and spending. Opposition to the welfare state grew more vocal in the 1970s, when most industrial countries encountered economic stagnation, inflation, and unemployment. Under adverse economic conditions, more and more questions were raised concerning the ability of western economies to afford the ever-increasing burden of social services. The cost of welfare seemed to outrun available resources. Explanations offered ranged from the rising costs of provisions due to technological progress (especially in the health field), through the "explosion of expectations," to the presumed adverse impact of welfare provisions on the work ethic.

Political controversy, which has accompanied the welfare state from the beginning, has intensified in the last two decades. This has led to a growing demand for accountability and evaluation. Policymakers and the public, increasingly inclined to raise questions regarding the feasibility and efficiency of

EVALUATING THE WELFARE STATE:
SOCIAL AND POLITICAL PERSPECTIVES

policies and programs, were also increasingly willing to allocate resources to program evaluation. This was especially true in the United States in the 1960s and 1970s, where practically all major new programs were either preceded by controlled experimentation or accompanied by ongoing evaluation research, often quite extensive and ambitious. The generous allocation of resources led to the growth of evaluation research as an interdisciplinary field of practice. The dramatic development of this field since the mid-1960s is reflected in an avalanche of texts, readers, and monographs, in the appearance of journals devoted exclusively to evaluation, and in the proliferation of training programs, conferences, and associations.

The institutionalization of the field has been accompanied by real progress in the methodology of evaluation. A comparison of texts published in the 1960s (Suchman 1967) or early 1970s (Weiss 1972) with those published toward the end of the decade (Rossi, Freeman, and Wright 1979) shows evidence of the growing ability of the field to deal with issues of measurement and causality, and to a growing awareness of the organizational and political context of evaluation. The direction of these developments was influenced by the disciplinary origins of evaluation research. Although a large proportion of those practicing evaluation were trained in the social sciences, the intellectual and methodological roots of this field can be traced to public health, medicine, agricultural science, education, and experimental psychology. More recent influences include economics and administrative science. The links to disciplines dealing with society per se, such as history and political science, have been much weaker. This may explain a tendency to focus on the implementation and outcome of specific programs rather than on the overall economic and political consequences of social policies. Thus we find only weak links between the field of evaluation, as reflected in its current literature, and the field of social policy (Gil 1976), which has accompanied the welfare state from the beginning.

In addition to a tendency to focus on the trees rather than the forest, evaluation researchers have been faulted for the atheoretical bent of their work (Chen and Rossi 1981). While putting the methodology of the behavioral sciences to good use, evaluation research seems to be only weakly grounded in theories of social organization, social change, and individual behavior. Are these limitations of evaluation research inevitable given the political structure of the welfare state and the rigid boundaries between the behavioral sciences? We shall not attempt to address this issue directly, but it has guided the selection of chapters for this volume. An attempt has been made to relate the current concerns of evaluation research to an assessment of historical trends and social processes, and to the discussion of basic conceptual issues.

The book is divided into five parts. The first is devoted to the political antecedents and consequences of the welfare state and to the social and psychological processes that affect the development of social policies and reactions to them. This is followed in Part II with an analysis of the discontinuity between policies that are the subject of public debate and the programs that affect the well-being of populations and the distribution of resources. The chapters included in Parts III and IV represent current developments in the practice of evaluation and explore the frontiers of this field. Part V focuses on the relationship of evaluation to policymaking. This involves examinations of the culture of political debates, the nature of choices facing policymakers, and the impact of research on policy.

The chapters included in this volume, written from a variety of theoretical and methodological perspective, all reflect, to a greater or lesser extent, the concerns of the late 1970s. Time alone will tell whether, at this point in history, the welfare state had reached a stage of consolidation, whether we witnessed the beginning of retreat, or whether these years, with their political and economic turmoil, were just a wrinkle in the curve of progress toward greater equality and welfare.

# References

Bruce, Maurice. 1961. *The coming of the welfare state.* London: B. T. Batsford.

Chen, H. T., and Rossi, Peter H. 1981. The multi-goal theory-driven approach to evaluation. *Social Forces* 59: 106–122.

Gil, David G. 1979. *Unravelling social policy.* Cambridge, Mass.: Shenkman.

Rossi, Peter H., Freeman, Howard H., and Wright, Sonia R. 1979. *Evaluation research: A systematic approach.* Beverly Hills, Ca.: Sage Publications.

Suchman, Edward A. 1967. *Evaluative research: Principles and practice in social service and public action.* New York: Russell Sage.

Weiss, Carol H. 1972. *Evaluative research: Methods of assessing effectiveness.* Englewood Cliffs, N.J.: Prentice Hall.

# I

# The Welfare State:
# Causes and Consequences

*The welfare state can be studied and evaluated from a number of different perspectives. From a Marxist orientation of class-conflict, Shalev sees the welfare state as "defining normative criteria of distribution in opposition to property rights and market dictates." Hence, he expects much of the observable variation in welfare state emergence and growth to be accounted for by the political strength of the "left," that is, social democratic labor movements. Shalev finds support for this hypothesis in his secondary analysis of a number of recent studies. King, from a different perspective, sees the welfare state as essentially conservative in intentions and outcomes. He argues that, contrary to expectations of critics and supporters, the welfare state helped maintain political stability and individual freedoms.*

*How then can one explain a certain malaise that seems to permeate the public in most Western industrialized democracies and that is attributed, at least partly, to disenchantment with the welfare state? The most common explanation is that of rising expectations, resulting in an overload of demands that, in the long run, inevitably leads to economic and political crises. Struempel endeavors to unravel the results of public opinion polls to show how sentiments are related to economic conditions and to issues of growth, equity, and quality of life. Yuchtman-Yaar subjects the concept of rising expectations to conceptual and empirical tests. He shows that this concept has two distinct components—expectancies and entitlements, of which only the second is related to feelings of deprivation. Both chapters suggest that at times of relative economic stagnation, issues of equity and justice may deserve greater, not lesser, attention.*

*Wilensky sees the "crisis of the welfare state" as related to the elementary structure of the political system. The crisis is most severe in those societies, such as the United States and the United Kingdom, in which the main interest groups (i.e., labor, capital, government) are not organized for "peak bargaining." In these societies, policymaking tends to be fragmented and conflictual, and the welfare state becomes an object of political controversy. Within this conflictual context, evaluation research may contribute to a general sense of malaise rather than to the advancement of social policy.*

# 1

# The Political Consequences
# of the Welfare State

## ANTHONY KING

In early 1981, the modern welfare state celebrated its centenary. It was on February 15, 1881, that Kaiser Wilhelm I of Germany proposed in a message to the Reichstag that social insurance be used to protect German workers against losses of income resulting from industrial accidents and old age. Later in the year, in November 1881, health insurance was added to the list of proposed reforms, and by 1889 the entire structure of Bismarckian social insurance had been established. The welfare state subsequently came to Britain between 1908 and 1911, to the United States in the mid-1930s, and to France shortly after World War II. Today, welfare provision in one way or another absorbs between one-fifth and one-third of the gross domestic products of most advanced industrial nations.

On the occasion of its hundredth anniversary, however, the institutions and practices of the welfare state are under widespread attack. They are blamed for inflation; they are associated with sprawling state bureaucracies and alleged bureaucratic rigidity; they are said to have created a vast problem of human dependency in all industrial nations. In a famous article in *The Public Interest*, Peter Drucker (1969) wrote about "the sickness of government." Among the symptoms of this sickness, he maintained, none was more apparent than "the fiasco of the welfare state."

> The welfare state turns out at best to be just another big insurance company, as exciting, as creative, and as inspiring as insurance companies tend to be .... The best we get from government in the welfare state is competent mediocrity. More often we do not get even that .... And the more we expand the welfare state, the less capable even of routine mediocrity does it seem to become [p.7].

EVALUATING THE WELFARE STATE:
SOCIAL AND POLITICAL PERSPECTIVES

Such criticisms have since been echoed not just in journals like *The Public Interest* and *Encounter* but in the campaigns of conservative politicians on both sides of the Atlantic (see also Flora, 1981).

It would be inappropriate for a mere political scientist to try to assess the economic, social, and psychological consequences of the welfare state. Instead this chapter concentrates on the welfare state's specifically political consequences. How is the political order of advanced industrial societies different from what it would have been had the welfare state not been invented by Bismarck and Kaiser Wilhelm a century ago? But before trying to answer this question, we need to ask and answer another question: What *is* "the welfare state"? As will emerge, the term has been used very loosely in much recent discussion.

## What Is "The Welfare State"?

In the 100 years since 1881, the activities of the state in industrial societies have tended to expand in five separate directions. It is important to take note of all five; it is also important to note that they are indeed separate.

In the first place, in most industrial countries the size of the "public sector" has expanded. That is to say, whereas 100 years ago most, though not all, productive economic activity was in the hands of privately owned firms, today a large portion is in the hands of the state. The British public sector, to take an extreme case, scarcely existed at the end of the nineteenth century; by 1980 it included coal, steel, the railways, gas and electricity supply, shipbuilding, aerospace, the country's largest airline and its second largest car manufacturer, and much more. The public sector has grown less rapidly in most other countries, but even in the United States it includes parts of the electricity supply industry, some of the railways, and a wide range of municipally provided services such as public transport. Government ownership of this kind was what most people had in mind a generation ago when they spoke of "socialism."

Second, in most industrial countries the state has also become involved in "macroeconomic management." That is to say, governments use their taxing and spending powers and their control over the money supply to try to pursue objectives that typically include full employment, relatively stable prices, and a surplus (or at least not too large a deficit) on the balance of payments. The state's involvement in macroeconomic management is usually associated with Keynesian economic doctrines; but a monetarist or, indeed, a socialist planner is engaged in the same kinds of activities, even though the means are different.

Third, in most countries the state has recently been more concerned than in the past with supervising and controlling many of the details of economic activity. That is to say, the state has become deeply involved in the business of "regulation." Thus, in the United States, for example, there exists a huge number of federal agencies concerned with regulating everything from railway rates, through water pollution, to the materials used in the manufacture of children's kites. These agencies include the Interstate Commerce Commission, the Federal Trade Commission, the Food and Drug Administration, the Occupational Health and Safety Administration, the Consumer Product Safety Commission, the Environmental Protection Agency, and so on. The regulations in question are intended to serve a wide variety of purposes—product safety, price fixing, maintenance of adequate public services, protection of the rights of minorities, protection of the environment, and the like—but all take the form of instructions issued by one state agency either to other state agencies or to private individuals and firms. Such detailed regulation of economic activity is reminiscent of the mercantilism of the seventeenth and eighteenth centuries.

Fourth, governments in industrial countries in modern times have been engaged in what can probably best be labeled "social engineering." That is to say, they have used the apparatus of the state to try to bring about desired changes in the structure of society: the elimination of poverty, racism, sexism, and crime, the creation of more socially just societies, more egalitarian societies, and so forth. Regulations of the kind just described have been used for these purposes; but so have redistributive taxes, expanded educational systems, laws against racial and sex discrimination, and changes in the penal system, to name but a few. *Brown* vs. *Board of Education* was an essay in social engineering, as was the setting up of the Equal Opportunities Commission in Britain. Social engineering is most commonly practiced in the United States and Anglo-Saxon countries; there is a good deal less of it in countries like Italy, Spain, and Portugal.

Finally, since the time of Bismarck, the state in almost every country has emerged as the guarantor of certain minimum standards of material well-being. That is to say, the state has become involved in the business of "welfare provision." Governments insure their populations against a variety of hazards: sickness, accidents, unemployment, old age. They may be the major suppliers of health care, as in the case of Britain's National Health Service. They intervene actively in the housing market. They increasingly assume pastoral functions, with the social worker replacing the priest. They are in most countries the major providers of education.[1]

It is important to understand that, although almost all modern states are active in all five of these fields, the fields themselves are best thought of as being separate. To be sure, in practice they frequently overlap; special educational facilities for the disadvantaged may serve both social-engineering and welfare

[1] It is not entirely clear where education should be slotted in. On the one hand, its welfare-provision aspect is fairly obvious; on the other, it has very often been used for purposes of social engineering —for instance, in the United States, where education was seen as one of the major instruments for socializing immigrants from diverse backgrounds into the national culture. If this chapter were concerned with providing a taxonomy of government activity, there might be something to be said for making education a sixth category.

purposes, just as an expansion of the public sector may be intended to improve the state's capacity for macroeconomic management. It is probably also the case that the expansion of state activity in any one field is likely, as a matter of contingent fact and in the long run, to lead to an expansion of state activity in other fields; once a government is committed to paying unemployment insurance, it is likely to find itself sooner or later committed to trying to maintain full employment, the provision of welfare services thus leading to a concern with overall economic management.

Nevertheless, there are two good reasons for wanting to distinguish quite sharply among the five fields. The first is that they are separate logically: one can easily think of a government's being involved in any one of the fields without its being involved in any—let alone all—of the others. Social insurance could coexist with an almost entirely private-enterprise economy, that is, with a tiny public sector; macroeconomic management could be undertaken in the absence of extensive detailed economic regulation; providers of welfare might not be at all concerned with social engineering, for example, with bringing about racial or sexual equality; and so on. The fact that governments are frequently active in more than one of these fields should not lead the observer to confuse them. States active in the field of welfare provision are usually also active in building extensive networks of public highways; but most people find it useful to keep welfare provision and highway construction separate in their minds.

The second reason for wanting to distinguish among the five fields is, if anything, even more important. Not only are the five fields separate logically; they can easily be distinguished empirically. It is simply not the case that states active in one or more of the fields are invariably active in any or all of the others. The passage of the Social Security Act in the United States in 1935 preceded by at least a generation any governmental commitment to Keynesian economic management; in France, by contrast, state welfare provision tended to lag behind governmental intervention in the economy; in Britain, again by contrast, the introduction of old-age pensions and various forms of social insurance took place before World War I, but it was not until after World War II that a major expansion of the public sector took place; and it was likewise not until after 1945 that British government became involved in what is here being called social engineering. Readers can provide many other examples, but one further illustration may be in order. Table 1.1 sets out the proportions of gross domestic product that nine Western European countries devoted to governmental expenditure on health and social security in the mid-1970s, together with a somewhat rougher indication of the size of their public sectors (in the sense of major industries owned and operated by the state). As can be seen, the rank order of countries in terms of welfare expenditure bears no relationship to the rank order in terms of the size of their public sector. Old-age pensions and nationalization are not the same thing.

The point in making these distinctions is that people who write about the welfare state, whether as critics of it or as protagonists of it, often fail to make

**TABLE 1.1**
**Level of Health and Social Security**
**Expenditure and Size of Public Sector of Nine**
**European Countries, 1970s**[a]

| Health and social security expenditure as percentage of GDP | | Size of public sector (rank order only) |
|---|---|---|
| Netherlands | 21.5 | Austria |
| Sweden | 20.5 | Great Britain |
| Belgium | 19.0 | Italy |
| Italy | 17.5 | France |
| France | 17.0 | Sweden |
| Great Britain | 15.5 | West Germany |
| Austria | 14.0 | Switzerland |
| West Germany | 13.0 | Netherlands |
| Switzerland | 11.0 | Belgium |

[a] *The Economist* 1978. Europe's economies: The structure and management of Europe's ten largest economies, 19, 26.

them. They typically lump together under the heading "welfare state" just about everything that modern governments do in every field of domestic policy. Thus, Peter Drucker in the article quoted earlier (1969) associates the welfare state with "the mess of the big cities" and with failures in transportation as well as in education (p. 7). Similarly, in a recent article, Fritz Sharpf (1977) uses the term *welfare state* in connection not merely with transfer payments and the direct provision of social services but with "the provision of infrastructure facilities on which profitable economic activities directly or indirectly depend," "the provision of subsidies and incentives to initiate or maintain desirable private sector activities whose profitability would otherwise be too low or too risky to attract sufficient private capital," and "the management of cyclical patterns of inflation and unemployment in the private enterprise system through the manipulation of macroeconomic parameters. [p. 340]"[2] Sharpf thus associates welfare provision with the expansion of the public sector and macroeconomic management, and attaches the label *welfare state* to all three.

Now there are no property rights in language, and writers like Drucker and Sharpf are perfectly entitled to use the term *welfare state* in any way they like. Sharpf, in his article, uses the term quite self-consciously and perfectly precisely. The disadvantages, however, of using this particular term in such an omnibus fashion are that important distinctions tend to be obscured, that matters of contingent fact are reduced to matters of definition, and that something called the welfare state is apt to be made the object of all manner of loves and hates that may, or may not, properly pertain to it. In this chapter,

[2] Sharpf also includes, rather surprisingly, "internal and external security."

*welfare state* will be taken to refer strictly to what was earlier labeled welfare provision. There is ample warrant for using the term in this limited way. Thus, Harold Wilensky (1975) remarks that the "essence of the welfare state is government-protected minimum standards of income, nutrition, health, housing, and education assured to every citizen as a political right, not as charity [p. 7]." Two students of comparative public policy (Siegel and Weinberg, 1977) similarly suggest that "the welfare state involves policies and programs designed to place at least a safety net under most residents. This net ensures that people will not be compelled to do without . . . basic human needs [p. 200]." For what it is worth, *The Concise Oxford Dictionary* concurs, defining a welfare state as a "country seeking to ensure the welfare of all citizens by means of government-operated social services." The dictionary makes no mention of nationalization, regulation, social engineering, or macroeconomic management. (See, also, Flora and Heidenheimer 1981.) I shall follow suit.

## Identifying the Welfare State's Political Consequences

Offering a reasonably satisfactory definition of *welfare state* is not, however, the end of our problems. Our task is to identify the consequences of a major social phenomenon over the span of an entire century. This would be formidable even if nothing else had changed in the interim; but, of course, much else has changed. Few of the countries of Western Europe and North America were liberal democracies in the 1880s; all of them are today. The public sectors of most Western countries were relatively small in the 1880s; most of them are now much larger, to the point where most modern economies are referred to as mixed economies. The last 100 years, and in particular the last 30 years, have witnessed what must be the highest rates of economic growth in human history; ordinary people are far richer now than they were in 1881, or even in 1951. The rise of the welfare state has thus coincided with the spread of democracy, the development of the mixed economy, and a period of unparalleled material prosperity. The phrase used was *coincided with*, but there is every reason to believe that all of these phenomena are related to each other in subtle and complex ways. The coming of political democracy undoubtedly promoted the development of the welfare state; the welfare state may well have made Western economies grow faster than they would otherwise have done; and so on. It follows that disentangling the consequences of the welfare state from the consequences of these other related phenomena is not going to be easy.

In addition, the analyst has to contend with the problem of counterfactuals. To ask questions about the consequences of any phenomenon in the real world is to ask what the world would have been like if the phenomenon had never come into existence or had operated differently. To say that one of the consequences of the Yom Kippur War was a sharp rise in the world price of oil is to say that the price would not have risen but for the war. Counterfactuals are hard enough to deal with in relatively simple cases like this; they are, of course, far trickier to handle when the phenomenon being considered, like the welfare state, is itself highly complex and has existed for a long time. The conclusions that one draws under these circumstances are inevitably speculative; the most that anyone can do is support his or her speculations with good arguments.

Finally, in this particular context, in talking about the political consequences of the welfare state, we need to be alert to the significance of the word *political*. The welfare state has undoubtedly had all sorts of consequences, some economic, some social, some, quite possibly, psychological. It is, moreover, perfectly possible that these economic and other consequences have in turn affected politics. If, for example, the welfare state has promoted the material prosperity of the West, this has almost certainly had political consequences; equally, if the welfare state has in the past retarded, or is now retarding, the growth of the West's prosperity, then this, too, is likely to have had, or to be having, political consequences. All one can do, given all these problems, is to ask the question in a reasonably precise form—How is the political order of advanced industrial societies different from what it would have been had the welfare state not been invented?—and to answer it in as plausible a way as possible. Thought experiments in history, as in other fields, are worth running even if the results are inevitably inconclusive.

## Hopes and Fears

A good way of approaching our question is to ask what the founders of the welfare state hoped its political consequences would be, and what its original opponents feared its political consequences would be. The welfare state, in fact, would seem to have had few wholly unintended or unexpected consequences; almost everything that has happened since 1881 was at least foreseen, if not precisely intended, by somebody.

Everyone knows that Bismarck, in introducing social insurance in Germany, had politics uppermost in his mind. (He always did.) The Kaiser's message to the Reichstag in February 1881 was explicit. The healing of social ills, it said,

> cannot be achieved exclusively by way of repressing socialistic excesses but must be sought simultaneously through the positive promotion of the worker's welfare. . . . The institutions which until now were to protect the worker who found himself in a helpless state because he had lost his ability to work, either by accident or on account of old age, have proven to be inadequate. This inadequacy has not been a minor factor in inducing members of this social class to seek the road of relief by supporting Social Democratic aims [Rimlinger 1971, pp. 112–113].

In another message to the Reichstag, toward the end of the year, the Kaiser, again using words put into his mouth by Bismarck, expanded on the same theme:

The cure of social ills must be sought not exclusively in the repression of Social Democratic excesses, but simultaneously in the positive advancement in the welfare of the working classes. We regard it as our imperial duty to urge this task again upon the Reichstag, and we should look back with the greater satisfaction upon all the successes with which God has visibly blessed our government if we are able one day to take with us the consciousness that we left to the fatherland new and lasting sureties for its internal peace and to those needing help greater security and liberality in the assistance to which they can lay claim [Rimlinger 1971, p. 114].

Bismarck in private was less verbose: "One who can look forward to an old-age pension is far more contented and much easier to manage [Snyder 1967, p. 281]."[3]

Political judgments like these were, to be sure, not the only or even the main considerations in the minds of many of the founders of the welfare state. Many of them were moved chiefly by humanitarian considerations; later, especially after World War II, many political leaders believed that transfer payments could have a stabilizing, countercyclical economic effect. But, to a greater extent than is sometimes realized, most of the founders of the welfare state were conscious of its possible political implications. "In pre-democratic Sweden...," according to Heclo (1974), "social insurance was seen as a palliative technique to prevent social unrest and diminish the appeal of socialism. [p. 231]" In Britain, too, the man who imported social insurance from Germany, Lloyd George, believed that social reforms were essential to the future of his party. In a speech in 1908, Lloyd George said that British Liberalism

is not going to repeat the fate of Continental Liberalism. The fate of Continental Liberalism should warn them of that danger. It has been swept on one side before it had well begun its work, because it refused to adapt itself to new conditions. The Liberalism of the Continent concerned itself exclusively with mending and perfecting the machinery which was to grind corn for the people. It forgot that the people had to live whilst the process was going on, and people saw their lives pass away without anything being accomplished. British Liberalism has been better advised. It has not abandoned the traditional ambition of the Liberal Party to establish freedom and equality; but side by side with this effort it promotes measures for ameliorating the conditions of life for the multitude [Bullock and Shock 1956, p. 212].

Nearly thirty years later, in 1936, Franklin Roosevelt, opening his campaign for reelection as president of the United States, emphasized his belief that the New Deal was as much a conservative as a radical undertaking.

Who is there in America who believes that we can run the risk of turning back our Government to the old leadership which brought it to the brink of 1933? Out of the strains and stresses of these years we have come to see that the true conservative is the man who has a real concern for injustices and takes thought against the day of reckoning. The true conservative seeks to protect the system of private property and free enterprise by correcting such injustices and inequalities as arise from it. The most serious threat to our institutions

[3]On Bismarck's reasons for promoting social insurance, see also Craig (1978, pp. 150–151), Stern (1977, pp. 218–221), and Pinson (1954, pp. 240–246).

comes from those who refuse to face the need for change. Liberalism becomes the protection for the far-sighted conservative. . . . In the words of the great essayist, "The voice of great events is proclaiming to us. Reform if you would preserve" [Rosenman 1938–1950, pp. 389–390].

Similarly, at the end of World War II, the Gaullists, according to two historians of the French welfare state, "perceived social security as a means of maintaining social peace and stability, first as a cushion against the full impact of fluctuations in economic activity, and second as an example of the association between capital and labor—the ideal form of social organization in Gaullist ideology [Cohen and Goldfinger 1975, p. 59]."

The nonrevolutionary proponents of the welfare state were thus moved by two separate, albeit closely related, political considerations. The first was simply to maintain the stability of the existing political order. A hungry person, an unemployed person, a person suffering from a deep sense of injustice or insecurity was a danger to the state; social insurance was thought of as a suitable means of reconciling that person to the state. Second and more specifically, conservative and old-fashioned liberal politicians, especially in Europe, were worried, on partisan as well as constitutional grounds, about the rise of left-wing parties like the SPD in Germany, the Labour party in Britain, and the Communists in France. They hoped that social insurance and similar welfare measures would reduce the support for left-wing parties at elections. Working-class voters were, in the nicest possible way, to be bought off.[4]

The views of the opponents of the welfare state are a little harder to discern, chiefly because there were so few opponents. As noted in King (1973, pp. 302–313), old-age pensions and social security became a matter of high-level ideological debate only in the United States. In most other countries, welfare reforms were often criticized on practical grounds—they would cost too much, undermine existing insurance arrangements, or whatever—but they were seldom attacked as being wicked, or subversive, or likely to undermine the foundations of the existing social order. Conservatives actually inaugurated the welfare state in Germany, Sweden, and some other continental countries; they welcomed it, or at least professed to welcome it, in Britain.[5]

[4]The phrase is cynical, but there is no need to be overly cynical. As was said earlier, most of the early proponents of the welfare state—notably Lloyd George and Roosevelt—were probably motivated at least as much by humanitarian as by political considerations. This was certainly true of social democratic politicians in countries like Britain and Sweden.

[5]On the day that Lloyd George introduced his national insurance bill in the House of Commons, a contender for the leadership of the Conservative party, Austen Chamberlain, wrote in his diary: "Confound L.G. He has strengthened the [Liberal] Government again. His sickness scheme is a good one, and he is on the right lines . . . . I must say I envy him the opportunity, and I must admit that he has made good use of it [Braithwaite 1957, p. 156]." Some years earlier, A.J. Balfour, subsequently to become a Conservative prime minister, said in a speech in Manchester: "Social legislation, as I conceive it, is not merely to be distinguished from Socialist legislation but it is its most direct opposite and its most effective antidote. Socialism will never get possession of the great body of public opinion . . . among the working class or any other class if those who wield the collective forces of the community show themselves desirous to ameliorate every legitimate grievance and to put Society upon a proper and more solid basis [Fraser 1973, p. 129]."

Those few, chiefly in the United States, who did advance general propositions against public welfare provision were quite clear what they were afraid of: that welfarism would in time destroy liberty. "Bureaucracy," warned Herbert Hoover, "is ever desirous of spreading its influence and its power. You cannot extend the mastery of the government over the daily working life of a people without at the same time making it the master of the people's souls and thoughts [Romasco 1965, p. 14]." Neither Hoover nor anyone else, however, was very specific about how government-supported welfare measures were to bring about the destruction of liberty. They knew that the road to hell was steep, but they did not have any very clear vision of the terrain through which it would pass; they did not spell out possible scenarios. They seem to have thought, rather vaguely, that in time the welfare state would make everyone personally dependent upon the state and that dependence on this scale would lead to tyranny; or that (as Hoover implied) the vast bureaucracy created by the welfare state would itself become an instrument of dictatorship; or that the welfare state would undermine the social foundations of freedom by depriving intermediate organizations like charities and other voluntary associations of their raison d'être. The welfare state was thus feared as monopoly employer, or as Big Brother, or as creator of an anonymous, highly atomized mass society. Whatever the details, it was the threat to liberty that was thought to be crucial. Echos of Herbert Hoover's fears can still be found in the writings of critics of the welfare state—in phrases like "the monster state" and "the Frankenstein state," used by the English publicist Paul Johnson (1980).

In short, the proponents of the welfare state hoped and believed that it would prove a bulwark of the political status quo. Its opponents believed that it would be destructive of liberty. Who was right?

## The Welfare State's Actual Consequences

Suppose that in the 100 years since the time of Bismarck most Western nations had become democracies, had acquired more or less mixed economies, and had, at least recently, enjoyed high levels of material prosperity. But suppose further, however improbably, that most Western nations had not at the same time become welfare states in the sense in which the term is being used here. Suppose that state-sponsored unemployment insurance did not exist, that old-age pensions paid by the state did not exist, that state accident and invalidity insurance did not exist, and that the delivery and financing of health care were entirely in the private sector. Under these circumstances, would the politics of the Western world have been more or less stable than in fact they have been?

Merely to ask the question is to suggest the answer. From some points of view, the twentieth century in Europe, even in Western Europe, has been a period of extreme political instability. Norway and Sweden have parted company; the Austro–Hungarian Empire has broken up; France has had three republican regimes, with a fascist interlude between two of them; Italy, Spain, and Portugal have all been governed by a succession of authoritarian and then liberal–democratic regimes. In addition, virtually the whole of the continent has been ravaged twice by modern industrial war. Yet this appearance of gross instability is in some ways misleading. At least six countries of Western Europe—Sweden, Denmark, the Netherlands, Belgium, Switzerland, and Great Britain—are governed today in much the same way that they were at the beginning of the century. Three others—Norway, Finland, and Ireland—have enjoyed long periods of political stability since acquiring their independence. The regimes of present-day Austria and France have been disrupted chiefly, though not solely, from outside. Only Germany plus the three Mediterranean countries—Italy, Spain, and Portugal—have undergone political upheavals generated largely from inside the country. Against a twentieth-century background of economic vicissitudes, expanding populations, high rates of social and geographical mobility, and devastating world wars, such a large measure of political stability might be thought remarkable.

More to the point, there is every reason to believe that Europe's political instability in the twentieth century, great though it has undoubtedly been, would have been even greater had welfare state measures not been introduced. The disruptions in Italy, Spain, and Portugal largely preceded the coming of the welfare state in those countries. With regard to Britain, where social insurance was introduced before 1914 and was substantially expanded in the 1920s, it is reasonable to ask whether a liberal–democratic constitutional regime could have survived the great depression in the absence of very extensive (by the standards of its time) social welfare provision. Certainly Conservative governments in Britain did not think so; they were responsible for most of the welfare reforms of the interwar period (Heclo 1974). Germany, of course, suffered two violent changes of regime, in 1918 and in 1933, despite the best efforts of Bismarck. The changes were caused by defeat in war, by economic chaos, and by the failure of the Weimar regime to establish its legitimacy in the eyes of the military, the upper classes, and large sections of the general population. Without Bismarck's reforms, the Wilhelmian and Weimar regimes, especially the latter, might well have fallen before they did; in an odd way, Bismarck's reforms may have damaged Weimar by making the previous Wilhelmian regime seem the more attractive in retrospect (Allen 1965).

One other indicator of what might be thought to be the welfare state's success in conducing to political stability is the almost total failure of antiregime political parties to make electoral headway in advanced welfare states. The last 100 years have been an era of enormous, indeed unparalleled, social and economic upheaval; yet on only one occasion in any welfare state has any antiregime party or combination of antiregime parties ever won a majority or anything like a majority of the votes in a free election. We take this fact so much for granted that we are apt to cease to wonder at it. Antiregime parties have been unsuccessful in the United States, Canada, Australia, New Zealand, Britain,

Ireland, Sweden, Norway, Denmark, the Netherlands, and Switzerland. They have done rather better in Italy and France. Even so, in Italy by far the highest percentage of the total vote amassed by antiregime parties since the introduction of welfare state measures in the late 1940s was the 40.5%—substantially less than half the electorate—gained by the Communists and the national-right parties in 1976, a figure that has since declined (Mackie and Rose 1977, p. 322).[6] In France the antiregime parties' highwater mark came in 1956, when the Communists and the Poujadists together won 37.6% of the vote (Mackie and Rose 1974, p. 137). Given the circumstances of these two countries, it would be a brave man or woman who would say that antiregime parties of Left and Right would not have done substantially better if both countries did not possess reasonably well-developed systems of social insurance. The one exception to our general rule is, of course, Germany, where the Nazis and Communists together won half or more of the votes at all three elections in 1932 and 1933 (Mackie and Rose 1974, p. 157). The German exception is well remembered because it is wholly unique in the experience of advanced welfare states (as well as for other, more sinister reasons).

Many of the founders of the welfare state were concerned with maintaining the stability of their political regimes. Many of them, as we have seen, had another, more specific objective: to stem the rise of left-wing political parties. Kaiser Wilhelm referred to "Social Democratic excesses"; Lloyd George warned British Liberals that they were in danger of being supplanted by Labour. In this connection, it goes without saying that the more extravagant hopes of the conservative founders of the welfare state have failed to be realized. The Social Democratic party in Germany continued to make progress after 1881, winning more than one-third of the popular vote in 1912, 1961, and 1965 and more than 40% at every election since 1969; the Social Democrats were in power in Germany in 1981. In Britain, the Labour party had replaced the Liberals as the main opposition to the Tories by 1929, and has been in office for seventeen of the thirty-five years since the end of World War II. Left and left-center governments have indeed held power in almost every democratic country with a welfare state except Italy, Spain, Ireland, Switzerland, and (depending on one's definition of *left-center*) the United States and Canada.

Still, two obvious points about the progress of the Left in democratic countries are worth making. The first is that in most democratic countries the Left in the 1980s is not what it used to be; it has become domesticated. The SPD of Helmut Schmidt was not the SPD that had the German bourgeoisie shaking in its boots in the 1870s; the British Labour party, always rather tame by continental standards, became even tamer as time went on. Most social democratic parties in Western countries have felt compelled to become more moderate, either in order to win votes, or because they have discovered that

---

[6] If the votes for the Proletarian Unity candidates are added, the total antiregime percentage rises to 42%.

revolutionary or quasi-revolutionary policies are not in conformity with real-world requirements. The second, related point is that, although the moderate Left has done well electorally in the era of the welfare state, the Communists and the extreme left-wing have done badly. No Communist or extreme left-wing party has ever won half the votes in a democratic election. In the two Western European countries with the strongest Communist parties, Italy and France, the Communists and their allies have succeeded in winning as much as 30% of the vote on only four occasions—in Italy in 1946, 1948, 1976, and 1979 (Mackie and Rose 1974, p. 219; 1977, p. 322; 1980, p. 352). Again the extreme Left's lack of success is so well known that we tend to take it for granted. The manifest failure of revolutionary parties, and indeed of revolution, in the West almost certainly owes much to social insurance and related government social provisions.

To sum up: Can Bismarck, looking down (or up) from wherever he now is, take some pride in his invention, the welfare state, conceived of as an essay in practical politics? Surely he can. Any conclusions about the effects of the welfare state on the long-term political stability of the Western world must be speculative, for the reasons already given; but it seems reasonable to suggest that state-sponsored welfare provision has contributed a great deal to making advanced industrial nations more stable—or, if one prefers, less unstable—than they would have been otherwise. Certainly this is the view of most Marxists, who ruefully concede that state welfare provision has consistently damped down popular support for left-wing causes. In the words of one recent British Marxist commentator:

> Once universal suffrage and the other major liberal rights are established, these provide a crucial channel through which to obtain welfare improvements. Indeed, welfare becomes a means of integrating the enfranchised working class within the capitalist system. . . . [Gough 1979, pp. 60–61]."

Quite so. Bismarck himself could not have put it better.[7]

The predictions of political doom made by the original opponents of the welfare state can be dealt with more briefly, since they must be among the worst political predictions ever made. Hoover and others believed that the welfare state would destroy liberty. To be sure, manifestations of the welfare state such as compulsory insurance schemes do restrict liberty in the sense that a citizen forced to contribute some part of his or her income to a state insurance fund is thereby no longer free to spend it on something else; Milton Friedman (1962, Chapter 1) and others make what they can of this and related points. But the

---

[7]Though Bismarck probably would have substituted *imperial* for *capitalist*. The view that the welfare state is a promoter of stability has also been expressed by Wilensky (1975). "The welfare state is in the process of humanizing industrial society. Over a century it has meant great gains in economic and psychological security for the less privileged; in the short run of each generation it produces some income redistribution. It is a prime source of consensus and social order in modern society, pluralist or totalitarian [p. 119]."

experience of the welfare state overall suggests that, far from resulting in any substantial diminution of liberty, it has, on the contrary, coincided with (though it may well not have been the cause of) very substantial expansions of liberty— indeed a veritable libertarian explosion—throughout the Western world. Conservative critics of the welfare state still talk of tyranny; but they are equally likely to talk, not altogether consistently, of licentiousness and permissiveness.

Consider the following list of "rights and prerogatives," as he calls them, recently put forward by Charles Lindblom (1977): "freedom to form and join organizations; freedom of expression; right to vote; eligibility for public office; right of political leaders to compete for support; right of political leaders to compete for votes; alternative sources of information; free and fair elections . . . which decide who is to hold top authority; institutions for making government policies depend on votes and other expressions of preference [p. 133]." To these one might add: freedom to travel at home and abroad; freedom to publish and read whatever one likes; freedom from restrictions arising from normally irrelevant considerations like race or sex; sexual freedom, including equal rights for homosexuals, the right to divorce, and the right of women to abort unwanted pregnancies.

These lists probably include the kinds of freedoms that Hoover had in mind. In addition, they probably include freedoms that never occurred to Hoover (and that he might not have approved of if they had). The only freedom that clearly mattered to Hoover that the lists do not include is the freedom to run one's own business exactly as one likes, and to make as much money as one possibly can, more or less irrespective of the consequences. Unfortunately, rights and freedoms of the kind listed here are not reported year by year in international statistical tables; no political Keynes has arisen to provide us with a system of national political accounts comparable to the national economic accounts that we are all familiar with. If, however, such political accounts did exist, measuring outputs of political as well as economic goods, they would almost certainly show that the boundaries of freedom have been pushed out in just about every welfare state (and been contracted in almost none).

Britain is a good case, although readers can supply data from their own knowledge for other countries. The British welfare state began to be constructed in 1908; it was more or less complete by 1948. Since 1948, theater censorship in Britain has been abolished, laws have been passed making it more difficult to prosecute authors on grounds that their books are obscene, the voting age has been lowered to 18, the BBC's television and radio monopolies have been abolished, restrictions on travel arising out of restrictions on foreign exchange have been lifted, legal steps have been taken to establish racial and sexual equality, the law prohibiting homosexual acts between consenting adults in private has been repealed, the grounds for divorce have been extended, and abortions have been made much easier to obtain. Herbert Hoover might or might not like modern Britain; but he could hardly maintain that its citizens had been deprived of their liberties. By almost any standard, Britain is a much freer country today than it was in 1948, let alone in 1908. The same is true of the great majority of welfare states.

The interesting question, since Hoover and most of those who agreed with him were intelligent, is how they came to be so mistaken. It would seem that, perhaps partly because they failed to think through alternative scenarios for the destruction of liberty, they were guilty of at least three separate failures of political imagination.

In the first place, they failed to see that, although it is indeed the case that in a welfare state many citizens become dependent on the state, it is also the case that in a welfare state the state becomes dependent on many of its citizens. When most doctors work for the government, they are indeed dependent on the government for their salaries; but the government is at least as dependent on them for the delivery of medical services. Doctors, in fact, are much better placed to go on strike than the government is to fire them. In a developed welfare state, dependence is a two-way street (King 1975, pp. 290–293). In the second place, the welfare state's opponents seem to have imagined that, as the number of state employees grew, so they would increasingly become merged into a single, large, monolithic entity—in other words, that the state really would become "the state." In fact, however, as we know, a whole host of factors— immense problems of coordination within governments, the desire of professional bodies to retain their professional autonomy, legislatures' suspicion of executives, empire building by bureaucrats, the development of strong agency– client relationships, and the like—have led the typical welfare state to be large all right, but to be neither single nor remotely monolithic. In Washington and London, even in Paris, the modern state looks far more like a big, sprawling, squabbling, extremely messy family than like Big Brother. Finally, in so far as the opponents of welfarism were fearful of the disappearance of groups intermediate between the isolated citizen and overweening state power, they need not have worried. We now know that the larger and more active the state, the larger, more numerous, and more active are likely to be the interest groups that spring into being in order to do business with it. Sometimes welfare states even create such interest groups precisely in order to have somebody to do business with. Politics in welfare states may be pluralistic; they may even be corporatist. They are hardly, in practice, tyrannical.

Indeed, viewed from the 1980s, there is an element of irony in the early debates about the welfare state. The fear of its opponents was that it would destroy liberty and lead to tyranny. That has not happened. Liberty has on occasion been destroyed, but by brownshirts, stormtroopers, and German and Russian tanks, never by welfarism. Instead, the common complaint of critics of the welfare state today is that it leads not to tyranny, but to something like its opposite: to overload, to ungovernability, to political bankruptcy, to crises of legitimacy. Whether such crises actually exist, and whether, if so, they can be attributed to the welfare state, we shall consider in a moment.

## An Inference and a Noninference

Bismarck, Lloyd George, and the others were right; Herbert Hoover and those who agreed with him were wrong. The welfare state has contributed to regime stability and to stemming the advance of extreme left-wing political parties; it has not resulted in the destruction of liberty. What inferences should be drawn from all this regarding the future?

One inference seems clearly warranted. The welfare state, in the sense of the maintenance by governments of certain minimum standards of material well-being, has been, and is likely to continue to be, a bulwark of political stability. If it did not exist, political conservatives would have to invent it. If, as Milton Friedman claims, capitalism is an essential condition of freedom, then the welfare state is probably just as essential a condition of capitalism. In the absence of extensive welfare provision, it is very doubtful whether the seemingly inevitable economic and social vicissitudes of the latter part of the twentieth century would be easily borne by increasingly well-informed, well-read, well-traveled, potentially restive urban populations. The welfare state has been a great cushion of change. Remove the cushion and the ground beneath would probably prove to be very stony. It is strange that in the 1980s people who call themselves conservatives should  be attacking the welfare state when it has proved such an admirably (or, from the Marxists' point of view, deplorably) conservative institution.[8]

In particular, it should be borne in mind that, despite its expense, despite the high taxes associated with it, despite the dead weight of bureaucracy that is allegedly dragging it down, the welfare state remains remarkably popular with Western electorates. In a recent comparative study of attitudes toward taxing and spending in the United States and Western Europe, Coughlin (1980) reports that "in all the nations for which we have data, antitax/welfare sentiments are nowhere expressed by clear majorities of national populations, and . . . continued popular support for improved programs is broadly based [p. 150]." In Britain, on the day of the May 1979 general election, a sample of voters leaving the polling stations were asked whether they would favor cutting taxes, even if it

[8]By no means all conservatives and neoconservatives are hostile to the welfare state construed in the way it is being construed in this chapter. See, for instance, Kristol (1977, especially pp. 197–198); and Plattner (1979, pp. 28–48). Kristol, in particular, argues that social welfare provision largely based on social insurance is perfectly compatible with liberal capitalism—even if conservatives are sometimes hard to persuade of the fact.

meant some reduction in government services such as health, education, and welfare, or maintaining government services such as health, education, and welfare, even if it meant that as a result taxes could not be cut. It had been clear for years that a majority of British people wanted taxes cut, at least in the abstract. A clear plurality of them in May 1979 voted for Margaret Thatcher and the Conservatives; Thatcher and the British Conservative party were, and still are, widely associated with hostility to the welfare state. Yet, confronted with the straight choice, fully 70% of the 1979 sample said they would prefer to maintain government services and to forego tax cuts, with only 30% saying the opposite.[9] To the extent that the British Conservatives are hostile to the welfare state (and their hostility is often exaggerated), they evidently won the 1979 election despite their hostility, not because of it.

If the inference can and should be drawn from what we have said so far that the welfare state is a politically stabilizing institution, another inference should not be drawn: that all is well with government in the modern democratic state. At the beginning of this chapter, a distinction was made among five fields in which most modern democratic states have been increasingly active: the public sector of the economy, macroeconomic management, detailed economic regulation, social engineering, and welfare provision. It was argued there that these five fields are separate, and should be kept separate, and that the label welfare state applies only to the last of them. It was further argued that welfare provision on its own had been a major factor contributing to political stability.

But, of course, it may still be the case that adverse political consequences are likely to result if modern governments are active in the field of welfare policy, and simultaneously in all four of the other fields. A country with a large public sector *and* a disposition to try to control its economy at the macro level *and* a penchant for detailed economic regulation *and* a tendency to engage in social engineering *and* a desire to provide welfare benefits on a large scale is very likely to find itself running into political difficulties as well as economic ones. These difficulties have been described and analyzed elsewhere, the best summary probably being that by Rose and Peters (1978). There is no need to go into detail here. Samuel Brittan probably put the point as well as anyone when he warned that excessive burdens should not be placed on the "sharing out" functions of the state, lest conflicts among social and economic groups, and between social and economic groups and the government, become insupportable. "Overload" and "ungovernability" remain useful concepts. This chapter is not concerned to deny the importance of these phenomena and the potential dangers inherent in them. What it does urge is that responsibility for

---

[9]Ivor Crewe/Gallup Poll, *BBC Election Programme Survey*, responses to question 45. The percentage of "don't knows," excluded from the calculation in the text, was 12.

these phenomena and these dangers should not be laid at the door of the welfare state alone. Far too many other factors are involved. It would help, at the very least, if people would stop using *welfare state* as an all-purpose, catchall phrase to denote everything in sight that they dislike about modern Western governments. The world is too complicated a place to be understood in such simple terms.

# References

Allen, W.S. 1965. *The Nazi seizure of power: The experience of a single German town 1930–1935.* Chicago: Quadrangle Books.

Braithwaite, W.J. 1957. *Lloyd George's ambulance wagon*, ed. H.N. Burbury. London: Methuen.

Brittan, S. 1975. The economic contradictions of democracy. *British Journal of Political Science* 5:130–131.

Bullock, A., and Shock, M., eds. 1956. *The liberal tradition: From Fox to Keynes.* London: Adam and Charles Black.

Cohen, S.S., and Goldfinger, C. 1978. From permacrisis to real crisis in French social security: The limits to normal politics. In *Stress and contradiction in modern capitalism: Public policy and the theory of the state*, eds. L.N. Lindberg et al. Lexington, Mass.: D.C. Heath. Pp. 57–98.

Coughlin, R.L. 1980. *Ideology, public opinion and welfare policy: Attitudes toward taxes and spending in industrialized societies.* Berkeley: Institute of International Studies, University of California.

Craig, G.A. 1978. *Germany 1866–1945.* Oxford: Clarendon Press.

Drucker, P.F.L. 1969. The sickness of government. *The Public Interest* 14:3–23.

Flora, P. 1981. Solution or source of crises? The welfare state in historical perspective. In *The emergence of the welfare state in Britain and Germany, 1850–1950.* London: Croom Helm.

Flora, P. and Heidenheimer, A.J. 1981. *What is the welfare state?* New Brunswick, N.J.: Transaction Books.

Fraser, D. 1973. *The evolution of the British welfare state.* London: Macmillan.

Friedman, M. 1962. *Capitalism and freedom.* Chicago: University of Chicago Press.

Gough, I. 1979. *The political economy of the welfare state.* London: Macmillan.

Heclo, H. 1974. *Modern social politics in Britain and Sweden: From relief to income maintenance.* New Haven, Conn.: Yale University Press.

Johnson, P. 1980. *The things that are not Caesar's.* Washington, D.C.: American Enterprise Institute.

King, A. 1973. Ideas, institutions and the policies of governments: A comparative analysis: Parts I and II. *British Journal of Political Science* 3:291–313.

King, A. 1975. Overload: Problems of governing in the 1970s. *Political Studies* 23:290–293.

Kristol, I. 1977. "Socialism: Obituary for an idea." In *The future that doesn't work: Social democracy's failures in Britain*, ed. R.E. Tyrell, Jr. Garden City, N.Y.: Doubleday. Pp. 186–199.

Lindblom, C.E. 1977. *Politics and markets: The world's political–economic systems.* New York: Basic Books.

Mackie, T.T., and Rose, R. 1974. *The international almanac of electoral history.* London: Macmillan.

Mackie, T.T. and Rose, R. 1977. General elections in Western nations during 1976. *European Journal of Political Research* 5:321–325.

Mackie, T.T. and Rose, R. 1980. General elections in Western nations during 1979. *European Journal of Political Research* 8:349–357.

O'Connor, J. 1973. *The fiscal crisis of the state.* New York: St. Martin's Press.

Pinson, K.S. 1954. *Modern Germany: Its history and civilization.* New York: Macmillan.

Plattner, M.F. 1979. The welfare state vs. the redistributive state. *The Public Interest* 55:28–48.

Rimlinger, G.V. 1971. *Welfare policy and industrialization in Europe, America and Russia.* New York: John Wiley.

Romasco, A.U. 1965. *The poverty of abundance: Hoover, the nation, and the depression.* New York Oxford University Press.

Rose, R., and Peters, G. 1978. *Can government go bankrupt?:* New York: Basic Books.

Rosenman, S.I., compiler. 1938–1950. *The public papers and addresses of Franklin D. Roosevelt.* Vol. 5. New York: Random House.

Sharpf, F.W. 1977. Public organization and the waning of the welfare state: A research perspective. *European Journal of Political Research* 5:340.

Siegel, R.L., and Weinberg, L.B. 1977. *Comparing public policies: United States, Soviet Union, and Europe.* Homewood, Ill.: Dorsey Press.

Snyder, L.L., ed. 1967. *The blood and iron chancellor.* Princeton, N.J.: Van Nostrand.

Stern, F. 1977. *Gold and iron: Bismarck, Bleichroder, and the building of the German empire.* London: George Allen and Unwin.

Wilensky, H.L. 1975. *The welfare state and equality: Structural and ideological roots of public expenditures.* Berkeley, Calif.: University of California Press.

# 2

# Class Politics and the Western Welfare State

## MICHAEL SHALEV

## Prologue: Socialism and the Welfare State

Does social democracy lead to socialism? That heated controversy of the first half of the century, which was, by the onset of the second half, presumed to have died a natural death along with other remnants of capitalism's ideological past, has in the last decade reared its head once again. This chapter is concerned with only one possible indicator of "transition to socialism" through peaceful political agency—the welfare state. Current intellectual concern with "crisis" and "backlash" has sparked considerable interest in the future of welfare states. But even before such catchwords became popular, neo-Marxists such as Miliband (1969) and Offe (1972), as well as occasional radical Weberians such as Parkin (1971, 1979) raised the more timeless question of whether social democratic governments have either the will or the capacity to adopt policies with equalizing effects on social welfare. Responding in the negative, they argued that the welfare state cannot effect a socialist transformation under liberal democracy because of the persistence of a fundamental imbalance—*irrespective* of patterns of political control—between labor and capital's economic and social power, and the existence of irresistible economic and political pressures exerted on nation-states by the international system.

Recently signs have appeared on the Left of the development of more conditional and complex views of the welfare state (e.g., Gough 1979; Westergaard 1978). For their part, democratic socialist sympathizers have not been slow to come to its defense (e.g., Korpi 1978; Maravall 1979; Stephens 1979). Of particular interest in this context is the recent emergence of a *class*

EVALUATING THE WELFARE STATE:
SOCIAL AND POLITICAL PERSPECTIVES

*conflict paradigm* of welfare state development in capitalist democracies, which
has been independently formulated by a number of European and American
political sociologists, and which seemingly lends support to the social
democratic claim to socialist potential. This paradigm has furthermore been
tested on a variety of (mostly cross-national) data sets with impressive results.
In addition to studies of redistributive state expenditures, recent research has
focused on a range of dependent variables including economic policy and
performance (e.g., Crouch, forthcoming; Hibbs 1977; Martin 1973; and Tufte
1978), income inequality (e.g., Dryzek 1978; Hewitt 1977; Jackman 1975,
1980), equality of opportunity (Erikson, Goldthorpe, and Portocarero 1979;
Parkin 1971; Scase 1977), and a number of specific domestic policy domains
such as housing (Esping-Andersen 1978), manpower planning (Webber 1979),
and workers' participation (Stephens and Stephens, forthcoming).

This chapter is intended as a preliminary review of the arguments and
evidence for the view that the bulk of the observable variation in welfare state
emergence and growth in Western nations can be accounted for by the
strength—especially the political strength—of social democratic labor movements. A synthetic representation of the class conflict paradigm under
consideration is presented in Figure 2.1 (cf. Korpi and Shalev 1979a, 1979b).
It is based on my reading of the work of Bjorn (1976, 1979), Castles (1978),
Flora (1976), Hanneman (1979a, 1979b), and Stephens (1979). The model is
designed for the rich capitalist democracies, and a number of "other things"—
especially economic growth rates—are treated as "being equal." On the left-
hand side of the model are several antecedents of class mobilization which are
not concerned with the present argument. Suffice it to say that they are
representative of the prevailing view (e.g., Lipset and Rokkan 1967) that
historically determined structural characteristics powerfully constrain the
organizational possibilities of both labor and capital in the twin arenas of class
conflict: politics and the market (work). At the same time, the model also
represents, in the form of feedback arrows, process approaches to mobilization,
which attribute considerable importance to the strategies and actions *chosen* by
class organizations. (For a comparison of structural and process theories of
political mobilization, see Shalev and Korpi 1980.)

From the right-hand side of the model, we learn that strong and coherent class
organizations are expected to provide the base for class control of the polity,
although the potential for translating mobilization into power is moderated by
various facets of the state, such as electoral participation laws, functional and
geographical centralization, cabinet autonomy, and civil service independence.
By virtue of political control, class organizations acquire the ability to promote
policies and ideas that are supportive of their own interests and the interests of
their constituencies. What all this means for social democracy is that under
permissive institutional arrangements, strong and coordinated socialist trade
unions and political parties, where they emerge, constitute the mobilizatory
springboard from which leap durable socialist governments capable of and
interested in expanding the welfare state.

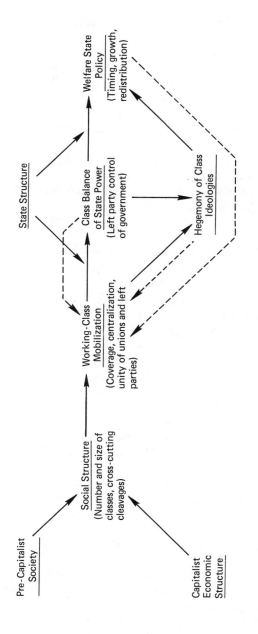

**FIGURE 2.1.** *A synthetic "class conflict paridigm" of welfare state development.*

# Theoretical Perspectives on the Welfare State

If welfare policies are indeed a reflection of the balance of class power, then it must be the case that they tap fundamentally conflicting class interests. Yet, *this is suggestive of a conception of the welfare that is at variance with most prevailing formulations.* Two representative conceptions may be described as the "social policy" and "public policy" approaches. The first, typical of the social policy literature, defines the welfare state in terms of its declared intentions—that is, some variant on the alleviation of poverty, in which "poverty" may be defined either in absolute terms or relativistically. Welfare policies emerge in this light as correctives to the critical insecurities, deprivations, and inequalities of a market economy; as, in fact, responses to functional needs of modern societies. Some interpretations conceive of these needs in terms of a public duty to alleviate private hardships, whereas others stress the contributions of public welfare to the smooth functioning of the (capitalist) political and economic status quo. In either case, the state is viewed as a rather mechanical problem-solving agent with little independent influence on the contours of policy. In contrast, students of public policy generally argue that state intervention, in relation to welfare or anything else, is the consequence of a political process that cannot be explained without reference to the interests and influence of politicians, pressure groups, and bureaucrats. Rather than seeing policy as the outcome of the declared or inferred motives of policymakers, such an approach directs our attention to the characteristics and behavior of the various policy actors in specific historical contexts.

Each of these broad aproaches to the dynamics of the welfare state offers an important but partial insight. On the one hand, it is of course true that, precisely because of what it aims to do, the welfare state is a rather unique policy area: It is on the whole more universal, more expensive, and less market rational than other areas of domestic policymaking. But this very uniqueness also carries with it a degree of contentiousness concerning the distribution of costs and benefits, which makes it impossible to ignore the elements of conflict and discretion in the formulation and implementation of welfare policy. The class conflict paradigm outlined earlier offers an account of both the ends of welfare states and the means by which they come into being and grow, of both their special socioeconomic purposes and consequences and the dynamic political forces that determine the parameters of the welfare state in specific national and historical contexts.

However, the effect is not merely to merge the insights of conventional students of the social policy and public policy schools, but also to recast them in terms of the interests and activities of *classes*. Whether or not it *actually* challenges the reward and opportunity structures of an abstracted capitalism, the welfare state unquestionably establishes normative criteria of distribution ("need," "fairness," "equality"), which are at a minimum independent of, and potentially in direct opposition to, those defined by property rights and market dictates and therefore are in presumed conflict with the interests of those who benefit most from capitalist distributive arrangements (loosely, the "dominant class"). Furthermore, the welfare state explicitly or implicitly sets out to correct what are, from the viewpoint of those who are both without property and without a commanding position in the labor market (the "working class"), serious deficiencies of the capitalist economy. It should therefore be viewed not as the state's inevitable response to developmental imperatives, but rather as a consequence of the evolution of classes and class struggle.

Like other policy instruments addressed to working-class interests, the welfare state has its origins in the problems of labor under capitalism, and specifically, the problem of distributive conflict between labor and capital over the division of income and other resources (Korpi 1980). The outcomes of this conflict, moreover, are by no means predetermined, by socioeconomic or any other "imperatives." Rather, they depend on the balance of class forces in the policymaking (political) arena. The polity, along with relations of production, is seen as an arena in which the conflicting classes struggle to realize their interests. Social democrats and scholars who implicitly share their assumptions go on to argue that in parliamentary democracies political control of the state is a consequence of electoral contests between political parties, and, hence, that the major political variable in welfare state development and growth is the relative strength of leftist parties. At the same time, their predisposition to link politics with the market on the grounds that both are arenas of distributive conflict leads class-conflict-oriented analysts to identify market-based class organizations (trade unions and employers' associations), as well as political parties, as being key actors in the struggle over welfare policy.

## Class Interests and the Welfare State

The conception of the welfare state that informs the class conflict perspective summarized in Figure 2.1 is, then, based on two assumptions: that the welfare state is a class issue (for the working class it constitutes a vehicle for the pursuit of its interests in the distributive arena of class conflict), and that the formation and growth (or contraction) of welfare states is a political process conditioned by the degree to which labor movements exercise control over the policymaking machinery of the state.

Beyond these generalities—important as they are in distinguishing the perspective under discussion from its chief competitors—lie a number of contentious choices which must be made in order to construct useful theories. In relation to the independent variables, it must be asked precisely which observable power resources are indicative of the relative leverage of the contending classes over welfare state policy. For example, leftist party control of the political executive—a favorite empirical referent for class power in cross-national research—never correlates perfectly with welfare state parameters. It is therefore incumbent upon researchers to identify additional or alternative causal variables and assess the degree to which these are independent of class power.

On the other side of the theoretical equation, it is necessary to identify an empirical policy domain that is more specific than "distributive conflict." Precisely which of the multitude of problems that capitalism presents to the working class are dealt with by the welfare state? And precisely which of the multitude of policies that it is possible to identify with the welfare state are likely to be sensitive to class interests and power? Attempts to link configurations of class power to welfare state policy outcomes are unlikely to be successful, or to be convincing even if they are successful, in the absence of specific a priori theoretical linkages between class and policy. A class conflict analysis worthy of the name must therefore begin with an examination of the nature of the labor–capital conflict, the problem areas for labor that arise out of this conflict, and the types of policy responses that labor movements have supported in attempting to address these problems. One possible framework of this kind is sketched in Table 2.1.[1]

Several observations are in order. First, in all three columns, each of the rows are obviously related. Control over growth-sustaining capital in principle guarantees the other forms of control; immunity from market fluctuations enhances labor's leverage over income distribution and the work process; legislation that protects or enlarges union power simultaneously enhances the possibility for labor to exert countervailing control pressure at several points. Obviously, this makes it difficult to tease the welfare state out from all the other state interventions.

Second, in the Marxian tradition Table 2.1 locates the sources of class conflict in the economic system. An important corollary is that the inequalities of power inherent in this system under capitalism set profound limits on the possibilities for working-class action in the (democratic) political arena. In particular, insofar as economic growth remains dependent on private capital accumulation, capital can mount very effective opposition to policies designed to make inroads into its other control rights, if necessary by threatening to halt or divert investment flows. Partly for this reason, the policy package associated with the welfare state conventionally addresses itself only to problems connected to employment and distribution, and not to the twin loci of control to which capital has historically assigned priority, namely, accumulation and the labor process. This in turn raises the perennial issue of whether it is structurally possible for the welfare state to be anything more than an appendage to— indeed, a source of reinforcement of—what remains a capitalist society. This issue has been widely discussed elsewhere, and the reformist position is ably put

---

[1]This scheme is in many respects similar to that of Stephens (1979), who is one of the few scholars in this area to predicate his study of the welfare state on a fully elaborated theory of class conflict.

TABLE 2.1

**Key areas of class conflict and corresponding welfare problems of labor under capitalism, with some democratic socialist policy responses**

| Conflict | Problem | Policy |
|---|---|---|
| Control over investment | Economic growth, and hence labor's future prosperity, is dependent on capital's ability and willingness to direct revenue into productive investments. | Direct investment, nationalization, or subsidization of capital to maintain investment levels and influence investment policy. |
| Control over employment | Labor's job security, and hence income security, are dependent on its ability to "sell" and capital's willingness to "buy" labor power, in the context of a volatile market. | Macroeconomic full employment policies, job creation, income maintenance schemes, job protection laws, support for trade unions. |
| Control over distribution | Labor's income claims are subordinate and in opposition to those of capital. Labor's rewards are dependent on market scarcity, human capital, and effort. | Income and consumption guarantees, income redistribution through taxing and spending, equalization of market situations (education), support for trade unions. |
| Control over work | Labor is both legally and factually subordinate to capital in the work process, although as a human "factor of production" its cooperation must be secured. | Codetermination and allied laws, support for trade unions. |

and defended by Korpi (1978), Stephens (1979), Maravall (1979), and others.

A third implication of Table 2.1, again arising out of the overlapping nature of the four loci of class conflict, is the problem of defining the precise boundaries of the welfare state's "working class" constituency. Our theoretical schema assumes that policies addressed to the same ends as the welfare state, as well as policies addressed to labor's other problems, are likely to be favored or opposed by similar class alignments (e.g., parties)—similar, but by no means identical according to Stephens (1979, pp. 53–54). In his view, whereas all employees without control have an objective interest in socialist control of investment and production, those who enjoy a relatively favorable market situation are likely to oppose reforms intended to equalize employment and income opportunities. On the other hand, Castles develops an argument that "rests on the assumption that welfare confers 'equality of status,' and that the only section of the community which has an unequivocal motive for opposing this type of equality, given that it may involve a redistribution of income and wealth, is that which is extremely privileged compared with the majority of the population [Castles and McKinlay, 1979b, p. 168; see also Castles, 1978, p. 75]."

A final difficulty arises in the identification of measurable facets of the welfare state that have well justified roots in class conflict. The decisions that have to be made here are important not only to meet the methodological desideratum of consistency between hypotheses and hypothesis testing, but also because in practice much controversy has arisen over whether researchers who fail to find class conflict effects on welfare policy have investigated the "wrong" policies, or whether those who do discern these effects have unconscionably "rigged" the dependent variable to suit their purposes. At least three different approaches to the problem of selecting welfare state indicators are discernible in the literature.

There is, first, a "maximalist" position that views the essence of the socialist welfare state as social control over the distribution of income, or more precisely, citizens' capacity to consume (Stephens 1979). To the extent that consumption capacities are determined by democratic political processes rather than by market mechanisms, inequality of condition and, in turn, inequality of opportunity are narrowed. Accordingly, welfare state "effort" can be proxied by measuring state spending in its entirety (with the exception of military expenditures), with appropriate adjustment made for economic capacity. However, other scholars have pointed out that many state expenditures are nonegalitarian in their consequences, and have argued instead for more narrowly focused indicators to explicitly capture *redistributive* welfare effort. Thus Wilensky (1975, 1976) chooses to omit the state's involvement in education from his measure of welfare spending; Bjorn (1979) leaves aside insurance-based social security schemes and utilizes only data for public assistance; whereas Hewitt (1977) attempts to isolate only that share of welfare expenditures that is financed by progressive taxation.

Each of these authors assumes that only those elements of the welfare state that contribute to the reduction of inequality truly contribute to social welfare. An alternative argument, suggested by Castles (1978), offers a third and more subtle approach to the meaning of equality. Consider the problem of education, for instance. Even if the rich enjoy a disproportionate share of the benefits of state education, the poor enjoy an equal *right* of access which would be denied them under a system of provision through the market. Similarly, the case for focusing on admittedly redistributive public assistance expenditures may be countered by pointing to the undesirable (from a socialist viewpoint) consequences of reliance on this form of provision, such as the fostering of political divisions within the working class and of "backlash" from the middle class (Korpi 1980), and the neglect of more permanent solutions to poverty, such as the provision of decently paying jobs (cf. Rainwater, Rein, and Schwartz 1979). Considerations of this kind led Castles to construct an index of "pure welfare," ranking nations not only in terms of the state's role in income allocation

(Stephens's measure), but also on the basis of indicators to capture "care for the weak" and "equality of citizenship rights."

The problem of choosing appropriate indicators is confounded by limitations imposed by the sort of research undertaken. Perhaps the most revealing and significant locus of class conflict over the parameters of established welfare states concerns not their size so much as who controls and benefits from social services (Gough 1979). This suggests a research program focused on quite precise and sophisticated dependent variables. The relative emphasis would be on selective versus universal programs, on subsidization of private schemes versus public provision, on earnings-related contributions versus revenue financing, on regressive versus progressive taxation, on cyclical welfare spending ("regulating the poor") rather than welfare-by-right, and so forth. In the meantime, however, we do not have measures of variables of this kind for large multinational samples. A more practical need is for cross-national researchers to recognize the absence of any necessary correlation between the three dimensions just discussed, and to attempt to simultaneously characterize welfare states in terms of state intrusion into the market, vertical redistribution, and security and equality of rights. One reason why a multidimensional approach is important is that the strategy of "socialist transformation" pursued by democratic socialist movements varies across nations and over time. This variation may also come through if researchers try to disaggregate various welfare state components (e.g., by differentiating expenditure categories) in order to reflect rather than obscure important strategic choices, such as those between income maintenance and demand management, between money and the provision of services, between redistribution of income and enlarging opportunity, and between intervention via the market and expansion of the state itself.

# The Pro-Social-Democratic Consensus and Its Shortcomings

It has been argued here that development of the hypothesis that the "democratic class struggle" can account for welfare state variations requires parallel development of our theoretical understanding of the origins of the welfare state in the conflicting class interests of labor and capital. But it emerges that the class-conflict-based theory outlined earlier poses serious logical and methodological obstacles to making the question of labor movement impacts on the welfare state researchable. I have suggested that these obstacles derive from the complex ties between the various interests of labor and among the various means for realizing these interests via state intervention. This makes it difficult to determine a priori what constituency will pursue what interests by means of what type(s) of policy and under what historical conditions. Without more precise specifications of the questions to be asked, the value of the answers we have concerning the impact of socialist movements on social policy is limited.

Nevertheless, it is of interest to know the interim state of the art in the field, particularly in view of the upsurge of research over the last decade. To begin with, half a dozen recent studies will be examined, all having in common the fact that they are informed by hypotheses derived from some variant of the model in Figure 2.1, they utilize large historical and/or comparative data sets and are committed to quantitative techniques of analysis, and they concur in supporting the claim that reformist socialist movements have contributed substantially to the achievement of socialist welfare state objectives.

I do not claim to have plundered the relevant literature in its entirety. For one thing, the focus here is deliberately confined to macrolevel research and excludes the vast literature on subnational variations in welfare provision. Case study investigations have also been explicitly omitted (but see Shattuck and Hancock 1978). Finally, a number of studies similar in nature to those to be reviewed could have been cited in further confirmation of the class conflict model (e.g., Dryzek 1978; Korpi 1980; Williamson & Weiss 1979). The research that has been selected is, however, certainly representative of its genre.

For brevity, the most essential features of the affirmative studies chosen for review have been summarized in Table 2.2. All six of the studies share the view that politically strong labor movements have hastened the advent and growth of the welfare state in the Western nations. Except for Flora, they are also agreed that the strength of parliamentary socialism is *more important* for welfare state development than other plausible influences, including economic growth. This consensus, furthermore, arises from studies that collectively are both cross-national and historical; which have investigated timing as well as scope, changes as well as levels, and overall as well as presumptively redistributive elements of welfare state commitment. At the same time, most of the researchers are agreed that the socialist impact on welfare is at least to some extent conditional upon such exogenous factors as economic conditions and characteristics of the political system. Furthermore, the majority of them (Stephens, Cameron, Bjorn, Flora) explicitly concede that state power, a la Scandinavian (and Austrian) social democracy, is by no means the only route to welfare state growth. Other apparent routes are the "consociational" corporatism of the low countries, the old regime Bismarckian welfare state, and the exertion of extraparliamentary pressures. In each of these cases the strength of the organized working class is only partially or "negatively" relevant to what is happening. Consociational democracies are generous to labor in part because of the importance of keeping the social peace in a context of divisive extraclass cleavages (McRae 1974); according to Flora, the Bismarckian strategy was predicated on the existence of a state bureaucracy that could operate social programs and landed interests that could pay for them, as well as fear of organized labor; and as Bjorn (following Piven and Cloward 1971) points out, the American case seems to demonstrate that mobilization of the disadvantaged can occur and affect policy quite outside of a labor movement framework.

Let us probe some of these cracks in the surface of the pro-social-democratic consensus a little further. As noted, Flora's is the weakest affirmation of the class conflict model, in that it suggests the following qualifications:

1.  The growth of socialist parties is not a requirement for welfare state breakthroughs. These have sometimes occurred as a direct spinoff from relatively high levels of socioeconomic modernization.
2.  Socialist influence alone cannot produce innovation, since no signs of the welfare state appeared anywhere before some floor level of indust-rialization and urbanization was reached (a less significant caveat than the previous one, since the class conflict model is itself predicated on "modernization" in the sense of the emergence of class-stratified capitalism).
3.  The argument of Figure 2.1 that the political mobilization of the working class only counts for policy when it results in direct control of the state is largely irrelevant to the formative period of the welfare state. Labor's influence then more frequently took the form either of threats to the stability of preparliamentary regimes or the impact of a socialist parliamentary presence on nonsocialist governments.[2]

One may add to this that several of the other studies (Bjorn, Cameron) show that even where socialist party entry into government has been institutionalized, its effects on policy are not necessarily proportional to the extent of entry. Higher welfare expenditures are sometimes associated with social democrats falling from power or participating in coalition governments.

There is another serious limitation to equating the class balance of state power with socialist party participation in government. As several of the studies (Stephens, Cameron) make plain, under "consociational corporatism" working-class interests are transmitted to the state and make themselves felt in policy in the absence of a governing working class party. In the Netherlands and to a lesser extent in Belgium, one observes a level of "welfare effort" comparable to that in the Scandinavian nations and Austria, where for decades social democratic parties have enjoyed a dominant or very prominent position in government. Nevertheless, several characteristics of the Dutch and Belgian cases suggest that they constitute only a partial deviation from the model. These are: (*a*) the existence of highly centralized labor unions integrated into corporatist structures (such as economy-wide wage bargaining); (*b*) routine participation of socialist parties in government; and (*c*) the quasi-social-democratic role played to some extent by the dominant Catholic parties, which

---

[2]On the basis of data on the coverage rather than timing of social insurance legislation, one of Flora's collaborators concludes that prior to World War I most of the variation is attributable to innovations by authoritarian regimes threatened by the growing electoral strength of socialist parties. In the post-1914 period *as a whole*, he finds that the significance of socialist party votes, now joined by leftist party incumbency, persisted (Alber 1980).

**TABLE 2.2**

**Empirical studies supportive of a pro-social-democratic class conflict model of the welfare state.**

| Study | Method | Sample | Welfare state indicator | Left strength indicator | Principal findings |
|---|---|---|---|---|---|
| Hewitt (1977) | Cross-national regressions | N = 17[a] | "Redistributive effect of government budgets" (social security expenditure as percentage of GNP, weighted by income tax as percentage of revenue, ca. 1973) | Socialist percentage of legislature, 1945–1965 | Equalizing welfare expenditures are fostered by powerful socialist parties, even net of the effects of economic development and growth and political democracy. |
| Stephens (1979) | Cross-national regressions | N = 17[a] | "Welfare State effort" (nonmilitary public expenditure as percentage of GNI, 1970) | Percentage of years Social Democrats or Communists in office, 1945–1970 | Social Democratic government (or corporatism under Catholic labor movements) advances "socialization of consumption rights" irrespective of economic or demographic conditions. |
| Cameron (1976) | Cross-national regressions | N = 13[a] | "Expansion of the extractive capacity of the state" (change in public revenue as percentage of GNP, 1956–1973) | Percentage of years Social Democrats and non-Communist allies with cabinet majority, 1956–1973 | Governments under Social Democratic influence or control expanded the public economy fastest, in turn using this economic leverage to reduce income inequality at the expense of private capital accumulation. |

| Study | Method | Countries | Dependent variable | Independent variable | Findings |
|---|---|---|---|---|---|
| Bjorn (1976, 1979) | Comparative historical analysis, 1920–1970 | Norway, Sweden, Australia, US, UK | "Government vertical redistribution of income" (public assistance expenditure as percentage of GNP, corrected for demand) | Percentage Social Democratic (or comparable) party members of cabinet | Under "class cohesive" party systems, pro-labor governments were more redistributive; otherwise expenditures probably fluctuate with popular insurgency. |
| Hanneman (1979a, 1979b) | Comparative historical analysis, 1870–1970 | Britain, France, Germany | "Vertical redistribution" (social insurance expenditure as percentage of GNP; income tax as percentage of revenue) | Various indicators of labor party and union strength | A highly mobilized working class produces greater redistributive intervention, provided state structures are open to incorporation of labor organizations into policymaking. |
| Flora (1976) | Comparative historical analysis, 1880–1970 | Western Europe (N = 12) | Inauguration of major social insurance programs | Vote share of left-wing parties | Socioeconomic modernization and working-class political mobilization were alternative and complementary sources of social policy innovation. |

[a] The basic sampling frame for the cross-national studies comprises all OECD members except those that were nondemocratic through most of the postwar period or had less than 1 million inhabitants (N = 18).

have substantial ties to the union movement and are flanked by strong competitors to their right.

These various qualifications add up to an admission that the mechanisms by which the interests and collective leverage of the working class are conveyed to the state and influence policy are much more variable than one would expect by interpreting strength of the Left as simply the extent of democratic socialist tenure in government.[3] There is also another set of considerations suggesting that the flood of pro-social-democratic findings cited earlier should be treated with caution, and these are methodological in nature.[4] Table 2.2 confronts us with a bewildering variety of operational conceptions of what the political strength of labor movements is (votes, legislative seats, office holding), and even of what these movements consist of (the problem of Communist parties). The samples and methodologies are also diverse, and in small-$n$ research of this kind, that diversity can make a great deal of difference.

There is some comfort to be taken from the fact that, despite the many dissimilarities between the studies, a broad convergence of findings nevertheless emerges. This in itself is no guarantee of their validity, however. Cross-national studies are beleaguered by difficulties of inferring comparability and causality. In addition, their characteristic reliance on linear tests of association can be misleading, since a few extreme cases in the distribution can produce attractively high correlations. In particular, it has not yet been clearly established whether social democracy, like nonsocialist America, is a species of "exceptionalism" or whether it is perhaps an underlying tendency of advanced capitalist democracies (Giddens 1973), which, in fact, behaves as a continuum. A further problem with cross-national correlations is their assumption of a contemporaneous causal relationship between office holding and policy. The partisan impact on policy probably takes time to develop, and its momentum may well persist even after a particular tendency leaves office. For all these reasons diachronic historical studies appear more suited to the present research task, and it is notable in this respect that the work of Bjorn and Flora produced by far the most heavily qualified affirmations of the pro-social-democratic interpretation of welfare state politics.

## Alternatives to the Social Democratic Interpretation

Paradoxically, it appears that the empirical consensus ranged behind the notion that socialist political power matters to welfare state outcomes is both impressive and riddled with qualifications and question marks. It must therefore

[3]For a fuller discussion of the weaknesses of, and desirable extensions to a rigidly social democratic interpretation of the role of class conflict in distributive policymaking, see my companion article (Shalev, forthcoming).

[4]More extensive discussions of methodological issues may be found in Borg and Castles, forthcoming; Carrier and Kendall 1977; Heisler and Peters 1978; Shalev, forthcoming; and Stonecash 1979.

be asked whether there are alternative theories that can make a better job of explicating observed variation in the relevant policy outcomes. Implicit or explicit alternatives to the thrust of the findings and interpretation so far described are to be found in a number of studies. Evidence purporting to demonstrate a lack of association between leftist strength and welfare state policy outcomes is variously explained as a consequence of the persistence of class power disparities deriving from the economic structure, the *embourgeoisement* of socialist politicians, the autonomy of the bureaucratic policy apparatus, or the irrelevance of old-fashioned distributive conflict to "post-industrial" societies (e.g., Heclo 1974; Heisler and Peters 1978; Jackman 1980; Therborn 1978). I propose to focus here on some critical alternatives to a pro-social-democratic analysis which do not necessarily deny the existence of an empirical link between social democracy and the welfare state, but radically reinterpret it. For, if it cannot be shown that labor movement strength is either a necessary or sufficient condition for welfare state development, it is indeed quite possible that the substantial empirical impact of the former upon the latter is actually due to some other, more inclusive variable with which it is correlated. At least three candidates for such a variable have been proposed in some recent cross-national studies: economic openess, Right strength, and "democratic corporatism." For the essential details, see Table 2.3.

After modifying and expanding his data base somewhat and rethinking his analysis, Cameron (1978) has come to a different conclusion than the one he reached in 1976. He now argues that the trade dependence typical of small economies can account for both the social democratic and consociational paths to public sector expansion. One of the reasons is that openess leads to a highly concentrated economy, which is viewed as a prerequisite for the emergence of governing leftist parties and/or strong union confederations, both of which press for increases in publicly funded income supplements.[5] The other reason—quite independent of labor organization—is that in order to counteract the potentially destabilizing effects of dependence on world markets, the state expands its economic intervention (e.g., using social services, labor market policies, and public investment as a buffer against imported cyclical shocks).

On reflection, neither of these arguments seriously challenges the original class conflict model, although openess (along with additional variables discussed by Cameron and others) may help to explain the model's "exceptional cases." Economic concentration is at best only one contributory influence on working-class mobilization (Shalev and Korpi 1980), and in three cases of exceptional openess/concentration—Ireland, Switzerland, and New Zealand—we fail to find strong unions and leftist parties. On the other hand, if Cameron were right on the second count—spending as a defense mechanism— he would presumably uncover a tendency over time for increases in economic dependence to foster increased public spending. This he is unable to do (p.

---

[5]The importance of concentration for labor organization goes back to Marx, but was more recently formulated by Ingham (1974) and subsequently by Stephens (1979).

**TABLE 2.3**

**Empirical studies rejecting the pro-social-democratic class conflict model of the welfare state**

| Study | Method | Sample[a] | Welfare state indicator | Left strength indicator | Principal findings |
|-------|--------|-----------|------------------------|------------------------|--------------------|
| Cameron (1978) | Cross-national regressions | N = 18 | "Expansion of the public economy" (change in government revenues as precentage of GDP, 1960–1975) | Average socialist percentage of government's electoral base, 1960–1975 | Economic openess, with or without leftist domination, is the source of rapid growth of the public economy. |
| Borg and Castles (1981) | Cross-national correlations | N = 16 | Policy commitment to welfare and equality (change in income maintenance expenditure relative to real p.c. income, 1962–1972; difference between pre- and post-tax income inequality) | Indicators of party unity, legislative strength, and office holding for socialist and rightist parties, 1962–1972 | Right-wing political weakness, with or without leftist control of government, explains variations in growth and equalizing effects of state revenue and expenditure. |
| Wilensky (1981) | Cross-national regressions | N = 19 | "Welfare effort" (social security expenditure as percentage of GNP, 1966 or 1971) | "Party power" (time in office plus legislative base plus prime ministership) of Left (including Communist) and Catholic parties, 1919–1976 or 1946–1976 | Catholic, not leftist, political power explains welfare state variations. |

[a]See note to Table 2.2. Wilensky's sample includes Israel.

1255n), despite the plausibility of this strand of the theory. There is also a minor methodological fault in Cameron's work. Judging by his scatterplots, the relationship of both leftist rule and economic openess to the expansion of the public economy is curvilinear. If this had been taken into account, it appears (at least to my eye) that openess is a better predictor than leftism for only a few cases, most notably the Netherlands.

A second significant attack on the pro-social-democratic consensus has been launched by Castles.[6] The essence of his argument is that a strong commitment to welfare is the product not of a strong political Left, but rather results from the absence of opposition from a strong and unified Right. Since weakness of the Right can be found even in the absence of strength on the Left, and since it is always associated with a strong and redistributive welfare state, the correlation between leftism and welfare must be regarded as spurious.

Interestingly, Castles adopts almost the same theoretical assumptions as the model of Figure 2.1, but with the addition of the unity and political strength of the Right at two different points in the causal chain. The argument is that a fragmented Right is a necessary condition for the emergence of a strong leftist party, *and* a strong Right is always "a major impediment to welfare state provision [Castles 1978, p. 77]." In most recent work (Borg and Castles, 1981),Castles extends the second of these arguments and claims to find an added element of asymmetry in the impact of Left and Right. Not only does the ideological posture of the Left fail to produce more welfare than when other nonrightist parties hold the reins of office, but, in addition, the Left only impacts on policy if it gets into office, whereas right-wing parties are able to effectively spread their antiwelfare message merely by speaking with a single voice (i.e., low rightist party fragmentation).

These claims probably overstretch the evidence. As Borg and Castles recognize, right-wing and left-wing strength are only weakly correlated across nations. If one computes averages for their welfare indicators separately for nations with a weak and a strong political Right, and then looks at variations within each category according to the Left's strength, it becomes apparent that leftism has a net positive influence on the dependent variables. True, "rightism" has a stronger effect overall than "leftism," although this margin narrows substantially if we set aside two apparently exceptional cases, New Zealand and Australia. These two "rightist" countries score so far below all the others on the available measures of welfare that some other or additional explanation appears to be called for. Castles's work also demonstrates rather clearly the significance of the researcher's choice of welfare state indicators for the substantive results obtained. The same countries are ranked quite differently, and the role of social democracy independent of Right strength emerges in quite

---

[6]After completing this chapter I obtained a more recent paper by Castles which somewhat modifies the argument summarized here.

a different light, as one moves between his different studies of the problem (e.g., Castles 1978; Castles and McKinlay 1979a, 1979b).

It seems to me that Castles's argument may well be significant, but probably only in its "moderate" version. What this version seems to say is that the same factors (cleavage structures, insitutional conditions) that weaken the Right also tend to strengthen the Left, and vice versa. But, one particular combination of contextual factors found in a few countries (especially the Netherlands) produces a fragmented, "coalescent" political system which (for reasons already discused) is associated with a level of welfare effort comparable to that observable in countries where the polity is dominated by the Left. Other than this, the message—which is an important one—is simply that the parliamentary expression of class conflict is not reducible to what working-class movements do, but rather is reflected in the party system as a whole.

The third alternative hypothesis to emerge from recent cross-national research is that of Wilensky. His earlier work (Wilensky 1975) was widely discussed, particularly its reliance upon the convergence hypothesis (welfare state growth was a product of "economic growth and its demographic and bureaucratic outcomes").[7] Subsequently Wilensky (1976) narrowed his focus solely to the "rich democracies," emphasizing the considerable *divergence* between them in welfare spending and attempting to account for this by invoking a theory of "democratic corporatism." His key proposition was that "centralization of government and of labor and employer federations permits the mobilization of consensus on major issues of political economy with minimal political fuss [1976, p. 43]." "Minimizing the fuss" means the avoidance of taxpayer backlash by reaching consensual peak bargains in which social policy plays a major role, and financing welfare expenditures by means sufficiently invisible that they will not arouse the ire of the citizens.

This study, however, left unsettled the question of what determines corporatism, while hinting (p. 34) that working-class mobilization might be a likely contender. Furthermore, it was criticized from many quarters for ignoring the possibility that Left political power, or at any rate the partisan composition of government, might be responsible for variations in welfare expenditure. In his most recent work, Wilensky (1981) responds to these criticisms with empirical extensions that purport to show that "cumulative left power has had no effect on welfare effort and output [p. 355]," except insofar as it has contributed (and then only weakly) to corporatism. Indeed, some powerful leftist parties may have impeded their spending capacity by raising working-class expectations and relying on "painfully visible taxes," a sure recipe for "tax-welfare backlash." A government that wants "to spend and yet keep cool" had better be Catholic than

---

[7]Subsequent research has called these findings into question. Miller (1976) showed that when rich and poor nations were differentiated, in the former, welfare effort *diminished* at higher levels of development. Across the developmental spectrum as a whole, Miller disconfirmed Wilensky's conclusion about the irrelevance of political system type, and Williamson and Weiss (1979) showed that the strength of unions and socialist parties contributed additional explained variance to that attributable to economic development predictors.

be leftist. Long-run Catholic party power is strongly supportive both of welfare expenditure and tax invisibility. More important, it makes a major contribution to the institutionalization of corporatist political exchange, which Wilensky continues to regard as the most important immediate influence on rich countries' spending.

The evidence in support of Wilensky's argument that Catholicism rather than socialism is the chief partisan contributor to welfare effort can be challenged. First, his dependent variable unwittingly stacks the odds against leftism. In his contribution to this book, Wilensky effectively makes the case that corporatist (presumably including *Left* corporatist) social policy is an integral part of a much broader package of state interventions with strong welfare implications. This would imply operationalizing welfare effort along "maximalist" lines (total government expenditure), with results already foreseeable from the work of Stephens and others. Instead, the measure used by Wilensky refers to long-established programs, the cost of which alters greatly in response to demographic changes over which governments of any complexion have little control, or else (in cases like unemployment insurance) to contingencies that leftist governments make great efforts to *prevent*.

Problems with Wilensky's coding of partisanship also serve to weaken the correlation between Left party government and social expenditure.[8] If these are taken into account it appears to me that welfare effort follows the Left–Right axis fairly closely except for five cases of "over-spending": Belgium, Netherlands, France, Italy, and Germany. Could it be that Catholic corporatism is responsible for these deviations? To answer this question, we need to distinguish between two varieties of political Catholicism and of corporatism. First, corporatism as Wilensky describes it (and as practised under social democracy) means the joint negotiation of economic policy (including wage fixing) by representatives of organized labor and capital and the state. This is what happens in Belgium and the Netherlands, but not in Italy and France, where there are no "social contracts" because the major parties of labor have been excluded from state power and the unions generally adopt a "contestational" posture toward both employers and the state. Germany falls in neither category, but is closer to the first.

In relation to Catholicism, there is a distinction to be made between Catholic parties that stand to the left of a sizeable conservative party and owe a special debt to working-class interests, and those in which Catholicism enters the polity in the form of what is, in fact if not in name, a right-wing party (Borg and Castles 1981, p. 7–8; Stephens 1979, Chapter 4). The first type of alignment is found in Belgium and the Netherlands, the second in Germany, Italy, and France. As we saw earlier, the first type is ideologically egalitarian, frequently governs along with left-wing parties, and produces a large and fairly redis-

---

[8]In my view, the parties in Israel, the United States, and Finland coded "leftist" by Wilensky do not properly belong in the democratic socialist category. He also seriously underrates Left strength in the Netherlands and, especially, Austria.

tributive welfare state. The second type of party, when dominant, has been responsible for considerable expansion of welfare but as a concession to the Left during spurts of working-class mobilization and capitalist weakness (e.g., immediately after the war in France and Germany). The cost to rightist interests is minimized as far as possible in such cases by emphasizing nonredistributive programs and methods of finance.

Thus Wilensky's study essentially just confirms the important (but by now no longer novel) insight that politics and policy in the Low Countries are special. True, "corporatism" accounts for more cases of commitment to welfare than social democracy does, yet it is after all only a description of certain institutional arrangements which can themselves hardly be understood without reference to class structure, power, and conflict (Panitch 1980).

## Epilogue: Socialism and the Welfare State

The welfare state emerges and grows in advanced capitalist societies with or without a strong and coherent social democratic labor movement. But its emergence is hastened, its growth is speeded, and its consequences for the interclass redistribution of resources and opportunities are arguably greater under social democracy. In the postwar period, the largest and most progressive welfare states are found only under social democracy or else where the corporatist structures normally associated with it have come into being as a result of a special combination of economic circumstances and politically articulated cleavages. These same factors in different combinations have undoubtedly contributed to the emergence of powerful reformist labor movements in Scandinavia and Austria, yet the evidence we have reviewed suggests that a politically and organizationally strong working class imposes an imprint on public policy which is greater than the sum of the preconditions that facilitated this strength.

Whether this is also taken to mean that social democracy leads to socialism depends of course on what one chooses to call socialism. If it means ameliorating the welfare problems of labor that result from capitalist methods of labor allocation and resource distribution, the answer is yes. If is means solving these problems by changing the fundamentals of capitalist labor allocation and resource distribution, the answer is probably no. And if it means challenging the ultimate source of capitalist power—its control over accumulation and the labor process—the answer is definitely no. Of course, committed social democrats see the welfare state as only one stage in a continuing process of transition, which will be followed by further and more decisive stages. In support of this contention they point to developments such as the Meidner proposal in Sweden for establishment of "wage-earners' funds" which would gradually transfer ownership and its prerogatives from capital to labor (Korpi 1978; Stephens 1979).

Critics on the more radical Left dismiss such claims, arguing that modern social democracy is in effect an important but transient stage in capitalist development, and that even its limited achievement of the full-employment welfare state was made possible by economic and political conditions unique to the first few postwar decades, conditions which served to temporarily obscure the contradictions inherent in corporatist compromise between labor and capital (Wolfe 1978). Some radicals go even further than this, contending that social democracy has merely institutionalized in the political arena the objective balance of class power determined by "the relations and forces of production" in the economic arena. For instance, Therborn and his collaborators attempt to show that in Sweden, nominal control over the state has added nothing in relative terms to the concessions wrested by the working class *prior* to the social democrats' ascension to power (Therborn *et al.* 1978).

The debate cannot be easily settled, particularly since the issues are to a large extent ideological rather than straightforwardly amenable to the tools of positivist social science. But the debate is an exciting one because it raises fascinating questions. What is the relative autonomy of the state from the power structure laid down by the social organization of production? Under what circumstances can movements of the subordinate class exploit the institutions of "bourgeois democracy" to transform the privileged position of the dominant class in distributive processes? To what extent is it generally true of domestic policymaking that conscious political agency, rather than more impersonal and less controllable forces, determine the outcomes of state intervention? And what is the true meaning and significance of the welfare state? The pro-social-democratic model of policy which has been reviewed here undoubtedly provides only partial and controversial answers to these questions, but it has the great virtue of inviting scholars from the fields of political science, sociology, economics, and social policy to join the struggle for better answers.

ACKNOWLEDGMENTS

I am indebted to Professor Harold Wilensky and the editors of this volume for helpful comments on an earlier draft of this chapter.

# References

Alber, J. 1979. The growth of social insurance in Western Europe: Has social democracy made a difference? Paper presented at the World Congress of the International Political Science Association, Moscow, August 1979.

Bjorn, L. 1976. *Labor parties and the redistribution of income in capitalist democracies.* Unpublished Ph.D. dissertation. University of North Carolina—Chapel Hill.

Bjorn, L. 1979. Labor parties, economic growth, and the redistribution of income in five capitalist democracies. *Comparative Social Research* 2:93–128.

Borg, S.G., and Castles, F.G. 1981. The influence of the political right on public income maintenance expenditure and equality. *Political Studies* 29:604–621.

Cameron, D.R. 1976. Inequality and the state: A political economic–comparison. Paper presented at the Annual Meeting of the American Political Science Association, Chicago, September 1976.

Cameron, D.R. 1978. The expansion of the public economy: A comparative analysis. *American Political Science Review* 72:1243–1261.

Carrier, J., and Kendall, I. 1977. The development of welfare states: The production of plausible accounts. *Journal of Social Policy* 6:271–290.

Castles, F.G. 1978. *The social democratic image of society: A study of the achievements and origins of Scandinavian social democracy in comparative perspective.* London: Routledge & Kegan Paul.

Castles, F., and McKinlay, R.D. 1979a. Does politics matter: An analysis of the public welfare commitment in advanced democratic states. *European Journal of Political Research* 7:169–186.

Castles, F.G., and McKinlay, R.D. 1979b. Public welfare provision, Scandinavia, and the sheer futility of the sociological approach to politics. *British Journal of Political Science* 9:157–171.

Crouch, C. Forthcoming. The conditions for trade union wage restraint. In *The politics and sociology of global inflation*, eds. C. Maier and L. Lindberg. (A volume reporting the Brookings project.)

Dryzek, J. 1978. Politics, economics and inequality: A cross-national analysis. *European Journal of Political Research* 6: 399–410.

Erikson, R., Goldthorpe, J.H., and Portocarero, L. 1979. Intergenerational class mobility in three western European societies. *British Journal of Sociology* 30: 415–441.

Esping–Andersen, G. 1978. Social class, social democracy, and the state: Party policy and party decomposition in Denmark and Sweden. *Comparative Politics* 11: 42–58.

Flora, P. 1976. On the development of the western European welfare states. Paper presented at the International Political Science Association Congress, Edinburgh, August 1976.

Giddens, A. 1973. *The class structure of the advanced societies.* London: Hutchinson.

Gough, I. 1979. *The political economy of the welfare state.* London: Macmillan.

Hanneman, R.A. 1979a. *Economic development and income inequality: A political–sociological explanation.* Ph.D. dissertation, Department of Sociology, University of Wisconsin—Madison.

Hanneman, R.A. 1979b. Inequality, redistribution, and the welfare state: Labor representation and government policy in Britain, France, and Germany 1870 to 1970. Paper presented at the Conference of Europeanists, Washington, March 1979.

Heclo, H. 1974. *Modern social politics in Britain and Sweden: From relief to income maintenance.* New Haven: Yale University Press.

Heisler, M.O., and Peters, B.G. 1978. Comparing social policy across levels of government, countries, and time: Belgium and Sweden since 1870. In *Comparing public policies: New concepts and methods,* ed. D.E. Ashford. Beverley Hills and London: Sage. Pp. 149–175.

Hewitt, C. 1977. The effect of political democracy and social democracy on equality in industrial societies: A cross-national comparison. *American Sociological Review* 42: 450–464.

Hibbs, D.A., Jr. 1977. Political parties and macroeconomic policy. *American Political Science Review* 71: 1467–1487.

Ingham, G.K. 1974. *Strikes and industrial conflict.* London: Macmillan.

Jackman, R.W. 1975. *Politics and social equality: A comparative analysis.* New York: Wiley.

Jackman, R.W. 1980. Socialist parties and income inequality in Western industrial societies. *The Journal of Politics* 42: 135–149.

Korpi, W. 1978. *The working class in welfare capitalism: Work, unions and politics in Sweden.* London: Routledge & Kegan Paul.

Korpi, W. 1980. Social policy and distributional conflict in the capitalist democracies. A preliminary framework. *West European Politics* 3:296–316.

Korpi, W., and Shalev, M. 1979a. Strikes, industrial relations and class conflict in capitalist societies. *British Journal of Sociology,* 30: 164–187.

Korpi, W., and Shalev, M. 1979b. Strikes, power and politics in the Western nations, 1900–1976. *Political Power & Social Theory* 1: 299–332.

Lipset, S.M., and Rokkan, S. 1967. Cleavage structures, party systems and voter alignments. In *Party systems and voter alignments*, eds. S.M. Lipset and S. Rokkan. New York: Free Press. Pp. 1–64.

McCrae, K., ed. 1974. *Consociational democracy: Political accomodation in segmented societies.* Toronto: McClelland & Stewart.

Maravall, J.M. 1979. The limits of reformism: Parliamentary socialism and the Marxist theory of the state. *British Journal of Sociology* 30: 267–290.

Martin, A. 1973. *The politics of economic policy in the United States: A tentative view from a comparative perspective.* Beverley Hills and London: Sage.

Miliband, R. 1969. *The state in capitalist society: The analysis of the Western system of power.* London: Weidenfeld & Nicholson.

Miller, L. 1976. The structural determinants of the welfare effort: A critique and a contribution. *Social Service Review* 50(1): 57–79.

Offe, C. 1972. Advanced capitalism and the welfare state. *Politics and Society* 2: 479–488.

Panitch, L. 1980. Recent theorizations of corporatism: Reflections on a growth industry. *British Journal of Sociology* 31: 159–187.

Parkin, F. 1971. *Class inequality and political order: Social stratification in capitalist & communist societies.* London: Paladin.

Parkin, F. 1979. *Marxism & class theory: A bourgeois critique.* London: Tavistock.

Piven, F.F., and Cloward, R.A. 1971. *Regulating the poor: The functions of public welfare.* New York: Pantheon.

Rainwater, L., Rein, M., and Schwartz, J. 1978. Income claims systems in three countries: A stratification perspective. Paper presented at the World Congress of Sociology, Upsala, August 1978.

Scase, R. 1977. *Social democracy in capitalist society: Working-class politics in Britain and Sweden.* London: Croom Helm.

Shalev, M. Forthcoming. The social democratic model and beyond: Two 'generations' of comparative research on the welfare state. *Comparative Social Research* 6.

Shalev, M., and Korpi, W. 1980. Working-class mobilization and American Exceptionalism. *Economic and Industrial Democracy* 1: 31–62.

Shattuck, P.T., and Hancock, M.D., eds. 1978 *Comparative Politics* 11. Special issue on "Policy problems of social democracy."

Stephens, E.H., and Stephens, J.D. Forthcoming. The labor movement, political power and workers' participation in western Europe. *Political Power and Social Theory 3.*

Stephens, J.D. 1979. *The transition from capitalism to socialism.* London: Macmillan.

Stonecash, J. 1979. Politics, wealth and public policy: The significance of political systems. *Policy Studies Journal* 7: 670–675.

Therborn, G. 1978. Sweden before and after social democracy: A first overview. *Acta Sociologica* 21 (supplement): 37–58.

Tufte, E.R. 1978. *Political control of the economy.* Princeton: Princeton University Press.

Webber, D. 1979. Social democracy as the midwife of change: A comparative survey of active manpower policy innovation in Sweden, Britain and West Germany. Paper presented at ECPR Conference, Brussels, April 1979.

Westergaard, J. 1978. Social policy and class inequality: Some notes on welfare state limits. In *The socialist register 1978*, eds R. Miliband and J. Saville. London: Merlin Press. Pp. 71–99.

Wilensky, H.L. 1975. *The welfare state and equality: Structural and ideological roots of public expenditures.* Berkeley: University of California Press.

*Michael Shalev*

Wilensky, H.L. 1976. *The "new corporatism," centralization and the welfare state.* London and Beverley Hills: Sage.

Wilensky, H.L. 1981. Leftism, Catholicism, and democratic corporatism: The role of political parties in recent welfare state development. In *The development of welfare states in Europe and America,* eds. P. Flora and J. Heidenheimer. New Brunswick: Transaction Books. Pp 341–378.

Williamson, J.B., and Weiss, J.W. 1979. Egalitarian political movements, social welfare effort and convergence theory: A cross-national analysis. *Comparative Social Research* 2: 289–302.

Wolfe, A. 1978. Has social democracy a future? *Comparative Politics* 11:100–125.

# 3

# Political Legitimacy and Consensus: Missing Variables in the Assessment of Social Policy[1]

## HAROLD L. WILENSKY

There is a spreading conviction among top policymakers in every rich democracy that in the 1980s we are confronting a crisis of the welfare state, an overload of social problems, an unprecedented prospect of economic ruin, and the rapid decline of the capacity to govern. Intellectuals, politicians, and bureaucrats are adopting the vocabulary of crisis. Only the phrasing differs, depending upon their political mood, ideological persuasion, or disciplinary affiliation.

If you go to a conference on public policy where economists dominate, you will hear that because of the acceleration of unit labor costs (especially fringe benefits) combined with an explosion of social security costs (the heavy fiscal burdens of the welfare state), the industrialized countries' competitive position is deteriorating and their economies are stagnating. Urgent trade-offs and dilemmas common to every rich country are sharply posed: job protection and social security versus a flexible labor supply and economic growth; economic equality and participatory democracy versus economic growth; the protection of the welfare state versus capital investment, economic performance, and the necessary structural adjustments, and the like. Or, if you attend a conference of neo-Marxists who discuss "the fiscal crisis of the state" or "the political contradictions of capitalism" (Habermas 1975; O'Connor 1973; Offe 1972a, 1972b; Offe and Ronge 1975), you will hear of the inevitable contradictions between the legitimacy of government bought through the welfare state and "the reproduction of capitalism" bought through state policies favoring private capital accumulation.

If they offer any prescriptions to cure the disease, conventional economists tend to favor cuts in social spending and job protection, reduction in taxes and benefits, and more income testing, that is, the selective targeting of income

[1]This chapter is based on research made possible by the support of the National Science Foundation (Grant SOC77-13265), the German Marshall Fund, the Russell Sage Foundation, and the Institute of International Studies and the Institute of Industrial Relations of the University of California, Berkeley. It is part of a forthcoming book on the politics of taxing and spending.

EVALUATING THE WELFARE STATE:
SOCIAL AND POLITICAL PERSPECTIVES

transfers and services. The neo-Marxists tend to favor basic changes in the structures of domination, in what they call the distributional, repressive, or ideological apparatus of the modern capitalist state. Insofar as they offer concrete prescriptions, they emphasize nationalization of industry or the collective control of capital; they view the expansion or reform of social policy as irrelevant or as merely another means of "capitalist hegemony." (Communitarian socialists, although they sometimes adopt neo-Marxist rhetoric, tend to favor formulas for decentralization and worker participation.)

Both conventional economists and neo-Marxists are tackling recurrent issues in the history of social science: freedom and order, hierarchy and equality, the causes and consequences of the wealth of nations. But neither group is sufficiently systematic and empirical. Economists dealing with social policy typically fail to consider long-run effects of various policies on social consensus; they underestimate or ignore political costs. Neo-Marxists, on the other hand, typically fail to make the comparisons necessary to justify their use of the adjective *capitalist* before their objects of attention—"crisis," "class relations," and so on. If they deal with more than one market oriented political economy, and need to show its imminent collapse, they tend to concentrate on the United Kingdom, the United States, and Italy, countries whose recent troubles are most obvious. Nowhere do we find systematic analysis of differences and similarities in problems of legitimacy and capital investment in "noncapitalist" countries at similar levels of development.

For many years I have been trying to unravel the structural and ideological sources and effects of welfare-state development among 19 rich democracies with a population of at least 1 million in 1966. My strategy is to examine a wide range of countries and to combine qualitative and quantitative data on the politics of taxing and spending. The aim is to explain variations in taxes, tax structures, social spending, and social policies, as well as their political and economic effects, and ultimately their effects on real welfare. (See Wilensky 1975, 1976, 1978, 1980; Wilensky and Lawrence 1979.)

This chapter draws on that research to argue three themes:

1. Unless we specify variations in the structure of modern political economies, we cannot assess general assertions about the fiscal crisis of "the" state, the collapse of consensus, or the various scenarios and trade-offs suggested in the literature on social policy evaluation. The very definition of economic and political constraints on social policy depends on which of three types of market-oriented democracies we are talking about. I shall label them "democratic corporatist," "corporatist without labor," and "least corporatist."

2. The trade-offs between job protection, social security, equality, and participatory democracy, on the one hand, and worker productivity, economic growth, and other measures of economic performance, on the other hand, are not so stark as suggested in the burgeoning literature on policy analysis. What is usually left out of the discussion of these big trade-offs are the costs and gains

in consensus or political legitimacy—a major concern of policy makers in corporatist democracies.

3. The obvious political functions of evaluation research are most prominent in least corporatist democracies. The experience with the War on Poverty under the Johnson administration in the United States and subsequent discussion of the "reprivitization" of the welfare state in several countries illustrate this ideological function of evaluation research. I would speculate that corporatism either reduces the fraction of government effort devoted to evaluation research, or integrates it more effectively into policy planning.

## Types of Political Economy among Market-Oriented Rich Democracies: Democratic Corporatism or the Mass Society?

In a recent paper (1976), I tried to solve the puzzle that countries sharing the problems of slow growth, inflation, unemployment, energy shortages, and rising aspirations for equality and security, as well as similar levels of taxing and social spending, vary greatly in the political protest they generate. For a solution, I developed a model of democratic corporatism. Variations in conformity to this model help explain national differences in tax structures (e.g., the balance among painfully visible taxes and other taxes) which, in turn, are powerful predictors of the intensity, duration, and success of tax–welfare backlash movements.

If we are to use this model to explain egalitarian social policies and their evaluation, we need at least three categories. The first is *corporatist democracies* such as the Netherlands, Belgium, Sweden, Norway, Austria, and perhaps West Germany. They are characterized by the interplay of strongly organized, usually centralized interest groups, especially labor, employer, and professional associations with a centralized or moderately centralized government obliged by law or informal arrangement to consider their advice. In essence, we see a consensus-making machine operating within a quasi-public framework to produce peak bargains involving the major issues of modern political economy, that is, economic growth, prices, wages, taxes, unemployment, and the balance of payments, as well as social policy (social security, education, housing, health, and now the environment and worker participation).

In these countries, social policy is in some measure absorbed into general economic policy. At a time of slow growth and rising aspirations, such an integration of economic and social policy tends toward an important result: Labor, interested in wages, working conditions, social security, and, to a lesser extent, participatory democracy, is forced to take account of inflation, productivity, and the need for investment; employers, interested in profit, productivity, and investment are forced to take account of social policy.

In devising a measure of the interplay between government and major private power blocs, as a clue to democratic corporatism, I used the appointment power of the central government weighted roughly equally with a measure of centralization of labor federations. (I could not locate comparable data on employer federations.) I added four indicators of the centralization of labor federations— the federation engages in collective bargaining, controls strike funds, has a large number of expert staff per 100,000 members, and collects big dues—and combined this score with the central government's appointment power.[2]

In an increasingly unfavorable economic environment, the need intensifies for a new consensus involving some coordination of contradictory social and economic policies. The corporatist democracies listed here have a chance to arrive at such consensus because they already provide top leaders of economic interest groups with channels for bargaining and influence in the broadest national context.

The second category I find useful for understanding variations in social policy is *corporatism without full-scale participation by labor*. Japan, France, and perhaps Switzerland have in varying ways developed quasi-public bargaining structures for the interplay of industry, commerce, agriculture, professional groups, and government. These structures permit some coordination and planning of social and economic policies, but they have kept labor federations at a distance. In all three countries, despite obvious differences in the strength of the state bureaucracy, the business community enjoys a privileged position in the definition and implementation of public policy. These countries are thus in a position to achieve good economic performance without adopting many public policies explicitly designed to increase economic and social equality. In view of the urgency of mass demands and the severity of economic constraints,

---

[2] For a detailed account of the model and measures, see Wilensky (1976), especially pp. 21–24, 48–51. As I noted on p. 51 there, my measures do not capture some tendencies in the German political economy. Structurally, although the DGB is relatively weak and there are important elements of decentralization in government, it can be argued that functional equivalents of corporatism would justify a higher score: industry-wide bargaining by moderately centralized unions informally coordinating their strategy, the growing professionalization of union staffs, the wage leadership of the metal workers, the presence of a big employer association, much centralized bargaining in the health industry, etc. During the decade of *Konzertierte Aktion* especially, German unions traded-off wage restraint for other nonwage gains (e.g., the growth of workers councils). (Cf. Lehmbruch 1979; Streeck 1978.)

In relation to my model of corporatism, the German case is ambiguous. Italy scores medium on my measures of corporatism, but its weak government and its system of clientismo ("surviving without governing") makes it problematic. Israel, although it fits the model, has uniquely heavy defense burdens, a major constraint on social policy development. Further, nothing is static: many observers of the Netherlands believe that since the strikes of 1973 the social partners will never again restore the strength of their consensus-making machinery. Whatever the variations and ambiguities over space and time, I would argue that without structures for bargaining approximating my model of corporatism, the minimum consensus essential for effective social and economic policies is unlikely for any rich democracy in the 1980s.

however, these three countries may one day be forced to move toward the full incorporation of labor into their bargaining arrangements, eventually joining the first group. Alternatively, they could swing toward authoritarianism—the increasing use of coercion to control a rising level of organized discontent focused on equality and security.

The third category includes countries that are least corporatist in their bargaining structures—*the fragmented and decentralized political economies* of the United States, the United Kingdom, Canada, and Australia—none of which are advanced welfare states. In these countries, the interest groups that elsewhere are constrained by the necessity of national bargaining and trade-offs are in a position to act out their most parochial strivings, reinforcing an already advanced state of *paralysis.*

This sketch of corporatism as a source of consensus ignores the role of political parties and the mass media, obvious determinants of public policy and its evaluation. Three interrelated trends are said to characterize all rich democracies: the decline of political party organizations and a weakening of the traditional party loyalties among voters; the increased dominance of the mass media, especially the broadcast media, in culture and politics; and the proliferation of single-issue groups, some of which are social movements without members (e.g., Nader's Raiders). These trends, however, are much more prominent in the least corporatist democracies, where the fragmentation of economic power blocs enlarges the vacuum created by party decline—a vacuum into which the strident media and single-issue groups have poured. Corporatist bargaining structures reduce the rate of decline of parties, which are often helpful in mobilizing consensus for peak bargains. At the same time they help control the policy agenda, framing media content and containing single-issue groups and other particularistic pressures.

Nothing here is entirely new and everything is a matter of degree: single-issue groups have always been active in the United States, from the abolitionists and the Ku Klux Klan to the suffragettes, from the temperance movement and the gun lobby to antiabortionists and gay rights activists. But where parties could once protect their leaders and members from such groups and exert pressure on them to reach accommodation, political leaders now stand exposed (Fiorina 1980, pp. 40–42). Add a fragmented, decentralized labor movement and similar employer and professional associations, themselves exacerbating the parochial pressures, and you end up with a fluid, massified polity incapable of collective responsibility for public policy. Surely the corporatist democracies are in a better position to offset or retard these tendencies toward mass politics and mass culture in the mass society.

To me, these distinctions—democratic corporatism (Sweden, Norway, Austria), corporatism without labor (France, Japan), and least corporatist political economies (United States, United Kingdom)—are necessary for formulating answers to several critical questions of social policy analysis.

## Corporatist Democracies Can Tax, Spend, and Yet Stay Cool

The questions concern the political and economic effects of the welfare state. First: Will no growth or low growth in the 1980s encourage the spread of a Hobbesian state of mind—whatever the poor or nonworking population gains from welfare expenditures, the nonpoor or working population loses? Or will it frighten the citizens into solidarity? The answer, of course, depends upon the structures in place for bargaining. The consensus-making machinery of corporatist democracies may or may not be able to meet the challenge. But it is virtually certain that the fragmented and decentralized political economies will fit Thurow's *Zero-Sum Society* (1980).

The second question is a more general version of the first: Is the welfare state a luxury of swift economic growth? Do the costs of job protection, income transfers, and personal social services characteristic of advanced welfare states block their future economic development? Again, there is no uniform relationship between the costs of such labor and social policies, on the one hand, and economic performance, on the other. Since World War II, by any major measure of economic performance, the heavy-spending corporatist democracies I have listed have done as well or better than the welfare state laggards. So far they have *not* been spending themselves into the grave. For instance, such big spenders and taxers as Germany, the Netherlands, Austria, Norway, and Belgium were in the better performing half of 19 rich democracies from 1950 to 1974, with good average annual real growth per capita, low unemployment, and medium to low inflation. (Sweden is a mixed case: very low in unemployment, average in inflation, but a bit below average in growth.) Even if we consider the crisis period of 1975–1979, the corporatist big spenders and taxers on average had a clear edge in inflation control and low unemployment, although they lost their edge in economic growth. If we take account of their much greater exposure to the Arab oil shock of 1973–1974, the excellent performance of Austria and France and the fair performance of Sweden look even better in cross-national perspective (based on Wilensky's unpublished data forthcoming; cf. similar findings in Cameron, 1982). Finally, none of them to this day has experienced strong antitax, antiwelfare, antibureaucracy movements—tax-welfare backlash movements like those of Glistrup in Denmark, Powell and Thatcher in Britain, or Wallace and Reagan in the United States.

Contrast the lean-spending, least corporatist democracies such as the United States, Canada, Australia, New Zealand, and the United Kingdom: From 1950 to 1974, they all had low growth per capita and a mixed performance by other measures. In the period 1975–1979, considering their lesser vulnerability to the Arab oil shock, these countries should have done better in economic performance than the corporatist big spenders but, in fact, did not. And the strongest tax–welfare backlash appears in the United States, a lean spender, and the United Kingdom, a middle-rank spender. (For details on measures and sources of tax–welfare backlash movements, see Wilensky, 1976.)

That the welfare state leaders with more corporatist bargaining structures have been able to combine good economic performance and high levels of taxing and social spending with relatively little political uproar is partly explained by their capacity to achieve social consensus.

## Corporatism, Consensus, and the Politics of Evaluation Research

There are no cross-national figures on the budgets and personnel of evaluation research units in or around government agencies making or implementing social policy. Where no source is cited, I base the following speculations on impressions from interviews with politicians, health and welfare officials, and experts in taxing and spending in 12 countries. I suggest three hypotheses:

1. The failure of researchers to include long-run costs and gains and hard to measure variables in their evaluations of social policies is more common and most misleading among least corporatist democracies.
2. Evaluation research is not by nature conservative, but it flourishes most as a substitute for program development and implementation in least corporatist democracies, where applied research is most politicized and most distorted by media amplification. The role of research in the war on poverty in the United States illustrates the point.
3. Slogans such as "reprivitization," "decentralization," "debureaucratization," and "empowerment," embraced by radicals and conservatives alike, are prominent in debates about the future of the welfare state in many countries. But the big trade-offs of values and resources implied by these slogans are better understood by elites in corporatist democracies than by elites in more fragmented and decentralized political economies.

Thus, it is in the corporatist democracies with advanced welfare states that we find the most promising adaptations to rising costs of pensions, job injury and unemployment insurance, and other social programs.

### THE SHORT-RUN SINGLE-ISSUE FOCUS OF EVALUATION RESEARCH

The more concentration on short-run costs and gains of particular social policies, the worse the long-run effects. One factor in the somewhat better economic performance of big-spending corporatist democracies is that they tend to choose the costs of active labor market policies and job protection rather than the other, perhaps more wasteful, programs of less corporatist welfare state laggards—reactive welfare programs that make no long-run contribution to human resource use.

There has been something of a natural history of the established programs that goes beyond the simple expansion of benefits and coverage experienced everywhere. For instance, consider job injury insurance, unemployment insurance, and pensions.

## Job Injury Insurance

In most developed welfare states the earliest welfare program, job injury insurance, has become a more general program for safety and health in the work environment. Obviously, if such program expansion cuts absenteeism, sick leave, and job injuries, the program costs can be offset by increased productivity per man hour, lower training costs for replacements, and lower health care and disability costs. Given the spreading ideology of participatory democracy, it can also provide a channel for worker participation that is at once meaningful to workers, helpful to management, and serves widely shared societal goals.

The Swedish safety ombudsman and subsequent laws on the working environment are a model of this innovative expansion. Contrast this to the United States, where similar concern about occupational injury and illness led to the creation in 1970 of the Occupational Safety and Health Administration (OSHA). In a study of the two systems, Steven Kelman (1981) observes that the two government agencies deal with the same issues, confront the same trade-offs between increased levels of protection and increased cost, the same problems of compliance, and make similar decisions regarding the content of regulations. Once again, the differences, fatal for the balance of costs and benefits, lie in the national bargaining machinery and related possibilities of consensus.

In the corporatist political economy of Sweden, regulations of the Worker Protection Board (*Arbetarskyddsverket*) are accepted by unions and employers; the atmosphere is one of negotiation and cooperation. In the United States, OSHA's regulations are constantly challenged in the courts; the atmosphere is confrontational. Unions complain of inadequate enforcement, employers denounce "overregulation" (their propaganda campaign pictures mindless bureaucrats issuing frivolous orders requiring split-seat rather than round toilets.[3]

Paradoxically it is in individualistic, decentralized America that government inspectors are intrusive and routinely fine employers for noncompliance. In collectivistic, centralized Sweden, inspectors are loath to punish employers; instead, they rely on consultation with health and safety professionals and other representatives of LO (the largest labor federation) and SAF (the employer

---

[3]In an atrocity tale the opponents of OSHA are fond of citing, it is estimated that OSHA regulations to limit worker exposure to coke-oven emissions cost industry and consumers several million dollars a year for each life saved—about $9000 a year for each coke-oven worker protected. (Of course, other regulations are more cost-effective, but the public debate centers on the dramatic case—whether fictional or true.)

federation) and look to local control—the institution of the safety steward or workplace ombudsman—for enforcement. They also set up joint research and development projects to produce innovative solutions to difficult problems of the work environment.

The contrast in the operations of OSHA could not be sharper: Adversary lawyers and environmental activists, often perform in front of TV cameras in open hearings, make verbatim transcripts, and escalate conflict, thereby fostering deadlock, delay, and resistance to final decisions. Huge amounts of money and time are expended in diversions from problem solving. Employer backlash is then mobilized to weaken the law.

Similarly, the history of German industrial accident insurance suggests that program expansion and innovation in the long run reduces costs (Alber 1980, pp. 9–10). The prewar system was restored in 1949. The principle of self-administration was introduced in 1951, with worker and employer representation split evenly. The major reform came in 1963: Benefits were indexed to wage levels, and several measures were introduced for the prevention of accidents. In 1971 the system was extended beyond workers to cover children in kindergartens and schools, and students. The law of 1973 further emphasized preventive measures, including the new position of "security engineer" for large workplaces. Despite the great expansion of industry, the number of industrial accidents, which had climbed from 1.3 million in 1950 to 2.7 million in 1960 before the reform, went down to 1.8 million by 1975. With the expansion of benefits and coverage, expenditures for accident insurance went up sharply.

The kind of social policy evaluation necessary to assess these cases has not been done, but I can offer a few clues to suggest that a cost–benefit analysis taking account of long-run effects would show a net decrease in welfare state costs in Sweden and West Germany. Consider the percentage of GNP spent on work injuries 1954–1974 and deaths from industrial accidents per 100,000 population. Expenditures declined for Sweden (.3% of GNP in 1954 to .16% in 1974), stayed steady in Germany (.71% in 1954 to .73% in 1974), and increased in the United States (.33% in 1954 to .51% in 1974).[4] What happened to the most dramatic and reliable measure of real welfare—deaths from industrial accidents? Comparable figures for the three countries are available only for 1968, 1971, 1975, and 1976. Sweden and West Germany

[4]From ILO, *The Cost of Social Security,* 1954, 1972–1974, and other years. Figures for Sweden and West Germany represent expenditures on "employment injuries." To make figures for the United States more comparable, expenditures on "workmen's compensation" were added to "temporary disability insurance" (the latter category comprises about 20% of the total work injury expenditure for the entire period 1954–1974). We also calculated per capita work injury expenditures in U.S. dollars, from 1960 to 1974; they show a sharp rise for all three countries. However, Sweden's expenditures remain low relative to those of Germany and the United States. The Swedish trend was $2.35 in 1960 to $5.02 in 1971 to $9.90 in 1974. The American trend was $8.98 in 1960 to $20.92 in 1971 to $31.08 in 1974. The German trend was $7.47 in 1960 to $21.89 in 1971 to $40.18 in 1974 (but much of the doubling from 1971 to 1974 is due to the sharply increased strength of the German mark against the dollar). GNP is at factor cost.

evidence a similar pattern of decline—from about 2.5 deaths from industrial accidents per 100,000 population in 1968 to about 1.5 deaths in 1976. The United States starts higher, 3.0 in 1968, and declines less, 2.4 in 1976 (UN World Health Organization, *Statistics Annual*, years indicated). Germany and Sweden's safety performance is all the more impressive in view of their industrial structure: the fraction of wage earners and salaried employees in the two most dangerous industries, mining and construction, is higher than that of the United States: In 1976 that of Germany was 9.6%, of Sweden, 7.6%, of the United States, 5.5% (OECD 1979, pp. 78, 222, 376).

In short, with far more direct regulation and intrusiveness, with far less participation by workers, the United States may spend more on accident insurance with less saving in safety and health than the big-spending, more corporatist welfare-state leaders.

### Unemployment Insurance

Like the expansion and reform of job injury insurance, unemployment insurance became an active labor market policy designed to improve the prospects of the hard to employ. In the more advanced welfare states of Western Europe, job protection has become a religion. Strong labor movements and social democratic governments (and in a few cases, Catholic parties and governments) have made it quite difficult for employers to fire anyone. They have also made it costly for employers who fail to take manpower planning seriously. By comparison, American employers are sloppy in planning and hard as nails in firing and layoffs.

Consultations or negotiations with unions or worker representatives on the need for and extent of layoffs is required by law or collective bargaining agreement in Sweden, Norway, Finland, Italy, and France. In France and the Netherlands, prior authorization by a public agency is required before any work force reduction may take place. In West Germany and Austria, an employer must consult a works council before dismissing anyone for cause; the Netherlands requires prior authorization from an employment office. To protect older workers in several sectors of West German industry there is outright prohibition of dismissal of workers between a given age and the age of retirement with pension (Delamotte 1972; International Labour Office 1974; Yemin 1976).

The methods employed by the Swedish Labour Market Board and its German, Norwegian, and Austrian counterparts are in sharp contrast to the rather casual process of linking people to jobs in less developed welfare states. The United States, for instance, has a weak, understaffed employment service whose operations are only loosely related to school counseling, testing, tracking, and guidance. School counselors are only slightly attuned to occupational information (Wilensky 1967a).

Thus, the trade-offs that must be measured in any serious evaluation of the effects of job protection include:

1. The employer's feeling of being hemmed in by laws and customs in the hiring, firing, and transfer of workers, and the real costs of those restrictions in the inflexibility of labor supply versus the worker's feeling of job security and the real gains in productivity that come from secure tenure. (There is some evidence that more secure workers are more productive—see Cole, 1979, and Vogel, 1979, on the employment practices of big corporations in Japan, and Wilensky, 1978, p. 97, for the general argument.)

2. Heavy unemployment insurance and welfare costs for the hard to employ minorities, women, and young, rather than the costs and gains of quotas and subsidies geared to rehabilitation and training, wage subsidies and tax incentives to employers, requirements that employers who lay off workers find them suitable alternative jobs, compulsory notification of job vacancies, work sharing, mobility allowances, and the like.

### Pensions

Similarly, pension reform is not inevitably a straight-line expansion in cost. Exploding pension costs and the increasing use of permanent disability benefits for discouraged middle-aged workers are now combining with political pressure from the prematurely retired to inspire hard thought about partial retirement programs, where taxpaying is added to benefit taking, second careers for the occupationally obsolescent and displaced (e.g., "cyclical life plans" with breaks in mid-career with older and younger workers filling in), and continuing education for all. Even in this difficult area, and even if we ignore the benefits to the morale of the target population, it is by no means certain that the long-run costs of these reforms will exceed the gains.

I feel least confident about a benign natural history of health insurance because the entrenched interests blocking health care reform are so powerful. Will the health care cost explosion frighten politicians and bureaucrats into emphasizing preventive medicine, nutrition education, and physical culture? If so, I suggest that the corporatist democracies are more likely than the least corporatist democracies to contain the bargaining power of physicians and other provider groups thereby moving the system toward real health outputs.

## CORPORATISM AND THE NATURE AND FUNCTIONS OF EVALUATION RESEARCH

The character of evaluation research and its effect on social policy depend upon the structure of the political economy in which it is financed and used: Fragmented political economies foster isolated single-issue research, typically focused on short-run effects and used for political ammunition rather than policy planning; more corporatist systems foster research in which a wider range of issues are connected, longer-range effects are more often considered, and findings are more often used for policy planning and implementation as well as budget justification. *Larger contexts for bargaining mean larger contexts for evaluation research.*

Consider the question of health care costs and real health. Evaluation of health care outputs (or the lack of them) has become a popular sport, especially in countries with poorly developed or poorly distributed health services. The single-issue formula is captured in the title of a special isue of *Daedalus*, "Doing Better and Feeling Worse: Health in the United States," taken from an article by a leading policy analyst, Aaron Wildavsky (1977). The assessment is admirably summarized by Wildavsky:

> According to the Great Equation, Medical Care Equals Health. But the Great Equation is wrong. More available medical care does not equal better health. The best estimates are that the medical system (doctors, drugs, hospitals) affects about 10% of the usual indices for measuring health: whether you live at all (infant mortality), how well you live (days lost due to sickness), how long you live (adult mortality). The remaining 90 percent are determined by factors over which doctors have little or no control, from individual life style (smoking, exercise, worry), to social conditions (income, eating habits, physiological inheritance), to the physical environment (air and water quality). Most of the bad things that happen to people are at present beyond the reach of medicine .... No one is saying that medicine is good for nothing, only that it is not good for everything. Thus the marginal value of one—or one billion—dollars spent on medical care will be close to zero in improving health [p. 105].

There is obvious truth in this—a partial truth emphasized in the most careful cross-national evaluation of the effect of "health care systems" in the literature (Anderson 1972). Comparing the United States, Sweden, and England, Anderson concludes that system contrasts in "input" are not connected in any direct way to any measurable output. Indeed, he abandons the attempt to link attributes of the system of medical care to customary indices of health and, in the end, argues that the main thing we can say with assurance is that Sweden is much superior to the United States in *equality of access* to doctors, dentists, drugs, and other medical facilities and personnel—whatever such equal access may mean for health—and that illness is more of a threat to family solvency in the United States. Although the British data on differences in access to medical facilities by income are somewhat fragmentary, the British appear to be like the Swedes in equality of dignified access to physicians.

Leaving aside the question of whether equal access is a worthy goal in itself, what all these studies and assertions overlook is the interdependence of all social policies. Sweden, like the Netherlands and similar big-spending corporatist democracies, not only distributes medical care more aggressively and fairly but also invests heavily in health-relevant programs of housing, safety, nutrition, health education, and child care, as well as environmental control, and draws the income floor for everyone higher and more uniformly; in short, it assures the least privileged of its population a higher standard of living. It is likely that the entire package—the interaction of all of these programs—is a major source of Sweden's superior health performance (Wilensky 1975, pp. 98–104).

A second problem that everyone recognizes but few evaluation researchers dwell on is the distinction between easy to measure short-run effects and hard to measure long-run effects. Consider the outcome of a large-scale national health service like that of Britain. There is some direct evidence that the National Health Service is used most intensively by the least well off—the old, the young, the poor, the single (Rein 1969)—although they do not tend to receive the highest quality service (Klein 1973). If, however, every other force making for the superior health of the upper half of the education and income distribution is not simultaneously equalized, the long-run effect of public health expenditures may be highly regressive. The poor die young—before they can contract the chronic diseases that dearly cost national health schemes. The more affluent citizens live to a riper age, chronically collecting health services paid for by the lifelong taxes of the deceased poor. A program that is highly progressive at a cross-sectional moment may be highly regressive in the lifetime of particular generations (Wilensky 1975, p. 96).

I have already given more positive examples where the short-run economic costs of social policies (e.g., active labor market policies) can be offset by long-run economic gains in fuller utilization of labor, by social gains in consensus, worker morale, and the reduced alienation of youth, and by political gains in the legitimacy of government.

## Adversary Expertise in Two Contexts

If corporatist democracies do, in fact, tend to integrate evaluation research into policy, and if that research does, in fact, put its results into larger contexts and longer time frames, with a vision of the interplay of issues and programs and a concern with long-run effects, it is because of a major characteristic of such systems—strong corporatist–technocratic linkages. When centralized unions and their federations interact with centralized employer federations, they try to match each other expert for expert, brief for brief (Wilensky 1956, 1967b), approaching government experts with the same ammunition. Such a process, once begun, tends to introduce a rational–responsible bias in bargaining. We see a kind of dialectic of expertise, part of a general tendency toward the interpenetration of rational–bureaucratic structures. If the employer association sends a top economist to bargain for it, the labor federation counters with its leading economist. If a parliamentary commission or government agency hires labor market experts to prepare for a hearing on the employment effects of technological change, the parties who testify will be attuned to labor market data. Such experts are preoccupied with rational argument and criteria; their technical competence compels opposing parties to be more careful or honest in the use of information and knowledge. It is still combat, but the spirit is, "*En garde!* We'll meet you with our statistics at dawn."

While this dialectic of expertise is evident in all modern countries, it is most developed and has most effect on policy planning and implementation where the adversary experts are enmeshed in a system that encourages consensus. Where the system is structured for confrontation, as in the least corporatist democracies, there will be fewer in-depth experts and more experts of two types: (*a*) narrow technicians with the single-issue, short-run disease; (*b*) experts skilled in histrionics and the uses of the media. Further, their expertise will have no solid base for policy impact.

Thus, there are plenty of ocupational health and safety experts in both Sweden and the United States, but as we have seen, the centralized consensus-making machine of Sweden both sets a bargaining framework for expert influence and ensures a high level of employer compliance via the participation and training of numerous rank-and-file safety ombudsmen, at least one in all but the tiniest enterprises.

In the United States, an inspectorate and adversary lawyers make voluminous records for delayed action in courts; in Sweden local safety ombudsmen and safety study circles learn and enforce, while top-level experts and the leaders of major economic blocs bargain and collaborate.

### The War On Poverty: Is Evaluation Research Conservative?

My theme that the type of political economy shapes the character and functions of evaluation research is nowhere better illustrated than in the War on Poverty, a collection of programs to deal with poverty and discrimination, education and training, and unemployment and inflation, especially prominent in the Johnson years. Because of its short duration and limited financing, this war would better be labeled a skirmish with poverty.[5]

The War on Poverty is also a dramatic illustration of Wilensky's law: the more evaluation, the less program development; the more demonstration projects, the less follow-through. For nowhere in the United States—not even in the Pentagon—have demands for rigorous evaluation research loomed so large. The new legislation setting up the Office of Economic Opportunity and similar programs in the Department of Health, Education, and Welfare required large-scale evaluation efforts; one of OEO's functions was to experiment and measure the outcomes of new programs. One student of this phenomenon, projecting the rate of increase of expenditure on poverty experiments in progress and proposed

---

[5]During the Kennedy-Johnson years, expenditures (cash and in kind transfers) focused on the poor rose from .8% of "full employment GNP" in 1961 to 1.4% in 1967; they peaked in 1973 at 1.8% in Nixon's first term, dropping back to 1.5% by 1976. The programs devoted to education, training, and other services designed to enhance the earning capacity of the poor directly never cost more than 1% of GNP, although this tiny effort produced a monumental fuss (Aaron 1978, pp. 6ff.; Haveman, 1977.)

in 1972, concluded that by the 1980s every citizen of the United States could be paid as a poverty researcher or as a subject in a poverty experiment—a novel way of clearing up "the welfare mess."

In the past decade or so, a remarkable consensus has emerged that the War on Poverty was a total failure. Radicals who never did believe that reform measures by "ideologically bankrupt liberals" could do anything to change "the basic structures of domination," self-flagellating liberals who read reports alleging the ineffectiveness of one or another anti-poverty program, fiscal conservatives who say that you cannot solve problems by throwing money at them, and old-fashioned reactionaries who believe that the poor should be punished for their lack of virtue, all agreed that the only winner of the War on Poverty was poverty. This consensus was remarkable because, as Aaron (1978) shows, neither the initial enthusiasm nor subsequent disenchantment were based on reliable information or scholarly analysis regarding the actual success or failure of the programs themselves. Along with the Vietnam War and the Nixon conspiracies, the negative consensus was part of the ideological climate for the passage of Proposition 13 in California in 1978 and the election of Ronald Reagan as president in 1980.

The poverty research itself was quite narrow, politically naive, and, in design and execution, often seriously flawed. It epitomized my picture of the single-issue evaluation focused on short-run effects used for political ammunition characteristic of least corporatist democracies. In a careful review of this period, an economist who later became the Assistant Secretary for Planning and Evaluation of HEW offers a careful review of this period. He describes research in and out of government as being guided by the "impulse to isolate individual influences; to make complex social and economic processes statistically and mathematically manageable through abstraction [Aaron 1978, p. 156]." The interdependence of policies is thereby obscured. Thus, in Aaron's words,

> improved education and training may be ineffective in increasing earning capacity unless steps are also taken to change the mix of available jobs, and efforts to change the the mix of available jobs may fail if low-wage workers lack training and education. Either taken alone might fail, when both together might succeed. Research and experimentation would detect the failures but have no way to indicate the hypothetical potential success. A rather vague assumption of such an interrelatedness marked early political rhetoric about the War on Poverty but was wholly absent from the precise, but partial, analyses of its effectiveness performed by social scientists [pp. 156–157].

Place the same social scientists in a corporatist democracy where the bargaining machinery forces an awareness of the interdependence of dozens of policies comprising an active labor market policy, and their evaluation research will do no harm. It may even be integrated into policy planning and implementation and do some good.

A second part of the War on Poverty story is the weakness in the United States of the "rational–responsible bias" typical of countries with tight corporatist–technocratic linkages. Without the constraining context of privately discussed research results and policy alternatives, evaluation research is fully politicized. Certain OEO programs, especially the Community Action Programs, Legal Services, and the Job Corps, were under constant political attack. The mixed results of evaluation and experimentation not only suffered from the single-issue short-duration disease, but also from the natural distortion resulting from political combat about redistribution of income and power. Did the Job Corps, which tried to train and place hard-core unemployed youth, raise subsequent earnings of Corps members? According to Aaron, the Job Corps received mixed marks by this and similar criteria, and probably yielded benefits greater than its costs. Yet its critics, noting the costs, called press conferences and delivered such lines as, "For the huge sums wasted on one Job Corps member we could send a student to Harvard," selectively adding some noncompletion or nonplacement rate from one of the reports (50%, 43%, 62%, or whatever); the program was sharply cut back. Similarly, evaluations indicated that the Community Action Programs had succeeded. (These were neighborhood self-help organizations designed to increase the political and economic power of the poor, with financing funneled through mayors of cities, bypassing outraged governors.) But "CAPs became the popular symbol of the failure of the War on Poverty [Aaron 1978, p. 32]." Conversely, Head Start, a program to provide preschool education and health care to young children of the poor, was pronounced a failure by the limited criteria of evaluation research; yet it remained politically popular.

Head Start illustrates not only the principle that nothing fails like success and nothing succeeds like failure, but also the fact that much of the evaluation research was seriously flawed. For instance, research concluded that a brief stint in a special school, as one might expect, brought only a small, temporary improvement in reading readiness, which faded after the first grade. A Rand Corporation evaluation of the evaluations, however, noted that research on Head Start and on similar programs for older children did not assign treatment and nontreatment children on a random basis, evaluated unrepresentative projects, were contaminated by "radiation effects" spilling over from project to nonproject children, or had other defects (Aaron 1978, p. 84). In the case of tests of reading achievement of older children the fading effect after a year (losing ground during the summer) ignored the differences between students in summer school and those whose only compensatory education was that administered by street gangs (Heyns 1978). Thus, although Head Start was at first an evaluated failure, follow-up studies, better designed, suggest more success. In fact, after sharp cuts in funding of all social programs, more recent, more sophisticated evaluation research—taking account of long-term effects and a wider range of gains and costs—has shown that *both* the Job Corps *and* Head Start were impressively cost-effective. (Lazar, 1979; Schweinhart & Weikart, 1980; Long, Mallar, and Thornton, 1981.)

In short, the newer innovative programs of the War on Poverty, typical of limited antipoverty action by welfare state laggards, were funded for such a short period at such a meager level that the fuss about their failure to solve some huge problem is absurd. These programs were hardly launched before they were shot down in a cloud of complaints about costs, corruption, and welfare scandals. In the rare case where careful evaluations were made and evidence was found of some modest success, the results were pronounced as benedictions at the graveside (Wilensky 1975, p. 111). Political success may have been inversely related to evaluated success. In the absence of effective coalitions of politicians, bureaucrats, and experts, in the absence of a system for aggregating interests, achieving consensus, and integrating social and economic planning, each interest group can interpret research results according to its preconceptions with no accommodation to opposing preconceptions. The voice of research, even scholarly analysis, is drowned out by the noise.

These considerations lead Aaron to conclude that evaluation research is, by nature, conservative: The inherent complexity of social policy insures that conflicting evidence will be available to policymakers and courts; programs have vague or multiple, or conflicting goals, which also insures conflicting research results ("what is an ordinary member of the tribe to do when the witchdoctors disagree?"); the prudent official will wish to defer action until more evidence is available or controversial issues are settled; there is a tendency for advocates using "forensic social science" to raise unrealistic expectations which are inevitably dashed, thereby producing an equally exaggerated hostility to any government action ("ideas that live by oversimplification die by oversimplification"); and so on. The trouble with this formulation is that it describes the nature of politics, programs, and applied research everywhere, including countries and times where research has had the reverse effect.

Again, we must remind ourselves that the functions of policy research vary according to the channels for its creation and diffusion (Wilensky 1967b, pp. 110–191). There are abundant examples of research that go beyond "window dressing" or the defense of established policy (pp. 16ff.) and, indeed, many of the policy goals and means of the War on Poverty had already been adopted or have since been instituted among the more corporatist welfare state leaders, with or without an elaborate machinery of evaluation.[6]

[6]If the effort of the Johnson administration had been somewhat larger and sustained longer, if political credibility had not been squandered in Vietnam and Watergate, Aaron might have been writing a book about the political genius of Lyndon Johnson, the amazing success of the War on Poverty, and the benign role of evaluation and experimentation. Two other peculiarities of American life noted by Aaron (1978) cannot be attributed to the conservative nature of evaluation research: the political dominance of lawyers and the committee structure of Congress.

"Most members of Congress are lawyers, more accustomed to dealing in mandates that require or prohibit behavior than they are to managing incentives that encourage or discourage behavior. Furthermore, the committee structure of Congress discourages the use of subsidies and charges to achieve substantive objectives. Such legislation must pass through the House Ways and Means and Senate Finance Committees. If committees

If I am right that larger contexts for bargaining mean larger contexts for evaluation research and more immediate policy impact with no intrinsic conservative bent, a systematic comparison of corporatist and least corporatist democracies would provide evidence. In the absence of such studies, here are two illustrative hypotheses. First, because corporatist democracies rely more on universal, categorical benefits financed by balanced tax structures, they create less public resentment of the undeserving poor and hence less demand for short-run, single issue, cost–benefit studies of the kind Americans saw in the War on Poverty. Second, when corporatist democracies undertake evaluation research it tends to be of two types: (1) general "level of living" surveys that emphasize the total effect of all social policies (such as those regularly done in Scandinavia); (2) professional cost-benefit studies of particular programs, with immediate policy impact, reflecting the greater centralization of government and the tighter connection between experts and politicians (e.g., a health economist in Norway does a cost–benefit study of a universal program of chest X-rays and concludes that a program screening for high risk populations would be more cost effective; the national policy is changed to fit the findings).

### *"Voluntarism," "Reprivitization," and "Empowerment": Slogans for filling vacuums*

One of the ideological exports of American intellectuals, now popular in the rhetoric of neoconservatives and some radicals, are theories of "empowerment" and of "reprivatization," often the product of fragmentary evaluation research. By empowerment they mean the replacement of government provision of services by mediating structures that stand between the state and the individual—voluntary organizations, ethnic, racial, and religious groups, neighborhoods, small businesses. At its extreme it means total reliance on voluntary associations and families as a way to strengthen democracy, cut the costs of government, and make services accountable to the consumer; policing power, education and social services—all would be delegated to such community groups (cf. Berger and Neuhaus 1977). By reprivatization of the welfare state, they mean greater reliance on the profit-making sector and market competition in the provision of social services. In both theories words like *voluntarism*, *private*, *independent*, *decentralized*, and *debureaucratized* are used to describe the benign effects expected to flow from these strategies.

Such theories have a resonance far exceeding their clarity or relevance. They are now providing an ideological base for a general attack on social services. Drawing on a detailed comparative study (Kramer 1981) of 75 voluntary agencies serving the handicapped in four countries—the Netherlands, Israel,

---

responsible for housing, education, health, training, safety, natural resources or any other "substantive" field wish to impose taxes or fees or offer subsidies, they normally must surrender exclusive jurisdiction and may lose all control over the legislation, [p. 162]."

Britain, and the United States—I shall offer a few reflections on these ideas in action.[7] I shall thereby highlight the possible conflict between a preoccupation with evaluation and experimentation, on the one hand, and adequate funding and services, on the other.

The advocates of voluntarism assign various meanings to the word *voluntarism*. We must distinguish two of the most common:

1. Voluntarism as voluntary associations that extend, improve, complement, supplement, or sometimes substitute entirely for the delivery of social services by government. These services are typically labor-intensive; they require both local intelligence (knowledge of particular needs of specialized clientele) and local consensus (community support of the program). The main targets: the aged, the young, and the handicapped of any age. Typical services for the handicapped are sheltered workshops, job training, transportation, day care centers, homemaker chore services, nutritional programs, and social, recreational, and camping activities. The expansion of the welfare state has, in fact, everywhere meant the growth of voluntary agencies with increased reliance on government funding. (Only in the United States and only until the 1930s did voluntarism as voluntary organizations retard the development of the welfare state.)

2. Voluntarism as volunteerism—the mobilization and deployment of volunteers, paid or unpaid, in money-raising campaigns or direct service, in private or public agencies. Advocates of greater volunteer participation say that it humanizes the welfare state, revives the sense of community, combats big government, and even reduces inflation. But, as Kramer suggests, the realization of one or another of these benign effects depends upon what kind of volunteers we are talking about: unpaid staff, unpaid fund raisers, paid service volunteers, peer self-helpers, mutual aid associations, neighborhood service organizations, religious institutions, etc. The label *volunteers* obscures these differences.

The advocates of "empowerment" in the United States are apparently unaware that the Netherlands, where voluntary agencies constitute the primary system of service delivery, has already tried one version of the theory. The cost, of course, is huge government subsidies out of current operating budgets and compulsory insurance premiums funneled through voluntary agencies—money to finance all their staff, administration, and services. In fact, the Netherlands has one of the costliest public sectors among modern democracies. What are the gains and costs? There are considerable gains in local autonomy, professionalism, and stable, high-quality services. The costs: the Dutch way is

---

[7]For a broader study of personal social services in international perspective, see Kahn and Kamerman (1976). Because I have discussed the complex topics of "decentralization" and "debureaucratization" elsewhere (Wilensky 1981) I shall confine these observations to "reprivatization" and "empowerment" and "voluntarism."

definitely not a way out of the fiscal crisis. Nor does it increase citizen control or participation. The Dutch agencies, dominated by professionals, have experienced a decline in citizen participation. Indeed, from Kramer's account, I infer that the almost complete reliance on voluntary agencies in the Netherlands has led to greater than usual fragmentation, duplication, and inflexibility. Some of Kramer's informants also claim that there is a lack of "quality control" but there is wide consensus that the Dutch are among the leaders in actual delivery of high-quality services.

American tendencies in the funding and delivery of personal social services resemble both "empowerment" and "reprivatization." In our increasing reliance on voluntary agencies and government subsidies, we move toward the Dutch model. In our emphasis on the profit-making sector and market competition to assure the best quality at the lowest price, we are embracing theories of reprivatization. The first tendency is evident in increased government funding of voluntary agencies, many with mandated citizen participation. The second tendency is evident in the spread of service contracts and payments to private vendors (e.g., the Job Corps, Medicare, day care, nursing homes, dialysis centers). Unfortunately, there is no evidence that they reduce the costs of delivering services, enhance consumer choice, or even improve "accountability."

Kramer reports that this politicized-grants economy, this alliance between voluntarism and vendorism, does not threaten agency autonomy or even advocacy as much as it deflects resources to the scramble for subsidies and then to rituals of reporting and accountability—the often meaningless counts of "outputs" such as number of interviews, hospital days, or meals served.

In no country has the government been able to monitor the activities of a maze of voluntary associations and private vendors. But the greater effort to do so in the United States has perhaps resulted in less service delivered at a greater unit cost—at least that is a hypothesis comparative research should explore. Apparently the United States is shooting for the Netherlands' level of dependence on voluntary agencies without the advantage of adequate, stable funding. The results: service functions are overwhelmed by grantsmanship, budget-justification research, and accountability rituals. The agencies become "fundraising instruments in search of a program"; agency volunteers are chiefly assigned to fundraising; public relations and marketing techniques are prominent. Kramer concludes that in the United States and, to a lesser extent, England, this arrangement diverts resources away from improved services, innovative programs, and leadership development, although it may increase citizen participation.

Because income from community campaigns is static, many voluntary agencies in the United States are engaged in a constant search for new funds; when approaching funding sources, public and private alike, the symbols "innovation" and "demonstration project" are expedient; the assumption is that new is better. In practice, the proposals are typically a means of carrying out the agencies' existing function. Here, as in the rest of American culture, the "cult of the new" runs rampant. In contrast, other countries place a higher value on government funding for implementation of existing programs. Again we have an illustration of Wilensky's law: the more demonstration, the less follow-through; the more entrepreneurial spirit, the less service delivery. As Kramer concludes, "The exaggerated emphasis on innovation by funding bodies may detract attention from other, more critical aspects of the social services system such as access, continuity, choice, coherence, effectiveness, equity, and efficiency."

Thus, the United States offers a preview of the kind of trade-offs the student of social policy will be evaluating in the 1980s if theories of "reprivatization" and "empowerment" are put into practice more widely.

## Conclusion

My model of corporatist democracy accents four interrelated tendencies in several modern political economies:

1. Bargaining channels develop for the interplay of strongly organized, usually centralized economic blocs, especially labor, employer, and professional associations with a centralized or moderately centralized government obliged to consider their advice.

2. The peak bargains struck by such federations both reflect and further a blurring of old distinctions between the public and the private.

3. These quasi-public peak associations bargain in the broadest national context rather than focusing only on labor market issues.

4. Consequently, social policy is in some measure absorbed into general economic policy, and chances for social consensus are enhanced. Such consensus-making machines are epitomized by Austria, Sweden, and Norway. A variant is corporatism without full integration of labor—epitomized by France and Japan. The least corporatist democracies include the United States, the United Kingdom, Australia, and Canada.

The decline of political parties as consensus builders is a general tendency in all modern democracies. Corporatism in part fills the resulting vacuum without exacerbating the trend. In contrast, the more numerous, fragmented, and decentralized interest groups of least corporatist democracies open the way for dominance by the media in symbiotic relation to single-issue movements and political demagogues, thereby hastening the decline of parties and the development of a mass society (cf. Wilensky 1964).

If we are to grasp the nature and functions of evaluation research and experimentation, we must take account of these variations in types of political economy. The bargaining structures of corporatist democracies provide much opportunity either to act without elaborate evaluation research or to integrate policy research into planning and implementation. Their centralization and broader bargaining focus make both elites and policy researchers more aware of the interdependence of public policies and the importance of long-run costs and gains. Their concern with the "social contract" encourages at least some attention to hard to measure variables such as political legitimacy and social consensus. Finally, corporatism encourages stronger links between knowledge and power—a dialectic of expertise, a rational–responsible bias, which itself is a force for accommodation among competing interest groups.

In contrast, the least corporatist democracies, with fewer technocratic linkages, politicize evaluation research more visibly and perversely. This can paralyze policy and reduce the capacity to plan, fund, and implement social programs. Although there is everywhere a rising distrust of science and government institutions, in fragmented, decentralized political economies the claims of policy research and politicians alike are discounted most vigorously. Two examples are (*a*) the bizarre relationship between evaluation research and experimentation in President Johnson's War on Poverty where modest successes (e.g., the Job Corps, Community Action Programs) were publicized as total failures whereas evaluated failures (e.g., Head Start) were pronounced successes; (*b*) the almost total lack of awareness among advocates of reprivatization, empowerment, and voluntarism of their likely costs in grantsmanship and government subsidies, weakened social consensus and political legitimacy—as is already apparent in the United States, which has begun to act out these theories. It is not evaluation research that is "conservative," it is the *immobilité* of least corporatist democracies.

A major question for the 1980s is whether the welfare state, with all its rigidities, its self-aggrandizing bureaucracies, its dedicated clientele (now a vast majority), can develop newer social policies more adaptively. What is the role of research and experimentation in this effort? Once again the answer depends on the type of political economy now in place. The past performance of the more corporatist democracies suggests that their centralized structures of bargaining permit considerable experimentation. In fact, the more advanced welfare states have already begun to extend their programs in ways that conceivably could contain costs, deal with newer issues, and emphasize real welfare outputs.

The short-run single-issue focus of evaluation research in least corporatist democracies obscures long-run trade-offs evident in these recent developments, specifically: trade-offs in such social policies as unemployment insurance as it is transformed into an active labor market policy designed to improve human resource use; job injury insurance as it becomes safety and health programs in the work environment; job protection as it improves the security and efficiency of workers; and pensions and disability insurance as they are supplemented and offset by programs for rescheduling work, work sharing, and flexible retirement. The single-issue short-run disease also obscures the interdependence of diverse social policies and their effects, as illustrated in the typical evaluation of the health outputs of health care systems.

In the end, the best strategy for social scientists in least corporatist democracies is to keep a steady focus on basic problems, avoid overselling the immediate policy relevance of their work, and guard against the fleeting political moods that infect the research of their more policy-excited colleagues.

## ACKNOWLEDGMENTS

I am grateful to Natalie Rogoff Ramsøy for a critical reading and to Susan Reed Hahn,Theodore M. Crone, James Jasper, and Cornelius W.R. Gispin for research assistance.

# References

Aaron, H.J. 1978. *Politics and the professors: The great society in perspective.* Washington, C.C.: The Brookings Institution.

Alber, J. 1980. A crisis of the welfare state? The case of West Germany. Paper presented at a workshop: A Crisis of the European Welfare States? ECPR Joint Sessions of Workshops, Florence, Italy (March 25–30).

Anderson, O.W. 1972. *Health care: Can there be equity?* New York: Wiley.

Berger, P.L., and Neuhaus, R.J. 1977. *To empower people: The role of mediating structures in public policy.* Washington, D.C.: American Enterprise Institute.

Cole, R.E. 1979. *Work, mobility, and participation.* Berkeley and Los Angeles: University of California Press.

Cameron, D.R. 1982. On the limits of the public economy. *The Annals.* 459:46–62.

Delamotte, Y. 1972. British productivity agreements, German rationalization agreements, and French employment security agreements. *International Institute of Labour Studies Bulletin* 9: 30–44.

Fiorina, M.P. 1980. The decline of collective responsibility in American politics. *Daedalus,* 109: 25–45.

Habermas, J. 1975. *Legitimation crisis.* Boston: Beacon Press.

Haveman, R.H., ed. 1977. *A decade of federal antipoverty programs: Achievements, failures and lessons.* Madison: Institute for Research on Poverty.

Heyns, B.L. 1978. *Summer learning and the effects of schooling.* New York: Academic Press.

International Labour Office. 1974. Termination of employment: General study by the committee of experts on the application of conventions and recommendations. International Labour Conference, 59th Session, Report III (Part 4B). Geneva: International Labour Office.

Kahn, A.J., and Kamerman, S.B. 1976. *Social services in international perspective: The emergence of the sixth system.* Washington D.C.: U.S. Government Printing Office.

Katzenstein, P.J. 1980. Capitalism in one country? Switzerland in the international economy. Cornell University. (mimeographed)

Kelman, S.J. 1981. *Regulating America. regulating Sweden.* Cambridge: MIT Press.

Klein, R. 1973. National health service: After reorganisation. *The Political Quarterly* 44: 316–5328.

Kramer, R. 1981. *Voluntary agencies in the welfare state.* Berkeley and Los Angeles: University of California Press.

Lazar, I. 1979. *Lasting Effects after pre-school: A summary report.* Washington D.C.: HEW Consortium for Longitudinal Studies.

Lehmbruch, G. 1979. Consociational democracy, class conflict, and the new corporatism. In *Trends toward corporatist intermediation*, ed. P.C. Schmitter and G. Lehmbruch. London, Beverly Hills: Sage Publications. Pp. 53–61.

Long, D.A., C.D., Mallar, and C. Thornton 1981. Evaluating the benefits and costs of the Job Corps. *Journal of Policy Analysis and Management* 1:55–76.

O'Connor, J.R. 1973. *The fiscal crisis of the state.* New York: St. Martins Press.

Offe, C. 1972a. *Strukturprobleme des kapitalistischen Staates.* Frankfurt am Main: Suhrkamp.

Offe, C. 1972b. Political authority and class structures: An analysis of late capitalist societies. *International Journal of Sociology* 2: 73–108.

Offe, C., and Ronge, V. 1975. Theses on the theory of the state. *New German Critique:* 6: 137–147.

Organization for Economic Cooperation and Development. 1979. *Labor force statistics 1966–1977.* Paris: OECD.

Rein, M. 1969. Social class and the utilization of medical care service. *Journal of the American Hospital Association* 43: 43–54.

Schweinhart, L.J. and D.P. Weikart 1980. *Young children grow up: the effects of the Perry preschool program on youths through age 15.* Ypsilanti, Mich.: the High/Scope Press.

Streeck, W. 1978. Organizational consequences of corporatist cooperation in West German labor unions: A case study. Berlin: International Institute of Management, discussion paper.

Thurow, L.C. 1980. *The zero-sum society.* New York: Basic Books.

Vogel, E. 1979. *Japan is number one.* Cambridge: Harvard University Press.

Wildavsky, A. 1977. Doing better and feeling worse: The political pathology of health policy. *Daedalus,* 106: 105–123.

Wilensky, H.L. 1956. *Intellectuals in labor unions: Organizational pressures on professional roles.* New York: Free Press–Macmillan.

Wilensky, H.L. 1964. Mass society and mass culture: Interdependence or independence? *American Sociological Review* 29: 173–197.

Wilensky, H.L. 1967a. Careers, counseling, and the curriculum. *The Journal of Human Resources* 2: 19–40.

Wilensky, H.L. 1967b. *Organizational intelligence: Knowledge and policy in government and industry.* New York: Basic Books.

Wilensky, H.L. 1975. *The welfare state and equality: Structural and ideological roots of public expenditures.* Berkeley: University of California Press.

Wilensky, H.L. 1976. *The 'new corporatism,' centralization and the welfare state.* London and Beverly Hills: Sage Publications.

Wilensky, H.L. 1978. The political economy of income distribution: Issues in the analysis of government approaches to the reduction of inequality. In *Major social issues: A multi-disciplinary view,* ed. M. Yinger. New York: Free Press. Pp. 87–108.

Wilinsky, H.L. 1980. Leftism, Catholicism, and democratic corporatism: The role of political parties in welfare state development. In *The development of welfare states in Europe and America,* ed. P. Flora and A.J. Heidenheimer. New Brunswick, N.J.: Transaction Books, Pp. 341–378.

Wilensky, H.L. 1981. Family life cycle, work, and the quality of life: Reflections on the roots of happiness, despair and indifference in modern society. In *Working life: A social science contribution to work reform,* ed. B. Gardell and G. Johansson. London: Wiley. Pp. 235–265.

Wilensky, H.L., and Lawrence, A.T. 1979. Job assignment in modern societies: A re-examination of the ascription–achievement hypothesis. In *Societal growth: Processes and implications,* ed. A.H. Hawley. New York: Free Press–Macmillan. Pp. 202–248.

Yemin, E. 1976. Job security: Influence of ILO standards and recent trends. *International Labour Review* 113: 17–33.

# 4

# Social Policy Evaluation and the Psychology of Stagnation

## BURKHARD STRÜMPEL

The trend in the popular attitude toward the economy in Western countries over the last decades clearly indicates that people are affected by a deep malaise. During the 1970s people's satisfaction with their economic situation, their confidence in their economic future, and their faith in the stability of the system and the competence and effectiveness of economic policies deteriorated, even in those countries that still registered increases in real incomes. The economy, which had been the mainspring of satisfaction during the postwar years of reconstruction, the burgeoning of pent-up consumer demand, and high population growth became a source of concern, causing disappointment, and even resignation. The decline in confidence in the polity, such as mistrust of government and of the competence and honesty of political leaders. And this malaise of the 1970s occurred despite spectacularly high levels of production and real income, and in a period of continued, although diminished, economic growth.

Although the above facts are hardly controversial, different implications for social policy are drawn from them by the adherents of different visions of society. For the curious coexistence of prosperity and gloom, several partly conflicting causes have been identified, of which three are discussed in this chapter, namely (a) rising expectations; (b) maldistribution; and (c) mal-allocation, that is, a qualitative mismatch between socioeconomic change and people's wishes, wants, and needs.

The proponents of an *industrial vision* of society strongly endorse greater

EVALUATING THE WELFARE STATE:
SOCIAL AND POLITICAL PERSPECTIVES

emphasis on capital formation, investment in production plants and technology, and efforts to improve productivity. They tend to claim that people are basically insatiable, that in industrial societies aspirations are rising quasi-automatically with income and consumption and are thus outrunning gratifications; that during the good times people learned to expect further income increases, and are naturally disappointed when these are not forthcoming.

The emphasis on maldistribution as the presumed cause of malaise is usually associated with an *egalitarian vision* of society's problems. Its partisans are concerned with an equitable distribution and redistribution of the wealth that society has produced. They define social justice in terms of rights and entitlements rather than as requiring special efforts aimed at earning benefits. They tend to argue that income inequality is more perceptible when average income levels, are stagnant than during a period of rising levels.

In the postwar era of historically unprecedented income growth, there were two avenues toward individual improvement: social mobility, implying an advance in one's own position relative to others in society, and rising general affluence, that is, increasing real incomes per capita in the economy. Whereas social mobility can be experienced only by some, the other avenue for income progress is open to the large majority of the population, including those whose social status remains stable. Their progress depends on the growth of the economy. The first decades after World War II were very generous in providing for real income increases. The 1970s, in contrast, brought income stagnation and deprived the nonmobile worker of the only, and highly cherished, source of participation in material betterment. At the same time, many more people had been affected by income declines and were thus tempted to engage in invidious comparisons with their more fortunate fellow citizens. Rather than by absolute income level or the absence of income increases, malaise is created by intensified social comparison and the more frequent experience of income decline. This situation, then, calls for interpersonal redistribution more than for growth.

Malaise is often seen as revolving around malallocation or a possible qualitative mismatch by those who endorse a *"quality-of-life" vision*. Their goal is to preserve what gains have accrued to the industrial society thus far, to fashion a low or moderate-growth society from this point onward, and to "live better with less" (Yankelovich 1980). According to them, what private and public sectors produce is no longer what people desire, and it entails costs that are not shown in any statistics—environmental damage, disruption of human bonds, depletion of resources. According to late British economist Fred Hirsch (1976), rising real incomes have resulted in a certain saturation with mass consumption goods. However, the dynamics of growth aggravate the competition for "positional goods," that is, goods that, unlike mass produced consumption goods, cannot be reproduced with diminishing marginal costs, such as a seaside villa, a flat in an exclusive neighborhood, or well-paying jobs with high social status. Consequently, we face increasing rates of inflation, or rationing, as evident in the barriers to entering certain professions or lines of work, or crowding, resulting in the diminution of quality as manifest in the educational system, road transportation, and urban planning.

Correspondingly, a family moving from a crowded inner urban location to an expensive suburb can hardly hope to achieve a better quality of dwelling than was provided ten years earlier by a much more modestly priced apartment located in a more densely populated area. The second car in the family only compensates for the deterioration—traffic noise, criminality, change in social composition—characteristic of large inner cities. In this case, the occurrence of stagnation of subjective well-being, despite higher real income and expenditures, needs no psychological explanation. Rather than the standard of the evaluation, the physical and social environment have changed. The thrust of socioeconomic policies, rather than centering on a potentially disruptive pursuit of growth or redistribution, must be toward improvement of the physical and social environment.

In order to gauge the merit of each of these explanations, I shall review three bodies of empirical evidence: (a) The subjective evaluation of the individual economic situation; (b) the evaluation of macroeconomic performance based on shorter term intertemporal comparison ("Consumer sentiment" in the Katona tradition); and (c) change in societal values and priorities—measures that must be considered indicators of what people would like to do or to see happen, rather than indicators of welfare proper.

## The Rising Expectations Hypothesis

Richard A. Easterlin (1974) analyzed the correlation between the gross national product of a country and the personal happiness scores of its inhabitants as collected by Cantril (1965). No correlation was found. For instance, in 1962 the average life satisfaction was higher in Cuba, Egypt, and Israel than in West Germany, and the United States, Yugoslavia, Brazil, and Poland ranked only slightly lower. Duncan (1975) reports that in the Detroit metropolitan area, representative cross-sections of the population were interviewed with the same questionnaire twice, first in 1955 and again in 1971, after the average real income per family had increased by 40%. Mean scores of satisfaction with income and level of consumption remained about the same during this period. On the other hand, practically all students of micro data pertinent here report that higher income earners consider themselves more satisfied than people receiving lower incomes (Abrams 1973, Easterlin 1974, Strümpel 1974).

These results are usually explained by referring to two concepts. First of these is the psychological adaptation level theory, which assumes an almost unlimited capacity of people to adjust their criteria situations to reality. As the environment becomes more pleasurable, subjective standards for gauging pleasurableness will rise (Brickman and Campbell 1972). The successful will be captives of the "hedonistic treadmill," but the unsuccessful may look forward, if not to a "humble but happy" life, at least to a certain degree of contentment.

The second explanation for the stagnation of the scores for subjective well-being despite increased income and consumption revolves around the concept of interpersonal comparison. People customarily evaluate their income more in relationship to others than to its absolute size. This phenomenon has been discussed under the heading "relative income hypothesis" by Duesenberry and has been used to explain why in many countries the rate of saving has stayed constant over time. Sociologists have developed the concept of "relative deprivation," and economists and statisticians have learned to look at poverty as a relative phenomenon.

So far, no support for the rising expectation hypothesis has been found. The two concepts previously discussed possibly explain why economic growth is not being translated into felt well-being, but they certainly do not explain why the absence or diminution of growth leads to malaise. There is, however, one psychological mechanism that relates to this: intertemporary comparison. People tend to judge their situation against past levels of their own accomplishment as much as against the levels that "relevant others" have reached. A significant correlation has been found between past income change and satisfaction with income even after the influence of absolute income is controlled for (Strümpel 1974). Moreover, the level of aspiration is more easily expanded than reduced (Campbell, Converse, and Rodgers 1976). Research of people's evaluation of their housing and neighborhood has shown that the optimal past experience (rather than, for instance, the most recent experience, or the worst past experience) is the most important standard for the pegging of aspiration levels, and that the distance between the latter and the perception of present status best predicts satisfaction (Campbell *et al.* 1976, Chapter 6). Let us further examine the relationship between income change and well-being on the macro level by turning to the oldest subjective indicator: surveys of consumer sentiment. This, however, shall carry us beyond the examination of the rising expectations hypothesis.

## Economic Sentiment and Changes in the National Economy

George Katona's quarterly surveys of consumer sentiment have been conducted in the United States since the late 1940s on the basis of interviews with representative cross sections of Americans. Respondents are asked to evaluate their present financial situation, whether or not they expect changes for the better of for the worse, how they judge the present general business conditions, and what expectations are for the economy as a whole. An index summarizes the results to these questions.

Figure 4.1 and 4.2 exhibit the contrast between the era of relative economic

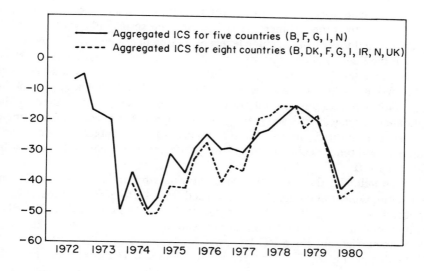

**Figure 4.1.** *This index of consumer sentiment for the five or eight members of the European Community Countries is weighted by population size. The index is composed of the frequencies of the answers to four questions—two dealing with the assessment of the individual economic situation, two dealing with the general economy. Higher index values express more optimistic assessments.*

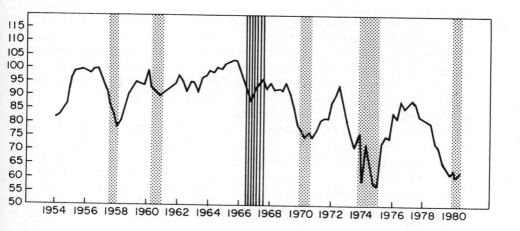

**Figure 4.2.** *This is an index of consumer sentiment in the United States. The shaded areas indicate recession. Since the American definition of the ICS is different from the European, the scale on the left is not comparable with the scale on the of Figure 4.1.*

success significant for the 1950s and 1960s, on the one hand, and the malaise of the 1970s, on the other. (Since the European time series only starts in 1972, only the last holdover from the high levels of sentiment documented elsewhere is visible in the figure.) As we know from other evidence (not exhibited here), the relatively high level of sentiment prevailing in Europe in 1972 is characteristic for the favorable state of economic psychology prevailing throughout most of the 1960s. Not only had the volatility of consumer sentiment, as measured by the amplitude of change, increased greatly, the average level of economic sentiment had also deteriorated. In the United States, the percentage of those who predicted good times declined from 47 to 17% between the end of 1966 and the middle of 1980.

Correspondingly, the proportion of pessimists who anticipated more extensive unemployment and depression increased from 14 to 66%, and there was a deterioration of conditions. Similar results have been obtained for other countries of Europe where triannual periodic surveys of consumer sentiment have been carried out since 1972.

Notwithstanding the fact that economic sentiment is the product of news developments in various spheres—the economy, the society, the world—there are some lasting sources of preoccupation shaping it: inflation, unemployment, and possible changes in size of consumers' disposable income. All of these are both measured and reported on the aggregate level and tend to impinge on the individual respondent's life experience.

To what extent did these macroeconomic variables shape Europeans' perceptions and expectations in the 1970s? Those observers who believe that decreasing rates of real growth intensify distributional conflict would most likely expect a high correlation between real income changes and changes in consumer sentiment. Those who attach highest importance to the transition from a "tight" to a "loose" labor market as the prime problem of economic welfare in this decade will expect the greatest impact on consumer sentiment from changes in unemployment. And finally, there are those who consider inflation the foremost economic problem of our times. They would probably expect the public to react most vehemently to increases in the rate of inflation, and to honor a return to stability with a distinct increase in optimism.

In a regression analysis of consumer sentiment to be predicted from the level of unemployment and the rate of inflation for the period of the 1970s, the relative strength of the inflation variables emerges clearly. Inflation comes in significantly in 7 of the 12 countries investigated, unemployment in only 1. A similar conclusion follows from a graphic representation of changes in consumer sentiment, inflation, and unemployment in the larger European countries. Although typically a mirror image of sentiment and inflation is apparent (see Figure 4.3) there emerges a surprising complacency toward the high plateau of unemployment plaguing all European countries since 1975 (Strümpel, Kuss, and Curtin 1980). The reason for this unusually strong sensitivity to inflation may be the following: In the highly inflationary environment of the 1970s,

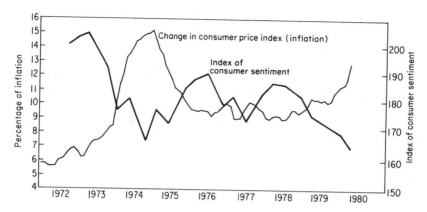

**Figure 4.3.** *This is a graph of economic sentiment and inflation in France. (From Strümpel, Kuss, and Curtin, 1980).*

nominal income increases were generally maintained, thus institutionalizing the anticipation of continuing real increases. The unexpectedly large inroads of inflation into real incomes were deeply resented. The individual, on the basis of earlier income progress, revised upward the notion about the value of his or her own input without seeing rewards being adjusted correspondingly. There is still another version of "money illusion" generated. Price increases also affect the sense of equity in that they inflate the individual's notion about the incomes of others. If everything becomes more expensive, someone must reap the benefit. Thus, others in the distributional game—who may only catch up with inflation—are perceived as gaining, thereby accentuating the sense of deprivation.

On the basis of the preceding evidence, it would be very shaky reasoning indeed to attribute the low levels of felt well-being of our still affluent societies to the absence of high rates of growth. The continuation of old-type industrial growth can be described as a temporary enhancement of welfare. But, it does not appear to be a viable long-term strategy, for two reasons: (a) because it exhibits only a very vague relationship to felt well-being: (b) we may not be able to get the old-type growth anyway, no matter how badly we want it. Economic growth as such does not make people happy, and income stagnation appears to be much less resented than institutional mismanagement, disarray, and a breakdown of equity, trust, and contractual security as caused by high rates of inflation. The miserable performance of the industrial economy in converting wealth into felt well-being is a feature of our social condition rather than of human greed. It must be seen as the result not of stagnation but of the inefficiency with which production is converted into satisfaction of needs. The evidence does not support the rising expectations hypothesis.

# The Maldistribution Hypothesis

Times of economic adversity, at least in modern history, have always stimulated the debate on equality as a maxim of social justice. Is inequality a luxury society can afford only in times of growth, and can maintain in times of stagnation only at its own peril? So the maldistribution hypothesis for the explanation of the present malaise would suggest.

Social research cannot hope to answer so broad a question. It may be able, however, to assess the extent to which a strategy of redistribution could indeed be implemented without arousing hostile reactions that would defeat the purpose of increasing the sense of well-being. We are no doubt witnessing an erosion of traditional notions favoring status and reward differentiation:

1. The norm of equality is increasingly being accepted—albeit not implemented—in some life domains: health care, public safety and protection by the law, universal suffrage, educational opportunity.
2. It is increasingly recognized that everybody, regardless of input, is entitled to a wage that ensures a "decent" minimum standard of living.
3. Western industrial nations have accepted progressive income taxation and thereby have consented to a massive correction of the market distribution.
4. There is more intense social comparison sensitizing participants in the distributional game.

Although these trends will remain far short of effecting or legitimizing radical redistribution in the near future, there is some evidence that moving toward more equality might meet with popular acceptance. Yuchtman–Yaar, in his contribution to this book (see Chapter 5) reports a significant negative correlation between income and the sense both of entitlement and of relative deprivation. However, the dynamics of aspirations differ among subcultures within a society. In the United States, professionals are more "saturable," that is, they tend to reduce the margin of material aspirations with rising income, in contrast to executives and people in business, who tend to retain high margins of unfulfilled aspirations even in the face of relatively high incomes (Strümpel 1976). This difference seems to be due to a specific value structure of professionals with college degrees who are more frequently oriented toward nonmaterial goals such as self-actualization and satisfying work than are other subgroups with about equal average income whose values and priorities are more strongly linked to monetary income.

These findings remind us that receiving less income in most cases leads to dissatisfaction and a sense of deprivation only to the extent that it is considered inequitable, that is, illegitimate. The standards applied for judging the fairness or equitability of a situation, while tainted by self-interest, express in part a social consensus about the rules of remuneration and their application. Sometimes, particularly during times of war or national emergency, austerity and even sacrifice is accepted as necessary or inevitable. The sense of equity then can be seen as a symptom of societal integration as manifested in the distribution of products and resources. If very many people disagree with the rules applied or feel that the rules agreed upon fail to be implemented, the orderly give and take that links individuals in any social system, is jeopardized.

Redistribution from the "haves" to the "have-nots" for the purpose of enhancing welfare within given resource constraints, then, seems to have a limited chance of success. It may have some promise in the long run and may offer the same slow gains in felt well-being as would a possible further shift in egalitarian norms of distribution. Such a shift is underway for women and disadvantaged minorities. Yet the emphasis here is not on the transfer of resources in order to equalize incomes, but rather on the equalization of opportunities and wage rates: equal pay for equal performance. Even implementation of this rule would hardly reduce vulnerability to income decline and job loss (Strümpel 1979).

The story does not end here. It is important to know what people mean by "performance": It is what one might call subjective performance, as measured by the ability and effort of the individual, rather than objective performance, that is, productive contribution as weighted by scarcity, such as market prices. Our evidence (Strümpel 1979) suggests that people tend to judge as equivalent the performances of a policeman and a fireman, with equal effort and equality demanding training, regardless of whether policemen happen to be in shorter supply at this particular moment than firemen. The lack of deference to the market mechanism revealed here is in line with the great sensitivity to inflation shown before. Inflation replaces implicit contracts by the unchecked rule of the market; only in an inflationary environment can debtors withhold part of the contracted real value of the amount to be repaid, can employers reduce the real value of wages without violating social norms, in other words, can a Manchester-type world be implemented.

## The Malallocation Hypothesis

Let us now turn to the malallocation hypothesis. When production and productivity rise, there should be more economic satisfaction, with both the individual and the aggregate economic situation, as well as a shift in value priorities from material to nonmaterial concerns. We have seen that there does not appear to be an improvement in the personal economic experience as expressed by subjective evaluation; however, a change in popular priorities and values is developing.

A far-reaching harmony between popular priorities and economic policy was characteristic of the decades following World War II. During the reconstruction period, expanding production, based on rapid capital formation, was of high priority to virtually all participants in the social game. In the public's evaluation, the positive concomitants of industrial growth weighed more heavily than the negative ones. In addition to satisfying the basic material needs, the economy provided for full employment, monetary stability, and a stronger sense of security and continuity. In its first phase, the construction boom replaced the ruins of wartime destruction, provided dwellings, and thus enabled the formation of families. The pollution of air and water, traffic congestion, and street noise remained below the threshold of importance, if not perception. The goal of economic growth reigned supreme. In order to speed up industrial reconstruction through capital formation, German trade unions in the 1950s consistently consented to a massive redistribution of income in favor of capital owners by accepting wage hikes far below the productivity increases.

Little is left of the honeymoon of the postwar era. There has been a distinct evolution of values and popular priorities related to the rise in mass affluence over the last decades. I summarize the still fragmentary evidence about this trend as follows. According to the surveys initiated by Ronald Inglehart and conducted in countries of Europe and the United States, postmaterial values (participation, self-actualization, and environmental protection) have been strongly on the rise in all countries, most notably among young respondents. Conversely, material values oriented toward achieving and securing command over material resources are more heavily represented among the older generation. The affluence characteristic of the period when the younger generation grew up brought to the fore higher-order needs, whereas the material deprivation that prevailed during the formative years of today's older people left lasting marks on their value structure, despite changed material circumstances (Inglehart 1977).

Within less than a decade *occupational* preferences in particular have changed greatly. Whereas in the middle of the 1960s a qualified majority of Germans and a strong simple majority of Americans rated economic security as the most important characteristic of a good job, in 1972–1973 the item "important work, feeling of accomplishment" had gained ground significantly (Katona and Strümpel 1978). Moreover, the traditional virtues of courtesy and subordination, diligence, modesty, and even respect for the employer's private property seem to have lost authority in both countries, particularly among younger people. The number of those who accept "hard work" as desirable and who subordinate pleasure to duty has diminished. The secular trend indicated by Inglehart appears to hold true even when monitoring changes between relatively short time intervals (Noelle–Neumann, 1978; Yankelovich 1974).

When asked to choose one of the two avenues for improving living standards—wage increases or reduced working time—the majority of workers in the member countries of the European communities (51%) preferred shorter work hours over higher wages (42%); in Germany the respective figures were 55% and 35% (Commission of the European Communities 1978). The desire for shorter work hours appears to be particularly strong in countries enjoying a relatively high real income per capita (see Figure 4.4).

It would be inaccurate to describe these changes as saturation. However,

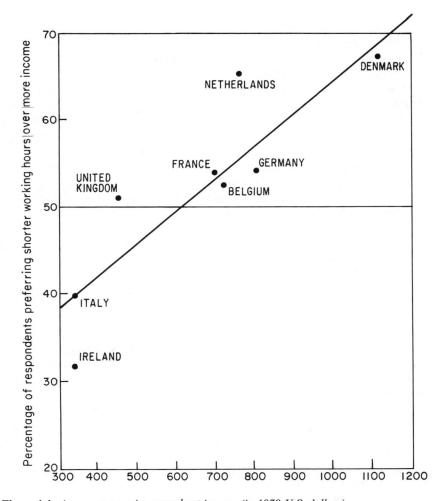

**Figure 4.4.** *Average per capita annual net income (in 1970 U.S. dollars).*

there seems to be a growing mismatch between the output of the economic system and people's aspirations, values, and preferences. There is a lack of feedback between people and both the market and the polity. What the industrial system has to offer in abundance—cars, refrigerators, air travel to the crowded Spanish coastline—is no longer attractive, and what would be attractive—an education offering social and economic mobility; a vacation in an unspoiled environment; a job that provides decent pay and a measure of self-determination, meaning, and flexibility—is harder to come by than in the past. This perspective of reality—to which could be added Ralph Dahrendorf's vision of the work society running out of jobs—indicates a need for institutional adaptation rather than GNP growth in order to align popular demands and system output. Choices between work, income, consumption, and leisure, between income and quality of employment, between material comfort and resource-saving consumer behavior are largely prevented by the well-known roadblocks of oligopolistic interests or sheer administrative inertia. They range from the failure of companies to offer attractive part-time jobs, the usual practice of making fringe benefits conditional on a large number of years of tenure, and product obsolescence planned by entire industries, to the failure to provide tenants with incentives to reduce their heat consumption. On the macro level we observe government deficit spending to counter the negative employment effect of labor-saving investment (or as in Germany, of rising rates of saving) instead of strategies to create employment without forcing production to rise, such as a reduction of working time.

## Conclusions

Various conclusions emerge from the preceding considerations.

First, a psychological explanation of the malaise characterizing the 1970s and 1980s does profit from considerations of *intraindividual* intertemporal comparison of change in real income. The first decades after World War II provided very generous real income increases. There were two avenues toward individual improvement: social mobility, implying an advance in position relative to others in society, and rising affluence, that is, increasing real incomes per capita in the economy. Mobility is facilitated or obstructed by the individual's standing in terms of social status, based mainly on education and occupation. Once formal schooling has been completed and an occupation chosen, the material future, relative to others in society, is largely preprogrammed by age and seniority. The other avenue for income progress was open to the large majority of the population, including those whose social status would remain stable, whose progress depended on the growth of the economy. The 1970s, in contrast, brought income stagnation and deprived the nonmobile worker of the only and highly cherished source of participation in material betterment; this transition was not inconsequential in terms of the subjective evaluations of both the economy and the individual's economic situation.

Second, the case for an explanation of the malaise based on unfulfilled aspirations for real income ("expectations") is strongest on the micro level. However, when the relationship between individual income change and felt economic well-being is considered, on the macro-time-series level, inflation rather than changes in aggregate income is likely to have the stronger influence on felt well-being. Income stagnation appears to be much less resented than institutional mismanagement, disarray, and a breakdown of equity, trust, and contractual security as caused by high rates of inflation.

Third, the initial question of this chapter—which of the three current explanations for the economic malaise of the post-postwar era (rising expectations, maldistribution, or malallocation) is most appropriate—is not answered simply. There is much evidence that in our era, unlike in the previous one, changing values and preferences with respect to the *mode* of work, employment, production, or consumption relative to their *quantity* have gained in importance, and that, unlike then, the most pressing priorities fail to elicit a sufficient and adequate response by economic institutions. This supports the malallocation hypothesis. In contrast, the support for both the rising expectations and maldistribution hypotheses is indirect. With regard to the former, it is rather a case of "constant expectations," the frequent failure to maintain *a given level* of income as characteristic of the current transition from growth to stagnation, that has been experienced. Perceived maldistribution, in turn, appears to be mediated by the sense of equity (or inequity) of income received. The norms of equity, rather than being based on the principles of equality or, conversely, on market values, tend to follow a particular calculus of personal merit—education, ability, effort. Prevalent high and rising rates of inflation—a hotbed of quick, upward and downward price and wage adjustments—do lead to a heightened sense of inequity and maldistribution.

# References

Abrams, M.A. 1973. Subjective social indicators. *Social Trends* 4:

Brickman, P., and Campbell, D.T. 1972. Hedonic relativism and planning the good society. In *Adaptation level theory: A symposium*, M.H. Appley, ed. New York: Academic Press.

Campbell, A., Converse, P.E., and Rodgers, W.L. 1976. *The quality of American life.* New York: Russell Sage Foundation.

Cantril, H. 1965. *The pattern of human concerns.* New Brunswick, N.J.: Rutgers University Press.

Duncan, O.D. 1975. Does money buy satisfaction? *Social Indicators Research* 2: 267–274. (Dordrecht, Holland)

Easterlin, R.A. 1974. Does economic growth improve the human lot? In *Nations and households in economic growth: Essays in honor of Moses Abramovitz*, eds. P.A. David and M.W. Reder. New York: Academic Press. Pp. 89–125.

Hirsch, F. 1977. *Social Limits to growth.* Cambridge: Harvard University Press, 1976.

Inglehart, R. 1977. *The silent revolution.* Princeton: Princeton University Press.

Katona, G., and Strümpel, B. 1978. *A new economic era.* New York: Elsevier.

Noelle–Neumann, E. 1978. Werden wir alle proletarier? Zurich:

Strümpel, B. 1974. Economic well-being as an object of social measurement. In *Subjective elements of well-being*, ed. B. Strümpel. Paris: OECD. Pp. 35–53.

Strümpel, B. 1976. Stagnation, welfare, and the efficiency of consumption. In *Frontiers in social thought—Essays in honor of Kenneth E. Boulding*, ed. M. Pfaff. Amsterdam: North Holland Publishing Co. Pp. 215–229.

Strümpel, B. 1979. Economic planning and the case for continuity. *Alternatives* 8:35–39.

Strümpel, B., Kuss, A., and Curtin, R.T. 1980. The use and potential of consumer anticipations data in the member countries of the European communities. Second report (unpublished).

Yankelovich, D. 1974. *The new morality—A profile of American youth in the 1970s.* New York: McGraw–Hill.

Yankelovich, D. 1980. Economic policy and the question of political will. Unpublished manuscript.

Yuchtman–Yaar, E. 1976. Effects of social psychological factors on subjective economic welfare. In *Economic means for human needs: Social indicators of well-being and discontent,* ed. B. Strümpel. Michigan: Institute for Social Research. Pp. 107–129.

Yuchtman–Yaar, E. Forthcoming. Social welfare and entitlements, in this volume.

# 5

# Expectancies, Entitlements, and Subjective Welfare

## EPHRAIM YUCHTMAN–YAAR

## Introduction

Students of advanced industrial countries have often argued that the economic growth and standard of living associated with this type of society stimulate the development of excessive levels of expectation so that the actual achievement of material well-being cannot satiate wants and aspirations. Edwards's (1927) early "rising expectations" hypothesis represents one of the influential statements on this issue: "As a group experiences an improvement in its conditions of life it will also experience a rise in its level of desires. The latter will rise more rapidly than the former, leading to dissatisfaction and rebellion [p. 30]." Perhaps in anticipation of the worldwide economic slowdown of the 1970s, Davies (1962) has reformulated Edwards's hypothesis: "Revolutions are most likely to occur when a prolonged period of objective economic and social development is followed by a short period of sharp reversal [p. 6]"

These hypotheses and related statements by political sociologists and social psychologists (cf. Bendix and Lipset 1959; Brinton 1938; Davis 1959; Geschwender 1964; Gurr 1970; Sorokin 1925; Urry 1975) have been incorporated into the debate over the processes and consequences of the welfare state. Wilensky's (1976) position in this context succinctly expresses a view widely shared: "I shall argue that at high levels of economic development the revolution of expectations must be channeled and contained because mass demands for benefits and services are outrunning the capacity of government to meet them [p. 8]."

Notwithstanding some important differences among its proponents, the theme

EVALUATING THE WELFARE STATE:
SOCIAL AND POLITICAL PERSPECTIVES

of rising expectations contains at least three related elements: first, that levels of expectation vary according to levels of economic well-being; second, that the rate of the former grows faster than the latter; and, third, that the resultant gap leads to feelings of relative deprivation and malaise.

These are forceful propositions which, if valid, have far-reaching ramifications for questions of welfare and its consequences at the societal and individual level. Their intuitive appeal, however, should not distract us from the need to examine the theoretical basis and empirical evidence upon which they are founded. Such an examination quickly reveals that much vagueness exists in the rising-expectations literature with respect to concepts, units of analysis, and specification of the underlying processes. For example, does the concept of expectations have unequivocal analytic and operational meanings? Is there an invariant direct link between objective economic circumstances and the subjective phenomenon of expectations? Do individuals and organized collectivities respond similarly to rising expectations? These and similar questions suggest that the rising-expectations argument may be deceptively simple and its premises and implications may warrant closer inspection.

This chapter is a preliminary effort at addressing some of these questions at the individual level with the aid of cross-sectional data collected in the United States.[1] Specifically, I will first discuss some concepts and propositions related to the theme of rising expectations and then apply them empirically in the context of job-earned income.

## Conceptual Considerations

Social scientists have usually treated the concept of expectations as an intervening variable, mediating between objective circumstances to which people are exposed and their subjective reactions to those circumstances. Katona's (1951) theory of the psychology of inflation illustrates this model in its application to the economic sphere:

inflation→ expectations→ consumers' sentiments and behavior

This schematic model has been adopted by virtually all theorists of rising expectations regardless of the specifications and operationalization of the independent or dependent variables included in them. However, the concept of expectations is, both semantically and psychologically, rather intricate. A distinction must be drawn between at least two different meanings of the term that, in my opinion, have important implications for understanding the role of

---

[1]The distinction between individual and collective levels is of utmost importance here since it is not altogether clear whether political demands, regarding, for example, the improvement of economic welfare, originate with widespread sentiments among individual members of a collectivity or whether they stem from institutionalized leadership (e.g., political parties, trade unions, professional associations.)

expectations as a theoretical construct. I will first discuss these meanings in the context of sociopsychological research, and move next to their relevance for socioeconomic issues.

One of the earliest systematic incorporations of expectations into sociopsychological theory appears in Merton and Rossi's (1968) essay on relative deprivation and reference group behavior. Drawing upon the empirical descriptions provided by Stouffer and his collaborators in the study of the American soldier in World War II (Stouffer, Suchman, Devinney, Stor, and William 1949), Merton and Rossi's analysis (1968) consistently demonstrates that levels of expectation are formed on the basis of certain objective features of the situation and that, once established, they tend to generate subjective responses independent of those features. For example: "A generally high rate of mobility induces excessive hopes and expectations among members of the group so that each is more likely to experience a sense of frustration in his present position and disaffection with chances for promotion [p. 291]."

This and similar illustrations analyzed in great detail by Merton and Rossi contain the main elements and describe the causal flow of the rising expectations theme: An objectively favorable condition (e.g., high rates of mobility) produces still higher ("excessive") expectations, and because of the resultant gap, feelings of frustration and discontent are aroused. A closer inspection of the empirical descriptions analyzed in this spirit reveals, however, two quite different processes disguised by the single term *expectations*. *Webster's Third New International Dictionary* (1976, p. 794) informs us that *to expect* means "to consider probable or certain . . . to suppose, think, believe." This definition pertains to purely cognitive processes involving estimations of possible outcomes or events based on subjective assessments of reality. But *to expect* is defined also as "to consider reasonable, just, proper, due." According to this definition, expectations involve normative considerations in the assessment of outcomes or events, that is, outcomes regarded subjectively as just or rightfully deserved. These two different usages of *to expect* seem critical for understanding the rising expectations argument; in order to keep them separate they will be referred to as expectancies and entitlements, respectively. Thus, levels of expectancy reflect a reality-bound process of evaluation whereas entitlement levels reflect a normative or moral judgment.[2] For the purpose of the present discussion expectancies can be accordingly defined as *subjectively attainable outcomes*; correspondingly, entitlements are *subjectively deserved outcomes*.

The relevance of the difference between expectancies and entitlements for the theory of rising expectations has been largely ignored by its students. Perhaps

[2]Both expectancy and entitlement should be distinguished from still another related concept—aspirations. The latter refers to desired events or outcomes that are not necessarily constrained by either perceived reality or criteria of justice; there exists, therefore, no inherent ceiling to levels of aspiration—as in how much money one would "aspire to" or like to have.

the major exception in this respect is Gurr's scholarly work, *Why Men Rebel* (1970). His analysis introduces a distinction between value expectations—"the goods and conditions of life to which people believe they are rightfully entitled,"—and value capabilities—"the goods and conditions they think they are capable of getting and keeping." Gurr's contribution is mostly theoretical, resting on little evidence from systematic empirical research. Nevertheless, his ideas and propositions provide an important conceptual basis for the potential fruitfulness of the distinction between value expectations and value capabilities—concepts which are essentially isomorphic to levels of entitlement and levels of expectancy.

Turning back to the empirical examples analyzed by Merton and Rossi (1968), it seems clear that both types of evaluation were involved in the subjective experiences of the individual soldiers—hence such expressions as *hopes and expectations* or *legitimate expectations*. In other words, feelings of relative deprivation were developed in these instances not simply because promotions did not come as fast as the soldiers believed they would; they must have also regarded those promotions as outcomes they rightfully ("legitimately") deserved. Without the existence of this sense of entitlement it is not altogether clear whether feelings of relative deprivation would have occurred. This convergence between levels of expectancy and entitlement that took place among these soldiers, however, does not necessarily have to occur as a general rule. The analytic distinction between the two concepts suggests that expectancies and entitlements might develop at least partially independently and, furthermore, that they may operate differentially either as causes or effects. Such a possibility implies that these variables may play a different role as mediators between objective circumstances and subjective responses. Specifically, it is proposed that *subjective well-being is related positively to the level of expectancy and negatively to the level of entitlement.* This hypothesis is empirically testable and, if validated, has some interesting implications for the theme of rising expectations. Before turning to the empirical realm, however, the rationale underlying this proposition and some related conceptual issues must be addressed.

It has been well established by sociopsychological research that an individual's sense of well-being is not determined solely on the basis of perceptions and evaluations of circumstances prevailing at present. Past experiences as well as those anticipated in the future are also usually taken into consideration. A higher level of expectancy with regard to positively evaluated outcomes implies a "better future," either in the sense that rewards are perceived as more likely to come, or that more of them are believed to be obtainable. Hence there is a hypothesized positive influence of expectancy level on subjective well-being. It is worthwhile to note in this connection that insofar as socially determined outcomes are concerned (e.g., salaries, benefits, and services), higher levels of expectancy might indicate that the "system" is perceived as responsive to wishes and needs so that feelings of anger and relative deprivation are *not* likely to develop.

The second part of the hypothesis can be similarly argued. A higher level of entitlement indicates a relatively large gap between the present position and that which is rightfully deserved. Placed in the framework of equity theory (Adams 1965; Homans 1961, 1974), this gap represents the discrepancy between the current level of rewards and the one the individual believes he or she should get without the obligation of further input. It is obvious, therefore, that the larger this discrepancy, the more likely that negative feelings will develop. In particular such a condition is conducive to the arousal of feelings of relative deprivation and social discontent (see Gurr 1970; Thurow 1973; Williams 1975).

Considering this argument in the context of rising expectations theory, it should by now become clear that failure to distinguish explicitly between levels of expectancy and entitlement is a serious flaw, limiting the usefulness of the theory. Specifically, two important conclusions are indicated: first, the negative consequences of rising expectations to which the proponents of this theme have called attention should be attributed only to discrepancies vis-a-vis entitlement rather than expectancy levels; second, if expectancies and entitlements exert contrasting influences on subjective welfare then the nature of the inter-relationship between the two variables must be understood in order to account for feelings of relative deprivation and discontent. Thus, for example, if there exists a complete overlap between levels of expectancy and entitlement, feelings of relative deprivation are not likely to develop even if available rewards lag behind, because the deficit vis-a-vis entitlement is fully compensated for by the prospect of its elimination.[3]

The specific case of a complete convergence between levels of expectancy and entitlement may serve to reemphasize the importance of understanding how these two variables are related. Unfortunately, there exists no coherent body of theory and research from which a general principle about this relationship can be deduced. Nevertheless, within the specific context with which the present study is concerned—expectancies and entitlements regarding job-earned income—it can be reasonably argued that they are positively associated and, moreover, that the formation of expectancy levels occurs prior to the development of feelings of entitlement. The reasoning behind this argument will now be considered.

## Expectancies and Entitlements with Respect to Pay

Income in the form of wages and salaries constitutes a vital ingredient in the

---

[3]To use the illustration from Stouffer *et al* (1949) once more, the feelings of frustration and disaffection prevailed not before but only after "legitimate expectations" failed to be realized.

economic welfare of most individual members of society and their families. Advanced industrial nations have frequently experienced harsh debates and severe conflicts about "proper" income levels and their rules of distribution. Since it is beyond the scope of this chapter to describe the different viewpoints on this problem (philosophical, economic, sociopolitical, etc.), I will only say that it has been of great concern in the more general complex of socioeconomic policies, especially in the domains of the labor market and welfare. For this reason a study of the rising expectations phenomenon in the context of pay is an interesting case in itself as well as being a pertinent aspect of more general processes of expectancies and entitlements.

To the best of my knowledge, only one empirical investigation has been conducted to date in which measures corresponding to the concepts of both expectancy and entitlement were employed in the sphere of work-pay (Behrend 1973). Although developed for different purposes, the variables and results of that study are highly relevant to this discussion. In particular, Behrend's analysis shows that (*a*) workers clearly distinguish between levels of pay expectancy (e.g., the amount of pay increase they think they will get) and pay entitlement (e.g., the pay increase they feel they rightfully deserve); (*b*) levels of entitlement tend to be higher than levels of expectancy; (*c*) the latter are developed according to the actual circumstances of the work environment, including the experience of past pay increases; (*d*) levels of entitlement are systematically related to levels of expectancy.

These interesting findings cannot, however, be indiscriminately accepted, for several reasons. First, they refer to an aggregated analysis, comparing statistics across groups. Second, Behrend's study does not examine the relationship between expectancy and entitlement directly, nor does it inspect their potential effects on workers' attitudes or behavior. And third, it is based on a unique sample.[4] An opportunity to overcome these limitations is provided by survey data collected by the Institute for Social Research (The Fall 1973 Omnibus Survey).[5] This data serves as the empirical base for the subsequent analysis.

## Measures

Three sets of variables, distinguished according to the empirical model presented here, can be described as follows:

[4]The sample consisted of the Dublin respondents who constituted a subsample of a national sample. The interviews were conducted in 1969.

[5]The sample in that survey was designed to yield some 1500 interviews with respondents 18 years of age or older, selected from housing units representative of the coterminous United States, exclusive of those on military reservations. A response rate of 74% resulted in 1210 interviews. For this analysis only full-time non-self-employed participants in the labor force were selected ($N = 714$). For a detailed description of sampling procedure and data set, see Struempel (1976).

*Measures of expectancy and entitlement*: Respondents were asked three questions, in the following order.

1. With regard to the income from your job, do you expect your wage rate or salary to increase, to decrease, or to stay about the same during the next year:

———increase

———stay the same

———decrease

———don't know

2. Few people know for sure, but approximately how large will the increase (decrease) be?——————————————(in percentages)

3. With regard to yourself, what amount do *you* think would be *fair* for next year's increase (decrease)?——————————————(in percentages)

The first two items were intended to provide information for the measurement of expectancy. Notice that the questions are formulated so as to elicit subjective estimates of one's change in pay level in the near future. This operationalization corresponds reasonably well to the definition of expectancy as presented earlier. The third item asks respondents to apply a subjective normative standard by which the amount of pay increase or decrease is evaluated. This process of evaluation is consistent with the definition of entitlement. These two indicators of expectancy and entitlement closely follow Behrend's (1973) measures of expected and equitable pay changes.

*Socioeconomic position*: Seven indicators were included to represent workers' objective socioeconomic characteristics.

1. Income level—self-reported job-earned income, categorized into an 18 interval scale

2. Income change—percentage increase or decrease in this year's as against last year's income, scaled as in 1

3. Education—a dichotomous variable, with respondents having nine years of schooling or more coded 1, and the rest, 0.

4. Occupation—a nine-point scale of occupational status according to the one-digit classification of the 1970 census book

5. Race—a dichotomous variable, with whites coded 1 and nonwhites, 0

6. Sex—a dichotomous variable, with males and females coded 1 and 0, respectively

7. Age—categorized into three age groups: 35 and below coded 1, 36 to 54 coded 2, and 55 or older coded 3

*Indicators of subjective economic welfare*: In accordance with the theoretical reasoning of rising expectations theory, two measures were selected to represent feelings of economic welfare.

1. *Relative social deprivation (RSD)* is an index composed of the linear combination of two questionnaire items:

    a. "How fair is what you earn on your job in comparison to others doing the same type of work you do?"

    b. "How fair is what people in your line of work earn in comparison to how much people in other occupations earn?"

An identical response scale was provided along with these questions, ranging from "much less than others" (scored 1) to "much more than others" (scored 5).[6]

2. *Income satisfaction*: This variable is tapped by a single questionnaire item, "How satisfied are you with the income you (and your family) have?" The response scale for this measure ranges from "delighted" (7) to "terrible" (1).[7]

## Empirical Model

The specific model empirically tested consists of independent, intervening, and dependent variables, the causal order of which is treated as being fully recursive. To begin with, it is assumed that employed workers typically assess prospects for pay changes on the basis of personal experience, perceptions and knowledge about the conditions of the labor market, the workplace, and their own "bargaining" position vis-a-vis these environments. For example, in a market or an organization that discriminates against women, it is reasonable to assume that women working in it have some knowledge about such reality, either through direct experience or transmitted information. Under such conditions, then, female workers are hypothesized to develop—ceteris paribus—lower pay expectancies than their male peers. Similarly, in an economic system that places higher value on youth than on age, it is expected that higher levels of expectancy will be found among younger employees.

As is the case in these two instances of sex and age, the remaining indicators are conceived as independent variables which represent important—albeit incomplete—aspects of the socioeconomic position of individual workers. Accordingly, they are presumed to have an appreciable influence on levels of expectancy. More specifically, it is expected that the more favorable the objective circumstances of workers are, the higher workers' levels of expectancy

---

[6]These measures were derived conceptually from Runciman's (1966) distinction between "egoistic" and "fraternal" deprivation. Despite the analytic difference between the two types of deprivation, they were combined into a single index in view of their relatively strong association ($r=0.56$).

[7]Thus the measure of relative social deprivation refers to job-earned income only, whereas the satisfaction item pertains to total income.

will be, as implied by the literature on rising expectations. This general proposition does not distinguish between the static and dynamic meanings of relative position. The first pertains to one's position vis-à-vis others' at a given time; the second reflects changes in a position over time. The rising-expectations hypotheses have been especially formulated in relation to the dynamic dimension. The present proposition encompasses both of these dimensions by measuring both income level and income change.

The formation of entitlements in relation to socioeconomic position is probably a more complex process. We are concerned here essentially with people's sense of justice in the realm of pay—an intriguing phenomenon about which little is known. Equity theory (Adams 1965; Homans 1961, 1974) represents the major systematic effort by behavioral science to address this question both conceptually and empirically. The most important proposition of equity theory is the principle of fair exchange according to which justice in the distribution of rewards is maintained if people get out of an exchange proportionately what they have put into it. Despite its generality, the equity principle is helpful in suggesting plausible connections between objective attributes of individuals and their sense of entitlement. For example, in a system that regards education as an asset, it is likely that employees having higher levels of education will have higher levels of entitlement.

But beyond such general guidelines much is left to be desired in the understanding of how people arrive at one level of entitlement or another. In particular, little is known about the relationship between income differentials and entitlement. For example, do people who earn more believe that they rightfully deserve to get still more? In attempting to answer such questions it becomes clear that equity theory is insufficient and that the larger social context must be considered first. A vivid illustration of this kind of contextual relevance is given by the case of black Americans. Students of the racial scene in America have commonly observed that prior to the Civil Rights Movement black workers generally accepted their inferior position in the labor market, as reflected in job and wage discrimination. One of the major consequences of the Civil Rights Movement was precisely the undermining of such a belief system and the inculcation of the black community with the realization that its position was not inevitable and that a drastic change in its condition was a legitimate claim (see Pettigrew, 1967).

The historical case of black Americans is consistent with the conclusions reached by Merton and Rossi (1968) on the basis of their survey analysis of the American soldier. Accordingly, perceptions of and knowledge about reality precondition the development of "legitimate expectations." More generally, this process is most vividly captured by George Orwell in his *The Road to Wigan Pier* (1937): "Talking once with a miner I asked him when the housing shortage first became acute in his district; he answered: 'When we were told about it' [p. 64.]"

These examples, along with Behrend's (1973) empirical findings, seem to suggest that expectancy tends to develop prior to entitlement and to function as

*Ephraim Yuchtman-Yaar*

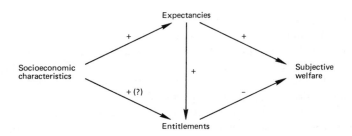

**FIGURE 5.1.** *This is a schematic model of the relationships among expectancies, entitlements, and subjective welfare.*

These examples, along with Behrend's (1973) empirical findings, seem to suggest that expectancy tends to develop prior to entitlement and to function as a cognitive yardstick against which levels of entitlement are formed. Accordingly, it is proposed that level of pay entitlement is positively affected by level of expectancy. This proposition, together with the hypotheses regarding the contrasting influences of expectancy and entitlement on subjective well-being, imply a causal model which will be schematically represented here. This is a path analytic model the signs of which indicate either positive $(+)$ or negative $(-)$ influences. The question mark attached to the path between socioeconomic characteristics and entitlement reflects my uncertainty with regard to the directionality of specific characteristics, though the rising expectations hypothesis, if we read it correctly, implies an overall pattern of positive effects of this kind. This model, presented in Figure 5.1, is examined as part of the empirical findings and analysis to which we now turn.

# Results

Beginning with some descriptive statistics, it might be of some interest to note the distributions of expectancy and entitlement. The means of these variables are 11.54% and 22.03%, respectively, with corresponding standard deviations of 34.91% and 39.46%. These figures imply that at the time of the survey the average American employee felt deserving of a pay increase of just over one-fifth of salary, but anticipated an actual increase of about one-half that rate. The immediate questions associated with these numbers concern the evaluation of their magnitude and the understanding of their origins. For example, should a discrepancy of 22% between present and just income levels be viewed as small or large? Is the anticipated pay increase big enough to ameliorate the gap vis-à-vis entitlement? The answers to such questions depend, of course, on the context in which they are placed. They may be related, for instance, to macroeconomic trends, such as the rates of inflation or unemployment during that year. Since the available data are based on a one-shot survey, it is impossible to engage here in any time-oriented analysis. Put in more general terms, in the absence of data collected systematically over long time periods it is difficult to assess whether expectancy and entitlement levels as obtained in this survey are "excessive" or "moderate," unique or typical. Moreover, with no such data available, we are in no position to find out to what extent these levels are influenced by structural and policy changes at the societal levels. Finally, having no similar measures for other societies, the findings concerning the distribution and determination of pay expectancies and entitlement cannot be understood in a comparative cross-national perspective.

On the other hand, it is useful to examine the findings of this survey in relation to the cross-sectional composition of its respondents. From this viewpoint the measures of dispersion, on first scrutiny, are informative. We note, first, that the standard deviations of both expectancy and entitlement are relatively large and, second, that the standard deviation of entitlement—in comparison to the mean—is smaller than that of expectancy. The large interemployee variation in estimation of pay increase or decrease raises the question as to whether this reflects mostly idiosyncratic individual differences or whether it stems from sytematic differences in the socioeconomic position, as the preceding discussion has suggested. The second result, namely, the relatively small variance in the distribution of entitlements, raises the question of whether normative considerations in the assessment of fair income set some upper and lower limits, and whether these are connected to both socioeconomic position and levels of expectancy. Table 5.1 provides an initial answer to these questions.

**TABLE 5.1**
**Zero-order Correlations between**
**Socioeconomic Characteristics**
**and Measure of Pay Expectancies**
**and Entitlements**

|  | Expectancy | Entitlement |
|---|---|---|
| Income | −.10 | −.43** |
| Income change | .27** | .35** |
| Education | .18* | −.14* |
| Occupation | .05 | −.19* |
| Race[a] | .04 | −.25** |
| Sex[a] | .13* | −.03 |
| Age | −.29** | −.18* |

*$p < .05$.
**$p < .01$.
[a]Whites and males represent the higher categories of these dummy variables.

The results presented in Table 5.1 are rather mixed with regard to the anticipated directionality of the effects of the independent variables and their relative strength. We note, first, that the relationship between income and expectancy levels is weak and negative. On the other hand, income exerts an appreciable influence on feelings of entitlement, this influence being, in fact, the strongest of all the independent variables included in this analysis. Of greater interest, however, is the negative direction of this association, meaning that employees with lower income apparently feel they have a right to rectify their inferior position through higher *rates* of pay increase. This result calls into question the often documented finding that American workers tend to be satisfied with their jobs. The reason might possibly be that the latter findings were based on measures that were not sensitive enough to workers' concern with the issue of fair pay.

In contrast to the static quality of socioeconomic position as indicated by income level, the measure of income change reflects recent fluctuations in the wages and salaries of our respondents. The correlation coefficients obtained for this measure imply that such fluctuations operate in an opposite direction to that of income; that is, those who have improved their lot financially tend to think that they will do still better in terms of pay increase—and they feel that they rightfully deserve this pay increase. This result provides probably the clearest empirical support, at the individual level, for the rising expectations hypothesis as formulated by Edwards (1927) and others.

The relationships between employees' levels of education and the two dependent variables are unexpectedly weak though statistically significant. Not surprisingly, more-educated workers anticipate higher rates of pay increase. However, in contrast to the hypothesis derived from equity theory, having more education does not entail higher levels of entitlement. The effects of occupational status are similar to those of education, and since neither of them is measured optimally, the results associated with them are probably underestimated.

No differences appear to exist between white and nonwhite employees regarding pay expectancies, but the racial distinction is clearly relevant for the issue of entitlement. The percentage of pay increase that nonwhites feel they deserve is significantly higher than that of white employees.[8] This finding may reflect the enhanced awareness among black workers of their deprived condition in the labor market, as noted in the preceding discussion.

The pattern of correlations for sex may be contrasted with the results obtained for race. Men tend to have higher levels of pay expectancy than do females—an indication probably of the actual differences between the sexes

---

[8]Since we are concerned here with zero-order correlations, it is possible that this result is an artifact of the relationship between race and income level (see table in the appendix). This problem applies to most of the correlations reported in Table 5.1, insofar as the independent variables are intercorrelated, and will be examined in the subsequent multivariate analysis.

with regard to income opportunities in the labor market. Despite this reality, however, working women have not developed a higher sense of entitlement. The comparison between the characteristics of race and gender on this issue is instructive since both blacks and females have traditionally experienced significantly lower earnings than the privileged groups of white and male employees. More recently, pay differentials have been documented to be more pronounced along sex rather than race lines, a trend which is replicated in these data as well. The finding that our female respondents have not, nevertheless, formed higher levels of pay entitlement may indicate insufficient awareness of their condition, or, alternatively, its acceptance as normatively legitimate.

The last indicator of this group of socioeconomic characteristics is age. This variable reveals a consistent tendency in that older workers are likely to have lower levels of both expectancy and entitlement. The negative effect of age on pay expectancy may be interpreted as a response to the actual career trajectories associated with age, since higher rates of increase in earning usually occur at earlier rather than later stages of occupational career. The decreased levels of entitlement as a function of age probably indicate a psychological adjustment to this experience. This interpretation is consistent with studies concerned with the relationship between age and job satisfaction. These studies have consistently reported that job satisfaction tends to be higher among older workers, and one of the competing explanations for this association has been the "moderation" effect of age. At the same time, alternative explanations for these results must be acknowledged. For example, it is possible that they express cohort rather than age effects, and given the nature of our data, such a confounding influence cannot be isolated.

The next set of findings to which we turn deals with the interrelationships among expectancy, entitlement, and the two measures of subjective economic welfare. In accordance with the rationale presented earlier, levels of expectancy and entitlement tend to vary together ($r=.37$); that is, employees who believe they will enjoy higher pay increases are also likely to feel they rightfully deserve them—and more—as the mean differences between the two variables would suggest. But with respect to the relationships between expectancy, entitlement, and subjective well-being, our a priori considerations are supported only in part.

**TABLE 5.2**
Intercorrelations among Measures of Expectancy, Entitlement, Relative Deprivation,
and Income Satisfaction

|  | 1 | 2 | 3 | 4 |
|---|---|---|---|---|
| Expectancy | — | .37 | −.06 | .02 |
| Entitlement | — | — | .27 | −.36 |
| Relative deprivation | — | — | — | −.48 |
| Income satisfaction | — | — | — | — |

As anticipated, subjective welfare is adversely related to level of entitlement, as indicated by the latter's positive association with relative social deprivation ($r=.27$) and negative correlation with income satisfaction ($r=-.36$). Unlike our argumentation, however, workers with higher levels of pay expectancy do not necessarily feel comparatively less deprived or more content financially, as indicated by the near-zero correlations of these relationships. Before dwelling on these results, however, it should be kept in mind that a correlation matrix does not enable the separation between gross versus net, or direct versus indirect effects among variables that are presumed to be causally interrelated. In order to facilitate these distinctions, all the correlations were subjected to a multivariate regression analysis according to the path analytic model presented in Figure 5.1. The results of this analysis are reported in Table 5.3.

Following the same order of discussion as in the previous section, we may notice that only four of the seven socioeconomic characteristics exert independent influences on level of expectancy. Level of expectancy is positively affected by income change, education, and sex, and negatively by age. The absence of significant net effects for income and occupation is due, probably, to multicolinearity, since both variables are related to most of the remaining socioeconomic characteristics. In general, however, these results do not differ markedly from the pattern depicted by the correlation matrix, and the relative strength of the four independent effects is quite similar, ranging from a beta coefficient of .12 (for sex) to .24 (for income change).

Considering next the determination of entitlement levels, we note that income change retains a small direct influence, but the most pronounced effects on

**TABLE 5.3**

Standardized Partial Regressions (Path Coefficients) for the Model Describing the Determination of Expectancy, Entitlement, and Subjective Economic Welfare

| Independent variables | Dependent variables | | | |
|---|---|---|---|---|
| | Expectancy[a] | Entitlement[a] | Deprivation[a] | Satisfaction |
| Income | −.05 | −.33[c] | −.03 | .07 |
| Income change | .24 | .16[c] | −.16[c] | .12[c] |
| Education | .14[c] | −.08 | −.05 | .05 |
| Occupation | .08 | −.08 | −.06 | .07 |
| Race[b] | .04 | −.21[c] | −.06 | .14[c] |
| Sex[b] | .12[c] | −.06 | −.07 | .03 |
| Age | −.20[c] | −.07 | −.04 | .05 |
| Expectancy | — | .30[c] | −.17[c] | .04 |
| Entitlement | — | — | .38[c] | .26[c] |
| Relative social deprivation | — | — | — | −.36[c] |

[a] These variables are entered both as dependent and independent, according to the path analytic model described. Satisfaction with income is treated as the "ultimate" dependent variable in this scheme.

[b] Whites and males represent the higher categories in these dummy variables.

[c] Coefficients are at least twice as large as their standard errors.

sense of entitlement are exerted by income level $(-.33)$ and by level of expectancy $(.30)$. These results are especially relevant for the issues of welfare policy, and are addressed in the final section of this chapter. The moderate yet clear independent effect of race $(-.21)$ is also meaningful in this context, particularly when compared with the nonsignificant effect of sex.

With regard to the direct influences on relative social deprivation, the results of the path analysis present a somewhat different and more intriguing pattern than that drawn from the correlation matrix. More specifically, it appears that levels of expectancy and entitlement have opposing, though unequal, effects on this variable, with path coefficients of $-.17$ and $.38$ respectively. This finding bears on the conceptual considerations underlying the basic model advocated here in two respects: first, it is consistent with our initial hypothesis that expectancies, per se, affect the sense of economic welfare positively; and second, it provides support to the causal order regarding the relationships among expectancy, entitlement, and subjective welfare as depicted by the model (see p. 98). This conclusion is based on the comparison between the zero-order correlations and the multivariate analysis, as follows. The near-zero correlation between expectancy and relative social deprivation versus the moderate but significant effect of the former as indicated by the path coefficient suggests that the third variable in this triangle—level of entitlement—operates as a "suppressor" with regard to the relationship between the other two variables. Once its intervening role is controlled for, the suppression effect is removed, and the underlying effect of expectancy on deprivation is uncovered through the path coefficient connecting these two variables. Since the size of this effect is, however, quite small, I will not elaborate on its potential implications for issues of socioeconomic policies. Nevertheless, I believe that the empirical confirmation concerning the differential impact of expectancy and entitlement on subjective economic welfare is of some theoretical importance and deserves further attention.

The second measure of subjective well-being—income satisfaction—shows relatively strong dependence on relative social deprivation and on level of entitlements, in the expected direction. Given the additional indirect effect of entitlement on satisfaction via social deprivation, its overall influence on this variable should be emphasized. Table 5.3 also indicates that income change still exerts an independent influence on satisfaction, as well. In fact, it is the only socioeconomic characteristic that directly affects all subsequent variables in this model. The theoretical relevance of this result for the behavioristic approach as represented particularly by Homans (1961, 1974) cannot be overlooked, but discussion of it goes beyond the limits of this chapter.

## Summary and Some Implications

Social science research is sometimes faced with the dilemma of "social relevance" versus "scientific elegance." That is, a desire to arrive at significant statements about social reality may interfere with commitment to rules of theory building and empirical inquiry. The propositions made about the revolution of rising expectations tend to reflect a preference for the first of these alternatives. At the same time, they provide a clear demonstration that insufficient sensitivity to conceptual clarity and empirical validity can nevertheless be richly compensated for by insightful observations and provocative ideas. This chapter is an attempt to systematize some aspects of these ideas conceptually and empirically. Conceptually, it suggested that the phenomenon of expectations is more complex than generally recognized, and that it can be more fully understood through the analytic distinction between cognitive and normative (or affective) elements which may be involved in it. The specific concepts and hypotheses derived from this distinction were aimed at showing that qua sociopsychological process, expectations may consist of both reality bound expectancies and normatively based entitlements which are differentially related to anteceding factors and potential consequences at the individual level.

With respect to the empirical problem, the specific purposes were, first, to attempt one plausible mode of operationalization of these concepts; and, second, to examine their fruitfulness in understanding the determination of subjective economic welfare as reflected in the domain of job-earned income.

It was noted earlier that the data set that served the empirical analysis is limited in terms of social space and time (dealing with a single society at one point in time), in addition to its exclusive focus on expectancies and entitlements with respect to job pay. Despite these restrictions, I believe that some of the empirical findings are worthy of further comment because of their potential relevance for broader issues of socioeconomic policies in the context of the welfare state. For brevity, only two such implications are addressed here.

The incorporation of the rising-expectations argument into the debate over the functioning and future of the welfare state has been characterized by the conviction of many that widespread and excessive claims for economic benefits constitute an inherent problem in this type of society. D. Bell (1975), a vigorous critic of the welfare state, has gone so far as to warn that "the ultimate problem presented by the revolution of rising entitlements is not that it will cost a lot of money—although it will certainly do that. What is potentially more dangerous is the threat that the revolution presents to our political system. It threatens to overload the system, to confront it with far more grievances than legislators and judges know how to cope with [p. 98]."

Although Bell's notion of entitlements ("claims on government to implement an array of newly defined and vastly expanded social rights") differs in some important ways from the definition of this concept in this chapter, my findings seem to bear on the general concern of Bell as well as other students of the welfare state (see, for example, Wilensky 1976, p. 8). This relevance appears in at least two different ways (see Table 5.3). On the one hand, the results of my analysis are supportive of such a concern in showing that a socioeconomic background that nourishes an optimistic outlook about future economic outcomes (e.g., level of expectancy) is also likely to encourage, directly and indirectly, heightened demands for entitlements and, consequently, feelings of relative deprivation and discontent. This conclusion is based, primarily, on the positive relationship between levels of expectancy and entitlement, and on the effects of the latter on subjective economic welfare. A significant aspect of this finding is that it reflects "genuine" sociopsychological processes rather than expressions of interest groups or institutionalized leadership in the political arena. To the extent that this finding is not unique to the circumstances of its data base, the implication might be that socioeconomic policies for the improvement of people's welfare facilitate—as an unintended consequence— the development of subjectively legitimate claims for still higher standards of economic well-being. From this perspective, then, the problem of rising and insatiable entitlements is inherent in the commitment to welfare and their implementation.

But, on the other hand, the results also suggest some other processes which caution against a one-sided view on the problem of rising expectations. I have already noted that the empirical findings show that the analytic distinction between expectancies and entitlements resides in the minds of people and that the two phenomena, though positively related, do not fully correspond to each other. This empirical observation implies that claims of entitlement may develop independently of expectancies and of the specific socioeconomic characteristics underlying them. The question is, therefore, whether the large variation in levels of entitlement which is unaccounted for by these factors stems mostly from idiosyncratic individual attributes, or from people's location in the socioeconomic hierarchy. The results presented by Table 5.3 point to systematic relationships of this kind, as indicated by the direct paths from income and race to entitlement. Specifically, levels of entitlement are more likely to be higher among certain deprived categories of employees, such as people with lower income or people of nonwhite origin. These trends may indicate a state of nonacceptance by these groups of what they consider to be excessive inequalities. Higher levels of entitlement for these people express, accordingly, legitimate demands for a more egalitarian redistribution.

In light of these findings and this interpretation, it is difficult to avoid the suggestion that the critical evaluation of the welfare state by Daniel Bell and his colleagues is oversimplified and could reflect an ideological preference, because if the trend of rising levels of entitlement reflects in part a movement toward greater equality of outcomes, then it is not the welfare state as such that is in danger. What might be at stake are the specific forms of economic institutions that safeguard existing inequalities. Indeed, one does not have to read between the lines in order to infer that such a thought did not escape Bell. The short abstract of his 1975 article in *Fortune* reads as follows: "More and more Americans are demanding that the government make them 'equal' to other

## TABLE 5.4

### Intercorrelations among Socioeconomic Characteristics, Levels of Expectancy and Entitlement, and Measures of Subjective Economic Welfare ($NNN = 714$)

| | 1 | 2 | 3 | 4 | 5 | 6 | 7 | 8 | 9 | 10 | 11 |
|---|---|---|---|---|---|---|---|---|---|---|---|
| Income | | -.32** | .21* | .34** | .13 | .43 | .18* | -.10 | -.43** | -.15* | .21* |
| Income change | | | -.01 | -.05 | -.04 | -.02 | -.19* | .27** | .35** | -.06 | .06 |
| Education | | | | .40** | .19* | -.02 | -.23* | .18* | -.14* | -.12* | .15* |
| Occupation | | | | | .15* | .04 | -.03 | .02 | -.19* | -.13* | .12* |
| Race | | | | | | .05 | -.04 | .04 | -.25** | -.12* | .25** |
| Sex | | | | | | | -.08 | .13* | -.03 | .00 | .02 |
| Age | | | | | | | | -.29** | -.18* | -.05 | .05 |
| Expectancy | | | | | | | | | .37** | -.06 | .02 |
| Entitlement | | | | | | | | | | .27** | -.36** |
| Relative social deprivation | | | | | | | | | | | -.48** |
| Income satisfaction | | | | | | | | | | | |

*$p < .05$
**$p < .01$

Americans. The demand may endanger our political system [p. 103]."

To conclude, this analysis suggests that rising claims of entitlement and, subsequently, feelings of deprivation and discontent, may be caused by a variety of factors, some of which have to do with the development of expectancies, others with various dimensions of people's position in the labor market and, more generally, in the stratification order of society. Socioeconomic policies probably have a profound influence on the development of these processes, directly and indirectly, but the nature of this influence is apparently not simple or uniform. What is needed, therefore, is more empirical data about other domains of expectancies and entitlements (e.g., housing, education, and employment) for different societies and over time. The systematic accumulation of such data would permit the development of a theory about rising expectations, social structure, and welfare policies.

# References

Adams, J.S. 1965. Inequity in social exchange. In *Advances in experimental social psychology* Vol. 2, ed. L. Berkowitz. New York: Academic Press. Pp. 267–299.

Behrend, H. 1973. *Incomes policy, equity and pay increase differentials.* Edinburgh and London: Scottish Academic Press.

Bell, D. 1975. The revolution of rising entitlements. *Fortune* April: 98–103, 185, 187.

Bendix, R., and Lipset, S.M. 1959. *Social mobility in industrial society.* Berkeley: University of California Press.

Brinton, L. 1938. *The anatomy of revolution.* New York: Norton.

Davies, J.C. 1962. Towards a theory of revolution. *American Sociological Review* 27: 5–19.

Davis, J.A. 1959. A formal interpretation of the theory of relative deprivation. *Sociometry* 22: 280–296.

Edwards, L.P. 1927. *The natural history of revolution.* Chicago: University of Chicago Press.

Geschwender, J. 1964. Social structure and the Negro revolt: An examination of some hypotheses. *Social Forces* 43: 248–256.

Gurr, T.R. 1970. *Why men rebel.* Princeton: Princeton University Press.

Homans, G.C. 1961. *Social behavior: Its elementary forms.* New York: Harcourt, Brace and World.

Homans, G.C. 1974. *Social behavior: Its elementary forms.* Second Edition, New York: Harcourt, Brace, Jovanovich, Inc.

Katona, G. 1951. *Psychological analysis of economic behavior.* New York: McGraw–Hill.

Merton, R.K., and Rossi, A.S. 1968. Contributions to theory of reference behavior. In *Social theory and the social structure*, ed. R.K. Merton. New York: The Free Press. Pp. 279–335.

Orwell, G. 1937. *The road to Wigan Pier.* London: Victor Gollancz.

Pettigrew, T.F. 1967. Social evaluation theory convergence and application. In *Nebraska symposium on motivation 1967*, ed. D. Levine. Lincoln: University of Nebraska Press. Pp. 241–311.

Runciman, W.G. 1966. *Relative deprivation and social justice.* Berkeley: University of California Press.

Sorokin, P. 1925. *The sociology of revolution.* Philadelphia: J.B. Lippincott.

Stouffer, S.A., Suchman, E.A., Devinney, L.C., Star, S., and William, R.M., Jr. 1949. *The American soldier. Vol. 1: Adjustment during army life.* Princeton. Princeton University Press.

Struempel, B., ed. 1976. *Economic means for human needs: Social indicators of well being and discontent.* Ann Arbor: University of Michigan Institute for Social Research.

Thurow, L. 1973. Toward definition of economic justice. *Public Interest* 31: 56–80.

Urry, J. 1975. *Reference groups and the theory of revolution.* London: Routledge & Kegan Paul.

Webster's third new international dictionary. 1976. Chicago.

Wilensky, H.L. 1976. *The new corporatism: Centralization and the welfare state.* Beverly Hills: Sage Publications.

Williams, R.M. Jr. 1975. Relative deprivation. In *The idea of social structure*, ed. L. Coser. New York: Harcourt, Brace, Jovanovich. Pp. 355–378.

# II

# Boundaries of the Welfare State and the Foci of Policy Evaluation

*Government is not the sole organ of welfare provision. A significant portion of benefits and services is provided by economic institutions, voluntary agencies, and kinship groups. Rainwater and Rein suggest that the claims that can be made on all of these be taken into account in the evaluation of trends in the development of* welfare societies, *a term they prefer to* welfare state.

*The Government's share in welfare is only partly reflected in data on taxing and spending. These, Aharoni argues, represent only the "tip of the iceberg." The submerged part, which is less readily accessible to scrutiny and evaluation, consists of the sponsorship of semigovernmental agencies and the use of the government's power to regulate benefits to some at the expense of others. This phenomenon is not necessarily undesirable. In his chapter, Wilensky argues that the most stable and successful welfare states are the ones using the less visible forms of taxing and spending.*

*The welfare state can be seen as the sum total of a large number of specific programs and policies designed to redistribute resources in order to enhance the well-being of various segments of society. The more visible among these policies become the subject of public debate. These debates are, however, only partly relevant to the redistributive processes occurring in the real world. Edelman argues, for example, that employment and welfare are often affected to a greater extent by the hidden actions of such agencies as central banks than by the employment policies that are the object of public scrutiny and debate. He argues that, contrary to rhetoric, government policies tend to reinforce existing inequities. Along the same line, Doron calls for greater attention to the "microallocation" of resources. Whatever the intentions of policymakers, important decisions as to "who gets what" are made by the professionals and bureaucrats who are entrusted with the day-to-day administration of welfare programs.*

# 6

# The Growing Complexity of Economic Claims in Welfare Societies

## LEE RAINWATER AND MARTIN REIN

The modern welfare state is generally thought to consist of two types of government programs. One transfers ("redistributes") income from some individuals to others with a view either to ensure minimum protection from various risks or to provide income adequacy. The second type directly provides services to citizens—these range from social protection (e.g., health programs) to improvements in human capital (e.g., education, job training), to provision of cultural advantages.

In preindustrial times, in the world of the countryside and small village, access to economic resources involved a complex of rights and duties which allowed one to receive, and produce for one's own use, various kinds of goods and services. In such an economy, money and formal market exchange had a small role. In modern times the claim to economic resources is substantially the claim to money income which is then exchanged for the goods and services families use as raw material in creating their standard of living. Claims for income, of course, have varied historically—claims based on might, service, loyalty, ownership, rent, sovereignty, God's will, interest, kinship, labor, and charity have all been important at various times.

The modern welfare *state* can be understood as embodying a particular claims structure that organizes income claims distributed ("redistributed") through government agencies. The welfare state has been defined as a "state that makes itself responsible for the social security and welfare of its citizens (Penguin 1969)." That is, it is a state that seeks to assure the security and adequacy of the standard of living of its citizens. The idea of such a state evolved through a series of social inventions in a 2-century-long struggle that

EVALUATING THE WELFARE STATE:
SOCIAL AND POLITICAL PERSPECTIVES

began in earnest in the last decades of the eighteenth century and continues today. That broader struggle, Karl Polanyi (1944) has argued, is basically a struggle between social forces that seek to have society operate according to the principles of a self-regulating market, and the varied, often opposing, forces that seek to contain the destructive effects of a pure market system.

Just as business and institutions identified with it have consistently fought to keep labor in the market, forces concerned with the protection of working people and their families against the destructive effects of a self-regulating market system have struggled in various ways to "take labor out of the market."

Although a great deal of the struggle involved in this transformation seems to deal most directly with the relationship of worker to capitalist, in fact, much of the struggle has been not only about the individual worker but about the family. Certainly the concern with the standard of living has been centrally one of families' welfare. But, also, a good deal of the struggle in the workplace has— and still does—involve family issues and relationships.

The goal of those who sought to transform the market mechanism that defines labor as a commodity was to break the dependence of workers and their families on the market-determined daily wage for the maintenance of their standard of living. They invented and institutionalized social means by which security and adequacy of the standard of living can be guaranteed.

By the end of World War II the welfare state was well established legally and administratively in most European countries, and it was beginning to be established in the United States as a legacy of the New Deal. However, in terms of its impact on people's lives, even in European countries, the pre-1950s welfare state was, in fact, a relatively marginal part of most families' set of income claims. Beginning in 1950, there was an explosive growth of welfare state funding. Before then, the proportion of the population affected at any one time and the proportion of GNP devoted to such expenditures (especially if we exclude old-age pensions and consider the impact of the welfare state on families headed by working age men and women), had relatively minor impact until the 1950s and 1960s.

## The Welfare Economy

In this chapter we draw attention to the commonly ignored role of employee benefits in contributing to economic welfare. Although there has been a great deal of attention devoted to the growth of government provided benefits, there has been little attention given until recently, to the parallel growth of employee benefits.

Government intervention affects the welfare economy in complex ways. The artificial separation between "public" and "private" benefits has made for serious difficulties in understanding the modern welfare *society*. These difficulties inhibit our understanding of the distribution of resources within a country, distort perceptions in cross-national comparisons, and blunt our ability to grasp the future development of the welfare state.

By *welfare society* we refer to the totality of welfare-oriented activities in the polity (welfare state) and the economy (welfare economy). We do not mean to imply that the welfare society is necessarily an egalitarian society—indeed the activities of the welfare economy may well undermine egalitarian welfare state programs. What is distinctive about the welfare society is that a high proportion of its resources are committed to institutions concerned with protection against economic risk and provisions to maintain family living standards that are not contingent on current family labor supply—whether that labor supply be withdrawn for reasons of ill health, old age, or leisure (as in the case of vacations and holidays).

In modern societies three major *institutional* frameworks distribute economic resources to individuals and nuclear families: the kinship system, the economy, and the state. The concrete expression of these generalized systems are the family and household, the firm or enterprise or governmental employer, and federal, state, and local governments in their relation with citizens. A *claims rationale* justifies the way in which these institutions distribute economic resources to households. For example, we think of family loyalty, marketable skills, and equity. Sometimes these rationales are implicit, sometimes explicit. They are never consensual or static. Rationales change over time and are subject to a considerable amount of controversy within each country. Moreover, there is considerable debate about the possibility and desirability of substituting types of resources within a sector and across sectors. Actors in each institutional system express their *interests* by attempting to use and modify the rationales in a bid to control and utilize economic resources of different types. There is a constant struggle for control and influence over the distributive processes within each institution. Actors with institutional interests activate a process of claiming. Other's accommodate and resist these claims. In this process, at least three factors play a role: the operation of market forces such as the dynamics of supply and demand; prevailing customs and traditions; and the political power to impose one's interest on others.

It is useful to distinguish types of economic resources in terms of the form in which the resource is transferred from institution to family. Although two types of resources are commonly differentiated in discussing government benefits—cash transfers and in-kind transfers—the elaborate diversity of benefits in the modern welfare state is probably better captured by three categories: unrestricted cash grants, restricted cash grants, and goods and services. Unrestricted grants refer to cash payments that the individual is free to spend in any way, for example, a grant given because of a situation of sickness or of ill health but which may be spent on anything. Restrictive grants refer to cash payments that the individual must spend for some particular purpose—for medical expenses, to buy food, to pay college tuition. This dichotomy is relatively unambiguous as long as we keep in mind that the difference between restricted

**TABLE 6.1**
**Types of Economic Resources Received by Families from Three Institutional Sectors**

| Form of resource | Formal institutional sector | | Household sector— kinship group |
| --- | --- | --- | --- |
| | Economy | Government | |
| Unrestricted cash grants | Factor income | Transfer income | Allowances and gifts |
| Restricted cash grants, vouchers and subsidies | Employee or fringe benefits | Earmarked transfers or subsidies | Expense payments and gifts for particular purposes |
| Goods and services | "Perks" | Social and personal services | Reciprocation and gifts of goods or services |

and unrestricted cash grants has to do with the *purpose* for which the money is spent, rather than the basis of the entitlement (which may also be related to some particular situation).

Each of the three institutional systems provides resources in all three forms. That is, government, economic institutions, and kinship groups provide unrestricted cash, restricted cash, and goods and services. Table 6.1 shows the nine types of economic resources that derive from combinations of the institutional sector and form of resource.

Each type of resource is reasonably amenable to definition in the framework of national account statistics. Therefore it is possible to assess the proportion of a country's product that is distributed to families in each of these ways. It is reasonably straightforward to distinguish economy and government in national accounts (understanding economy to include the relationship of employer to employee in governmental organizations as well as private ones). The kinship group is within the household sector; therefore, interfamily transfers (i.e., all transfers from one nuclear family to another) escape detection in the national accounts—even when these interfamily transfers may be legally mandated and regulated by law or court order.

# Employer-Provided Welfare Benefits

Benefits provided by the job are of two types: those which are viewed as shelter against the risk of income loss or high consumption costs and those viewed as part of the conditions of employment. The first type are known as employee benefits and include pensions, life insurance, health insurance, sick pay, vacations, and supplemental unemployment benefits. Generally speaking, employee benefits are tax exempt.

These benefits can be contrasted with those arising as part of the conditions of employment. These include, for example, subsidized cafeterias, recreational facilities such as sauna and squash courts, use of the company car, martini lunches, and employee discounts. In the national income accounts, these benefits are described as material and services consumed in production. But, in principle, these benefits can account for an important component of personal consumption; employees who receive them are often required by law to add them as income for tax purposes although in practice this is seldom done. We call these benefits which are part of the condition of employment "perks." Many take the form of a direct service rather than a cash supplement.

There is considerable difficulty in deciding how to classify employee benefits where the state is the employer. For a variety of reasons, employee benefits in the government sector have generally tended to be larger relative to wages. Welfare state programs have often started out as welfare programs for government employees and only later have been extended either to all employees or to the general population. This history has an important effect on national accounts statistics. In these statistics, social security contributions and benefits include employee benefits to government employees. But this is misleading because the government is acting as an employer. Therefore when one examines comparative data on the proportion of the gross national product devoted to social security or the rate of growth of social security, transfer income to the general public is confounded with government employees' benefits. We will seek to distinguish "real" transfers (that go to broad categories of the population) from government employee compensation, but it is not always possible to do so given existing statistical data series.

## The Redefinition of the Territory of Social Policy

The increasingly intermingled activities of the economy and the polity involving issues of social policy call into question the dominant social policy model. The image of the welfare state which was forged after World War II, particularly in Britain and the United States, held that there existed in the economy a "pre-fisc" distribution of income (that is to say, an original distribution of income) against which the redistributive effect of government intervention would be measured—the "post fisc" distribution. Most studies of income distribution examine the distribution of earnings as if this distribution were pure and uncontaminated by government intervention, and they accept the implicit theory of the welfare state.

This perspective assumed a sharp distinction between economic and social policy. Each policy is governed by a different rationale. Social policy is equated with the welfare state. Its mission is to undo the dysfunctional inequalities generated by the economic system. The latter obeys the natural laws of the market with minimum government involvement. Some exceptions, such as the government mandating minimum wage level, were accepted as necessary evils. But such interventions are controversial, because it is widely assumed that they have perverse effects—such as, for example, in the case of the minimum wage, drying up the volume of low-wage jobs and thus undermining their purposes.

But, there remained a kind of consensus that a desirable social policy should deal with specific government efforts to relieve want, poverty, or to achieve a measure of redistribution through taxation, education, housing, income support, medical care, and other public services. There was a considerable amount of faith in the positive role of government in offsetting the negative effects of the market. Government could play this role directly and actively by financing and administrating a broad range of social services.

And yet, in the mid-1950s, the French economist Jean Marchal (1957) already observed that this picture of the way the economy operates hardly fit even the first half of the twentieth century, let alone the emerging second half. He characterized the conventional model of income determination as follows:

> Isolated individuals buy and sell labor. Their relations in markets which are largely competitive give rise to wage rates which, together with other elements, ultimately contribute to the determination of profit rates. Subsequently, some of these individuals are required to shoulder a tax burden which channels incomes to other individuals. But these taxes are small. In such circumstances it is possible to begin with a study of the mechanism of wage formation and with the various incomes derived directly from production, only later to proceed to governmental actions resulting in a redistribution of these incomes. However, it should be stressed that this approach cannot be dissociated from two circumstances which no longer exist today: the isolation of the buyers and sellers of labor and the modest size of the transfers.
>
> Buyers and sellers of labor today are organized into large groups and their discussions take place on the national plane, in the framework of markets, as they are still called, or of public institutions. Moreover, the taxes and transfers involved have become much larger. The workers now have to balance everything they receive and spend and to regulate their behavior accordingly. A worker cares little whether he receives a higher pay packet from the firm where he is employed, or benefits from a reduction in the tax he has to pay the government out of his wages. In either case his purchasing power increases. Similarly, an entrepreneur may complain and try to raise his sales prices when a collective agreement or a public wage award forces him to pay higher wage rates; but he will react in exactly the same way to any increase in the taxes which affect his activities .... The distinction between incomes due to production and incomes due to transfers becomes obscured and is no longer usable. The reactions of the labor group, just as those of the entrepreneur or any other group, are functions of its total income, that is to say, of everything it receives, both at the moment of its contribution to a productive service and on any other occasion .... What is needed is the theory of the total income of labor, a theory of wages in the widest sense [Marchal 1957: 155–156].

During the same decade, a Royal Commission on Taxation of Income and Profits pointed to the growing importance of occupational welfare benefits: "Modern improvements in the conditions of employment and the recognition by employers of a wide range of obligations toward the health, comfort and amenities of their staff may well lead to a greater proportion of an employee's true remuneration being expressed in a form that is neither money nor convertible into money [quoted in Titmuss 1974: 140]. Yet the arguments of Titmuss, Marchal, and the Royal Commission by and large went unheeded by social policy specialists.

Slowly the picture began to change, and there emerged a redefinition of the meaning of social policy to include government initiatives designed to alter directly the behavior of employers and employees. Of course, any effort to enlarge the meaning of social policy must draw the line somewhere. In practice we note that in a modern economy, direct and indirect government expenditures permeate virtually all aspects of the economy.

As awareness of the growing complexity of interaction between government and economic institutions in the provision of economic resources to families has grown, observers have sought to develop frameworks for organizing the multifaceted transactions that go on between economic and governmental institutions and the household's recipients of these resources. If benefits are provided either by government or by business, and if the money to pay for the benefits is either generated within the economy or transferred to government through payroll or other kinds of taxes, the problem of conceptualizing the system is no longer a simple one. The enormous range of different types of programs leads to the need to develop a framework to make sense of, and to do an accounting of, the different kinds of resources that are being generated and transmitted to households.

The development of a framework for dealing with all aspects of economic and political interactions around the provision of concrete economic resources to families must take into account the particular roles which each of these two institutions can play vis à vis the provision of economic resources to households, and then measure the interaction between those two. Let us touch briefly on a set of categories for the roles government and economic institutions play vis à vis the economic resources families receive—a paycheck, a universal transfer like the family allowance, and employee benefit like an entitlement to borrow money at a reduced interest rate, or whatever.

This scheme is oriented toward accounting for the *mechanisms* by which resources end up in individual hands. However, we have left out an important dimension—the *rationale* for the provision of the resource. Resources are transferred for different "reasons," and description of rationales represents separate perspective on transactions among the various institutions.

First let us consider eight roles the government can play in the provision of a particular economic resource.

1. It can play no role at all.
2. It can regulate the provision of the resource by a nongovernment institution.
3. It can mandate some other institution to provide the resource.
4. It can encourage other institutions to provide the resource by lowering the cost through tax exemptions.

5. It can pay for, but not provide, the provision of the resource out of general tax revenues.
6. It can directly provide benefits in the form of cash.
7. It can directly provide goods and services.
8. It can both pay for and provide cash, goods or services.

What about the role of economic institutions? They have no regulatory or mandating authority; they operate by contract rather than legal power. But they can have the following five roles:

1. They can have no role in providing economic resources.
2. They can provide the financing for the resource but take no other role.
3. They can provide cash resources directly to families.
4. They can provide services directly to families.
5. They can both pay for and provide cash or services.

A description of the relevant economic role and the relevant government role with regard to a particular resource will amply specify the transactions between the two institutions in relation to the family in the provision of the resource. If we can measure the value, the cost, and the number of people involved, we can describe a society in terms of the relative importance of the government and the specific role of economic institutions. Let us briefly consider some examples to illustrate how this categorizing would work.

First, with respect to some resources both government and employers may play no role. Such resources are left completely up to the individual to provide. To have a retirement income, for example, the worker must purchase an annuity. This is the image of welfare provision offered by the early advocates (and their successors) of self-regulated markets. For them, there is no appropriate relationship between government and individuals with respect to these resources; and, the only appropriate relationship between the economy and the individual is cash payment for the use of his or her productive factors.

In fact, of course, even during times when this liberal economic theory has dominated, there have had to be other kinds of provisions. There has always been the spending of general tax revenues to provide charity. Here the economy plays no role; the government provides cash to the destitute. This is the simple binary model of the minimal welfare state which the Poor Law Reform of 1834 sought to establish.

In the modern welfare states, however, the territory sketched by the several intersections of government and economy roles is very richly populated. Where the government plays no role, the employer may still provide and pay for important resources both in the form of cash and, no less importantly, goods and services. This is the world of pure employee benefits. But government has played an even larger role in creating employer provided benefits through regulation and by legally requiring employers to provide the benefit at their own cost. For example, in Germany, sickness coverage moved from being a program paid for by employers but provided by government sickness funds to one both paid for and provided by employers with the government having only a mandating role.

The initial role of government in the welfare economy was one of regulating and mandating, as in the development of wage and hours laws and the regulation of collective bargaining and minimum wage laws. The mandating of employee benefits is a more recent development. We observe that the ERISA regulations in the United States do not require employers to provide employee benefits, but do require that if they choose to provide them to some employees they must provide them to all. Another example of mandating is the French law which requires employers to devote a small proportion of their payroll to paying for educational expenses of their employees; the employees themselves are relatively free to choose the kind of further education they would like.

There is a strong possibility that a major area of the welfare society in the future will involve exactly this kind of mandating of benefits to be provided by employers. We can expect this line to be taken both because of the growing importance of employer provided fringe benefits in broadening the economic resources of individuals and families, and for the much more straightforward reason that mandating may prove to be politically more appealing than the invention of new welfare programs which require higher general or payroll taxes. Note the recent interest in the United States in mandating the provision of insurance against catastrophic medical costs by employers. In the United States, where health insurance is principally an employee benefit, one would expect a great many innovative efforts along this line.

Reversal of the traditional welfare state pattern (business pays, government provides) is becoming increasingly apparent in the area of unemployment policy. Here we are seeing more and more programs in which the employer provides the service—a job and the rewards that go with it—but the cost is carried by the government. Where the job is fully subsidized employers do not pay for the economic resource at all: they merely provide it.

Probably much more common are systems involving partial subsidization so that both government and the employer are footing the bill, but the resource is to be provided by the employer. This is true of public service employment as well as of employment in the private sector.

## The Development of Employee Benefits and Government Transfers in the United States since 1929

It is possible to make a gross observation of the evolution of employee benefits ("other labor income" in the national accounts), and government transfers from 1929 to the present, using tables published each year in

Appendix B of the Economic Report of the President. Table 6.2 shows components of economic resources from those tables as a proportion of gross national product from 1929 to 1977. The table shows total social security contributions by employers and employees; other labor income; total government transfers, retirement benefits to government employees (which are counted as part of total government transfers), and other transfers (i.e., excluding government employee benefits); and disposable personal income and, as an approximation of disposable factor income, disposable personal income minus transfers and other labor income.

In the table we observe a steady increase in the proportion of GNP represented by social security contributions and by employee benefits (other labor income). Over the period from 1940 to the present, social security contributions as a proportion of GNP have increased at an average rate of 3.2% a year. We notice that the first large jump in the share of social security contributions in GNP came in the 1950s, a 5% growth rate, and that the annual growth in share of GNP has declined ever since.

Employee benefits as indexed by other labor income had their most rapid growth during the 1940s, increasing at an average rate of 8% per year. In that decade they more than doubled as a proportion of GNP. Then the rate of growth slowed through the 1960s to pick up again in the 1970s.

Overall, by 1977 employee benefits as a proportion of GNP had increased more than ninefold. Since GNP in constant dollars increased 4.25 times during

**TABLE 6.2**

**Components of Economic Resources in the United States as a Proportion of Gross National Product 1929–1977[a]**

| Year | Social security contribution | Other labor income (OLI) | Government transfers | | | Disposable personal income | |
| | | | Total | Government employees retirement benefits | Other transfers | Total | Minus transfers + OLI |
|---|---|---|---|---|---|---|---|
| 1929 | 0.2 | 0.5 | 1.5 | 0.1 | 1.4 | 79.6 | 77.6 |
| 1940 | 2.3 | 0.6 | 3.1 | 0.3 | 2.8 | 75.2 | 71.5 |
| 1950 | 2.5 | 1.3 | 5.3 | 0.3 | 5.0 | 71.8 | 65.2 |
| 1960 | 4.2 | 2.2 | 5.7 | 0.6 | 5.1 | 69.1 | 61.2 |
| 1970 | 6.0 | 3.3 | 8.1 | 1.0 | 7.1 | 69.8 | 58.4 |
| 1977 | 7.4 | 4.7 | 10.9 | 1.5 | 9.4 | 69.2 | 53.6 |
| Annual rates of growth | | | | | | | |
| 1940–1977 | 3.2 | 5.7 | 3.5 | 4.4 | 3.3 | −0.2 | −1.0 |
| 1950–1960 | 5.3 | 5.4 | 0.7 | 7.2 | 0.2 | −0.4 | −0.6 |
| 1960–1970 | 3.6 | 4.1 | 3.6 | 5.2 | 3.4 | 0.1 | −0.5 |
| 1970–1977 | 3.0 | 5.2 | 4.3 | 6.0 | 4.1 | −0.1 | −1.2 |

[a] Economic Report of The President

that period of time, the constant dollar value of other labor income has increased almost 40 times in the 50 years since the late 1920s.

All government transfers also increased throughout the period—roughly at the rate of 3.5% a year since 1940. But we observe that there was little growth during the 1950s and an accelerated rate into the 1970s.

If one removes government employee retirement benefits from the transfer category, one finds overall a slightly lower rate of increase in government transfers, and the rate of growth is lower in each period. One risks distortion if one uses the official national account figure for government transfers as a proxy for the welfare state expenditures. Government employee benefits have an increasing effect on that figure as time goes on, rising from 7% of transfers in 1929 to 14% in 1977.

Overall, we observe that other labor income has been the most rapidly growing of these economic resources; the second most rapidly growing is government employee retirement benefits. In each decade since 1950 these two categories grew faster than the more traditional welfare state benefits of general government transfer and social insurance.

The very low rate of growth in government transfers during the 1950s reflects complications due to the collapse of many different programs into one category. From 1950 on, there was a decline in veterans' benefits. If it were not for this there would have been quite rapid growth in transfers. Even excluding veterans' benefits, however, total government benefits have always grown faster than transfers per se.

We find that disposable personal income (after-tax income) as a proportion of GNP declined steadily up to 1960; since then the proportion has been quite stable. However, if we adjust disposable personal income by subtracting out government transfers and other labor income we see that not only has disposable income as a proportion of GNP declined throughout the whole half century, but the rate of its decline increased in the 1970s.

Fifty years ago almost 80% of the GNP went directly into people's pockets, so to speak. By the 1980s, only half of disposable personal income reaches them directly in the form of after-tax primary factor income. Clearly the trend has been toward collective provision, whether by the private sector in employee benefits, or by government through taxes, transfers, and public services. Note that in 1929 just over 1% of the GNP was going into all three kinds of social benefit, whereas by 1977, 23% was going into social security, transfers, and other labor income. It is important to note that we are missing one component of social protection resources—that is, income from private plans (which is buried in capital income). Therefore the 23% is only a part of the full social benefit amount.

We can get a somewhat better understanding of this evolution from a more detailed breakdown of employee benefits and government transfers. Our source assembled these figures for the purpose of calculating the tax expenditures represented by the fact that these benefits are not taxable (except when cash

**TABLE 6.3**

**Employer Contributions for Major Social Insurance Programs and Employee Benefits as a Percentage of Gross National Product, Selected Years, 1955–1975[a]**

| Contribution or benefit program | 1955 | 1960 | 1965 | 1970 | 1975 |
|---|---|---|---|---|---|
| **Employer contributions** | | | | | |
| Pension and profit sharing | 0.8 | 1.0 | 1.1 | 1.3 | 1.9 |
| Federal civilian employees' retirement | * | 0.2 | 0.2 | 0.2 | 0.3 |
| State and local employees' retirement | 0.2 | 0.4 | 0.4 | 0.5 | 0.6 |
| Group health insurance[b] | 0.4 | 0.7 | 0.9 | 1.2 | 1.5 |
| Group life insurance | 0.1 | 0.2 | 0.2 | 0.3 | 0.3 |
| Workmen's compensation[c] | 0.4 | 0.4 | 0.4 | 0.5 | 0.5 |
| Cash sickness compensation[d] | e | e | e | e | e |
| Supplemental unemployment | e | e | e | e | e |
| Total employer contributions | 2.1 | 2.8 | 3.2 | 4.0 | 5.0 |
| **Benefits paid** | | | | | |
| Pension and profit sharing | 0.2 | 0.3 | 0.5 | 0.7 | 0.8 |
| Federal civilian employees' retirement | 0.1 | 0.2 | 0.2 | 0.3 | 0.5 |
| Military retirement | 0.1 | 0.1 | 0.2 | 0.3 | 0.4 |
| State and local employees' retirement | 0.2 | 0.3 | 0.3 | 0.4 | 0.5 |
| Group health insurance[b] | 0.6 | 0.9 | 1.1 | 1.5 | 1.5 |
| Group life insurance | 0.2 | 0.2 | 0.2 | 0.3 | 0.2 |
| Workmen's compensation[c] | 0.3 | 0.3 | 0.3 | 0.3 | 0.3 |
| Cash sickness compensation[d] | e | e | e | e | e |
| Supplemental unemployment | 0.0 | e | e | e | e |
| Total benefits paid | 1.6 | 2.3 | 2.9 | 3.9 | 4.4 |

[a]From Sunley 1977.
[b]Includes most group disability insurance.
[c]Includes government social insurance funds and private plans.
[d]State and local temporary disability insurance.
[e]Less than .05%.

income is from retirement pensions). This means that we do not have information on the contributions that individuals make to their employee benefits, but this probably involves a fairly small amount. We see in Table 6.3 the same story of steady increase in various kinds of benefits over the 20-year period from 1955 to 1975.

Comparing each 5-year period in Table 6.3, we find (ignoring workmen's compensation, which is a social insurance program) that employee benefits grew very rapidly in the late 1950s, more slowly in the early 1960s and then began to pick up speed again, particularly in the first half of the 1970s. It would be very interesting to know something of the reasons for this pattern of growth. To what extent does it involve an increase in average benefits per employee, and to what extent does it involve changes in the coverage of employees. Further analysis of the details of growth in the different kinds of programs could suggest something of the historical pattern by which health insurance, private pensions plans, and government pension plans (which consume the lion's share of these benefits) were phased in.

Comparing the top and bottom panel of the table, we note another important fact. Contributions grow more rapidly than benefits in the early stages of the expansion of a program. Thus, we see that contributions exceeded benefits by almost 30% in 1955, whereas by 1975 they only exceeded benefits by about 14%. Until retirement systems are fully mature, it is hard to know exactly how to evaluate what they represent as an economic resource to households, since there is a very real question—at least in the way many U.S. pension funds are organized—as to whether the individual will be able to collect a pension, or will instead be a victim of the employer's bankruptcy or some other unfortunate event or crime.

Overall, then, we can say that the past half century has seen rapid growth in collective provision for economic need. Everyone is well aware of the growth in government programs, but we have also seen that programs for employees, in both the government and private sectors, have shown a very rapid growth rate. By the mid-1970s these social benefits accounted for about 25% of the GNP. Using the figures in Tables 6.2 and 6.3, we arrive at an estimate that employee benefits (government and employees combined) accounted for about one-third of total social benefits, and government transfers accounted for about two-thirds. Around 1940 these resources in relation to GNP were about one-fourth that size. At that time the employee sector accounted for somewhat less than 20% of total benefits. Thus the two systems have both grown very rapidly, but employee benefits have grown more rapidly than have governmment transfers.

We have outlined a scheme for describing structures of social protection that includes both private and public resources and programs. Table 6.4 shows the

**TABLE 6.4**
**Social Protection Receipts—International Comparisons**[a]

| | Percentage of gross domestic product | | | | |
|---|---|---|---|---|---|
| | 1962 | 1965 | 1970 | 1975 | 1977 |
| France | 16.5 | 18.2 | 19.2 | 22.9 | 23.9 |
| Germany | 19.4 | 19.9 | 21.4 | 27.8 | 27.4 |
| Belgium | 15.8 | 16.7 | 18.5 | 24.6 | 25.1[b] |
| Italy | 14.4 | 17.6 | 20.0 | 24.7 | 23.1 |
| Netherlands | 14.1 | 17.3 | 20.8 | 27.8 | 28.8 |
| Great Britain | — | — | 16.4 | 20.6 | 19.7 |
| Ireland | — | — | 13.2 | 19.7 | 19.2[b] |
| Denmark | — | — | 19.5 | 25.9 | 25.3[b] |
| United States[c] | 9.2 | 9.3 | 13.1 | 16.6 | 17.0 |

[a]From (except for U.S.) *Les Comptes de la Protection Sociale: Methodes et Series 1959–1978.* Paris: INSEE, 1979.
[b]1976.
[c]Our estimates.

proportions of gross domestic product devoted to social protection in European Community countries from 1962 to the present. We have added rough estimates for the United States.

Taking the most recent figures, we see that overall the Netherlands has the highest portion of GDP devoted to social protection, but is followed very closely by Germany. Comparing these proportions with those for social transfers (in Kohl 1981), one sees that the range is much narrower for total social protection than for social transfers. With social transfers the highest country has 2.3 times the percentage of GDP of the lowest country, whereas for social protection the top to bottom range is only 1.74, three-fourths as much. Also, there are three countries that rank quite differently. In both series the Netherlands is at the top and Britain and the United States bring up the rear. But Germany, which ranks fifth in transfers, is at the top in the social protection series, and Denmark, which ranks sixth in transfers, comes fairly close. On the other hand, France drops to sixth place in the social protection series. The most important observation, however, is that with the exception of Great Britain, Ireland, and the United States, the other countries are very, very close to one another ranging by 1977 from 23.1% in Italy to 28.8% in the Netherlands. Clearly, Great Britain, Ireland, and the United States are low in their provisions for social protection, the United States markedly so.

How do countries compare on the question of who finances social protection? In Table 6.5, we see data organized in terms of the contribution of enterprises, households, and government agencies. The enterprise sector includes all productive organizations, whether government or private. Therefore the government sector includes only government agencies that are not engaged in the production of ordinary goods.

We see that there are quite marked differences from country to country. Denmark generates almost all of the finances for social protection in the

**TABLE 6.5**
**Percentages of Social Protection Receipts by Sector Financing Them, 1976[a]**

|  | General government | Enterprises | Households | Total |
|---|---|---|---|---|
| France | 30.4 | 46.9 | 22.7 | 100 |
| Germany | 41.1 | 31.7 | 27.2 | 100 |
| Belgium | 43.2 | 35.1 | 21.7 | 100 |
| Italy | 31.1 | 55.8 | 13.1 | 100 |
| Netherlands | 41.6 | 21.5 | 39.6 | 100 |
| Great Britain | 60.8 | 21.1 | 18.1 | 100 |
| Ireland | 72.3 | 12.8 | 14.9 | 100 |
| Denmark | 91.3 | 6.8 | 1.9 | 100 |

[a]From *Les Comptes de la Protection Sociale: Methodes et Series 1959–1978*. Paris: INSEE, 1979.

government sector: in Ireland and Britain this figure is also very high. In contrast, France generates far more in the enterprise sector, and the lowest proportion in the government sector. Italy depends even more heavily on the enterprise sector. The Netherlands is distinctive for the high proportion of financing that comes from households themselves.

Obviously, at a given proportion of GNP devoted to social protection, claiming structures can vary a great deal in terms of how much different institutional sectors are brought into play. Germany and the Netherlands are very similar in the proportion of GDP devoted to social protection, but Germany finances by a heavier reliance on enterprises, whereas in the Netherlands there is a heavier reliance on households. Denmark and France are quite similar in overall level but differ widely in the structure of financing, with France generating 70% of the financing *outside* of government and Denmark only generating 91% *inside* government.

However, we need to know more than who pays the bills. We also need to know on what basis the bill is paid, and, in particular, within government we need to be able to separate financing to support employees from financing for transfers to the general public. Within the enterprise sector we would like to know the balance of financing in the form of payroll tax for general social security versus contributions to special plans for employees. We discuss this issue at the end of this chapter.

Let us return now to the question of claims structures by considering labor cost variations among countries. In Table 6.6 we see that there is a very wide range in the degree to which labor costs other than pay for time actually worked vary from one country to another. These data also bear on the question of the balance between state benefits and those derived from enterprise sector social policy.

The ratio of legally required personnel costs to contractual and voluntary ones, is quite different from country to country. In the United States the costs not legally required are 53% greater than the legally required ones. In all other countries but Austria, the former costs are less than the legally required ones, ranging down to a low in Ireland of only 30% of the legally required costs. Thus countries differ a very great deal in the relative weight of the legal versus contractual mechanisms for establishing claims. This is in line with our expectation. Presumably, the more a state is a welfare state, the higher the degree of legal requirement and the less the role of contract and voluntary choice in these matters.

Another way of assessing country variations and changes over time in the balance of legal versus contractual benefits is to look at two items in standard comparative national account series: contributions to social security in relationship to employers' contributions to private pensions and other funds. As shown in Table 6.7 we find a very large difference between France and Germany, on the one hand, and the United Kingdom and the United States on the other. In the first two countries, the contributions to social security are about

TABLE 6.6
Average Other Labor Costs as Percentage of Hourly Wage
for Industrial Workers in Selected Countries

| Country (year) | Total other labor costs | Vacations and other paid free time[a] | Other legally required personnel costs | Other contractual and voluntary costs |
|---|---|---|---|---|
| Italy (1972) | 87.2 | 18.6 | 48.2 | 20.4 |
| Austria (1975) | 79.1 | 13.3 | 29.7 | 36.1 |
| France (1972) | 66.2 | 13.9 | 32.1 | 20.2 |
| Netherlands (1972) | 65.7 | 19.6 | 23.4 | 22.7 |
| Germany (1977) | 65.5 | 21.4 | 26.8 | 17.3 |
| Belgium (1972) | 64.7 | 20.4 | 32.2 | 12.1 |
| Sweden (1975) | 39.8 | 11.1 | 24.3 | 4.4 |
| United States (1975)[b] | 36.1 | 13.8 | 8.8 | 13.5 |
| Great Britain (1973) | 23.7 | 11.2 | 6.9 | 5.6 |
| Ireland (1975) | 22.1 | 9.0 | 10.1 | 3.0 |
| Denmark (1975) | 20.4 | 12.5 | 4.4 | 3.5 |

[a] Includes legally required minimum vacations in countries which have them (most European countries). Most of these costs are legally mandated.

[b] Large firms only. Total amount for all industrial workers probably lower, legally required proportion higher, and other two categories lower.

5 times those to private funds, whereas in the United Kingdom and the United States they are only 1.5 to 1.9 times as much. Clearly in the United States proportionately much more of social protection is derived from private contributions than in the other two countries. Conversely, the continental countries make much heavier use of legally mandated, social-security-type programs to provide for employees' needs.

However, it is difficult to go very far with this kind of comparative analysis because the so-called private funds confound activities that are legally mandated and those that are arrived at by contractual agreements between employers and employees. This seems to be particularly a problem in the continental countries where some of the funds accounted for in the comparative national account series as private funds in fact involve contributions that are legally mandated.

A rough approximation can be made using the European social protection accounts, where there is a distinction made between basic plans that are either general or statutory, and those that are complementary or fully voluntary. It is possible that even some of the so-called complementary plans of private employers may in some ways be so subject to legal regulation thay they are in effect mandated, but for purposes of this comparison we have assumed that

**TABLE 6.7**

**Ratio of Social Security Contributions to Employers' Contributions to Private Funds in France, Germany, The United Kingdom, and the United States, 1960, 1970, and 1976[a]**

|  | Ratio of social security contributions | | |
|---|---|---|---|
|  | 1960 | 1970 | 1976 |
| Employers plus employees' contributions |  |  |  |
| France | — | 5.3 | 5.8 |
| Germany | 5.0 | 4.5 | 5.0 |
| United Kingdom | 1.5 | 1.9 | 1.7 |
| United States[a] | 1.9 | 1.9 | 1.7 |
| Employers' contributions only |  |  |  |
| France | — | 3.8 | 4.1 |
| Germany | 2.6 | 2.3 | 2.6 |
| United Kingdom | 0.7 | 1.0 | 1.0 |
| United States | 1.1 | 1.0 | 0.9 |

[a] From United Nations National Accounts .
[b] For earlier periods the ratios were: 1940 = 3.8; 1950 = 1.9.

complementary plans in the enterprise sector are in fact contractual and not legally required.

Table 6.8 gives the results of this approximation. Employers' contributions to social protection schemes fall into three categories. In the private sector there are complementary and voluntary plans, mandated plans (basic social security and other kinds of mandated plans). The government sector includes provision for its own employees. One could separate household contributions into those for mandated plans and those for contractual ones, but, in fact, in most countries only a very small proportion of household contributions go to mandated plans. Although we do not have exactly comparable data, we have made rough estimates for the United States of the distribution of receipts among these five categories.

We find that although the ratios derived from the standard national accounts for France and Germany suggest that employers put up 2.5–4 times as much money for mandated plans as for contractual ones, by this accounting in Germany 10 times as much money is spent on mandated plans as contractual ones, and in France 4.5 times as much. Thus, the ratios for employers' contributions are, in fact, far too low. This tells us that what is called social security and what is called a private fund is to some extent a convention that can become outmoded with the elaboration of the welfare society.

The figures for complementary and voluntary private plans in Table 6.8 show only two countries—the United States and the United Kingdom—in which a significant proportion of the financing for social protection plans comes via

## TABLE 6.8
### Source and Type of Financing for Social Protection in Selected Countries in 1974[a]

| | Percentage of financing by source and type | | | | |
|---|---|---|---|---|---|
| | Employers | | | | |
| | Private | | | | |
| Country | complimentary and voluntary plans | mandated plans | Government | Households | General government finance |
| Germany | 3.5 | 31.5 | 12.8 | 26.5 | 25.7 |
| France | 8.5 | 38.8 | 13.5 | 20.7 | 18.5 |
| Italy | 0.4 | 47.1 | 13.2 | 14.8 | 24.5 |
| Belgium | 1.5 | 36.7 | 7.0 | 22.0 | 32.8 |
| United Kingdom | 12.5 | 13.2 | 10.1 | 18.2 | 46.0 |
| Ireland | 0.7 | 0.7 | 20.4 | 13.6 | 64.6 |
| Denmark | 3.8 | 3.6 | 4.2 | 2.3 | 86.1 |
| United States[b] | (20) | (21) | (10) | (18) | (31) |

[a] From (Except for United States) Statistical Office of The European Community, *Social Accounts 1970–1975*, Tables 13–21.

[b] Not based on the same system of social accounts. The figures are merely indicative, being derived in a rough way from several different sources.

market arrangements in which the government does not play a controlling role. In France there is a moderate place for this kind of financing, amounting to 8.5%. In the other countries, it seems truly trivial.

It should be noted that in countries with highly developed social insurance systems, even where complementary plans may be contractual and not legally mandated, employers may prefer to make use of social security funds rather than providing benefits directly. Thus, in France 80% of the money in the complementary plans is, in fact, channeled through a social security *caisse*. Of the total social protection money spent in France, less than 3% involves direct provision of cash or services from private employers to their employees.

## Conclusion

Scholars who seek to understand and explain the evolution of the modern welfare society will have to pay a great deal more attention to the complex interactions among families, employers, and government which lead to the extremely rich pattern of social protection programs in both the private and public sectors. It is quite possible that simple indices of welfare state expenditures are more misleading than useful for comparative analysis.

Given the very large size of welfare society expenditures as defined in the broad sense discussed here, it becomes understandable that a society's managers seek to minimize the demand for them and complain that the public does not appreciate the necessity of reducing its welfare demands. Thus, for example, when asked whether "the West German welfare policy might end like the British welfare catastrophe" Karl Otto Poehl, Bundesbank President, told an interviewer in the summer of 1980:

> I do think there is a tendency to overdo it in . . . all Western industrialized countries, including the United States or Britain, Italy, and France. But at least in Europe there is a growing danger that we are exaggerating the benefits of the welfare state and the result is that [the] efficiency, productivity of our economies is slowing down and that the built-in inflation is becoming stronger and stronger. I am not advocating a reduction in the welfare state—that's very difficult—but I think it should be reformed and we should be very cautious in not expanding it even more. We may be reaching the limits of the expansion of our welfare system and maybe even have already done a little bit too much in that direction [*International Herald Tribune* 1980].

Managers are concerned about these demands in exactly the same way as they are concerned about the wage demands—and for the obvious reason that the two are of a piece, as Jean Marchal (1957) argued 25 years ago.

# References

*Economic Report of the President* 1978. Washington, D.C.: U.S. Government Printing Office.
*International Herald Tribune*, August 25, 1980. P. 9.
Kohl, J. 1981. Trends and problems in post-war public expenditure development in western Europe and North America. In *The development of welfare states in Europe and North America*, ed. P. Flora and A. Heidenheimer. New Brunswick, N.J.: Transaction Books. Pp. 307–344.
Marchal, J. 1957. Wage theory and social groups. In *The theory of wage determination*, ed. J.T. Dunlop, London: St. Martins. Penguin Books. Pp. 148–170.
*Penguin English Dictionary 1969*.
Polyani, K. 1944. *The great transformation*. Boston: Beacon Press.
Sunley, E.M., Jr. 1977. Employee benefits and transfer payments. In *Comprehensive income taxation*, ed. J.A. Pechman, Washington, D.C.: The Brookings Institute. Pp. 75–114.
Titmuss, R.M. 1959. *Essays on the welfare state*. New Haven: Yale University Press.

# 7

# Systematic Confusions in the Evaluation of Implementing Decisions

## MURRAY EDELMAN

Political systems allocate values, and they also legitimize themselves. The two functions can be independent of each other because governmental value allocations are always markedly unequal, requiring that the great majority who get the least of whatever is valued receive psychological attention, promises, and reassurances which, together with some coercion, maintain their loyalty, docility, and services. If value allocations were more nearly equal and equitable, they would more surely constitute their own legitimation.

Though value allocation and legitimation are analytically separate functions, the most widely accepted model of policy formation masks the distinction between them and can do so persuasively because political institutions combine and confuse the two functions. Readily made observations nonetheless make it possible to distinguish the governmental activities that legitimize from those that allocate, and so to see legislation and implementation in a new light.

At its most basic level the issue is whether the actions of "implementers" of public policies are responsive to public wants, demands, and supports as expressed in elections and legislative actions; or whether they are responsive instead to existing inequalities in resources, while elections and legislative bodies shape public opinion and legitimize bureaucratic actions. The first view is taught in elementary civics classes and is implicit in David Easton's (1971) systems theory. This position sees "system maintenance" as dependent on the system's capacity to reflect public wants adequately and to deal with the tensions generated by conflicting demands. Survival is taken as evidence of successful conversion of demands into policy and of coping with stress. Because the demise of a political system is an uncommon event and because "survival"

EVALUATING THE WELFARE STATE:
SOCIAL AND POLITICAL PERSPECTIVES

and "maintenance" are ambiguous concepts, history serves, in this mainstream model, to justify established political institutions.

The alternative view also asks how the system maintains itself, but without assuming that public demands and supports are inputs or that governmental actions are outputs. I call attention to observations that point to a less reassuring set of hypotheses:

1. Public discussion and debate, expression of popular preferences, and most controversial legislative actions often have little effect on administrative "decisions," though they do legitimize incumbents in public offices and established social, economic, and political institutions.
2. Public and private actions that are labeled "implementation" decisively shape value allocations and the quality of life; but most such actions are not widely discussed or controversial, and are not significantly constrained by elections, legislation, policy statements, or public rhetoric.
3. The formal goal definitions and the formal structure of public administrative organizations are chiefly forms of legitimation, with little relevance to the values administrative actions allocate.

The term *system* is used in very different senses in these two models. In David Easton's work and in most political science writing, the system is composed of abstract, reified political processes, not of people. It consists of inputs (public demands and supports), conversion processes (legislation, adjudication, execution), outputs (laws, orders, decisions), and feedback. *These terms predetermine the observations and the valuations of their users.* To fit the individual and governmental actions into the model these concepts create is to see the actions of administrative agencies as the empirical and moral consequences of public wants; but the perception emerges from an abstract set of concepts with fixed meanings, not from logic or from observation of human actions.

In the alternative model, the system is composed of people whose diverse roles and class positions are maintained through stable or recurring economic and psychological interactions. Social structure shows itself in the lives of individuals as opportunities, advantages, temptations, constraints, or deprivations. To put the point another way, differences in economic and social positions give rise to both psychological and governmental traits, especially "implementing," responses that maintain the differences. There is a "system," then, in the fundamental sense that publicized activities create confidence in governmental responsiveness to the will of the people, while the unpublicized activities that allocate benefits and deprivations reflect established inequalities in economic and psychological resources.

## Publicized Governmental Actions with Little Effect on Value Allocations

The domestic public programs that are most intensely debated and most widely discussed involve laws that promise to eliminate or minimize inequalities. They deal especially with civil rights; affirmative action; regulations of business to protect consumers, workers, or people who live near industrial plants; and welfare programs. These are also the problems that are never solved, and the forms of law that are largely symbolic or tokenistic. Because they highlight the social inequalities that are a profound source of anxiety to the deprived and to the elite, they are continuing objects of attention, revision, hope, and fear. But it is the publicity, the controversy, the discussion, and the formal enactment or defeat of legislation that captures public attention, not the effects of any of these actions upon inequalities or upon how well people live; for legislation and speculative rhetoric in themselves make little change in inequalities. What such laws (words) mean for the quality of life depends entirely on the actions of those whose behavior they are supposed to change, especially administrators, employers, landlords, and corporate officials. I shall argue in this chapter that there is good reason for these elites to continue their past practices, and usually little reason for them to change.

Widely publicized legislation plays a critical role in the social system, but it is psychological, not social or economic, in character. These laws amount to a form of word magic, purporting to remedy problems and to erase established privileges by proclaiming that the problems and privileges will no longer exist: no more denials of civil rights or discrimination against women or minorities, no more corporate pollution of the environment, no more welfare fraud, and so on. Attention is focused upon a future free of the practices that deny benefits to most and confer advantages on some, not on the poor record of such liberal reforms in the past and the systematic reasons for the poor record. Symbolic governmental language and legislation keep alive the expectation of change, and conservative opposition reinforces belief in the reality of symbolic political battles.[1] These governmental actions reassure many and threaten a few, but change little, very largely because the general public remains bemused or encouraged by the reassurances and the threats and by marginal or tokenistic action that leaves the inequalities underlying the increments very much as they

---

[1] In a few policy areas, notably tax policy, implementing decisions are partly incorporated in legislative action, especially through technical statutory provisions that shape the degree of progressivity or regressivity, exemptions, and ease of avoidance. It remains true in such policy areas that the rhetoric and symbols that justify policy and constitute the terms of public discussion and debate typically have little bearing on actual impact; and that administrative enforcement decisions are major determinants of the impact. My argument about the disjunction between public discussion and value allocations remains valid regardless of the branch of government that does the implementing. I analyzed this issue as it applies to tax policy in *The Symbolic Uses of Politics* (*Edelman 1964*, pp. 28–29).

With respect to general well-being, some individuals improve their situations dramatically, others suffer declines in status and well-being, but these shifts are typically the result of individual good fortune, illegal or opportunistic actions, or extraordinary talent or lack of it in an area that brings high monetary rewards. They are not the intended result of public policy and they do not substantially or lastingly lessen social and economic inequality. Public policy does occasionally increase it substantially, as through the grant of tax favors to people who receive particular forms of income.

were. The persistence of gross inequality, the outcome that determines well being, is recognized as a historical fact, but discounted as a picture of the future. Although conditions may improve for much of the population, there is no consistent secular diminution in inequality (De Lone 1979; Lindert and Williamson 1976; Miller 1976).

## Implementation That Maintains Established Inequalities

No aspect of politics better demonstrates its largely symbolic character than the slight public attention ordinarily given to the specific actions of administrators. Party platforms, campaign rhetoric, presidential promises and proposals, and legislative programs are continually in the news and are accepted as evidence of victories or defeats for causes, interest groups, and individuals. Yet this controversial language rarely makes any difference in how well or how badly any individual lives except as it affects his or her state of mind through reassurance or threat. That psychological effect is typically its only effect.

The governmental actions that shape the quality of people's lives appear in the decisions we classify as "implementation": actions that affect income, living costs, surveillance of daily lives, employment opportunities, social bonds, freedom to act and to express opinions, intellectual autonomy, and stimulation or constriction of art and of science. These actions come in the decisions of such agencies as the Federal Reserve Board, city police departments, private corporations, school boards, funding agencies, the Defense Department, parole boards, and the Agriculture Department. They are presented as the judgments of professionals, technicians, policy analysts, and other specialists with the skills to achieve the policy goals of legislatures, high executives, and high courts. Thousands of such actions occur every day at every level of government, most of them unnoticed by the press, few of them discussed, debated, or known outside the enclaves of professionals, corporate managers, technicians, and interest-group representatives who continually interact with one another to formulate them and change them.

It has been fashionable for several decades to qualify or reject the Goodnow (1897) distinction between policy and administration; but the logic of that distinction has continued to dominate both popular and academic thought about public administration. Although everyone recognizes that administrators exercise discretion when choosing the premises that shape decisions, academic writing, civics textbooks, and popular oratory typically ignore the logical implication of that view. We downplay the abundant evidence that the "policymaking" organs of government create rhetoric more than value allocations; that the "implementing" organs of society allocate values; and that the two kinds of activity are linked to one another because legislation and executive statements mainly legitimize what implementers do, not because they shape what implementers do.

Just how this division of labor among authoritative rule makers functions should become clear from a consideration of some hypotheses about organizational decision making:

*Where large inequalities exist, it is usually "efficient" and "rational" to maintain them.*

Efficiency and rationality are the key concepts for the justification of administrative actions. The Weberian ideal-type model of bureaucracy offers the rationale that implementers naturally accept. It takes values as given by a rational–legal code and focuses upon bureaucratic implementation.

This orientation perpetuates existing inequalities, for the terms in which issues are posed require that result. If discourse about values is not part of the decision-making process, administrators can only accept the social structure within which they operate as the appropriate one; there is no incentive and no opportunity to reconsider questions of equity or ethics. Implementers act within a framework that brings them rewards or penalties according to the effects of their policies on groups that wield large resources, although these actions are rationalized by abstract or "long-term" goals that typically emphasize redistribution or help for the disadvantaged. Every controversial policy area illustrates the point. Inflation that itself reflects the strong market power of sellers vis-à-vis buyers presents a "problem" to the Federal Reserve Board, which sees tight money and high interest rates as the rational and efficient course of action, although those devices slow investment, create unemployment, and thus hurt the people with the least money and the most fragile hold on their jobs, while rewarding large investors. The Federal Communications Commission decides that it is rational and efficient to award television or radio licenses to the groups with the largest capital resources, for they can most credibly promise good equipment and good programs.[2] Traffic administrators and experts on highway safety determine that it is rational to require inspections of passenger automobiles, thereby denying transportation or making it costly to the poor while benefiting automobile dealers and manufacturers. It is rational and efficient to award procurement contracts to the established firms with large resources and experience with similar contracts.

In such cases implementers cannot be concerned with how strengthening oligopolies and killing competition will in the long run affect economic prosperity, television quality, or national security, but only with rationality in the context of established social structures and existing inequalities.

[2]Cf. Edelman (1950), Chapters 4 and 6. My argument that rationality is defined by the social structure within which policy implementers function means, of course, that where the social structure places egalitarian incentives and pressures upon them, they will respond to that structure. My examples in this chapter are drawn almost entirely from the United States. In a capitalist society, egalitarian goals are formal and rhetorical, whereas an inegalitarian social structure shapes implementing decisions. By the same logic, however, democratic socialist institutions subject administrators to a more egalitarian set of incentives, as Alex Radian has pointed out to me is often the case in Israel.

In each instance the "implementing" decision wins political support from the groups that benefit from it and from a wide and inattentive general public impressed with its symbolic benefits, and in doing so, it advances the careers of the administrators who make the decision. By the same token, the occasional implementing decision that substantially improves the bargaining position of the weak is denounced as damaging the efficiency of the system and thus it hurts the careers of its implementers, as recent experiences of the Federal Trade Commission and the Occupational Safety and Health Administration neatly illustrate.

The established structure of benefits, opportunities, and coercions shapes perceptions of efficiency and rationality and provides the premises upon which implementing decisions are made. The role of implementer systematically creates responsiveness to some linguistic appeals and insensitivity to others, amounting to identification with some people's interests and alienation from others. The policy implementer's distinguishing presentation of self highlights the efficient and rational specialist who takes account of information laypersons either do not know or cannot properly interpret. Although the ideological motive of preserving established statuses and the related motive of protecting or augmenting the implementing agency's budget may be critical, they are likely to be subconscious. To ignore common talk or appeals that call attention to personal advantage or suffering is a way of asserting a professional stance and distinguishing it from a naive one. The efficient implementer makes this point by reducing issues to quantitative statements whenever that is feasible.

A prototypical case involved a public utility's application to the Wisconsin Public Service Commission for a substantial increase in rates for electricity and gas in the fall of 1979. A hearing examiner responded to petitions claiming that elderly and poor people would have to choose between heat and food if the increase were granted. He declared that the commissioners would be "aware" of the petitions and letters opposing the application on the ground that it would cause suffering and starvation, but that it would be illegal for them to base their decision on such testimony; for the law requires the regulatory agency to authorize rates that yield a fair profit to the utility in the light of its increased costs (*Madison Press Connection*, September 26, 1979, pp. 1, 3). The discourse that is included and excluded by this kind of interpretation means that the interests of stockholders are protected materially, whereas those of ratepayers are protected rhetorically. Reduction of issues to numbers systematically precludes attention to suffering, humiliation, and cold houses. The personification of a suffering client unable to pay higher rates is not experienced as a threat, but rather defines the victim as less than competent, playing upon and reinforcing widespread class-based prejudices. The inclusion and exclusion of forms of discourse places the implementer in a world in which some human beings become significant and other human beings become nonentities, undeserving, or self-seeking.

This imperative to define the efficient and rational so as to maintain the established social structure is overdetermined. It flows at the same time: (*a*) from pressures from the groups that can help or cripple an agency's operations and the careers and reputations of its staff; (*b*) from socialization of the population into holding certain beliefs about which statuses and which kinds of people are respectable, meritorious, and competent and which are suspect, pathological, undeserving, or inefficient; (*c*) from cues regarding current threats to interest groups or to class position, both of which are rationalized in terms "the public interest"; (*d*) from the ease with which actions defined as rational and efficient can be reconciled with an agency's formal goals, which are always stated in ambiguous language. Though these various perceptions are experienced as separate, reasoned judgments, they manifestly define and reinforce each other.

*The organizational structure for administrative decision making and the formal definitions of agency goals and jurisdictions are key legitimizers of policy outcomes.*

This issue is almost certainly the most mystifying and the least understood in the literature of administrative enforcement and implementation. Yet it becomes considerably clearer if some readily made observations are taken seriously.

First, the actions and inactions of every agency have substantial effects upon issues and people not subject to its jurisdiction, reflecting the complex links among different issues. Defense Department actions formally justified as protecting national security are also grants and denials of profits, jobs, and status for millions of people, both in the United States and abroad. School boards and school administrators' decisions about curricula, buildings, and closing of schools are formally educational, but they influence the growth and decline of neighborhoods, the self-esteem of minorities, and the incomes of contractors. In both examples, the list of substantial effects could easily be extended. The point is that formal goals and jurisdictions fix the terms within which administrative policy is judged and interest groups consulted; but the effects of every agency's actions are far more extensive than its formal jurisdiction.

Second, the abstraction of organizations from the other administrative units with which they have empirical and logical ties masks and distorts the evaluation of controversial governmental actions. In organizational analysis we conventionally see structure as an influence on action; but it also influences public perceptions and therefore political support. This effect is subtle, powerful, and pervasive.

Several examples illustrate the effect. In the U.S. federal government there are separate agencies to deal with major social and economic problems. The Federal Reserve Board, the Treasury, and Alfred Kahn's office in the Executive Office of the President focus chiefly on inflation and on unemployment. The

Department of Labor includes subunits concerned with manpower, apprentice-ships, skills, and job placement. Welfare agencies deal with poverty. Prisons deal with criminals. The list could be extended.

From one perspective the establishment of agencies to deal with particular social problems evinces public concern with those problems and an effort to solve or ameliorate them. But a closer look at the powers of such agencies and their effects on each other yields some less reassuring observations. Some of them can influence the welfare of the groups they are supposed to protect, and others cannot. The Federal Reserve Board wields an arsenal of weapons to cope with inflation and unemployment: open market operations, changes in the discount rate, and changes in reserve requirements. These devices directly influence interest rates, investment decisions, and economic booms and downturns, even if they do not permit the "fine tuning" the more optimistic economic technicians claimed for them in the 1960s. Welfare agencies, in contrast, can do nothing to solve the basic problems of *their* formally designated clientele, the poor. They cannot influence the supply of jobs or wage rates or the illnesses and other handicaps that force people to apply for welfare benefits. The Department of Labor is similarly without jurisdiction to solve the basic problems of the clientele it is supposed to help: the labor force. It has no power to deal with unemployment, with the maintenance of real income, or even with union organization and collective bargaining.

For the reasons just noted, it is the Federal Reserve Board that can most materially help or hurt workers, welfare recipients, consumers, and every other economic grouping in the United States, although each such clientele is formally and symbolically aligned with a different agency. Yet the Federal Reserve Board is the least publicized, the least understood, and so, symbolically, the least important of the federal economic agencies. The others symbolize protection against publicized threats, but have limited power or no power to provide the protection. The "Fed" is defined and perceived as a specialized, technical agency; but it helps shape the quality of life for everyone. Influence on its decisions is tightly restricted, though the consequences of its decisions are wide-reaching. Structurally, and as a result of the channels of recruitment of members of the Board of Governors of the Federal Reserve System and the members of its key committee, the Federal Open Market Committee, the interests of the banking community, of corporations, and of corporate agriculture are systematically protected by Federal Reserve Board policies. The much larger sector of the public whose welfare depends on its decisions are systematically excluded from influence while symbolically being protected by organizations without powers or jurisdiction to take more than token actions.

*Because formal jurisdiction is unrelated to empirical links or tangible consequences, organizational units systematically create problems for which they are not held accountable.*

The Federal Reserve Board is again a conspicuous example, for this effect is a corollary of the one just discussed. In adopting measures to combat inflation, as it did in 1979 and 1980, the "Fed" increases unemployment and extends its duration, especially in regions and cities in which joblessness is already high. These policies increase crime, divorce, alcoholism and other drug abuses, and other manifestations of social disorganization. The prison system, law enforcement authorities, and mental health agencies are responsible for coping with a small set of the effects of these Federal Reserve Board policies, but are powerless to do anything about their causes. The Board is symbolically in a different universe; it is not expected to consider these consequences of its policies. Staff members who did so would be defined as unreliable or incompetent.

Consider another example. If a federal agency responsible for conservation or environmental preservation (e.g., the Environmental Protection Agency) were to propose a policy that would preempt a large portion of the land in Utah and Nevada for federal use, appropriate a major portion of the scarce water in the area, create massive housing, health, schooling, and other problems flowing from a sudden increase in population, increase the chance the area would become a bombing target in time of war, and cost at least $30 billion, the adverse public reaction would be widespread, strong, and doubtless quickly successful, with conservatives leading the attack. When the Defense Department and the National Security Council made exactly that proposal in the case of the MX missile, there was some local adverse reaction and some opposition to further escalation of the arms race, enough to convince the Defense Department to modify the proposal; but national support remained strong, especially among conservatives, and the project may be implemented. An agency identified with the goal of national security elicits a very different pattern of support and opposition from one formally identified with ecology. In each case some problems created by administrative action are masked, minimized, or ignored when legitimized by widely supported formal goals.

*Commercial organizations largely escape accountability for the problems they create when they are part of an empirically linked organizational structure that includes governmental organizations as well.*

One revealing example involves the Immigration and Naturalization Service (INS), Los Angeles garment industry subcontractors, and large clothing manufacturers. The name brand manufacturers subcontract cutting, sewing, pressing, and other operations to marginal firms that hire undocumented (illegal) Mexican labor, pay them rates that violate minimum wage laws, and ignore health and safety codes. If workers in these sweat shops complain or show interest in union organization, the contractor reports them to the INS as illegal aliens. The restive workers are then deported and are replaced by greener or more docile ones, for the supply of illegal labor is large and constantly replenished.

Operating here is an integrated social structure of opportunities and coercions that cuts across the governmental–private distinction. The system produces high profits for garment manufacturers, relatively low prices for consumers, intense financial pressure on contractors to violate laws and on illegal workers to submit to unlawful pay rates and unlawful working conditions, and legal pressure on the INS to thwart union organization and to negate the efforts of other governmental agencies to implement minimum wage and health and safety laws. In a sense, the "energy source" for the whole system is Mexican poverty and overpopulation. That energy is channeled so as to yield advantages for some and deprivations for many others, and to immobilize public criticism. Insofar as the general public is aware of the system at all, it chiefly blames the two groups with the least choice, the strongest pressures, and the fewest advantages (the undocumented Mexicans and the garment subcontractors); it supports the futile efforts of the INS to enforce the immigration laws; and, in the form of purchases and goodwill, it supports the clothing manufacturers who reap the greatest benefits from the complex structure. Because they are part of a structure that is empirically linked but formally distinct, the INS is not perceived as union busting, and the manufacturers are not perceived as creating unlawful conditions and poverty.

Consider another example. Private employers enjoy the formal right to hire as many employees as they choose, fire them whenever it becomes unprofitable to keep them on the payroll, and pay them as little as necessary to induce them to accept employment so long as the wage rate does not violate minimum wage laws. Welfare agencies are distinct from this commercial world. The two forms of organization are evaluated in the light of separate criteria and different formal goals.

But close ties between the two types of organizations appear as soon as the question of empirical links is raised. Virtually all welfare recipients are unable to support themselves, either because industries cannot provide jobs, or pay less than a subsistence wage, or have impaired workers' earning ability through accident or occupational disease. In that realistic sense, public welfare agencies both socialize the costs of maintaining a labor force for industry and socialize the public to see their taxes as doles to undeserving recipients rather than as subsidies to industry.

There is a related empirical link as well. Welfare agency staff members are under constant pressure to keep welfare costs low by keeping benefits low, by adopting burdensome and demeaning procedures that discourage many from applying, and by withholding information about the availability of benefits (Piven and Cloward 1971). Unemployment insurance offices deny the claims of applicants who have not sought work or have refused "suitable" work; staff members are constantly under pressure from business and conservative groups to define "suitable" so as to force applicants to accept jobs under their skill level or prior pay level. Welfare organizations, unemployment insurance offices, and other governmental administrative units accordingly help provide a large supply of reserve labor for industry: people forced by their poverty and the absence of alternatives to accept wages and working conditions that they would otherwise refuse and that regularly employed workers reject.

These corporations and the governmental organizations are part of an integrated structure in practice, though not in terms of their formal goals, names, or symbolic import. The structure systematically requires taxpayers to bear some major costs of operating corporations, and it provides surplus labor at low cost for inefficient marginal firms. At the same time the structure systematically subjects the staffs of public welfare offices and employment offices to policy constraints that maintain established economic privileges and disadvantages and symbolically reassures taxpayers that the poor are being protected, even while welfare costs are kept low and private enterprise is promoted. The disparity between formal policy goals, on the one hand, and material value allocations, on the other, is wide; but, the symbolism inherent in formal rhetoric and in organizational structuring masks and mystifies the value allocations.

Academic analysis becomes even more involved with the symbolism than most public opinion; the ostensible beneficiaries of welfare and other governmental protections display a skepticism and ambivalence about their symbolic or tokenistic rewards that rarely appears in the public administration or political science textbooks and journals.

*It is typically in decisions of small enclaves of specialists, often at low hierarchical levels, that discretion to promote the values of the implementers is greatest.*

These decisions have the most potent impact on the quality of people's lives. The decisions in question are defined as impersonal, for Weber's model does legitimize, even if it does not describe (Gerth and Mills 1958, pp. 196–266). Examples are: sentencing in trial courts; helping professionals' treatments of clients or inmates; police officers' handling of suspects; noncommissioned officers' treatments of private soldiers, both in battle and in peacetime "training"; and implementation of legislative policies by low-level administrative staff (cf. Mechanic 1966, pp. 96–206). The lower in the governmental hierarchy such decisions are made, the less public discussion, and the more intense the impact on the lives of people subject to the administrative actions is likely to be. Except for the occasional case the media portray as shocking, low-level bureaucratic actions and those made in specialized enclaves are not noticed or publicly discussed, for they epitomize mechanical implementation and supervision by responsible superiors.

This effect comes into play regardless of the contrary intentions or the formal goals of policy planners. The Law Enforcement Assistance Administration established state planning agencies in order to guide and coordinate local law enforcement; but county and municipal police departments quickly developed control over the state agencies and have used them as a funnel to acquire federal funds (Feeley and Sarat 1980). The resources for asserting influence and for planning lie with the local police agencies, not with a newly created "planning agency," no matter how honorific its symbolic resonance or how logical its "mission."

Perhaps the polar instance of value allocation by hierarchical subordinates appears in cases of physical abuse, torture, and killing of people perceived as evil or as political dissidents. The third degree in the back rooms of police stations is one example. Political repression and torture under the Iranian Shah, in Argentina, in South Korea, and in many other contemporary states are more blatant examples.

The political framework and communication patterns in such situations are revealing about the symbolic as well as the material uses of hierarchies. Although the officials and the social groups with the highest status are the ones who benefit most substantially from such repression, their bureaucratic subordinates typically carry on their abuses without direct orders and without the specific knowledge of their superiors. The higher-ups typically do not ask and the lower-downs do not tell, but both benefit from the results. Indeed, the absence of specific communication about a public policy on which the survival of a regime depends itself becomes a signal that the policy is unmentionable and that is is sanctioned, though communication about it is not. Such forms of state terror are bound to be largely random, for their arbitrary character is necessary to their intimidating effect; but it is the subordinates who choose specific victims, specific punishments, and specific indulgences.

Noncoms in armies, foremen in industry, teachers in schools, and low-level authorities in other hierarchies occasionally resort to less blatant forms of random terror and indulgence for essentially the same reason and with essentially the same results. Such actions are likely when elites fear insubordination, resistance, or revolt and when a hierarchy legitimized by formal goals is functioning.

## The Free Market in Creating Regulatory Agencies

For reasons already considered, regulatory agencies are a necessary component of the intricate structure of advantage, reassurance, legitimation, and inequality that characterizes the modern welfare state. Their rules and decisions reflect and reinforce the balance of benefits and deprivations with which concerned interests can live; and they help to reestablish the balance when unanticipated economic or political developments disrupt it. But there is often conflict or uncertainty regarding what a politically acceptable balance is, and regulatory agencies occasionally disrupt an established modus vivendi by too blatantly taking the role of one of the adversary groups, as the Federal Trade Commission did in the 1970s.

Though regulatory agencies are rarely abolished, their powers, influence, jurisdiction, and budgets are vulnerable if they operate in a controversial area; so there is recurring political pressure to establish additional agencies, overlapping with existing ones in jurisdiction but responsive to a different pattern of interest.

Examples are easy to find. The Federal Communications Commission has periodically been subjected to severe attacks on its budget and its jurisdiction. Its influence on telecommunications policy has varied over the years. The Nixon White House established an overlapping telecommunications office in the Executive Office of the President responsive to political and economic groups critical of the FCC and the television network news programs. In the antitrust field there has long been overlapping jurisdiction among the Antitrust Division of the Department of Justice, the Federal Trade Commission, and state agencies to curb restraint of trade.

One of the more complex sets of overlapping agencies operates in the field of banking, doubtless because a wide range of groups with conflicting interests wield resources in that area and because banking policy affects everyone's well-being, directly or indirectly. The Comptroller of the Currency, the Federal Deposit Insurance Corporation, the Federal Reserve Board, and state banking authorities all exercise significant powers. One of the more astute and more conservative recent chairmen of the Federal Reserve Board, Arthur Burns, characterized the relationship among these banking regulators as "competition in laxity," because all the agencies have an incentive to go easy in lowering the boom on the regulated banks in order to appease pressures to remove banks from their jurisdiction or weaken their powers or cut their budgets or give a competing agency greater powers. When dealing with groups with clout, such possibilities are constant threats: a structural reason regulatory agencies must remain relatively docile in order to survive and prosper. The status, income, and promotion opportunities of an agency's staff hinge upon how this defensive game is played.

There is a related reason that "regulation" usually means something different in its consequences from its conventional connotation: It helps maintain inequalities rather than remove them.

Politically weak groups do win some protection from regulatory agencies in some of their decisions, of course; but the net outcome of their various policies reflects established power relationships, as a long series of studies has shown. Although the language in which regulation is conventionally discussed defines regulated businesses as vulnerable, the historical record defines the regulating agency as vulnerable whenever it takes its formal goals seriously: whenever it confuses support for its legitimation function with support for redistribution of values.

## The Symbolic Uses of Formal Goals

The publicized goals of administrative organizations rarely coincide with the benefits and deprivations that flow from those agencies' actions. The latter are always more problematic, more diverse and diffuse, and their chief benefits go to elites, though these consequences are masked from public scrutiny by the publicized statements of goals.

Education of the young, liberation of their minds, and provision of wide opportunities in life are the formal goals of public schools; they win support and legitimacy for free public education. Some students benefit from their schooling in these respects, but schools have other consequences for most students. They teach the basic skills and the specialized skills useful in modern industry, government, and armies: skills these organizations would have to provide themselves if the taxpayers did not do it for them. Schools inculcate loyalty, patriotism, docility, and appreciation of the rewards of conformity, especially in working-class students (Litt 1963). Schools delay the age at which young people enter the labor market, masking the problems created by high levels of unemployment among the young. For many working parents they provide daytime baby-sitting, making it easier for more family members to work when one income will not support the family; schools mask the social costs of substandard wages. Most of these effects of schooling are inconsistent with the publicized goal of liberating the minds of the young and evoking their full potentialities. The formal goal must be understood as serving a different purpose from description of what schools do. Its consequence is legitimation. From another perspective, it focuses public attention on a valued but remote and abstract objective and in doing so diverts attention from the values schools confer and deny in everyday life.

The armed forces are justified as a means of defense, as protection of the national security, and they do provide such protection on occasion. They also provide other values that are little noticed and not regarded as respectable topics of discussion. The army is both an outlet for the poor and the unemployed and a means of controlling and disciplining that potentially volatile group. Its increasingly frequent use in brushfire wars enhances the bargaining power of multinational corporations when they encounter popular or governmental resistance abroad. Its contracts are a major source of profits for domestic industry, in some cases the only source. It evokes willingness to sacrifice by most of the population. It frequently wins public support for the regime in control of the executive branch.

Here again, the organization's formal and publicized goal is a potent legitimating device but not adequate as a *description* of organizational activities or their consequences. In these examples and in others that might be cited, the potency of the formal goal depends on its ambiguity and abstractness: on the impossibility of reaching agreement about what constitutes "education" or "national security" or of finding unambiguous tests of when they have been achieved or have failed.

The term that expresses a political goal is a symbol, not a guide to future actions or outcomes. It reflects dissatisfactions and anxieties about established institutions, past outcomes, and current value allocations. In reassuring the anxious and focusing attention on language and on hopes, the "goal" as symbol fixates thought and intelligent play with ideas and observations: it constrains reflection on the meaning of experience, the combination of theory and praxis that offers hope of liberation from the intellectual constrictions of past institutions and from condensation symbolism.

## Issue Networks as Masked Regulators

Hugh Heclo's study (1978) of issue networks calls attention to a recent organizational development that reinforces the policy effects I have been analyzing. In each controversial policy area, a small group of concerned and informed people repeatedly come together to negotiate, bargain, and influence one another: representatives of law firms that specialize in such fields as health, education, environmental policy, or telecommunications; lobbyists for concerned interest groups; staff members of legislative committees; administrative agency staff with credentials as lawyers, engineers, policy analysts, and other forms of expertise. Heclo concludes that enclaves of such "technopols" are increasingly responsible for decisions and policy directions, while the affected publics, including the groups the technopols formally represent, are more and more thoroughly excluded from influence.

Social relationships and sharing of knowledge of the issues and of one another within the network of issue experts is bound to develop understandings and symbiotic ties that negate conflicts based on incompatible formal goals. Inequalities among participants in influence, resources, and ties to centers of power would become so well understood that formal bargaining within the issue network would often be unnecessary, for outcomes could be anticipated and therefore accepted, in practice if not in public rhetoric. Such pragmatic agreement based upon marginal advantages in resources is agreement to *reflect* established inequalities in policy rather than the use of governmental processes to change power relationships in line with public values.

Heclo (1978, pp. 105–106) sees the rise of issue networks as reason for the decline of public influence. "More than ever," he writes, "policy making is becoming an intramural activity among expert issue-watchers, their networks, and their networks of networks." The issue network becomes the true locus of decisions that affect private and public well-being. In yet another way, then, the formal administrative structure as symbol reassures interested groups that they are represented in technical decision making, while the social dynamics and resource inequalities of issue networks preempt the field, insulating action both from public discourse about values and from the organizations most intimately concerned with the issues.

## Governmental Organizations as Political Reinforcements

The focus in public debate and in policy analysis upon the goals of new and proposed governmental programs blurs recognition of a critical organizational outcome. New programs reflect established political resources, and so are likely to strengthen the groups that are already strong. The interstate highway system built almost entirely with federal funds in the 1950s and 1960s was a political victory for the "highway lobby" of auto manufacturers and dealers, oil companies, construction contractors, and truckers; and by strengthening their numbers, their financial position, and their political importance in every community, the highway program has made the highway lobby far more potent than it had been. The same spiral of influence that produces governmental programs that yield still more influence is apparent in arms procurement, in airport financing, and in the many other governmental subsidies to business. It is not as apparent, but just as real, in welfare programs. The Appalachia Program of the 1960s gave far more money to large highway construction firms than to the unemployed ex-miners and ex-farmers of Eastern Kentucky and West Virginia who were its ostensible beneficiaries, its "goal." The AFDC program keeps ghetto real estate profitable for landlords, and the Medicaid program helps enrich affluent physicians.

Organizations as symbols yield public support, while organizations as creations, and creatures, of political-bargaining relationships yield more tangible benefits for those who can use them as bargaining counters.

These observations suggest that governmental value allocations and legitimations take masked and mystified forms, and that the viability of the political system rests in part upon the mystifications. The conventional view of legislation as value choice and of administration as rational decision making is a central contributor both to system viability and to evaluative confusion.

This analysis also highlights the normative element in the conventional model of the political process, just as it calls attention to its own normative presuppositions. If value-free social science is an illusion, the ultimate mystification is surely the pretence of objective social science, just as the chief protection against mystification lies in self-consciousness about the problematic empirical and normative postulates on which analysis rests.

## References

De Lone, R.H. 1979. *Small futures: Children, inequality, and the limits of liberal reform.* New York: Harcourt Brace Jovanovich.

Easton, D. 1971. *The political system.* 2nd ed. New York: Knopf.

Edelman, M. 1950. *The licensing of radio services in the United States.* Urbana: University of Illinois Press.

Edelman, M. 1964. *The symbolic uses of politics.* Urbana: University of Illinois Press.

Feeley, M.M., and Sarat, A. 1980. *The policy dilemma: The crisis of theory and practice in the law enforcement assistance administration*. Minneapolis: University of Minnesota Press.

Gerth, H.H., and Mills, C.W. 1958. *From Max Weber*. New York: Oxford University Press.

Goodnow, F.J. 1897. *Comparative administrative law*. New York: G.P. Putnam's Sons.

Heclo, H. 1978. Issue networks and the executive establishment. In *The new American political system*, ed. A. King. Washington, D.C.: American Enterprise Institute for Public Policy Research. Pp. 87–124.

Lindert, P.H., and Williamson, I.G. 1976. Three centuries of American inequality. University of Wisconsin–Madison, Institute for Research on Poverty, Discussion Paper 333-76.

Litt, E. 1963. Civic education, community norms and political indoctrination. *American Sociological Review* 28: 69–75.

Mechanic, D. 1966. Sources of power and lower participants in complex organizations. In *Readings in organization theory*, ed, W.A. Hill and D. Egan. Boston: Allyn and Bacon. Pp. 196–206.

Miller, H.P. 1966. *Income distribution in the United States*. Washington, D.C.: Government Printing Office.

Piven, F.F., and Cloward, A. 1971. *Regulating the poor*. New York: Atheneum.

# 8

# The Welfare State: Issues of Rationing and Allocation of Resources

## ABRAHAM DORON

The welfare state in most industrial societies is at present undergoing a serious crisis. This crisis is a result of a number of social, economic, and political factors. The most obvious are the economic stagnation experienced by most industrial countries in the last decade, the crumbling of the ideological support for the welfare state among large sectors of the population,[1] and the weakening of the sense of social solidarity that supplied the moral foundation for it (Pinker 1979). As a result, the welfare state faces a serious problem of how to avoid increasing erosion of its role in assuring the social and economic security of large segments of the population, and especially of the weaker strata of society.[2]

The most obvious sign of this crisis is the continual decline of resources allocated for welfare activities in almost all industrial countries, where there is an ongoing public debate on how to further curb the flow of funds for the activities of the welfare state. The outlook for the immediate future is not bright: Already limited resources will continue to dwindle, greatly reducing the availability of social welfare services. Whether we like it or not, we must prepare ourselves to face the problems resulting from these policies. The question is, How this can be accomplished without compounding the problems already facing large segments of the population?

---

[1]David Donnison used this phrase in his lecture "The Discovery and Development of Knowledge," at the 19th International Congress of Schools of Social Work, August 14–18, 1978, Jerusalem, Israel.

[2]For an interesting discussion of these issues, see Horowitz (1978) and Logue (1979).

EVALUATING THE WELFARE STATE:
SOCIAL AND POLITICAL PERSPECTIVES

In order to deal with this situation, it is necessary to examine more carefully not only the overall strategies in allocating resources for the various welfare activities (i.e., the issues of macrosocial distribution) but also to give greater attention to the processes of actual distribution of these resources to families and people in need at the point of access to the social services (i.e., the issues of microsocial distribution) (See Glennerster 1975; Heclo and Wildavsky 1974; Judge 1979).

In the context of the current political economy, the issues of macrosocial and microsocial distribution are perceived as two different and mostly unrelated processes. One is involved with the ongoing struggle for the overall allocation of resources to the totality of social welfare programs, which is the product of complex political and social forces. The other concerns the process of actual delivery of the services to families and individuals at the ground level—that is, at the point of contact between the social services system and the individual in need of a particular service, which is the product of organizational and professional policy and practice (Algie 1980; Judge 1978).

Until quite recently, public debate, academic research, and political thinking focused primarily on the macrosocial allocation of resources to the various welfare programs and their distribution to the different bodies responsible for the implementation of social welfare policies. The macropolicy decision directed toward the social welfare services field tended to overwhelm the micropolicy decisions at the ground level. Only limited thought has been given to the processes of microsocial distribution of resources to the people in need and to the actual delivery of the social services. Politicians and social administrators felt much more confident with the former than the latter and therefore neglected the crucial issues of microsocial distribution (Heclo and Wildawsky 1974, Chapter 8). Indeed, most economic theory still does not deal with these micro issues.

It is only in the last few years that the importance of the micropolicy decisions have become recognized and that this allocative process has been seen as a process of service rationing of paramount importance. Moreover, in view of the virtually unlimited nature of social needs and the subsequent demand for social services on one side, and the limited availability of money, manpower, and service facilities on the other side, service rationing at the ground level is one of the most important functions of all social service systems (Judge 1978; Parker 1967; Scrivens 1979). This process is, according to A.G. Stevens (1972), "the unseen factor which enables the social services to operate," or "the oil which enables the machinery to work and without which it would grind to a halt."

Microsocial distribution or service rationing is important because it is in this process that the critical decisions are made as to who will receive the service, the amount and quality of the service, and who will receive any other benefit at the disposal of the system. The decision as to who will receive service, both in amount and quality, establishes not only the outcome of the rationing process but actually produces the social effect of the service on the welfare of the various population groups (Glennerster 1975).

Another major problem in the macro and the micro allocational processes is that the strategic priorities established at the macro level as to the overall allocation of resources for welfare activities are mostly established in the general political process of formulating a country's economic and social policies and budgetary planning. This process is generally overt and explicit, and is therefore open to public debate and control. The operational priorities established at the micro level by organizational and professional policy and practice are, however, usually unseen, frequently unconscious, and rarely explicit. Even more important, the professional and political practice of denying the service-rationing process that makes up the microsocial priorities removes the subject from public debate and leaves it chiefly in the hands of the service suppliers (Powell 1976; Stevens 1972).

Consider the medical care services provided by Israel's sick funds—they all claim that every insured person in need of medical care will receive all the services required, both in quantity and in quality. Like their counterparts elsewhere, the Israeli sick funds strongly deny any form of rationing in the allocation of services. But limitations of money, manpower, and facilities inevitably cause these organizations to use various rationing devices at the point of access. In the Israeli case, this is effected at the level of the local clinic, the individual physician, or at the hospital emergency room. Denial of the existence of rationing at the point of access thus makes it impossible to control openly who will receive what amount on quality of service.

The problems thus created are of a threefold nature: first, it makes it very difficult to assure that the strategic priorities established on the national level are actually adopted and implemented at the ground level; second, it makes it impossible to guarantee that the (hidden) process of service rationing will ensure a fair distribution of service to the population in need; and third, it makes it very hard to predict the distributional outcome of social welfare policies (Algie 1980; Davies 1978, Chapter 7; Forder 1974, p. 81; Foster 1979).

It is thus increasingly recognized that to make the working of social policies more effective, it is necessary to develop theories and models that will clarify the processes of microsocial distribution. This would transform the problems of micro distribution into policy issues, a dimension they lack at present (Parker 1967). Moreover, as already indicated by Judge (1978) and Algie (1980), it is also necessary to develop a conceptual integration of the macro and microsocial distribution—that is, to link in a more coherent way the allocation of resources for welfare activities at the national level with the middle and ground-level processes of distribution at the point of service delivery.

In the last decade there has been a growing awareness of these issues, and initial outlines of service-rationing theories have begun to appear. Although a unified theory has not yet been formulated, the outlines have significantly contributed to the understanding of the dynamics of service rationing and the implications for the user population of the access barriers they can produce.

The theory outlines can be classified into types. One, which can be discerned in the writings of, among others, Parker (1967), Rees (1972), Scrivens (1979), and Stevens (1972), divides the microsocial rationing process into two major categories. One category includes the strategies designed to reduce demand for the various social services. Scrivens calls these demand inhibitors, and sees their goal as being to reduce in various ways the number of people with which the services have to deal. The other category includes the strategies which reduce the supply of services when there already has been a demand expressed for them. Scrivens calls the latter supply inhibitors, and they attempt to bring into balance the demand for services with the existing supply.

Among the demand-inhibiting strategies, the most common are deterrence, denial, and withdrawal of information. Deterrence includes the various forms of imposing stigma—feelings of shame or guilt—either directly or indirectly, among people who are actual users or may become users of the service; and procedures within the services that in themselves have a deterrent effect, such as poorly equipped offices, inconvenient hours, irksome rules, long queues, waiting lists, unfriendly personnel.

Denial usually takes the form of pretending that needs that should be catered to by a particular service do not actually exist; or in the event that the existence of the needs cannot be disproved, pretending that they are the concern of another service or of a different unit, and referring the claimant elsewhere. Referral of clients from one service to another and "red tape" are part and parcel of the denial tactics. Withdrawal of information is also a common demand-inhibiting strategy. Failure to provide adequate and relevant information about a service and its functions and thus allowing people to remain ignorant as to under what circumstances they can make proper use of it is undoubtedly an important factor in reducing demand. (Examples of this in the Israeli context are discussed in Doron, 1978a).

Among the strategies that restrict the supply of services are eligibility conditions (which may include citizenship and nationality), the discretion of the service supplier in deciding upon the amount and character of service provided, charging for serivces, dilution of both quantity and quality of service, and the various forms of red tape. The simplest and most evident strategy to restrict the supply of service is to set eligibility criteria. To the extent that these criteria are openly spelled out and clearly defined, they are the accepted and democratic way of putting limits to the supply of a particular service. Basically, there is therefore nothing wrong in using this rationing strategy. The problems arise when these criteria remain undisclosed or unclear, or can be changed by the service at will.

Disretion of service suppliers, whether accorded to the service administrators, professional staff, or other personnel, serves clearly as a supply inhibiting strategy. Service administrators can use their discretion to screen the claimants as to which services should be given; professional such as physicians, psychologists, or social workers can control access to services (Donnison 1977; Foster 1979; Titmuss 1971); even nonprofessional personnel such as secretaries or receptionists can used their discretion to screen applicants, either to ease or to hinder their access to service (Blau 1963; Hall 1974).

An accepted strategy to restrict the availability of a service is to charge for its use. This is, of course, the classical economic approach to equate supply with demand. It is derived from the model of the market, where price regulates demand. On the face of it this is an openly declared and clear rationing strategy. The problem is that it is very difficult to determine the inhibiting effect of charges on the users of services. It is not always clear on whom the burden actually falls—that is, to what extent the users shift this burden to others, and to what extent the charges fall on the users themselves. Another problem in using charges involves the elasticity of demand for a particular service and its social importance with regard to its cost to various population groups. The effectiveness of this strategy is therefore not as unequivocal as its supporters claim (Maynard 1979; Parker 1976; Stewart 1980).

Frequently, charging for services plays a symbolic role of responding to political values or to fiscal requirements (of raising revenue) rather than being a pertinent solution for controlling demand. As Parker (1976) indicates, the symbolic value of paying which marks the bilateral, quid pro quo transaction in the economic market fits the dominant values of our society, and there is therefore a powerful urge to use it as a remedy without weighing its actual effectiveness in the microsocial distribution of resources.

The diluting strategy includes a variety of methods to lower the level of service as a way of dealing with increased demand: reducing the time made available to clients, erosion of professional standards, utilizing inadequately trained staff, disregarding problems raised by clients, limiting the amount of information provided, premature termination of care, and the like (Foster 1979). Red tape (i.e., the various forms of bureaucratization and inefficiency in the service delivery process) can also serve as a deliberate rationing strategy aimed at reducing demand.

Another typology can be derived from the writings of Algie (1980), Davies (1978), Gruber (1980), Judge (1978), and Stone (1979). They tend to divide the microsocial rationing process into priority categories. These categories can be professional, territorial, and/or related to selected population groups at risk.

The strategy of establishing microsocial priorities at the ground level on the basis of professional assessment of need is commonly accepted, and both politically and administratively convenient. Its acceptability derives from the social and cultural consensus that professionals—whether physicians, teachers, psychologists, or social workers—possess objective criteria to identify needs in their field of competence, and that they are therefore best fitted to establish the existence of such needs. On the face of it, we have here a conscious and explicit strategy of rationing.

However, the assumption that professionals are capable managing a need-based distribution system has no firm foundation. This basis is lacking for a number of reasons. First, the knowledge and skills of the "helping professions" have far to go before it will be possible for them to use objective, clear, and unequivocal criteria of diagnosis and classification in order to establish need for a particular service (Algie 1980). Second, professions have an internal logic of their own. Members of all professions tend thus to adopt criteria for granting their services which reflect the hierarchy of their professional values, and not necessarily criteria that take into account the individual needs of those who require their services, or the intention of those responsible for formulating macrosocial policy (Doron 1978b). Third, it is becoming more evident that the process of professional diagnosis and classification, made mystifying by technical nomenclature, is actually a status-awarding process biased by class, ethnicity, and personal predilection. The distributive system thus effected is not geared to allocate services to meet social needs in an objective way, but rather to allocate statuses and services in ways that run parallel to the existing stratification system and thus reinforce it (Gruber 1980). Fourth, the placement of the microsocial distribution of services in the hands of professionals thus transfers to them the control over the operation of these services. The inevitable result is that the scarce service resources are to a large degree used to meet the requirements of the professionals rather than the needs of their clients (Foster 1979; Kolberg 1978).

The setting of geographical priorities constitutes an integral part of national strategies in allocating resources for social welfare services. The main goal is to prevent the creation and existence of inequalities in the services available in different parts of a country. The importance of this macrosocial distribution strategy is not questioned, the issue to be dealt with here is related to the *microsocial* strategies that derive from the territorial priorities. The macrosocial allocation of resources on the basis of territorial priorities requires the granting of resources to local authorities responsible for the microsocial distribution within their localities. Only in a small part of the social welfare services, as, for example, in the field of social security, are both macro- and microsocial distribution the responsibility of the national government. Local authorities have a large degree of autonomy in the distribution of their services. As a result, it is extremely difficult to assure that the social priorities guiding the national government will also guide the local authorities in the distribution of social services at the ground level (Davies 1968; Department of Health and Social Security 1976; Judge 1978).

An example of this dilemma is provided by certain happenings in Tel Aviv that were highlighted in a dramatic television broadcast. In one of its moves to cut public expenditure, the government reduced its welfare allocation to the Tel Aviv municipality. As a result the municipality decided to phase out the meals-on-wheels service to the aged and chronically ill. Although the Israeli government has recently pursued a policy of curtailing its welfare activities, it has repeatedly stressed its priority commitment to continue to provide necessary social welfare services to the most needy sections of the population. There was no question that the aged and chronically ill in need of hot meals belong to this category. The microsocial distribution of resources allocated for this purpose rests, however, with the local authorities; it is they who are responsible for the provision of the social welfare services on the local level. In this example, the municipality opted for another order of priorities, and decided to cancel services for a most vulnerable group in the population.

It is important to emphasize here that it would be too simplistic to complain about the choice of priorities of the Tel Aviv municipality in this case. One can envisage a situation in which other local authorities would choose not to provide hot meals to the needy aged and chronically ill, for the national government has accorded every local authority to autonomy to determine its own expenditure priorities in the field of social welfare, as well as in other fields. It is thus the considerable freedom and autonomy enjoyed by local government that constitutes the central problem with microsocial distribution.

The significance of this is that within the context of local government autonomy, it is extremely difficult to achieve the objective of territorial justice: There appears to be a conflict between attaining territorial justice and maintaining local freedom of choice. As long as the local authorities are free to determine their priorities in the areas for which they are responsible, it is impossible to assure that their order of priorities will concur with that of the national government (Judge 1978).

Beyond the issue of local autonomy and choice, it has also to be remembered that equalizing financial resources between regions and localities may not necessarily equalize the distribution of social welfare services (Maynard and Ludbrook 1980, p. 290). The macrosocial strategy of geographical priorities in allocating resources provides only an additional avenue through which the objective of territorial justice can be pursued (Maynard and Ludbrook 1980, p. 312). Territorial justice as defined by Davies means "an area distribution of provision of service such that each area's standard is proportional to the total needs for the service of the population [Davies 1968, Chapter 1]." However, the factors involved in the definition and identification of needs and generating demand for services to meet those needs are extremely complex.

The strategy of setting priorities for at-risk population groups is mainly used as a selective strategy to confine the provision of social service benefits to the most needy. The rationing mechanisms used in this strategy are the principle of need, and means testing. On the face of it the rationing here is clear and explicit, but in practice the situation is far more complicated (Reddin 1977). The problem with the selective rationing process is that it is very difficult to define unequivocally who is a person in need, and to carry out the means testing to establish that an individual or a family actually are in need. The inevitable lack of clarity of these parameters leaves the service providers at ground level a very large degree of discretion, some of which have already been discussed. It is, however, important to add that discretion in establishing financial need too often involves the injection of a moral judgment by the service supplier as to whether a person applying for service is deserving or not deserving. The recourse to moral judgments in the rationing process unavoidably produces additional distortions in the microsocial distribution of services and brings about unintended distributive outcomes.

Clearly, selectivity has many other limitations as a service-rationing strategy. The danger of imposing stigma, their socially and divisive effects, the high effective tax rates it puts on low incomes, the negative incentives to work it produces, and so forth, are all issues that cannot be dealt with here. In any event, the selective strategy is far from being efficient and effective in the microsocial distribution of social welfare services (Garfinkel 1980, pp. 65–66).

One example of the use of the selective strategy is the cash subsidy provided to low-wage earners in Israel in the early 1970s. In a follow-up study on this program it was found that the chief causes of performance inefficiency were "strategic," and involved "namely the principle of selectivity that required a combined test of means and family situation." The conclusion of the study was that when the selectivity principle is translated into operational eligibility rules and implementation tactics, much of the efficiency theoretically expected tends to disappear at the ground level of implementation. As a result of these findings the subsidy program was eventually phased out, but advocacy of the selective strategy continues to persist (Doron and Roter 1978, pp. 10–11).

The rationing strategies included in these typologies are not necessarily exclusive. They can and do operate to complement each other, and are constantly interacting. As one strategy is relaxed or rejected, another is almost automatically applied to replace it (Stevens 1972, p. 9). They all create selective processes of service provision and delivery which go beyond the acknowledged intentions and declared policies in most social welfare services (Scrivens 1979, p. 63).

It is difficult to assess the impact in recent years of the emerging service-rationing theories on the working of social policies. On the whole their influence seems to have remained rather limited, and they have barely started to make inroads in the making of social policy. Under the present conditions of diminishing resources for welfare activities and declining support for the welfare state, it is imperative that the problems of microsocial distribution to brought more into the open, and that more use be made of the increasing knowledge of service rationing so as to assure a more equitable and more efficient distribution of scarce resources.

Significant progress has been made in the development of service-rationing theories, and this has brought greater awareness to the problems of microsocial distribution. Much less advance has been achieved in the conceptual integration and linking of the macro- and microsocial distribution process. The only field of social service in which these two processes have become closely integrated is that of social security services. It was made possible in this field because most social security systems operate as an integral part of national government and provide their service directly to the population: Their functions are not divided between a variety of particularistic agencies as in other social service systems, or between various levels of government, or between the policymaking function and implementation functions. The processes of macro- and microsocial policymaking here are highly centralized and integrated. Moreover, the social security benefits are provided mainly in cash, and are provided on the basis of clearly defined eligibility rules. Thus, very little discretion is left in the hands of the service providers at the point of access. Also, by their nature, the social security services require only minimal involvement of professionals in the provision of benefits. All these factors facilitate a more rational rationing of these services.

Means testing and the principle of need play only a minor and residual role in advanced social security systems. Relinquishing these rationing devices does not mean that social security benefits could not be selective in their incidence and geared to improve the circumstances of vulnerable population groups, for the redistributive goal of transferring larger resources to groups in need is mainly obtained by means of eligibility rules. Although these rules are universal in their relation to defined population groups, the very definition of these populations can make these services highly selective in their incidence and progressive in their redistributive effect.

Generally speaking, an integrated policy that includes the establishing of macrosocial priorities and microsocial eligibility criteria as part of national policy in the field of social security have, for the most part, assured that the overall strategic priorities are implemented at the ground level, and that the distributional outcomes of these policies can to a large degree be obtained. No such results can be claimed for other social service systems.

The main difficulty in achieving a more coherent integration of macro- and microsocial distribution in other social service systems, and in particular in the health and personal social services, lies in the assumption that the professionals in these services are capable of identifying social needs and providing benefits to meet these needs. The evidence available on the concrete operation of these social service systems makes it clear that by the very logic of such systems, professionals are constrained to accept and implement strategic priorities established at the national level. It is also quite evident that the mechanisms of professional assessment and discretion cannot guarantee a fair and equitable distribution of service at ground level.

To deal with this situation it is necessary to develop clearer criteria of professional service rationing, and in this way to circumscribe the extent of professional power in the allocation of scarce resources. The social security service systems can, with the necessary modification, provide such a model. In view of the prospective circumstances of growing scarcity of resources in the field of social welfare, the development of such criteria seems more urgent than ever.

# References

Algie, J. 1980. Priorities in personal social services. In *The yearbook of social policy in Britain 1978*, eds. M. Brown and S. Baldwin. London: Routledge and Kegan Paul. Pp. 179–205.

Blau, P.M. 1963. *The dynamics of bureaucracy: A study of interpersonal relations in two agencies*. Chicago: Chicago University Press.

Davies, B. 1968. *Social needs and resources in local services*. London: Michael Joseph.

Davies, B. 1978. (in association with Reddin, M.). *Universality, selectivity and effectiveness in social policy*. London: Heinemann.

Davies, B. 1980. Policy options for charges and means tests. In *Pricing the social services*, ed. Ken Judge. London: Macmillan. Pp. 132–153.

Department of Health and Social Security. 1976. *Priorities for health and personal social services in England*. London: HMSO.

Donnison, D. 1977. Against discretion. *New Society*, September 15.

Doron, A. 1978a. Public assistance in Israel: Issues of policy and administration. *Journal of Social Policy* 7: 456–457.

Doron, A. 1978b. The dilemma of services versus income transfers in the process of social development. In *Human well-being: The challenge of continuity and change*, Jerusalem: The Conference Organizing Committee for the Nineteenth International Council on Social Welfare. Pp. 70–83.

Doron, A. and Roter, R. 1978. *Low wage earners and low wage subsidies*. Jerusalem: The Hebrew University, Baerwald School of Social Work and the National Insurance Institute, Bureau of Research and Planning.

Forder, A. 1974. *Concepts in social administration*. London: Routledge & Kegan Paul.

Foster, P. 1979. The informal rationing of primary medical care. *Journal of Social Policy* 8: 489–509.

Garfinkel, I. 1980. *Welfare reform: A new and old view*. Institute for Research on Poverty. Reprint Series, No. 373.

Glennerster, H. 1975. *Social service budgets and social policy*. London: Allen and Unwin.

Gruber, M.L. 1980. Inequality in the social services. *The Social Service Review*, 54: 59–75.

Hall, A. 1974. *The point of entry*. London: Allen and Unwin.

Heclo, H. and Wildavsky, A. 1974. *The private government of public money*. London: Macmillan.

Horowitz, I.L. 1978. Social welfare, state power and the limits of equity. In *Policy studies review annual*, Vol. 2, ed. H.E. Freeman. London: Sage Publications. Pp. 341–358.

Judge, K. 1978. *Rationing social services*. London: Heineman.

Judge, K. 1979. Resource allocation in the welfare state: Bureaucrats or prices? *Journal of Social Policy* 8: 371–382.

Kolberg, J.E. 1978. Limits to welfare. *Acta Sociologica* 21: 113–123. Supplement—The Nordic welfare state.

Logue, J. 1979. The welfare state: Victim of its success. *Daedalus*, Fall: 69–87.

Maynard, A. 1979. Pricing, insurance and the national health service. *Journal of Social Policy* 8: 157–176.

Maynard, A. and Ludbrook, A. 1980. Budget allocation in the National Health Service. *Journal of Social Policy* 9:290.

Parker, R.A. 1967. Social administration and scarcity. *Social Work* (U.K.) 12: 9–14.

Parker, R.A. 1976. Charging for the social services. *Journal of Social Policy* 5: 359–373.

Pinker, R. 1979. *The idea of welfare.* London: Heineman.

Powell, J.E. 1966. *A new look at medicine and politics.* London: Pitman Medical.

Reddin, M. 1977. *Universality and selectivity: Strategies in social policy* Dublin: National Economic and Social Council, The Stationery Office.

Rees, A.M. 1972. Access to the personal health and welfare services. *Social and Economic Administration* 6: 34–43.

Scrivens, E. 1979. Towards a theory of rationing. *Social Policy and Administration.* 13: 53–64.

Stevens, A.G. 1972. Rationing in the social services. *Welfare Officer* 21: 5–12.

Stewart, M. 1980. Issues in pricing policy. In *Pricing the social services*, ed. K. Judge. London: Macmillan. Pp. 7–23.

Stone, D.A. 1979. Diagnosing and the dole: The function of illness in American distributive politics. *Journal of Health, Politics, Policy and Law* 4: 507–521.

Titmuss, R.M. 1971. Welfare rights, law and discretion. *Political Quarterly* 42: 113–132.

# 9

# Charting the Iceberg: Visible and Invisible Aspects of Government

YAIR AHARONI

## Introduction

Throughout the developed world, the public sector has experienced enormous growth over the last 3 decades. Both the scope and the range of services supplied by this sector have been expanded. Citizens rely on their government for the solution of a myriad of economic, social, and cultural problems and exert pressures on government to mitigate almost every type of individual risk. At the same time, opportunities for new programs are limited. Existing service levels cannot be cut without adversely affecting countless vested interest groups, and substantial real increases in governmental revenues are unlikely, as the public is unwilling to pay an increasing proportion of its income to the public pool. Moreover, the widely held perception of the government as being inept and gripped by special interest groups limits the political acceptability of increased government spending. Under these conditions, the endless crusade against government inefficiency has gained renewed intensity, and the vision of reducing waste in government has gained appeal.

In the United States, one result has been a movement demanding a constitutional amendment for setting up a balanced budget each year. James Buchanan (1975) proposed a constitutional amendment that would limit the governmental budget to a given percentage of the GNP. The creation of independent legal bodies has also been recommended as one way of limiting the degree to which the legislature may succumb to pressures from various groups. The autonomy of these bodies is advocated to protect them from both political favoritism and political oscillation, thus ensuring greater efficiency.

EVALUATING THE WELFARE STATE:
SOCIAL AND POLITICAL PERSPECTIVES

Since the size and scope of publicly financed services is growing, any prescription that reduces their costs through higher efficiency must be carefully considered. The major purpose of this chapter is to compare the different ways in which services are supplied by the public sector, and to analyze the reasons for and consequences of these differences.

## The Growth of the Public Sector

Concern about the size of public expenditures is hardly new. As early as 1860, Gladstone pointed out in his budget speech that England's national wealth had grown by only 16.5% between 1853 and 1859, whereas public expenditures had increased by 58%. He concluded, "I may at once venture to state frankly that I am not satisfied with the state of public expenditure and the rapid rate of its growth. I trust, therefore, that we mean in a great degree to retreat our steps [quoted in Klein, 1976]." Public expenditures in the United kingdom at that time were approximately 11% of GNP; thereafter, they declined as a proportion of GNP until the end of the nineteenth century. In the twentieth century, the proportion began to rise again, and by the 1960s it had reached approximately 60% of GNP. A steady growth in the government's share in GNP was recorded in other Western countries as well.

There are various explanations for the increase in the size of the public sector. Economists tend to explain the increase in public expenditures as resulting from structural changes in society, technological complexity, urbanization, and similar factors. In an interdependent and complex society, they argue, there are many externalities, and an increasing number of market failures. Government action is needed to neutralize the effects of those failures caused by economic and technological factors that are exogenous to the political system (see Mueller, 1979, and the citations therein).

In the Marxian view of society, the increase in public expenditures is a response to the growing internal contradictions of the capitalist system. Capitalism, being inherently destructive, resorts to public expenditure as an investment in social control. O'Connor (1974) points out, quite correctly, that public expenditures can be viewed as a system of conflict. To the extent that the political system is faced with demands based on high expectations and to the extent that scarcity persists, the system cannot meet all its expectations; it must devise means either to reduce expectations or to decide on priorities.

Some political scientists explain the growth of the public sector as stemming from increasing demands for services by powerful interest groups competing for more government services. Others stress the increasing power of the bureaucracy, or the increasing participation of more groups in the political activities of the country and the resulting competition among parties to attract votes. According to the latter view, expenditures and taxes are allocated to guarantee political support. Downs (1957) and Breton (1974) argue that voters are more conscious of taxes than they are of government benefits. As a result, visible government budgets in a democracy are smaller than they would be if all citizens had perfect information. Moreover, the allocation of resources is distorted, since the "purer" the public good, the less attractive it is from the politician's point of view.

Since the end of World War II, the main reason for the growth of the public sector has been the increase in political participation. This caused a tremendous surge in the demands on government to supply services, and mainly to protect individuals against all kinds of risks. Changing definitions of fairness and justice have brought about some significant changes in the role of the government in most Western nation-states. Government has increasingly been expected to protect the poor, the weak, and the unfortunate against a growing list of misfortunes. In addition to these changing values, there has been a gradual shift in the distribution of political power away from the bureaucracy and propertied classes.

As a result of increasing public demands, the size and scope of operations of the public sector and its functions have grown. In addition, since the 1930s, government has been perceived as being responsible for the total management of the economy: It is now expected to maintain full employment, to promote economic growth, to protect the economy from the vicissitudes of business cycles, and to arrest the crises of economic recession. Moreover, the government is expected to achieve an equitable distribution of income, wealth, and economic and social opportunity. Since the 1950s, the growth in government has stemmed largely from demands to reduce individual risks. The welfare state has been turned into an insurance state, as all individuals are protected against an array of risks by shifting the burden of their consequences to the community at large (Aharoni 1981).

Two conflicting considerations come into play in determining the desirable size of the public sector: On the one hand, most people want the government to provide more social services and to help mitigate private risks; on the other hand, there is a fear of a "big government" that is inefficient, interfering, and corrupt. The unclosed gap between demand for increasing services and public unwillingness to pay for them causes inflation as well as social and political tensions.

## Indirect Spending by the Government

Funds are needed for government to obtain resources from the economy to undertake public expenditure and supply various services. In a simple economic model of social choice, all services supplied by the public sector are financed through taxation. In a democratic society, public revenues and expenditures are both assumed to appear in the budget, and this budget is assumed to be thoroughly scrutinzed by elected representatives. In reality, this assumption does not hold. Many of the services supplied by the public sector are financed not by taxes by by nonfiscal means, and are carried out through the coercive powers of the government, exercised by the bureaucratic apparatus. These costs are incurred involuntarily in the sense that in the absence of law, regulation, quota, or license they would not have been incurred at all.

The trend toward a bigger role for government, as measured by its share of employment, use of resources, output, or taxes collected as a percentage of GNP, has been commented on by economists and political scientists alike. Governmental expenditures are only a partial indication of government supplied services, but, in fact, these figures represent only the tip of the iceberg. The changing balance between decisions made in the market place and those made in the political arena is reflected not only in the growing share of government expenditure in GNP, but also in the increasing importance of services supplied by state-owned authorities and by the largely neglected growth in what may be termed "invisible government." Therefore, in order to document the shift from small government to the welfare state and then to the insurance state, one has to examine three distinct phenomena: the growth of visible expenditure; the swelling of invisible government; and the increase in the operations of state-owned enterprises.

## The Invisible Government

Through interference with the market mechanism, the government can increase the services provided to particular groups without affecting its budget. To see this, consider the following example. The Israeli government wants to increase the income of disabled war veterans. One way of achieving this goal would be to pay them additional sums of money in the form of educational allowances. These allowances are part of the governmental budget, and are shown in its published expenditures. Instead, the Israeli government chose to restrict the issuance of taxi licenses to disabled veterans only. Since the number of licenses is restricted, an artificial scarcity is created and the wealth of those who receive the licenses is increased. The rising income of the licensees is not shown in the budget, nor is it recognized as a government expenditure; it is simply buried in the increased costs to taxi users. The demand for taxi services is relatively elastic and a monopoly on taxi licenses is not a guarantee of unlimited income. However, it certainly guarantees additional income without affecting the government budget at all. Moreover, it seems a fair hypothesis that most people are less disturbed by this licensing policy (and may even be totally ignorant of its existence) than they would be by an equivalent increase in government expenditures. A similar method is used for gas stations: The construction of such stations is restricted by the government, and licenses are granted only to disabled war veterans.

Such methods enable the government to hide much of their expenditures. Costs of publicly supplied services are shown in the official statistics as outlays of the private sector, but these expenditures are made solely and exclusively because of government power of regulation.

Almost any government service or policy can be achieved through cross-subsidization, tax expenses, licensing, granting of special rights, tariff and nontariff protection, and many other devices. Thus, low water prices to farmers can be cross-subsidized by higher prices to city dwellers. Various methods have been employed to emasculate liberal trade agreements. Subsidies, guaranteed government procurements, incentives, taxes, and nontariff barriers have been used by many countries facing domestic recession and unemployment. Governments have also used tie-in agreements in foreign aid and have negotiated "voluntary" agreements to curb imports. These policy tools were used to support a particular sector, industry, region, or even firm. Costs are borne by consumers in the form of higher prices. Because benefits accrue to few and costs are paid by many, those carrying the additional burden, even if they know its total size, do not bother to complain.

Governments all over the world subsidize certain declining firms to ensure employment. In Israel, when the owners of a textile plant in a development town threatened to close it, the government agreed to give them a direct subsidy from the budget. The Belgian government, in a similar situation, decided to nationalize the firm in question; its losses are not shown in the budget. The U.S. government aided its textile industry through restrictions on foreign trade. The increasing costs of clothing to the consumer are not shown in any budget.

The compliance costs associated with government regulations are another example of invisible government. These costs are not borne by taxpayers in general, but by the consumers of the regulated products. In some cases the burden is quite clear, as in the case of a regulated industry where all expenses for tax-withholding, compliance with government information requirements, and the like, are recognized as part of the cost of doing business and are reflected in the firm's rate structure. In these cases, the cost (minus tax reduction) is borne by the customers (e.g., the purchasers of electricity or telephone services) rather than the taxpayers as a whole. In other cases, the burden is less obvious. Compliance costs in a more competitive industry may or may not be shifted to the consumers of the products.

Over the last two decades, the invisible government appears to have grown faster than its visible counterpart. This growth came about not only because costs can be hidden (thus avoiding possible public discontent), but also because of administrative and ideological factors. Many people believe that the market, even if it is distorted by governmental directives, is a superior mechanism for allocation than direct supply by the government.

Thus, for instance, many governments used to solve the housing problems of the poor by building them houses; today, they use other methods. In Israel there is no significant aspect of the housing market that is not affected by government action in one form or another. The government supplies housing aid in so many ways that it is almost impossible to untangle the maze of cost-increasing regulations on the one hand and subsidies on the other. The government owns houses and rents them to certain segments of the public at highly subsidized rents through state owned enterprises. The government also builds house for sale, sometimes through state owned enterprises, sometimes through private contractors. In other cases, the contractor may be granted a special permit to utilize a higher percentage of the lot for building than that usually allowed under the building code, and this largesse is traded against the sale of some apartments at a lower rate for young couples. Indeed, the increased involvement of government in the supply of services has not only augmented the opportunities for benefits but has also created a maze of methods of supply that are difficult even to catalog.

Note that invisibility is not synonymous with lack of accountability. Accountability implies "that those who wield power have to answer in another place and give reasons for decisions that are taken [Miller 1971]." A method may be invisible in that the true costs and benefits are not recorded in the budget, but the costs may have been approved by the legislator. For example, when a government procurement order is used to boost the profits of a certain firm, there may be full accountability, even though the costs and benefits of the order will not be recorded. If a decision is made to withhold taxes at source, a significant portion of the cost of tax collection is shifted from the public to the private sector, but with full accountability.

Note that the term *invisible* is used here in a strictly descriptive sense, no pejorative meaning is intended. It is not implied that government expenditures recorded in the budget are "better" than expenditures that are shifted to the private sector. Pollution, for example, may be reduced by collecting taxes from the polluters and paying subsidies to those who suffer from pollution. It can also be fought by regulation.

## THE ROLE OF STATE-OWNED ENTERPRISES

Over the past 10–20 years, state-owned enterprises (SOEs) have assumed an increasingly important role in the world economy. In many developing countries, they have become a principal vehicle through which the state attempts to achieve its development goals. In Europe, SOEs have been used to advance a wide variety of state goals. Whatever the original reasons for their creation, these enterprises have been used to shift risks to the public sector by protecting declining industries, by bailing out ailing firms, by guaranteeing input prices to the private sector, or by shielding workers against unemployment. Many of these enterprises have suffered heavy losses, partially at least as a result of their function as a protector and insurer.

In the 1940s and 1950s, state-owned enterprises were created in Western Europe to save public utilities from going under, or to ensure that the commanding heights of the economy remained in public hands and subject to government directions. In the 1960s and 1970s these enterprises were used to protect workers against the risk of unemployment and to save private entrepreneurs in declining industries from suffering losses. Dozens of private enterprises were acquired by governments in Germany, France, Italy, the Netherlands, Sweden, and the United Kingdom in order to prevent the collapse of the firms. Thus, the hard-coal industries in Britain, France, Italy, Spain, and West Germany were brought under state ownership to avoid closure; three-quarters of the Swedish shipbuilding industry was brought under government control. Other SOEs were created to assure guaranteed employment to thousands of workers. In many of these cases, the new plants suffered heavy losses, yet were not allowed to reduce their work force. Railroads all over the world continue to lose $billions annually, yet their work force is not materially reduced.

Because of a very strong bias against governmental ownership, in the United States, state ownership is relatively restricted and is concentrated at the state rather than the federal level. Presumably for ideological reasons, the U.S. government tends to shield workers against the risk of unemployment by granting contracts to private enterprise or by the creation of pseudo-private enterprises, such as CONRAIL, rather than resorting to state ownership. Public services are also supplied through government by contract. According to one authority on the subject, the major advantage of contracts is that

they offer a detour around a conservative belief system. . . . They permit elected officials to claim balanced budgets and conservative economic policies while distributing projects and contracts funded by public debt. . . . Incentives for efficiency, productivity, and management improvement are weak in that portion of the private sector for which the government is the major customer and in which the cost-plus contract and variations of it are commonplace . . . These efforts put free enterprise rhetoric to work in extracting private profit from government expenditure [Walsh 1978].

In Israel, where free enterprise ideology is much weaker, the government has bypassed the budget when instituting new programs. Thus, "free" high school education has been financed by increasing the National Insurance levies, and billions of Israeli shekels are granted as subsidies for low rent housing through an SOE charging rents 10% of the market level. These foregone rents appear nowhere, not even in the books of the SOE.

# The Advantages and Disadvantages of Various Forms of Government Control

Public services may be financed by (*a*) general revenues, government deficits, or an increase in public debt, all of which are unrelated to the supply of the service itself; (*b*) earmarked taxes, designated to cover the costs of that service, or fees paid by the users of the service; or (*c*) the government's coercive power to force cross-subsidization of SOEs or regulated firms or to force the private sector to finance the service indirectly. Thus, defense or police services are covered by general revenues, and the cost of the service is budgeted. Toll roads in some countries, social security or the broadcasting services in others, are financed through earmarked compulsory taxes that may or may not be shown in the budget. Services such as ports, electricity supply, or the issuance of passports may be financed by collecting fees from the users. In contrast, many of the safety arrangements in factories are financed by the owners of the factory, who are compelled by law to provide such services and to finance their provision. The costs are absorbed by consumers through higher prices for protected goods, for example, for cars with safety belts. Costs of increased producers' liability for their products, for example higher insurance, are passed on to the consumer; other kinds of costs may be paid through a cross-subsidy scheme; public transportation services to thinly populated areas are cross-subsidized by higher ticket prices on other routes.

The preferred financing method for public services has been extensively discussed by economists, who have attempted to establish normative rules for public finance. It has been shown that general-fund financing can create a "fiscal illusion" on the part of the voters who have to decide separately on the size of taxes and that of expenditures. At least from that point of view, earmarked taxes should be preferred and each expenditure should be tied to its own tax (Wicksell 1896). On the other hand, Richard Wagner (1976) has posited that the more dispersed the sources of government revenues the greater the fiscal illusion would be. His hypothesis was supported by the finding of an inverse relationship between the level of local government expenditures and the degree of concentration of their tax revenues on a few (visible) tax sources. To that one might add that, to the extent that taxpayers are aware of payments for services only when they pay them directly in cash, charging for services through higher costs of goods or through losses of SOEs would be less resisted and would have less of an effect on elections. Governments in democratic societies should prefer invisible methods of raising revenues.

What are the determinants affecting the choice of organizational methods? In a world of full information, no institutional constraints, and equal distribution of talents, the organizational form used may not make any difference. In the real world, however, differences are significant. First, organizational forms differ in the degree of visibility of information about the distribution of costs and benefits, and therefore of voters' awareness of this distribution. Second, organizational forms differ in their efficiency and in the degree of discretion enjoyed by managers over such things as workers' salaries, rules for the distribution of the benefits, and vulnerability to political oscillations. Therefore, different stakeholders will prefer different organizational forms. Third, the use of certain organizational forms increases the quantity of services supplied at the expense of other costs and affects resource allocation. Fourth, different forms of organizations differ in the perception of choice rendered to the users. Finally, reorganization is sometimes used to disguise the failure of public policy to achieve its ends. Governments use a multitude of organizational forms: They supply some services directly; some through authorities, enterprises, or wholly or jointly owned legal bodies; some through voluntary organizations; some through local authorities; some through invisible methods. We focus here on the major differences between direct supply of the service, use of autonomous agencies, and invisible methods.

## DIFFERENCES IN THE DEGREE OF VISIBILITY

By definition, the supply of services is most visible when its costs are registered in the budget. Hidden costs (and revenues) are perceived as causing fewer direct confrontations, protests, and conflicts than do revenues and costs explicitly revealed. Therefore, invisible types of revenues are preferred when the size of the government is under attack, or when it is limited by constitution, or when the benefits accrue to a small group. If the public is ignorant of hidden taxes, their size and existence will not affect election results. Therefore, invisible methods enable the government to pursue policies that are contrary to its avowed goals, and to redistribute costs and benefits in ways that will not increase its size, as officially calculated. Therefore, in countries with a strong leftist bias, government services and controls are maintained openly, whereas in more conservative countries, where the belief in the superiority of the "free enterprise system" and "small government" is strong, governments are more apt to disguise taxes. As one example, Pennsylvania constitutionally restricted municipal borrowing to 7% of assessed valuation. However, government-owned corporations are exempt from this municipal debt limit. By 1973, Pennsylvania had 1872 such municipal authorities, most of which issue revenue bonds, invest the proceeds in the construction of projects designed by the sponsoring government bodies, and then lease the completed construction to a government agency for the life of the bonds. In all countries, the wider the distribution of benefits, the higher the probability that the service will be supplied through a budget-recorded outlay, either by the civil service directly or through contracting. Outlays for services that benefit the whole population, such as education, will be supplied directly by government, whereas benefits that accrue to one industry or a favored region are more likely to be disbursed in ways that are not easily traceable.

## DIFFERENCES IN EFFICIENCY AND IN VULNERABILITY TO POLITICAL OSCILLATIONS

Different stakeholders may receive greater benefits under one organizational form than under another. This point was demonstrated with regard to the invisible part of government; it is also true for state-owned enterprises, where salary scales are often higher than those of the civil service. Unlike enterprises operated directly by the government, state-owned enterprises generate their own funds. Such funds will usually be used to finance further expansion of their own services, rather than those of others.

In theory, state-owned enterprises are autonomous, flexible, and more efficient than government-bureaucracy in performing a job requiring managerial discretion, expenditious decision making, and quick reactions to changing environments. In practice, the degree of autonomy is a function of the ability of the firm to generate its own sources of fund and/or its dependence on government. Further, in practice, these enterprises have been used to increase salaries or "to avoid the vagaries of the budget" (Vernon and Aharoni, 1981; see also Anastassopolous, 1980).

SOEs are less vulnerable to political oscillation: Their operations are much less affected by changes in the administration than those operations shown in the budget. Invisible methods are even less vulnerable: Since no automatic mechanism exists for their periodic review, grants and largesse through invisible methods may continue undetected for long periods of time.

## DIFFERENCES IN THE QUANTITY OF SERVICES SUPPLIED

When a government service is provided by the civil service, its size may be limited not only by budgetary considerations but also by limits to the administrative capabilities of the government. However, when the supply of the service is moved to the market and subsidies are offered, the volume of the service has a tendency to increase: Administrative capabilities do not constrain its size, and many additional constituents have a stake in the increase of the service. Once the administrative and manpower constraint is removed, the volume of the service is expanded. Thus, when low-income housing projects were replaced by subsidized renting, a powerful lobby of contractors set to work to demand more money for such a service; when hospitalization is paid for by a national insurance scheme to private hospitals, health service costs soar. All insurance schemes involve moral hazard; that is, since the event against which insurance is taken remains at least partially under the control of the insured, the very existence of insurance may reduce the incentive to avoid carelessness.

When programs have no budgetary constraints, the actual costs to the country may be even higher. Thus, if government aids a failing industry by nationalizing it, it must formally request funding from parliament. This causes at least some public debate. If, however, the industry is aided by tariff protection, quotas, or other invisible methods, there is rarely any interest group to represent the scattered and unorganized consumers who pay more for their clothing, shoes, or television sets. Consequently, the program can burgeon, and its ability to withstand changing times without a policy change is strengthened. Of course, the story is somewhat different when another interest group is affected. Thus, a powerful car industry may lobby against higher prices for steel. Much less political pressure can be expected when the final consumer pays the cost, as, for example, in the subsidization of mail services to newspapers and other strong interest groups at the expense of first-class mail users. Invisible types of aid can thus be expected to be used to grant government largesse to small and powerful groups; the larger the dispersion of those financing the subsidy, the smaller the probability of its being reduced. In this sense, a government that is really interested in reducing the adjustment shock and not in perpetuating the infancy status of infant industries or the ailing status of declining ones, may be better off to nationalize them, thereby subjecting their subsidies to annual examination by the legislative body. Of course, in doing so the same government opens itself wide to charges of inability to manage state-owned enterprises properly, of ineptitude, and of failure to achieve desired objectives. Civil servants therefore prefer invisible methods of aid over outright nationalization.

## ORGANIZATION AND FREE CHOICE

Capitalism, when left to the discipline of the market place, has shown itself to be harsh and heartless. The deprivations suffered during depressions, the inhuman work conditions imposed in British factories during the nineteenth century, or, more recently, the problems of the near insolvency of many American cities represent the adverse effects of the unfettered operation of the market. Government intervention is widely believed capable of eliminating or alleviating the burden of such effects. Moreover, it is often argued that the government can achieve optimality where the market has failed (e.g., Baumol 1952). The latter belief sometimes fails to recognize that there are also externalities and failures in government itself.

Consider the case of health insurance. In many countries, national health services were recommended to assure that no one is deprived of health care because of inability to pay. It was widely believed that the cost of medical services would be reduced as a result of the economies of scale attendant on nationalization. According to Jewkes and Jewkes (1963, pp.59–60), such a belief turned out to be a "colossal misconception." In fact, the cost of health services soared. In the United Kingdom, a country with one of the finest national health services, costs were controlled by arbitrary ceilings. The market mechanism was replaced by queuing. The heartless decisions of the market were replaced by equally heartless decisions by government executives attempting to limit the use of medical services by allocating fewer funds.

Accumulated evidence appears to indicate that economies of scale in the field of public administration are illusory. It is important to recognize that redundancy in the number of agencies dealing with a problem does not necessarily imply inefficiency. Competition among the agencies may seem chaotic, but may also result in better systems, more experimentation, and more innovation. Moreover, the larger the public sector, the more important it is to avoid the standardization and centralization of all systems, in order to preserve individual freedom. Thus, unless there is compelling evidence to the contrary, a large number of competing agencies is preferable to one large agency. The market mechanism, even when distorted to allow for equitable distribution of income, has long been recognized as the best allocator of scarce resources.

Choice is enhanced when decisions regarding the use of services are left to the individual. A well-known example is Friedman's (1962) suggestion of a voucher system in which individuals can choose the institution in which their children will be educated. The same choice can be allowed to suppliers. The United States government aids charitable institutions by recognizing contributions made to them as tax deductions. It keeps track of the cost to the treasury, but without showing it in the budget. The ability to write off charitable contributions gives the rich much more power than the poor in allocating resources to nonprofit institutions and may benefit universities or museums more than old-age homes. However, the decisions are made by millions of individual taxpayers, and thousands of organizations have a chance of appealing for their cause. In contrast, direct distribution by the government may appear more equitable, but may, in fact, cause petty tyranny by allowing a government official to be the only judge of a worthy cause. If government wants to allocate these resources, an allocation of the funds among several competing government agencies may be a superior solution.

## REORGANIZATION AS A MEANS OF SHIFTING RESPONSIBILITY

In many cases, services are moved to another organization because the organization previously responsible failed to accomplish its task. In several countries, post office departments were made autonomous agencies because of public complaints, if not outcries, about the level of the service. Similarly, the U.S. government designed the Model Cities program to give responsibility to local authorities for objectives such as urban redevelopment and hardcore employment after having failed to achieve results itself. The new agencies may not have greater success in solving the problem, but the very act of reorganization shifts responsibility and gives the impression that the problem can be solved, or that a solution is about to be achieved.

## OBJECTIVES AND ORGANIZATIONAL FORM

No organizational form is well suited for all purposes and no organizational form consistently dominates all others. Goals must be clearly stated before one method can be selected over others. Objectives in the public sector are often vague and conflicting. Different persons emphasize different objectives and therefore advocate different organizational solutions. For example, if the objective is to ensure that government hiring practices are based on objective standards of merit rather than on political patronage, the standardization of internal hiring procedures is a desirable policy. If on the other hand, the objective is to increase the efficiency of a given service, then standardization of hiring procedures may hinder the achievement of the goal. It may be desirable to offer higher salaries to accountants to attract them to the government, or to allow instructors to experiment with different educational innovations, or grant money incentives to managers. If one believes that government should centrally allocate all resources, one would oppose any kind of organizational shelter that allowed a certain part of the government to use the proceeds of an earmarked tax or the revenues from the sale of a service it grants, to improve or expand the service in question. If one views accountability as the preeminent value, one would have different prescriptions for the way state-owned enterprises should be operated than if one looks for pure economic efficiency.

## Conclusion

The prescription of a particular organizational system depends upon one's objectives, one's priorities, and the degree of transparency sought. The supply of services directly by the government ensures the greatest degree of standardization. It also ensures the greatest degree of visibility and accountability. State-owned enterprises, being independent bodies, may be more efficient in supplying a specialized service that calls for more autonomy, less standardization of procedures, and an ability to make expeditious decisions. They are generally more flexible in adapting themselves to a changing environment. Such enterprises, however, achieve their autonomy mainly because they are not subject to the general civil service and other regulations in areas such as personnel policies and procurement, and from their ability to finance themselves. Therefore, when standardization of these policies is important, SOEs are not desirable.

Self-financing is the basis for autonomy of an enterprise. If the enterprise is financed through revenues, fees, or earmarked taxes, it can hope to achieve autonomy. The more funds the enterprise generates, the greater the degree of autonomy. It can use these funds to achieve prescribed goals, and to increase payments to certain stakeholders, notably its employees. Not surprisingly, there is a tendency to shift the supply of services financed through earmarked taxes or fees to services supplied by independent authorities. Thus, employees of such bodies as the post office, airports, or the railroad will press for independence in the hope that this will bring them higher salaries.

To be sure, in many cases there are much more mundane reasons for the use of a certain organization: historical accident, tradition, the desire to allow participation of nongovernment sources of funds in a certain venture. Governments seem continually to be reorganizing the way they supply their services and the way they combine their different parts. The commissioning of a reorganization play may provide the government with a respite; it justifies government's declining to act until the reorganization is over. Reorganization can also be used to delay a program or to create the impression that a cure is available. Reorganizations are not designed to achieve discernible cuts in governmental size. Organizational changes are justified by improved operations rather than by reduction of expenditures. Those hoping for a swift reduction in government size and a dramatic diminishing of its scope of operations should attempt to reduce the demands on the government rather than look for a cure through changing organizational methods.

# References

Aharoni, Y. 1981. *The no risk society.* Chatham, N.J.: Chatham House Publishers.

Allison, G. 1971. *Essence of decision.* Boston: Little Brown and Co.

Anastassopolous, J.P. 1980. *La strategie des entreprises publiques.* Paris: Dalloz.

Baumol, W.W. 1952. *Welfare economics and the theory of the state.* Cambridge, Mass.: Harvard University Press.

Breton, A. 1974, *The economic theory of representative government.* London: Aldline Treatises in Modern Economics, Macmillan.

Buchanan, J. 1975. *The limits of liberty: Between anarchy and leviathan.* Chicago: University of Chicago Press.

Downs, A. 1957. *An economic theory of democracy.* New York: Harper and Row.

Friedman, M. 1962. *Capitalism and freedom.* Chicago: University of Chicago Press.

Jewkes, J., and Jewkes, S. 1963. *Value for money in medicine.* Oxford: Basil Blackwell.

Klein, R. 1976. The politics of public expenditure: American theory and British practice. *British Journal of Political Science* 6: 410–411.

Miller, A.S. 1971. Accountability and the federal contractor. *Journal of Public Law* 20: 473.

Mueller, D.C. 1979. *Public choice.* Cambridge, England: Cambridge University Press.

O'Connor, J. 1974. *The corporation and the state.* New York: Harper and Row.

Vernon, R., and Aharoni, Y. 1981. *State-owned enterprises in the Western Economies.* London: Croom Helm.

Wagner, R.E. 1976. Revenue structure, fiscal illusion, and budgetary choice. *Public Choice* 25: 45–61.

Walsh, A.H. 1978. *The public's business: The politics and practices of government corporations.* Cambridge, Mass.: MIT Press.

Wicksell, K. 1896. A new principle of just taxation. In *Classics in the theory of Public Finance,* ed. R.T. Musgrave and A.T. Peacock. New York: St. Martin's Press. P. 73.

# III

# Evaluation Research:
# Concepts and Issues

*This section is devoted to evaluation research as a field of practice. Rossi and Berk review the "state of the art" in evaluation research at the beginning of the 1980s, and they show how evaluation can be adapted to stages of policymaking. They point to the issues with which evaluators have to grapple: accuracy of measurement, alternative causal explanations, the generalizability of findings, etc. These authors point to the potential contribution of social science theory to the improvement of policy evaluation. Specific methodological and theoretical issues in the evaluation of organizational performance are the common focus of two very different chapters. Spilerman and Litwak examine the manner in which the reward systems of institution affect the quality of service and the well-being of inmate. Doron and On see organizational slack as a key to the evaluation of organizational performance and propose that experience curves serve as tools for the measurement of slack.*

*The two remaining chapters in this section concern the implementation of social policies and programs in specific areas. Aviram uses published data on budgets, patients, and manpower to assess the implementation of a reform in the field of mental health. Spiro and Liron use a variety of methods to assess the target efficiency of a recreation program. Their work provides empirical evidence for some of the arguments raised in the chapters of Edelman and Doron in Part II while raising some methodological issues relevant to the evaluation of equity in welfare programs.*

# 10

# The Scope of Evaluation Activities in the United States

## PETER H. ROSSI AND RICHARD A. BERK

The purpose of this chapter is to provide a detailed introduction to the variety of purposes for which evaluation research may be used and to the range of methods that are currently employed in the practice of that field. Specific examples are given wherever appropriate to provide concrete illustrations of both the goals of evaluation researches and the methods used.

While the coverage of this chapter is intended to be comprehensive in the sense of describing major uses of evaluation research, it cannot even pretend to be encyclopedic, so references to more detailed discussions of topics are provided. In addition, there are several general references that survey the field of evaluation in a more detailed fashion (Cronbach 1980; Guttentag and Struening 1975; Rossi, Freeman, and Wright 1979; Suchman 1967; Weiss 1972).

## Policy Issues and Evaluation Reseach

Virtually all evaluation research begins with one or more policy questions. Evaluation research may be conducted to answer questions that arise during the formulation of policy, in the design of programs, in the improvement of programs, and in testing the efficiency and effectiveness of programs that are in place or being considered. Specific policy questions may be concerned with how widespread a social problem may be, whether any program can be enacted that will ameliorate a problem, whether programs are effective, whether a program is producing enough benefits to justify its cost, and so on.

EVALUATING THE WELFARE STATE:
SOCIAL AND POLITICAL PERSPECTIVES

Given the diversity of policy questions to be answered, it should not be surprising that there is no single "best way" to proceed and that evaluation research must draw on a variety of perspectives and on a pool of varied procedures. Thus, approaches that might be useful for determining what activities were actually undertaken under some educational program, for instance, might not be appropriate to determine whether the program was worth the money spent. Similarly, techniques that may be effective in documenting how a program is functioning on a daily basis may prove inadequate for the task of assessing the program's ultimate impact. In other words, appropriate evaluation techniques derive and must be linked explicitly to each of the policy questions posed. Although this point may seem simple enough, it has been far too often overlooked, often resulting in forced fits between an evaluator's preferred method and particular questions. Another result is an evaluation research literature padded with empty, sectarian debates between warring camps of "true believers." For example, there has been a long and somewhat tedious controversy about whether assessments of the impact of social programs are best undertaken with research designs in which subjects are randomly assigned to experimental and control groups *or* through theoretically derived causal models of how the program works. In fact, the two approaches are complementary and can be effectively wedded (e.g., Rossi, Berk, and Lenihan 1980).

To obtain a better understanding of the fit between evaluation questions and the requisite evaluation procedures, it is useful to distinguish between two broad evaluation contexts, as follows:

*Policy and program formation contexts*: Contexts in which policy questions are being raised about the natures and amounts of social problems, whether appropriate policy actions can be taken, and whether programs that may be proposed are appropriate and effective.

*Existing policy and existing program contexts*: Contexts in which the issues are whether appropriate policies are being pursued and whether existing programs are achieving their intended effects.

Although these two broad contexts may be regarded as stages in a progression from the recognition of a policy need to the installation and testing of programs designed to meet those policy needs, it is often the case that the unfolding of a program in actuality may bypass some evaluation activities. For example, Head Start and the Job Corps were started with minimum amounts of preprogram testing: Indeed, the issue of whether Head Start was or was not effective did not surface until some years after the program had been in place, and the Job Corps has just recently (1.5 decades after enactment) been evaluated in a sophisticated way (Mathematica 1980). Similarly, many programs apparently never get beyond the testing stage, either because they are shown to be ineffective or troublesome (e.g., contract learning, Gramlich and

Koshel, 1975) or because the policy issues to which they were addressed shifted in the meantime (e.g., as in the case of negative income tax proposals, Rossi and Lyall, 1976).

Unfortunately, a statement that evaluation techniques must respond to the questions that are posed at different stages of a program's life history only takes us part of the way. At the very least, it is necessary to specify criteria that may be used to select appropriate evaluation procedures, given one or more particular policy questions. For example, randomized experiments are an extremely powerful method for answering some of the questions posed as part of program design issues, but may be largely irrelevant to or ineffective for answering questions associated with program implementation issues. Yet, such terms as *powerful*, *relevant*, and *ineffective* are hardly precise; the four criteria offered here would seem far more instructive.

First, one must consider whether the measurement procedures that are being proposed are likely to capture accurately what they are supposed to measure. Sometimes such concerns with measurement quality are considered under the rubric of "construct validity" (Cook and Campbell, 1979), and are germane to *all* empirical work regardless of the question being asked.

It is important to stress that questions about measurement quality apply not only to program outcomes such as "learning," but also to measures of the program (intervention) itself and to other factors that may be at work (e.g., a child's motivation to learn).

Finally, although we will not get into a thorough discussion of measurement issues in evaluation research, two generic kinds of measurement errors should be distinguished. On one hand, measurement may be subject to bias that reflects a *systematic* disparity between indicator(s) and an underlying "true" attribute that is being gauged. (The role of *random* measurement error is sometimes addressed through the concept of "reliability.") On the other hand, measures may be flawed because of *random* error or "noise." Whether approached as an "errors in variables" problem as in the econometric literature (e.g., Kmenta 1971, pp. 309–322) or as the "underadjustment" problem in the evaluation literature (e.g., Campbell and Erlebacher 1970), random error can lead to decidedly nonrandom distortions in evaluation results. (for a recent discussion see Barnow, Cain, and Goldberger, 1980).

Second, many evaluation questions concern causal relations such as, for example, whether or not a specific proposed program of bilingual education will improve the English language reading achievement of program participants, that is, whether exposure to a program will "cause" changes in reading achievement. Whenever a causal relationship is proposed, alternative explanations must be addressed and, presumably, discarded. If such alternatives are not considered, one may be led to make "spurious" causal inferences; the causal relationship being proposed may not in fact exist. Sometimes this concern with spurious causation is addressed under the heading of "internal validity" (Cook and

Campbell 1979) and, as in the case of construct validity, is relevant regardless of stage in a program's life history (assuming causal relationships are at issue).

The consideration of alternative causal explanations for the working of social programs is an extremely important research design consideration. For example, programs that deal with humans are all subject more or less to problems of self-selection; often enough persons who are most likely to be helped or who are already on the road to recovery are those most likely to participate in a program. Thus, vocational training offered to unemployed adults is likely to attract those who would be most apt to improve their employment situation in any event. Or sometimes operators "cream the best" among target populations to participate in programs, thereby assuring that such programs appear to be successful. Or, in other cases, events unconnected with the program produce improvements which appear to be the result of the program; an improvement in employment for their parents, for instance, may make it more likely that adolescents will stay in and complete their high school training.

Third, whatever the empirical conclusions resulting from evaluation research during any of the three program stages, it is necessary to consider how broadly one can generalize the findings in question; that is, are the findings relevant to other times, other subjects, similar programs, and other program sites? Sometimes such concerns are raised under the rubric of "external validity" (Cook and Campbell 1979), and again, the question is germane to all program stages and regardless of evaluation method.

Generalization issues ordinarily arise around several types of extensions of findings. For instance, are the findings appliable to cities, agencies, or school systems other than the ones in which they were found? Or are the results specific to the organizations in which the program was tested? Another issue that arises is whether a program's results would be applicable to students who are different in abilities or socioeconomic background. For example, *Sesame Street* was found to help preschool children from lower socioeconomic families, but it also helped children from middle-class families (Cook *et al.* 1975). Or, curricula that work well in junior colleges may not be appropriate for students in senior colleges.

There is also the problem of generalizing over time. For example, Maynard and Murnane (1979) found that transfer payments provided by the Gary Income Maintenance Experiment apparently increased the reading scores of children from the experimental families. One possible explanation is that with income subsidies, parents (especially in single-parent families) were able to work less and therefore spend more time with their children. Even if this is true, it raises the question of whether similar effects would still be found now that inflation is taking a much bigger bite out of the purchasing power of households. Finally, it is impossible to introduce precisely the same treatment(s) when studies are replicated or when programs move from the development to the demonstration stage. Hence, one is always faced with trying to generalize across treatments that can rarely be exactly identical. In summary, external validity surfaces as a function of the subjects of an evaluation, the setting, the historical period, and the treatment itself. Another way of viewing this issue is to consider that programs vary in their "robustness;" that is, in their ability to produce the same results under varying circumstances, with different operators, and at different historical times. Clearly, a "robust" program is highly desirable.

Finally, it is always important to consider that whatever one's empirical assessments, the role of chance must be properly taken into account. Formal, quantitative findings are sometimes considered under the heading "statistical conclusion validity" (Cook and Campbell 1979) and the problem is whether tests for "statistical significance" have been properly undertaken. For example, although Head Start children appear to perform better in early grades, the observed differences in performance could easily result from chance factors having nothing to do with the program. Unless the role of these chance factors is formally assessed, it is impossible to determine if the apparent program effects are real or illusory. Similar issues appear in ethnographic work as well, although formal assessments of the role of chance are difficult to undertake in such studies. Nevertheless, it is important to ask whether the reported findings rest on observed behavioral patterns that occurred with sufficient frequency and stability to warrant the conclusions that they are not "simply" the result of chance.

Three types of factors play a role in producing apparent (chance) effects that are not "real." The first reflects sampling error and occurs whenever one is trying to make statements about some population of interest from observations gathered on a subset of that population. For example, one might actually be studying a sample of students from the population attending a particular school, or a sample of teachers from the population of teachers in a particular school system, or even a sample of schools from a population of schools within a city, county, or state. Yet, although it is typically more economical to work with samples, the process of sampling *necessarily* introduces the prospect that any conclusions based on the sample may well differ from conclusions that might have been reached had the full poulation been studied instead. Indeed, one could well imagine obtaining different results from different subsets of the population.

Although any subset that is selected from a larger population for study purposes may be called a sample, some subsets may be worse than having no observations at all. The act of sampling must be accomplished according to rational selection procedures that guard against the introduction of selection bias. A class of such sampling procedures that yield unbiased samples are called probability samples, in which every element in a population has a known chance of being selected (Kish 1965; Sudman 1976). Probability samples are difficult to execute and are often quite expensive, especially when dealing with populations that are difficult to locate in space. Yet there are such clear advantages to such samples, as opposed to haphazard and potentially biased methods of selecting subjects, that probability samples are almost always to be preferred over less rational methods. (See Sudman, 1976, for examples of relatively simple and inexpensive probability sampling designs.)

A second kind of chance factor stems from the process by which experimental subjects may be assigned to experimental and control groups. For example, it may turn out that the assignment process yields an experimental group that on the average contains brighter students than the control group. As suggested earlier, this may confound any genuine treatment effects with a priori differences between experimentals and controls; here the impact of some positive treatment such as self-paced instruction will be artificially enhanced because the experimentals were already performing better than the controls.

Much as in the case of random sampling, when the assignment is undertaken with probability procedures, the role of chance factors can be taken into account. In particular, it is possible to determine the likelihood that outcome differences between experimentals and controls are statistically significant. If the disparities are statistically significant, chance (through the assignment process) is eliminated as an explanation, and the evaluator can then begin making substantive sense of the results. If the process by which some units get the treatment and others do not is *not* a random process, one risks a "sample selection" *bias* that cannot be assessed with statistical inference. It is also possible to place confidence intervals around estimates of the treatment effect(s), which are usually couched as differences between the means on one or more outcome measures when the experimentals are compared to the controls. Again, an estimate of the "wiggle" is produced; in this case the wiggle refers to estimates of the difference in outcome between the experimental group and the control group.

A third kind of chance factor has *nothing* to do with research design interventions undertaken by the researcher (i.e., random sampling or random assignment). Rather, it surfaces *even if the total population of interest is studied and no assignment process or sampling is undertaken.* In brief, if one proceeds with the assumption that whatever the program processes at work, there will be also at work forces that have *some* impact, but not *systematically*, on outcomes of interest. Typically, these are viewed as a large number of small, random perturbations that on the average cancel out. For example, performance on a reading test may be affected by a child's mood, the amount of sleep on the previous night, the content of the morning's breakfast, a recent quarrel with a sibling, distractions in the room where the test is taken, anxiety about the test's consequences, and the like. Although these each introduce small amounts of variation in a child's performance, their aggregate impact is taken to be zero on the average (i.e., their expected value is zero). Yet, since the aggregate impact is only zero *on the average*, the performance of particular students on particular days *will* be altered. Thus, there will be *chance* variation in performance that needs to be taken into account. As before, one can apply tests of statistical inference or confidence intervals. One can still ask, for example, if some observed difference between experimentals and control is larger than might be expected from these chance factors and/or estimate the wiggle in experimental–control disparities.

It is important to stress that statistical conclusion validity tells us something about the quality of inferential methods applied and *not* whether some result is statistically significant. Statistical conclusion validity may be high or low independent of judgments about statistical significance. (For a more thorough discussion of these and other issues of statistical inference in evaluation research, see Berk and Brewer, 1978.)

In summary, evaluation research involves a number of questions linked to different stages in a program's life history. Appropriate evaluation tools must be selected with such stages in mind, and against the four criteria just discussed. In other words, at each stage, one or more policy-relevant questions may be raised. Then, evaluation procedures should be selected with an eye to their relative strengths and weaknesses with respect to: measurement quality, an ability to weigh alternative causal explanations, the prospects for generalizing, and their capabilities for assessing the role of chance.

In the next few pages the general issues just raised will be addressed in more depth. However, before proceeding, it is important to note that in the "real world" of evaluation research, even when an ideal marriage is made between the evaluation questions being posed and the empirical techniques to be employed, practical constraints may intervene. That is, questions of cost, timeliness, political feasibility, and other difficulties may prevent the ideal from being realized. This in turn will require the development of a "second best" evaluation package (or even third best), more attuned to what is possible in practice. On the other hand, practical constraints do not in any way validate a dismissal of technical concerns; if anything, technical concerns become even more salient when less desirable evaluation procedures are employed.

## Policy Issues and Corresponding Evaluation Strategies

This section will consider each of the major policy and program questions, in turn, and will identify the evaluation research strategies best fitted to provide answers to each of them.

As indicated earlier, the organization of this section does not mean to imply that policymakers always ask each of the questions raised, in the order shown. The questions are arranged from the more general to the more specific, but that is an order we have imposed; it is not intended to be a description of typical sequences, or even a description of any sequence. Indeed, often enough, for example, research that uncovers the extent and depth of a social problem may spark the need for policy change, rather than vice versa as may appear to be implied in this section.

## POLICY FORMATION AND PROGRAM DESIGN ISSUES

We first consider policy questions that arise in the policy formation and program design stage. Policy changes presumably arise out of dissatisfaction with existing policy or existing programs, or out of the realization that a problem exists for which a new policy may be an appropriate remedy. The information needed by policymakers and administrators is that which would make the policy and accompanying programs relevant to the problem as identified, and efficacious in providing relief from at least some of the problem's burdens.

It is important that it be understood that we do not presuppose that the solutions sought by policymakers are ones which would solve the social problems in question as seen in some objective sense, but only that the problem *as experienced and understood* by the policymaker is to be addressed. Thus, from the perspective of policymakers, eradicating poverty may not be the goal so much as lowering the level of expressed concern with the problem of poverty, as experienced by the decision makers. Problem oriented "rationality" on the part of decision makers is not one of the assumptions concerning policymakers maintained in this chapter.

It is also important to stress that defining a "social problem" is ultimately a *political* process whose outcomes are not simply an assessment of available information. Thus, although it would be hard to argue against providing the best possible data on potential areas of need, there is no necessary correspondence between patterns in those data and what eventually surfaces as a subject of concern. (See, for example, Berk and Rossi, 1976, for a more thorough discussion.)

### Where Is the Problem and How Big Is It? The Needs Assessment Question

These are questions that seek to understand the distribution and extent of a given social problem. Thus, it is one thing to recognize that some children are learning at a rate that is too slow to allow them to leave elementary schools sufficiently prepared for high school, and it is quite another to know that this problem is more characteristic of poor children and of minorities and more frequently encountered in inner-city schools. It does not take more than a few instances of slow learning to document that a learning problem exists. To provide sufficient information about the numbers of children who are in that deprived condition and to identify specific school systems with heavy concentrations of such children is quite another task. Similar questions arise with respect to other conditions that constitute the recognized social problems of our times, for example, the distribution of quality medical care, adequate housing, pressing poverty.

There are numerous examples of needs assessments that might be cited. Indeed, the monthly measurement of the labor force is perhaps the most extensive effort at needs assessment, providing monthly estimates of levels of unemployment and structural and area distribution. The Office of Economic Opportunity's 1968 Survey of Economic Opportunity was designed to provide a finer-grained assessment of the extent and distribution of poverty in urban areas than was available through the decennial census. The Coleman *et al.* (1967) report of educational opportunity was mandated by Congress to provide an assessment of how educational services and facilities were distributed by race and socioeconomic status.

The number of local needs assessments covering single municipalities, towns, or counties done every year must now mount to the thousands. The 1974 Community Mental Health legislation calls for community mental health need assessments to be undertaken periodically. Social impact statements to be prepared in advance of large-scale alterations in the environment often call for estimates of the numbers of persons or households to be affected or to be served. The quality of such local assessments varies widely, and is most likely quite poor on the average. The main problems in attaining high-quality needs assessments lie in the fact that the measurement of social problems of the more subtle variety (e.g., mental health) is quite difficult, and high-quality surveying methods are often beyond the reach of the talents and funds available.

It should be noted that the research effort involved in providing answers to the needs assessment question may be as inexpensive as copying relevant information from printed volumes of the U.S. Census, or may require several years' effort in the design, fielding, and analysis of a large-scale sample survey. Moreover, needs assessments do not have to be undertaken solely with quantitative techniques. Ethnographic research may also be instructive, especially in getting detailed knowledge of the specific nature of the needs in question. For example, the development of vocational training programs in secondary schools should respond to an understanding of precisely what sorts of job-related skills are lacking in some target population. Perhaps the real need has more to do with how one finds a job commensurate with one's abilities than with an overall lack of skills per se (Liebow 1967). On the other hand, when the time comes to assess the extent of the problem, there is no substitute for formal quantitative procedures. Stated a bit starkly, ethnographic procedures are likely to be especially effective in determining the *nature* of the need. Quantitative procedures are, however, essential when the *extent* of the need is considered.

Although needs assessment research is ordinarily undertaken primarily to develop accurate estimates of the amounts and distribution of a given problem, and hence is intended to be descriptive, often enough such research can also yield some understanding of the processes involved in generating the problem in question. For example, a search for information on how many high-school students study a foreign language may bring to light the fact that many schools do not offer such courses, and hence that part of the problem is that universally available opportunities to learn foreign languages may not exist. Or, the fact that many primary-school children of low socioeconomic backgrounds appear to be tired and listless in class may be associated with a finding that few such children ate anything for breakfast before coming to school. A program that provided in-school breakfast feeding of poor children may be suggested by the findings of this needs assessment.

Particularly important for uncovering process information of this sort are carefully and sensitively conducted ethnographic studies. Thus, ethnographic studies of disciplinary problems within high schools may be able to point out promising leads as to why some schools have fewer disciplinary problems than others, in addition to providing some indication of how widespread problems associated with discipline are. The findings on why schools differ might serve to suggest useful ways in which new programs could be designed that would help to bring all schools in line with those that are currently better at handling discipline issues. Thus, Conant's (1959) qualitative survey of American high schools suggested ways in which American high schools could be improved by contrasting the educational practices in "successful high schools" with "average" and "poor" schools.

Indeed, the history of ups and downs of public concern for social problems provides many examples of how qualitative studies (e.g., Lewis 1965; Liebow 1967; Riis 1890), and sometimes novels (e.g., Sinclair 1906; Steinbeck 1939), raised public consciousness about particular social problems. Sometimes the works in question are skillful combinations of the qualitative and quantitative, as in the case of Harrington (1962), whose *Other America* contained much publicly available data interlaced with graphic descriptions of the living conditions endured by the poor.

*Can We Do Anything about a Problem? Policy-Oriented General Research*

Knowing the distribution and extent of a problem does not of itself lead to programs that can help to ameliorate that problem. In order to design programs, we have to call upon two sorts of knowledge: first, basic social science understanding of a problem helps to point out the leverage points that may be used to change the distribution and extent of a problem. Second, we need to know something about the institutional arrangements that are implicated in a problem so that workable policies and programs can be designed. For example, our basic understanding of how students learn might suggest that lengthening the school day would be an effective way of increasing the rate of learning of certain skills. In constructing a program, however, we would have to take into account that lengthening the school day is a matter that would concern teachers and their organizations as well as factors involving the physical capacities of schools, and other persons involved, such as parents and school-infra structure personnel.

Another example may help to illustrate the complexity of the problems that arise in the design of appropriate programs. To know that there exist learning disabilities among school children does not of itself suggest what would be an appropriate policy response. To construct a policy response that has a chance to ameliorate educational problems typically means that one ought to call upon some valid theories about how such problems arise and/or how such problems could be reduced. Appropriate knowledge useful to policy formation would consist of theories that link learning disabilities to school experiences. Note that it is not crucial that learning disabilities be created by school experiences, only that school experiences influence to some appreciable degree the development of learning disabilities. There is little that policy can do (at least in the short run) about those causes of learning disabilities having their roots in factors that are traditionally thought to be outside the sphere of policy relevance. Hence, knowledge about the role of family relationships in learning disabilities is not policy relevant (at present) because it concerns matters with which the policy sphere traditionally has not concerned itself. In contrast, research and knowledge dealing with the effects of schools, teachers, educational facilities, and the like, are currently policy relevant because social policy has been directed toward changing schools, the supply of educational facilities, the quality of teachers, and similar issues.

This conception of policy relevant research is one that causes considerable misunderstanding concerning the relationships between basic and applied social research. A policy oriented research is one that tries to model how policy changes can affect the phenomenon in question. Knowledge about the phenomenon per se—the province of basic disciplinary concerns—may be important to understand how policy might be changed to alter the course of the social problem in question, but much basic research often is not. For example, laboratory studies of learning processes or of the development of aggression in persons may not be at all useful to educational policymakers or to criminal justice officials. Perhaps the clearest way to describe the difference is to say that policy oriented research and basic research are not contradictory or in conflict with each other but that, in addition to understanding basic processes, policy oriented research must also be concerned with the connections between the phenomenon and how policies and programs may affect the phenomenon in question.

Thus, although basic researchers may be most interested in accounting for as much of the variance as possible by positing general processes, policy oriented research is more likely to be interested in how much can be affected by policy factors that in total explain very little of the variance in human behavior. For example, researchers often find that some 80% of the explained variance in recidivism can be accounted for by a felon's previous record, whereas an effective policy may be one that accounts for at maximum 10% of the explained variance. Thus, basic researchers can safely ignore policy effects because they do not explain much, whereas policy researchers must search carefully for such relatively weak inputs into the problem in question (Rossi, *et al.* 1980).

In addition, to construct a program that is likely to be adopted by an organization, we need to have intimate knowledge of what could motivate that system to change and adopt the new procedure and to use it at an appropriate level of effort. Large scale organziations—schools, factories, social agencies, and the like—are resistant to change, especially when the changes do not involve corresponding accommodations in reward systems. For example, an educational program that is likely to work is one that provides positive incentives for school systems, schools, and individual teachers to support and adopt the changes in learning practices embodied in the program.

Inadequate attention to the organizational contexts of programs is one of the more frequent sources of program implementation failure. Mandating that a particular program be delivered by an agency that is insufficiently motivated to do so, or is poorly prepared to do so, and/or has personnel that do not have the skills to do so is a sure recipe for degraded and weakened interventions. Indeed, sometimes no programs at all are delivered under such circumstances (Rossi 1978).

Answers to the question, Can we do anything about the problem? can come from a variety of sources. Existing basic research efforts (whatever the method) aimed at understanding general social processes are one source, although mastering this diverse technical literature is often difficult. Commissioned review papers may be an easy way to bring together in a predigested form the set of relevant existing basic research findings.

It should be noted that basic research is often enough not useful to policy needs because policy relevant concerns have not been directly addressed in the research. For example, studies of children who present disciplinary problems in school may stress understanding the links between the family situations of the children and their behavior. But, for policy and programmatic purposes, it would be considerably more useful if the researchers had spent at least some effort studying how various school disciplinary systems affect the rates at which disciplinary problems appeared. Policy mutable variables (those that can be changed by policy) often tend to be slighted in basic research since policy is ordinarily only a small contributor to the total causal system that gives rise to a problem.

General research consciously linked to the roles that relevant major public institutions—schools, police, courts, and so on—generally play in modifying the incidence of social problems may be the best answer to policy needs. Such research would pay special attention to policy mutable conditions of individual and household behavior. Policy relevant general research may take a variety of forms, ranging all the way from systematic observational studies to carefully controlled randomized experiments that systematically vary the policy relevant experiences of subjects.

## Will Some Particular Program Work?

When some particular program has been identified that appears to be sensible according to current basic knowledge in the field, the next step is to see whether it is effective enough to be worth developing into a program. It is at this point that we recommend the use of *randomized* controlled experiments to test the candidate programs. This form of research is extremely powerful in detecting program effects, because randomly allocating persons (or other units, e.g., classes) to an experimental group (to which the tested program is administered) or to a control group (from whom the program is withheld) assures that all the factors that ordinarily affect the educational process in question are on the average distributed identically among those who receive the program and those who do not. Therefore, randomization on the average eliminates causal processes that may be confounded with the educational intervention and hence enormously enhances internal validity. That is, the problem of spurious interpretations can be quite effectively addressed.

We advocate the use of randomized experiments at this stage in the development of a program both because they are powerful and because a potentially useful program ought to have the best chance of working when administered in a program run by dedicated researchers. However, this commitment in no way undermines the complementary potential of ethnographic studies, particularly to document *why* a particular intervention succeeds or fails.

Developmental experiments should be conducted ordinarily on a relatively modest scale, and they are most useful to policy needs when they test a set of alternative programs intended to achieve the same effects. Thus, it would be more useful for an experiment to test several ways of ameliorating learning disabilities, since the end result would be to provide information on the relative effectiveness of several different methods that a priori seemed equally attractive.

There are many good examples of field testing through randomized experiments of promising programs, for instance, the five income-maintenance experiments conducted in the United States in recent years were devised to test under varying conditions the impact of negative income tax plans as substitutes for existing welfare programs (Kershaw and Fair 1976; Rossi and Lyall 1976). The Department of Labor tested the extension of unemployment benefit coverage to prisoners released from state prisons in a small randomized experiment conducted in Baltimore (Lenihan 1976). Randomized experiments have also been used to test national health insurance plans, as well as direct cash subsidies for housing to poor families. At issue in most of the randomized experiments were whether the proposed programs would produce the effects intended, and whether undesirable side effects could be kept at a minimum. Thus, the Department of Labor LIFE experiment (Lenihan 1976) was designed to see whether released felons' adjustment to civilian life could be eased through increased employment and lowered arrest rates. The most extended series of developmental experiments is that reported by Fairweather and Tornatzky (1977), a series that extended over 2 decades of consistent refinement and retesting, and resulted in an efficacious and replicable treatment that can be implemented in a variety of conditions.

### Can Agencies Deliver an Effective Program? Field Testing the Program

Once an effective treatment has been isolated, the next question is whether a program incorporating the treatment can be administered through some public or private agency. Implementation of programs is always problematic. Agencies are no different from other organizations in resisting changes that are unfamiliar and perhaps threatening. Interventions that work well when administered by dedicated researchers often fail when left to less skillful and less dedicated persons, in federal, state, or local agencies, or in the private sector. Hence, it is necessary to test whether agencies can deliver interventions at the proper dosage levels and without significant distortions. Randomized controlled experiments as previously described are again an extremely powerful tool, and appropriately designed randomized experiments should compare several possible modes of delivery.

Although implementations may be fruitfully studied through randomized experiments, descriptive accounts of implementation may be just as valuable and considerably less expensive. For example, just a few visits to high schools that were supposed to have implemented a widely publicized program designed to raise the academic motivation of poor black children revealed that the programs existed mainly on paper and in the public relations releases of the main sponsor (Murray 1980). Similarly, careful qualitative field visits to the sites of the celebrated Cities in Schools project brought to light that the project as implemented fell far short of original designs and intentions (Murray 1981).

For some programs, systematic field testing had to be undertaken on a large scale. For example, the Department of Housing and Urban Development commissioned 10 cities to carry out demonstrations of housing allowance programs in order to ascertain how best to administer such programs, leaving it to each city housing agency to set up its housing allowance program within the broad limits of specified payment levels and rules for client eligibility. Following up on the LIFE experiment noted earlier, the TARP experiments funded by the Department of Labor provide another example: Two states were chosen to run a program that provided eligibility for unemployment benefits to persons released from prisons. Each state ran the program as a randomized experiment with payments through its Employment Security Agency (Rossi, Berk, and Lenihan 1980).

## ACCOUNTABILITY EVALUATION

Once a program has been enacted and is functioning, one of the main questions that is asked concerns whether or not the program is in place appropriately. Here the issues are not whether the program is achieving its intended effects, as much as whether the program is running in ways that are appropriate, and whether problems have arisen in the field. Programs often have to be fine-tuned in the first few years or so of operation. (For this reason, estimates of effectiveness should be made only when any necessary "shakedown period" is over.)

### Is the Program Reaching the Appropriate Beneficiaries?

Achieving appropriate coverage of beneficiaries is also often problematic. Sometimes a program simply may be inadvertently designed so as to be unable to reach and serve significant portions of the total intended beneficiary population. For example, a program designed to provide food subsidies to children who spend their days in child care facilities may fail to reach a large proportion of such children if regulations exclude child care facilities that are serving fewer than five children. A very large proportion of children who are cared for during the day outside their own households are cared for by women who take a few children into their homes (Abt Associates 1979).

Although a thorough needs assessment of child care problems would have brought to light the fact that so large a proportion of child care was furnished by small-scale vendors, and hence should have been taken into account in drawing up administrative regulations, such might not have been the case. In addition, patterns of the problem might change over time, sometimes in response to the existence of a program. Hence there is some need to review from time to time how many of the intended beneficiaries are being covered by a program.

Experience with social programs over the past 2 decades has shown that there are few programs, if any, that achieve full coverage or near full coverage of intended beneficiaries, especially where coverage depends on positive actions on the part of beneficiaries. Thus, not all persons who are eligible for social security payments actually apply for them; estimates of nonapplication rates range up to 15% of all eligible beneficiaries. Still others may not be reached because facilities for delivering the services involved are not accessible to them; and so on.

There is also another side to the coverage problem. Programs may cover and extend benefits to persons or organizations that were not intended to be served. Such unwanted coverage may be impossible to avoid because of the ways in which the program is delivered. For example, although *Sesame Street* was designed primarily to reach disadvantaged children, it also turned out to be attractive to advantaged children and to many adults, beyond the group for which it was designed (Cook *et al.* 1975). Although the unwanted viewers of *Sesame Street* are reached at no additional costs, there are times when the "unwanted" coverage may turn out to severely drain program resources.

Studies designed to measure coverage are similar in principle to those discussed under "needs assessment" studies earlier. In addition, the problem of overcoverage may be studied through program administrative records. The study of undercoverage, however, often involves commissioning special surveys.

### Are Appropriate Benefits Being Delivered? Program Integrity Research

When program services depend heavily on the ability of many agencies to recruit and train appropriate personnel, or to retrain existing personnel, or to undertake significant changes in standard operating procedures, it is sometimes problematic whether a program will always manage to deliver to beneficiaries what had been intended. For many reasons the issue of program integrity often becomes sufficiently critical to warrant additional fine-tuning of basic legislation or of administrative regulations.

Several examples may highlight the importance of this issue for educational programs. Although funds can be provided for school systems to upgrade their audiovisual equipment, and schools may purchase it, such equipment often goes unused either because there are no persons trained to use the equipment or because audiovisual materials are not available (Rossi and Biddle 1966). Or a new curriculum may be designed and made available to schools, but schools may be unable to use the curriculum because teachers find it too difficult to use.

In other cases the right services are being delivered, but at a level that is too low to make a significant impact on beneficiaries. Thus, a supplementary reading-instruction program that on average results in only an additional 40 min per week of reading instruction is hardly sufficient to affect reading progress.

Evaluation research designed to measure what is being delivered may be accomplished easily, or may involve measurement problems of considerable complexity. Thus, it may be very easy to learn from schools how many hours per week their audiovisual equipment is used, but very difficult to learn precisely what is going on inside a classroom when teachers attempt to use technology requiring changes in teaching methods, classroom organization, or other services that are highly dependent on persons for delivery. Measurement that would require direct observation of classroom activity may turn out to be very expensive to implement on a large scale.

One of the best examples of systematic studies in difficult-to-observe situations is Reiss's (1971) study of police–citizen encounters. Research assistants were assigned to ride with police on patrol to systematically record each encounter between the officers under observation in the patrol cars and members of the public. Reiss's study provides basic descriptive accounts of how such encounters are generated, how the behavior of citizens affected police responses, and so on.

Often for the purposes of fine-tuning a program, it may not be necessary to proceed on a mass scale in doing implementation research. Thus, it may not matter whether a particular problem in implementing a program occurs frequently or infrequently, since if it occurs at all, it is not desirable. Hence, for program fine-tuning, small-scale qualitative observational studies may be most fruitful. For example, if qualitative interviews with welfare recipients reveal any instances in which husband–wife separations were undertaken solely for the purpose of retaining or increasing benefit eligibility, one might judge that this was sufficient evidence that the program rules should be altered to remove the incentive involved.

Programs that depend heavily on personnel for delivery, or that involve complicated programs calling for individualized treatments for beneficiaries, are especially good candidates for careful and sensitive fine-tuning research because such programs increase the difficulties of implementation. In effect, there may be problems in motivating personnel to deliver complicated, personalized human services appropriately and skillfully. (An outstanding example of this is provided in Fairweather and Tornatzky, 1977).

### Are Program Funds Being Used Appropriately? Fiscal Accountability

The accounting profession has been in operation considerably longer than program evaluation; procedures for determining whether or not program funds have been used responsibly and as intended are well established and hence are not problematic. However, it should be borne in mind that fiscal accountability measurements cannot substitute for the studies mentioned earlier. The fact that funds appear to be used as intended in an accounting sense may not mean that program services are being delivered as intended. The conventional accounting categories used in a fiscal audit are ordinarily sufficient to detect, say, fraudulent expenditure patterns, but may be insufficiently sensitive to detect whether services are being delivered in the requisite level of substantive integrity. It is in significant recognition of this difference that the General Accounting Office has recently set up an Institute for Program Evaluation, one of whose major roles is to instruct GAO personnel in appropriate evaluation procedures.

It is also important to keep in mind that the definition of costs under accounting principles differs from the definition of costs used by economists. For accountants, a cost reflects conventional bookkeeping entries such as out-of-pocket expenses, historical costs (i.e., what the purchase price of some item was), depreciation, and the like. Accountants focus on the value of current stocks of capital goods and inventories of products, coupled with "cash flow" concerns. When the question is whether program funds are being appropriately spent, the accountant's definition will suffice. However, economists stress opportunity costs defined in terms of what is *given up* when resources are allocated to particular purposes. More specifically, opportunity costs reflect the *next best* use to which the resources could be put. For example, the opportunity cost of raising teachers' salaries by 10% may be the necessity of foregoing the purchase of a new set of textbooks. While opportunity costs may not be especially important from a cost-accounting point of view, they become critical when cost-effectiveness or benefit–cost analyses of programs are undertaken. We will have more to say about these issues later.

## PROGRAM ASSESSMENT EVALUATION

The evaluation tasks discussed under accountability studies are directed mainly to questions dealing with how well a program is running. Whether or not a program is effective is a different question, one to which answers are not easily provided. Does a program achieves its goals over and above what would be expected without the program?

Many evaluators consider that the effectiveness question is quintessentially evaluation. Indeed, there is some justification for that position: Effectiveness assessment is certainly more difficult to accomplish, since it requires higher levels of skills and ingenuity than any of the evaluation activities previously discussed. However, there is no justification for interpreting every evaluation task as calling for effectiveness assessments—as apparently some evaulators have done in the past, aided in their misinterpretation by imprecise requests for help from policymakers and administrators.

### *Can the Effectiveness of a Program Be Estimated? The Evaluability Question*

A program that has gone through the stages described earlier in this chapter should provide few obstacles to evaluation for effectiveness in accomplishing its goals. But there are many human-services programs that present problems for effectiveness studies because one or more of several criteria for evaluation are absent. Perhaps the most important criterion, one which is frequently absent, is the lack of well-formulated goals or objectives for the program. For example, the effectiveness of a program designed to "raise the level of learning" among certain groups of school children through the provision of per capita payments to schools cannot be evaluated without considerable further specification of goals. What is meant by *levels*, and what kinds of learning achievements are deemed relevant.

A second criterion is that the program in question be well specified. Thus, a program designed to make social work agencies more effective by encouraging innovations is also not evaluable as far as effectiveness is concerned. First, the goals are not very well specified, but neither are the means for reaching goals. Innovation as a means of reaching a goal is not a method, but a way of proceeding. Anything new is an innovation; hence, such a program may encourage the temporary adoption of a wide variety of specific techniques and is likely to vary widely from site to site.

Finally, a program is evaluable from an effectiveness point of view only if it is possible to estimate in some way what the expected state of beneficiaries is in the absence of the program. As we will discuss, the critical hurdle in effectiveness studies is to develop comparisons between beneficiaries who have experienced a program and those who have not. Hence, a program that is universal in its coverage and that has been going on for some time cannot be evaluated for effectiveness. For example, we cannot evaluate the effectiveness of the public school systems in the United States because it is not possible to make observations on Americans, cities, towns, counties, and states that do not have (or recently have not had) public school systems.

This discussion of effectiveness evaluability is raised here because we believe that often evaluators are asked to undertake tasks that are impossible or close to impossible. Thus, it is not sensible for federal policymakers or program managers to call for effectiveness evaluations to be undertaken by all state and local program units, at least at this stage in the development of state and local capabilities. Nor does it make much sense to undertake large-scale evaluations of programs that have no nationwide uniform goals but are locally defined. Hence, the evaluation of Title I or of Head Start and similar programs should either not be undertaken or should be called for lightly.

Techniques have been developed (Wholey 1977) to determine whether or not a program is evaluable in the senses discussed here, and decision makers may well want to commission such studies as a first step rather than to assume that all programs can be evaluated.

Finally, it may be worth mentioning in passing that questions of evaluability have in the past been used to justify "goal-free" evaluation methods (e.g., Deutscher 1977; Scriven 1972). The goal-free advocates have contended that since many of a program's aims evolve over time, the "hypothetico-deductive" approach to impact assessment (Heilman 1980) is at best incomplete and at worst misleading. In our view, impact assessment necessarily *requires* some set of program goals, although whether they are stated in advance or evolve over time does have important implications for one's research procedures (Chen and Rossi 1980). In particular, evolving goals require far more flexible research designs (and researchers). In other words, there cannot be such a thing as a "goal-free" *impact assessment.* At the same time, we have stressed that there are other important dimensions to the evaluation enterprise in which goals are far less central. For example, a sensitive monitoring of program activities can proceed productively without any consideration of ultimate goals. Thus, goal-free evaluation approaches can be extremely useful as long as the questions they can address are clearly understood.

## *Did the Program Work? The Effectiveness Question*

As discussed, any assessment of whether or not a program "worked" necessarily assumes that it is known what the program was supposed to accomplish. For a variety of reasons, the enabling legislation by which programs are established often appears to set relatively vague goals or objectives for the program, making it necessary during the "design phase" (as discussed earlier) to develop specific goals.

In whatever way goals might be established, the important point is that it is not possible to determine whether a program actually worked without developing a limited and specific set of criteria for establishing the condition of having worked. For example, it would not have been possible to develop an assessment of whether *Sesame Street* worked without having decided that its goals were to foster reading and number-handling skills. Whether these goals existed before the program was designed or whether they emerged after the program was in operation is less important for our purposes than the fact that such goals existed at the time of evaluation.

Programs rarely succeed or fail in absolute terms. Success or failure is always relative to some benchmark. Hence an answer to "Did the program work?" requires a consideration of "Compared to what?" The development of appropriate comparisons can proceed along at least three dimensions: comparisons across different subjects, comparisons across different settings, and comparisons across different times. In the first instance, one might compare the performance of two sets of students in a given class in a specific classroom period. In the second instance, one might compare the performance of the same set of students in two different classroom settings (necessarily at two different moments in time). In the third instance, one might compare the same students in the same class, but at different moments in time.

(For convenience, in this discussion we use examples in which students, classes, and classroom periods figure strongly. The concepts being illustrated, however, are generally applicable; for example, you can substitute households, communities, and life-cycle stages in the discussion which follows without losing any essential meaning.)

As Figure 10.1 indicates, it is also possible to mix and match these three fundamental dimensions to develop a wide variety of comparison groups.[1] For example, comparison group 2 ($C_2$) varies both the subjects and the setting, although the time is the same. Or, comparison group 6 ($C_6$) varies subjects, the setting, and the time. However, with each added dimension by which one or more comparison groups differ from the experimental group, the number of threats to internal validity necessarily increases. For example, the use of

---

[1] We have used the term *comparison group* as a general term to be distinguished from the term *control group*. Control groups are comparison groups that have been constructed by random assignment.

| | Same subjects | | Different subjects | |
|---|---|---|---|---|
| | Same setting | Different setting | Same setting | Different setting |
| **Same time** | *a* | *a* | $c_1$ | $c_2$ |
| **Different time** | $c_3$ | $c_4$ | $c_5$ | $c_6$ |

**FIGURE 10.1.** *A typology for comparison groups.*

comparison group 4 (different setting and different time period) requires that assessment of program impact simultaneously take into account possible confounding factors associated with such things as differences in student background and motivation, and such things as the "reactive" potential of different classroom environments. This in turn requires either an extensive data collection effort to obtain measures on these confounding factors, coupled with the application of appropriate statistical adjustments (e.g., multiple regression analysis), or the use of randomization and thus, true control groups. Randomization, of course, will on the average eliminate confounding influences in the analysis of impact. On grounds of analytic simplicity alone, it is easy to see why so many expositions of impact assessment strongly favor research designs based on random assignment. In addition, it cannot be overemphasized that appropriate statistical adjustments (in the absence of randomization) through multivariate statistical techniques require a number of assumptions that are almost impossible in practice to fully meet.[2] For example, it is essential that measures of all confounding influences be included in a formal model of the program's impact, that their mathematical relationship to the outcome be properly specified (e.g., a linear additive form versus a multiplicative form), and that the confounding influences be measured *without error*! Should any of these requirements be violated, one risks serious bias in any estimates of program impact.

At the same time, however, random assignment is often impractical or even impossible. And even when random assignment is feasible, its advantages rest on randomly assigning a relatively *large* number of subjects. To randomly

---

[2]There are some research designs that, although not based on random assignment, do readily allow for unbiased estimates of treatment effects through multivariate statistical adjustments (e.g., Barnow, *et al.* 1980).

assign only two schools to the experimental group and only two schools to the control group, for example, will not allow equivalences between experimentals and controls to materialize. Consequently, one is often forced to attempt statistical adjustments for initial differences between experimental and comparison subjects.

The use of multivariate statistical adjustments raises a host of questions that cannot be addressed in detail here. Suffice to say that despite the views of some that anything that can go wrong will, extensive practical experience suggests a more optimistic conclusion. Quite often, useful and reasonably accurate estimates of program effects can be obtained despite modest violations of the required statistical assumptions. Moreover, available statistical technology is evolving rapidly and many earlier problems now have feasible solutions, at least in principle. (For a review of some recent statistical developments in the context of criminal justice evaluation, see Berk, 1980.)

It is sometimes possible to either solve or partially bypass comparison-group problems by resorting to some set of external criteria as a baseline. For example, it is common in studies of desegregation or affirmative-action programs to apply various measures of equity as a "comparison group" (Baldus and Cole 1977). Thus, an assessment of whether schools in black neighborhoods are being funded at comparable levels to schools in white neighborhoods might apply the criterion that disparities in excess of plus or minus 5% in per pupil expenditures indicate inequality and hence failure (Berk and Hartman 1972). However, the use of such external baselines by themselves still leaves open the question of causal inference. It may be difficult to determine whether it was the program or some other set of factors that produced the observed relationship between outcomes of interest and the external metric.

It is also important to understand that distinguishing between success and failure is not a clearcut decision, since there are usually degrees of success or degrees of failure. Whereas decision makers may have to make binary decisions whether, for example, to fund or not to fund, the evidence provided on effectiveness usually consists of statements of degree which then have to be translated into binary terms by the decision makers. Thus, a program that succeeds in raising the average level of reading by ½ year more than one would ordinarily expect—a considerable gain—may be less successful than one that has effectiveness estimates of a full year. This quantitative difference has to be translated into a qualititative difference when the decision to fund one program rather than the other has to be made. At this point, other considerations may surface, including costs, potential negative effects, public acceptability, and so on.

### Was the Program Worth It? The Economic Efficiency Question

Given a program of proven effectiveness, the next question one might

---

[3] Recall that opportunity costs address the *foregone* benefits of the *next best* use of the resources in question (Thompson 1980, pp. 65–74).

reasonably raise is whether the *opportunity costs* of the programs are justified by the gains achieved.[3] Or the same question might be more narrowly raised in a comparative framework: Is program A more "efficient" than program B, both otherwise equally acceptable alternative ways of achieving some particular goal?

The main problem in answering such questions centers around establishing a yardstick for such an assessment. For example, would it be useful to think in terms of dollars spent for units of achievement gained, in terms of students covered, or in terms of classes or schools that come under the program?

The simplest way of answering efficiency issues is to calculate cost effectiveness measures, dollars spent per unit of output. Thus, in the case of the *Sesame Street* program, different cost effectiveness measures were computed: (*a*) *dollars spent per child hour of viewing*; and (*b*) *dollars spent per each additional letter of the alphabet learned.* Note that the second measure implies knowing the effectiveness of the program, as established by an effectiveness evaluation.

The most complicated mode of answering the efficiency question is to conduct a full-fledged cost–benefit analysis in which all the costs and benefits are computed. Relatively few full-fledged cost–benefit analyses have been made of social programs because it is difficult to convert all the costs and all the benefits into the same yardstick terms. In principle, it is possible to convert into dollars all the costs and benefits of a program; in practice, it is rarely possible to do so without some disagreement on the valuation placed, say on learning an additional letter of the alphabet.

An additional problem with full-fledged benefit–cost analyses is that they must consider the long-run consequences not only of the program but also of the next-best foregone alternative. This immediately implies the need "discounting": taking into account the fact that resources invested today in some social program may produce over a number of succeeding years consequences that have to be compared to those that might have resulted from the next best alternative. For example, a vocational program in inner-city high schools must address (among other things) the long-run impact on students' earnings over their lifetimes. This in turn requires that the costs and benefits of the program and the next best alternative be phrased in terms of *today's* dollars. Without going into the arcane art of discounting, the problem is to figure out what a reasonable rate of return over the long run for current program investments and competing alternatives might be. And, one can obtain widely varying assessments, depending on what rate of return is used (Thompson 1980).

## EVALUATION IN EVOLUTION

The field of evaluation research in the social sciences is scarcely out of its infancy: The first large-scale field experiments were started in the mid-1960s; interest in large-scale national evaluations of programs also originated in the

War on Poverty; the art of designing large-scale implementation and monitoring studies is evolving just now; concern with the validity statuses of qualitative research has just begun; and so on.

Perhaps what is most important as a developing theme is the importance of social science theory for evaluation. It has become increasingly obvious that social policy is almost a blind thrashing about for solutions. Guiding the formation of social policy by sensitive and innovative applications of general social science theory and empirical knowledge is becoming increasingly frequent. This development is further enhanced by the increasingly held realization that errors in model specification are errors in theory. Hence, there is no good policy without good understanding of the problem involved and of the role that policy can play. Nor is there any good evaluation without theoretical guidance in modeling policy effects.

# References

Abt Associates. 1979. *Child care food program*. Cambridge, Mass.: Abt Associates.

Baldus, D.C., and Cole J.W.L. 1977. Quantitative proof of intentional discrimination. *Evaluation Quarterly* 1:1.

Barnow, B.S., Cain, G.G., and Goldberger, A.S. 1980. Issues in the analysis of selectivity bias. In *Evaluation studies review annual*, Vol. 5, eds. E.W. Stromsdorfer and G. Farkus. Beverly Hills: Sage Publications. Pp. 42–59.

Berk, R.A. 1980. Recent statistical developments with implications for evaluation of criminal justice programs. In *Handbook of criminal justice evaluation*, ed. M. Klein and K. Teilman. Beverly Hills: Sage Publications. Pp. 63–96.

Berk, R.A., and Hartman, A. 1972. Race and class differences in per pupil staffing expenditures in Chicago elementary schools. *Integrated Education* 10:52–57.

Berk, R.A., and Brewer, M. 1978. Feet of clay in hobnailed boots: An assessment of statistical inference in applied research. In *Evaluation studies review annual*, Vol. 3, ed. T.D. Cook. Beverly Hills, Sage Publications. Pp. 190–214.

Berk, R.A., and Rossi, P.H. 1976. Doing good or worse: Evaluation research politically re-examined. *Social Problems* 23:337–349.

Campbell, D.T., and Erlebacher, A. 1970. How regression artifacts in quasi-experimental evaluations can mistakenly make compensatory education look harmful. In *The disadvantaged child, Vol. 3. Compensatory education: a national debate*, ed. J. Hellmuth. New York: Brunner/Mazel. Pp. 185–218.

Chen, H., and Rossi, P.H. 1980. The multi-goal, theory-driven approach to evaluation: A model linking basic and applied social science. *Social Forces* 59:106–122.

Coleman, J., *et al.* 1967. *Equality of educational opportunity*. Washington, D.C.: Government Printing Office.

Conant, James B. 1959. *The American high school today*. New York: McGraw–Hill.

Cook, T., *et al.* 1975. *Sesame Street revisited*. New York: Russell Sage.

Cook, T., and Campbell, D. 1979. *Quasi-experimentation*. Chicago: Rand McNally.

Cronbach, L.J. 1980. *Towards reform of program evaluation*. Menlo Park, Calif.: Jossey–Bass.

Deutscher, I. 1977. Toward avoiding the goal trap in evaluation research. In *Readings in evaluation research*, ed. F. Caro. New York: Russell Sage. Pp. 221–238.

Fairweather, G. and Tornatzky, L.G. 1977. *Experimental methods for social policy research*, New York: Pergamon.

Gramlich, E.M., and Koshel, P. 1975. *Educational performance contracting.* Washington: The Brookings Institution.

Guttentag, M., and Struening, E., eds. 1975. *Handbook of evaluation research.* Beverly Hills: Sage Publications. (2 vols.)

Harrington, M. 1962. *The other America.* New York: Macmillan.

Heilman, J.G. 1980. Paradigmatic choices in evaluation methodology. *Evaluation Review* 4:693–712.

Kershaw, D., and Fair, J. 1976. *The New Jersey income maintenance experiment.* New York: Academic Press.

Kish, L. 1965. *Survey sampling.* New York: John Wiley.

Kmenta, J. 1971. *Elements of econometrics.* New York: Macmillan.

Lenihan, K. 1976. *Opening the second gate.* Washington, D.C.: Government Printing Office.

Lewis, O. 1965. *La Vida.* New York: Random House.

Liebow, E. 1967. *Tally's corner.* Boston: Little–Brown.

Mathematica. 1980. *Job corps evaluated.* Princeton: Mathematica Policy Research.

Maynard, R.A., and Murnane, R.J. 1979. The effects of the negative income tax on school performance. *Journal of Human Resources* 14:463–476.

Murray, S.A. 1980. The national evaluation of the PUSH for excellence project. Manuscript. Washington: American Institutes for Research.

Reiss, A.E. 1971. *The police and the public.* New Haven: Yale University Press.

Riis, J.A. 1890. *How the other half lives.* New York: C. Scribner.

Rossi, P.H. 1978. Issues in the evaluation of human services delivery. *Evaluation Quarterly* 2:573–599.

Rossi, P.H., Berk, R., and Lenihan, K. 1980. *Money, work and crime.* New York: Academic Press.

Rossi, P.H., and Biddle, B. 1966. *The new media and education.* Chicago: Aldine.

Rossi, P.H., Freeman, H., and Wright, S. 1979. *Evaluation: A systematic approach.* Beverly Hills: Sage Publications.

Rossi, P.H., and Lyall, K. 1976. *Reforming public welfare.* New York: Russell Sage.

Scriven, M. 1972. Pros and cons about goal-free evaluation. *Evaluation Comment* 3:1–4.

Sinclair, U. 1906. *The jungle.* New York: Doubleday.

Steinbeck, J. 1939. *Grapes of wrath.* New York: Viking.

Suchman, E. 1967. *Evaluation research.* New York: Russell Sage.

Sudman, S. 1976. *Applied sampling.* New York: Academic Press.

Thompson, M. 1980. *Cost–benefit analysis.* Beverly Hills: Sage Publications.

Weiss, C. 1972. *Evaluation research.* Englewood Cliffs, N.J.: Prentice–Hall.

Wholey, J.S. 1977. Evaluability assessment. In *Evaluation research methods,* ed. L. Rutman. Beverly Hills: Sage Publications. Pp. 41–56.

# 11

# Equity Criteria for the Evaluation of Social Welfare Programs: Mothers' Summer Recreation[1]

SHIMON E. SPIRO AND RUTH LIRON

The objective of this chapter is to propose and demonstrate an approach to the evaluation of social programs that focuses on their *distribution* rather than their *impact*. Issues of equity and target efficiency, which are central to discussions of social policy, have so far received only scant attention by students of program evaluation. Although some influential textbooks dealing with evaluative research (e.g., Rossi, Freeman, and Wright 1980; Tripodi, Fellin, and Epstein. 1978) discuss ways of assessing the success of programs in reaching their intended target populations, the main concern of evaluation research is with the impact of programs on their *actual* clients, rather than with their distribution among *potential* users. Thus, for example, two randomly selected volumes of the leading journal in the field (*Evaluation Quarterly* 1977; *Evaluation Review* 1980) contain 68 papers, but only five of them (7%) deal somehow with issues of distribution or allocation, whereas 39 papers (60%) are devoted to the methodology of impact assessment and to findings about program outcomes (the remainder deal mostly with the history, politics, organization, and ideology of program evaluation).

Social policy can be defined as a field concerned with the enhancement of equality of life chances (Rich 1977). All social programs have explicit or implicit redistributive goals and some redistributive effects, whether intended or unintended. Hence, the evaluation of social programs should concern itself with such issues as who benefits from them, and who pays for them.

[1] The study on which this chapter is based was commissioned by the Center for Demographic Issues, Prime Minister's Office, Israel.

EVALUATING THE WELFARE STATE:
SOCIAL AND POLITICAL PERSPECTIVES

These issues are conceptualized in the social policy literature in different ways. Weisbrod (1969) talks about the "target efficiency" of programs, defined as "the degree to which the actual redistribution coincides with the desired redistribution." He differentiates between "vertical" target efficiency," that is the proportion of the benefits of a program that reaches the intended target population, and "horizontal target efficiency," that is, the proportion of the target group actually being served. Kahn (1973), among others, is concerned with "creaming," that is, the tendency of programs to serve not the most needy potential clients, but the ones best equipped to utilize the program appropriately and successfully. For example, sheltered workshops intended to serve the unemployable blind may, in fact, employ those who could have coped with demands of employment in the open market (Scott 1967). Similarly, the utilization of many personal service programs may be dependent upon personal resources such as free time, social connections, and acquired skills, which are negatively correlated with indicators of deprivation and need.

The distribution of program benefits between potential clients is affected by a number of factors. First, there are the processes of resource allocation between central and local government (Judge 1978), or between government and the voluntary sector (Kramer 1981). These affect distribution of resources among different localities, different population groups (defined by religion, ethnicity, age, etc.), or different social networks. Second, there are the organizational and physical aspects of service programs, which may facilitate or obstruct access and utilization for different individuals. Third, there are the professional ideology and the professional practices employed by the personnel of service agencies, which affect the utilization of these services by different cultural and economic groups (Cloward and Epstein 1965). Finally, there are the attitudes, resources, and skills of potential clients as they affect their ability to utilize programs and benefit from them (McKinley 1972).

The extent to which issues of equity and target efficiency should be central to the evaluation of a program will depend on the scarcity of program benefits (relative to perceived need), and on the extent to which access to the program seems problematic because of one or more obstacles. In the remainder of this chapter we shall discuss the evaluation of a recreation program which, in our opinion, required evaluation of distribution more than evaluation of impact.

## Summer Recreation for Mothers

Since 1974, the Israeli government has sponsored day camps for mothers of large families. The program is intended for mothers of four children or more, with low income, who are too busy with their manifold responsibilities as housewives and mothers to devote time to themselves. The purpose of the camps is to provide the participants with a few days of relaxation and enjoyment. The sponsors claim that participation in the program may have some effect on the participants' self-image and on their functioning as mothers and wives, and some such effects have actually been detected in previous evaluative studies (Sharni 1979). However, the program's *raison d'être* is the enjoyment it provides to its participants. This being so, simple measures of client satisfaction, or even of the growing demand for the program, may be sufficient evidence of its value for the participants.

The more serious problem, in the case of this and similar programs, is its distribution among potential clients. Here there may be reason to suspect that the most needy women — those with the largest numbers of children, the lowest incomes, and the most difficult marital and family situations — may also be the ones least likely to utilize the program. They may lack initiative and information, and may find it difficult to mobilize the support of other family members for their participation in the program.

Issues of equitable efficiency seemed to be of special pertinence to this program for two reasons. The first is scarcity: The program could accommodate only a small fraction of those eligible and interested in it. In 1978 (the year of our study), the program provided places in day camps for only 5000 women, although Israel has some 120,000 families with four children or more. The second reason is organizational: The program, although sponsored and financed by the central government, was implemented by local branches of voluntary organizations, such as women's movements and community centers. These organizations handled the recruitment and selection of candidates for the program. The result of this arrangement was a highly decentralized program with a long chain of implementation and weak links. One would have to consider the possibility that despite rather detailed directives provided by the sponsoring government agency, access to the program may be affected by community ties and social skills rather than by the indicators of deprivation. These considerations were the motivation for an evaluative study focusing exclusively on the distribution of the program among potential clients (Liron and Spiro 1980).

In the evaluation of the distribution of this program, four strategies were employed:

1. An "armchair" examination of criteria for the recruitment and selection of clients: If implemented properly, could they be expected to result in equitable and efficient allocation? This could be defined as an assessment of the theoretical equitable efficiency of the program (Doron and Rotter 1976).

2. An examination of the process of implementation: Are those who recruit and select clients aware of the criteria and procedures, and do they accept them and implement them?

3. A study of the outcome of the recruitment and selection process through a comparison of a sample of participants with a sample of eligible

nonparticipants: Do the two samples differ in a manner defined by the goals of the program and the criteria for admission? That is, are participants more needy or eligible than the nonparticipants?

4. The use of ecological correlations, to examine the allocation of the program to communities: Is the allocation of the program to communities proportionate to the distribution of eligible potential clients, and are deviations from proportionate allocation correlated with aggregate indicators of need or eligibility?

The main body of this chapter will be devoted to a discussion of these four strategies and the presentation of findings based on them.

## Criteria and Procedures for Selecting Participants: The Theoretical Target Efficiency of the Program

The governmental department sponsoring this program[2] established several criteria for admission to the day camps: Participation was limited to mothers of four children or more, with at least two infants under the age of 6, who were not eligible for any workplace related holidays, could not afford to pay for a vacation, and had not attended a government sponsored day camp in more than a year. These criteria are obviously intended to assure that only the neediest are considered for admission, and that among the neediest, the benefits of this program are spread as widely as possible.

The sponsoring agency also prescribed procedures for recruitment and selection for the camps. Every day camp was to have a governing committee, made up of representatives of the voluntary organization running the camp and of the local public welfare, health, and education services. This committee was to request lists of potential participants from the local public welfare office and the local maternal and child health clinic. The composition of the committee and the mandatory sources of referral were to ensure equitable utilization of resources and easy access to the program for the most deprived segment of the population.

A closer examination of the criteria and procedures reveals a few potential problems. The criteria are defined as *dichotomous* variables. They do not differentiate between levels of need. They do not state that a mother of six should get preference over a mother of four, or that candidates should be ranked by family income (as an indirect measure of ability to afford a vacation). There is nothing in the criteria to tell the local organizers how they should choose among a large number of candidates all of whom answer the minimal conditions of eligibility.

[2]This was originally the Center for Demographic Issues at the Prime Minister's Office. In 1979, responsibility for the program was transferred to the Ministry of Labor and Social Welfare.

Furthermore, at closer inspection, most of the criteria are found to be rather imprecise, and open to various interpretations. Thus, for example, a mother of four or more could be one who has four or more children currently living with her, or one who has given birth to four children, some of whom may have left home. Similarly, the ability to afford a vacation may be a matter of judgment.

As for the procedures, the role played by the various local bodies may provide certain groups in the population (members of voluntary organizations, welfare clients, mothers of infants who attend the government's Mother and Child Clinic, etc.) easy access to the program, and discriminate against persons without specific institutional attachments. This problem is aggravated by the fact that organizers are not required to engage in any form of publicity that might have widened the circle of potential applicants.

Thus a mere examination of the criteria and procedures, prior to any collection of data on actual performance in the field, raises the possibility that accessibility to and utilization of the program may be affected not only by need, but also by supposedly irrelevant factors such as prior and ongoing contact with local organizations and agencies.

## Implementation of the Selection Process

This part of the study is based on interviews with the 40 local "organizers" who in 1978 were responsible for the organization of 48 day camps which took place in the 25 communities of the southern half of the country. The organizers were mostly either volunteers or paid employees of a local community center or a local branch of a women's group. In a few cases the organization of the camp was entrusted by the voluntary organization to an employee of some local agency, either a school principal or a social worker. The 40 organizers were interviewed, and asked for opinions and experience related to the process of recruitment to the camps.

The organizers were asked to list the criteria for admission to the program. Practically all remembered that only mothers of four children or more were eligible; almost two-thirds remembered that the program was meant for women who would otherwise have been unable to take a vacation, but less than half remembered that mothers who had attended a camp in the previous year were ineligible, or that the camp was intended for mothers who had to take care of at least two preschool children (Table 11.1). Not surprisingly, the criteria less often remembered were also the ones less consistently enforced.[3] Almost half

---

[3]The fact that the proportion enforcing a criterion may be larger than the proportion aware of it should not come as a surprise. A respondent may not recall a principle in response to an open question, even if he or she honestly claims (in response to a closed question) never to have violated it.

**TABLE 11.1**

**Organizers Awareness of, Adherence to, and Agreement with Criteria of Eligibility for Participation in Day Camps ($N = 48$)**

| The criterion | Percentage aware | Percentage enforcing | | | Percentage Agreeing |
|---|---|---|---|---|---|
| | | Very strictly | Quite strictly | Total | |
| Four children or more | 96 | 33 | 63 | 96 | 35 |
| Two Children under age 6 | 46 | 25 | 29 | 54 | 40 |
| Ineligible for workplace holidays | 63 | 65 | 13 | 78 | 65 |
| Unable to afford vacation | | 54 | 29 | 83 | 77 |
| Did not participate last year | 46 | 29 | 38 | 67 | 35 |

the organizers admitted they did not always make sure that a candidate had at least two preschool children, and a third did not strictly enforce the rule against "repeaters." We also found the level of agreement with most of the criteria to be rather low. Our respondents were asked, in relation to each criterion separately, whether it should stand as it is, be dropped, be changed, or whether organizers should be allowed greater judgment in applying it.

A majority agreed that the two criteria of need (or lack of alternative vacation resources) should stand as they are, but most respondents argued for flexibility as regards the other criteria (family composition and previous participation). They knew of mothers of three, or mothers with school-age children only, who needed recreation as badly as anyone. Many organizers felt that for some of the most needy women, annual participation was no luxury. Most felt that more leeway should be given to the local organizers, since they knew the applicants personally and were the best judges of merit and need. Actually, most organizers employed some additional criteria, which they used in exceptional cases. They would occasionally close their eyes to the fact that a woman did not meet all the criteria listed, if her physical or mental condition, or her home situation, were such as to justify special consideration. Some 25% of the organizers also admitted giving preference to members of the sponsoring organization, or to regular participants in some ongoing program.

In unstructured conversation following the interviews, the organizers expressed ambivalence about the criteria. On the one hand, they objected to the limitations on their judgment. On the other hand, they realized that the criteria protected them from pressures. It should be noted, however, that organizers differed in the extent to which they saw themselves as being under pressure. As we shall later show, the allocation of resources *between* communities was anything but equitable. Thus, there would be great differences between communities in the actual or perceived scarcity of places in day camps. Organizers also differed in the extent to which they publicized the program and encouraged demand for it. Hence, we found that some organizers reported having to turn back many applicants whereas, others, albeit a minority, had a hard time ensuring full occupancy. We found a modest, but positive correlation between perceived scarcity of places and adherence to the criteria dictated by the sponsors.

As for procedures, only two-thirds of the organizers reported having formed the required governing boards. Even then, the selection of candidates was done mostly in consultation between the organizer and a local social worker. Often one person (a school principal, social worker, or local organizer) handled the whole recruitment and selection process. Recruitment was done mostly by word of mouth, within local networks, with hardly any utilization of public notices or the media. Efforts were made, through home visits and similar means, to reach women who were known to be in need but did not apply, but little effort was made to reach potential candidates who were not part of local networks and who were not known to local agencies.

Although the decision and actions of the local organizers were, on the whole, congruent with the objectives of the program, one could say that decentralization—the implementation of a governmental program through local branches of voluntary agencies—necessarily results in some attrition of criteria and procedures, and may increase the discrepancy between the intended and actual clientele of the program.

## The Outcome of the Recruitment and Selection Processes in One Community

Who are the participants in the program? In what ways do they differ from nonparticipants? Information relevant to these issues was obtained from questionnaires administered to random samples of participants and nonparticipants in one community. For this part of the study we selected a middle-sized town, heterogeneous in the composition of the population, where five different organizations (four women's groups and a community center) had conducted day camps in the summer of 1978 for a total of 169 women and their youngest children. We took a random sample of 40 women from among the 169 who participated in the program and compared it with a random sample of 40 out of 1823 women, mothers of four children or more, who did not attend a day camp in 1978. The first sample was drawn from the lists provided by the camp organizers, the second from the files of the National Insurance Institute, which administers Israel's program of family allowances.

A comparison of the two samples (Table 11.2) yields a number of interesting observations. We find that the women who attended the camps had, *on the average*, more children than those who did not attend, but not more *children under the age of 18*. We find the mean number of children under 18 to be almost

TABLE 11.2

**Comparative Characteristics of Participants and Nonparticipants in the Day Camps of One Town (Two Samples of 40 Each, Summer of 1978)**

| Characteristic | Participants | Nonparticipants | $\chi^2$ | d.f. | $p<$ |
|---|---|---|---|---|---|
| | | | Significance[a] | | |
| Age: 26–35 years | 23% | 55% | 13.01 | 4 | .03 |
| Mean age | 39.4 years | 35.5 years | | | |
| Number of children: seven or more | 43% | 15% | 13.09 | 3 | .005 |
| Mean | 6.3 | 4.9 | | | |
| Number of children under 18 | | | | | |
| less than four | 33% | 10% | | | |
| four to six | 48% | 88% | 15.54 | 4 | .005 |
| seven or more | 20% | 3% | | | |
| Mean | 4.5 | 4.4 | | | |
| Economic conditions | | | | | |
| Enjoying work-related benefits | 8% | 15% | 1.21 | 2 | N.S. |
| Husbands steadily employed | 68% | 90% | 3.72 | 1 | .10 |
| Utilizing public welfare office | 33% | 13% | 4.59 | 1 | .05 |
| Having gone on vacation | 27% | 43% | 1.98 | 1 | N.S. |
| Previous attenance | | | | | |
| In 3 years | 70% | 10% | 28.17 | 2 | .005 |
| Preceding year | 28% | 5% | | | |

[a]$\chi^2$ were mostly computed from more detailed tables having two columns (representing the two samples), and a number of rows indicated by the number of degrees of freedom (+1).

equal in the two groups with the sample of participants tending to the extremes: more families with seven or more children under 18, but also more families with fewer than four children under 18. The differences in family composition are, undoubtedly, related to differences in age: The participants tended to be older, and consequently more of their children were over 18 (and may have left home). Thus it is not clear whether, in terms of family composition, the participants can be seen as more "needy" or eligible than the comparison group.

We find, however, that the participants may be economically more disadvantaged than the comparison group. Fewer of them hold jobs entitling them to social benefits (including paid holidays); fewer have husbands who hold a steady job. More of the participants reported getting some kind of help from the local public welfare office, and slightly fewer had taken a vacation away from home in the preceding year.[4]

The differences in economic conditions are in the direction implied by the goals and criteria of the program. They are, however, weak—and, at best, of

[4]The vacation mostly involved visits to relatives living in other parts of the country. The nonparticipants mostly traveled with their husbands and children; the participants mostly with their children. This may again serve as a weak indicator of less satisfactory family situations.

marginal statistical significance. The strongest difference found between the two samples was in the likelihood of previous participation. A majority of the participants, but only a small minority of the nonparticipants, had participated in a day camp in any of the 3 years preceding our study. Contrary to the regulations, 28% of the sample who participated in 1978 had also attended a camp in 1977.

The findings presented in Table 11.2 seem to indicate quite clearly that in the town studied, the program was utilized by a clientele that, in terms of need and eligibility, differed only slightly (albeit in the expected direction) from the rest of the relevant population. This is probably due, at least in part, to the process of implementation described earlier. The role played by local voluntary organizations, and the lack of any publicity, limited the utilization of the program to those who have been part of certain local networks. This impression is reinforced by the fact that approximately one-third of the nonparticipants had never heard of the day camps, and that very few (10% as compared with 43% of the participants) had heard of it from any of the "functionaries" of the program (local organizers, social workers, etc.). A majority (80%) of the nonparticipants indicated that nobody had invited them to attend the program. Lack of knowledge or encouragement were the most frequently mentioned reasons for nonparticipation (50%).

While the findings are drawn from a local survey conducted in one community, they are probably representative of conditions in the country as a whole.

## The Distribution of Resources among Communities

One meaning of equity is that individuals who are equally eligible should have equal access to a program, irrespective of nonrelevant factors such as community of residence. In other words, a program should be distributed equitably not only within, but also between communities.

To assess this dimension of equity, data were obtained regarding the scope of the program in all 62 towns and cities with a population of 5000 or more.[5] The number of places in day camps for 1978 were related to the number of families with four children and more. In Table 11.3, we present the distribution of the number of places per 100 mothers of large families. The median number of places for the semiurban and urban communities included in our analysis was 8 (i.e., 8 places in day camps for every 100 mothers). The proportion varied, however, considerably, between communities. It was as high as 25 (i.e., 1 place for every 4 mothers) at one extreme, or as low as 1 (1 place for every 100 mothers) at the other, ignoring 4 communities that did not take part in the

---

[5]Since the program was relatively underdeveloped in the Arab sector, only towns with a Jewish majority were included in this analysis.

TABLE 11.3
Distribution of Day Camps between
Communities (with Population
of 5000 or More)

| Number of places for every 100 mothers of four children or more | Number of communities |
|---|---|
| No day camps | 4 |
| 1–5 | 13 |
| 6–10 | 20 |
| 11–15 | 11 |
| 16–20 | 9 |
| 21–25 | 5 |
| Total | 62 |

program. The linear regression of the number of places in day camps on the number of families with four children or more was $Y = 39 + .0385x$, and the correlation coefficient (Pearson's $R$) was .83. The relatively large constant in the regression equation points to an advantage of small towns over larger cities in the allocation of this program.

Could the variations between communities be explained in terms of differing needs? To answer this question, three aggregated indicators of need were used: (*a*) the proportion of very large families (i.e., seven children or more) among all large families in a community; (*b*) the proportion of public welfare clients among all families in a locality; and (*c*) a composite index of "poverty dependency," published annually by the Ministry of Labor and Social Welfare, comprising the number of public welfare clients, the proportion of the municipal budget devoted to public welfare, the proportion of large families among all families in the locality, and the "dependency ratio," that is, the ratio between the working-age population, on the one hand, and children and elderly people on the other (Berman 1978).

From Table 11.4, we learn that all these variables are positively but weakly related to the ratio between day camp places and the number of large families. Jointly, these indicators of need explain just 7% of the variance in the allocation of resources.

Thus, aggregation of need or eligibility does not go very far in explaining variations among communities. These are probably related to the politics of program implementation. The camps are organized and administered by community centers and by local branches of national voluntary organizations. One of the goals of these organizations is to gain a foothold in every community. Since the program discussed is very popular, each organization would like to

**TABLE 11.4**

Correlation (Pearson's *R*) between three Measures
of Need and the Number of Places in Day Camps
for Every 100 Mothers of Four Children or More

| The measure | Correlation with number of places for 100 mothers |
|---|---|
| Percentage of families with seven children or more | .25 |
| Percentage of clients on public welfare | .27* |
| Poverty dependency | .20 |
| *Multiple* correlation of above three | .26 |

*Significant at $p < .05$.

operate at least one day camp in every community. Voluntary organizations also find it easier to manage the recruitment and selection processes in small towns. Thus the manner in which this program has been decentralized results in an advantage to small towns over large cities. Another probable source of variation is the interest and initiative of the local government and local leadership, a variable on which no data were obtained for this study.

## Conclusions

This evaluation of a recreation program for mothers of large, low-income families focused on the distribution of the program among potential users. Four separate but interrelated strategies of evaluation were used, with the following results:

1. *Criteria and procedures for recruitment and selection of participants were critically assessed,* and were found to be only partly consistent with the program's implicit redistributive goals.
2. *Examination of the processes of implementation of these procedures and criteria* showed some attrition in implementation, due to the decentralized nature of the program.
3. *A comparison of clients and nonclients* showed that the former tended to be only slightly more "needy" or "eligible"; due to the procedures employed and the decentralized nature of the program, benefits have tended to become concentrated within specific local networks.

4. *The distribution of the program between communities* was found to be inequitable, related to political and organizational factors rather than to indicators of "need."

The strategies employed in this study can be described as "primitive": They do enable us to point to problems in the allocation and distribution of the program, but they do not offer more exact measures of deviation from desired modes of distribution. A next step would be the employment of more specific models of the equitable distribution of specific program and measures of deviations from them. A more consistent concern with these issues should enhance the interaction between policy analysis and program evaluation, to the benefit of both fields.

# References

Berman, Y. 1978. *Social profile of towns and cities in Israel.* Jerusalem: State of Israel, Ministry of Labor and Social Welfare.

Cloward, R.A., and Epstein, I. 1965. Private social welfare disengagement from the poor: The case of family adjustment agencies. In *Social welfare institutions*, ed. M.I. Zald, New York: Wiley. Pp. 623–644.

Doron, A., and Rotter, R. 1976. *Low wage earners and low wage subsidies.* Jerusalem: The Hebrew University School of Social Work and the National Insurance Institute (in Hebrew).

Judge, K. 1978. *Rationing social services.* London: Heinemann.

Kahn, A.J. 1973. *Social policy and social services.* New York: Random House.

Kramer, R. 1981. *Voluntary agencies in the welfare state.* University of California Press.

Liron, R., and Spiro, S. 1980. Voluntary agencies as agents of a governmental program: The day camps for mothers of large families. *Society and Welfare* 3:66–82 (in Hebrew).

McKinley, J.B. 1972. Some approaches and problems in the study of the use of services: An overview. *Journal of Health and Social Behavior* 13:115–52.

Rich, R.C. 1977. Equity and institutional design in urban service delivery. *Urban Affairs Quarterly* 12:383–410.

Rossi, P.H., Freeman, H.E., and Wright, S.R. 1979. *Evaluation: A systematic approach.* Beverly Hills and London: Sage Publications.

Scott, R.A. 1967. The selection of clients by social welfare agencies. *Social Problems* 14:248–257.

Sharni, S. 1980. Day camps for culturally deprived mothers as a means of creating changes among participants. *Megamoth* 25:367–381 (in Hebrew).

Tripodi, T., Fellin, P., and Epstein, I. 1978. *Differential social program evaluation.* Itasca Ill.: Peacock.

Weisbrod, B.A. 1969. *Collective action and the distribution of income.* Reprint 34. University of Wisconsin, Institute for Research on Poverty.

# 12

# Community Mental Health in Israel: An Interim Policy Assessment

URI AVIRAM

## Introduction

The objective of this chapter is to present a method of interim policy assessment that is feasible and relatively inexpensive, and that is applicable to situations in which measurements of policy impact may be premature, but where policymakers and the public need to know whether, and to what extent, a policy is in fact being implemented. This approach is applied in this chapter to the field of Community Mental Health (CMH).

This evaluation reviews and examines inputs and process rather than the outcome of the program. With the aid of literature review and comparisons with other similar policies, objectives and boundaries are clarified, and the most critical elements of such a program are identified. Data sources are statistics and indices that are quite commonly gathered by administrative public agencies. Information about the extent of inputs and the direction of the critical elements of the system illuminate the trends of policy and monitor its direction. The major question is not how successful the program was but whether it was implemented at all and to what extent its course reflected the direction of its initial objectives. This type of interim assessment may allow for mid-course corrections and improvement if they are necessary. Such assessment should help policy decision makers, program planners, and administrators to monitor their services systematically, to improve operations, and to plan new services.

EVALUATING THE WELFARE STATE:
SOCIAL AND POLITICAL PERSPECTIVES

# Community Mental Health in the United States and Israel

CMH is considered a progressive departure from the traditional approaches in psychiatry. Some even view this movement as the "Third Psychiatric Revolution" (Hobbs 1964). The CMH movement has expressed itself in social policy in many countries in the Western world. Changes and innovations in the spirit of CMH occurred most specifically in England (Dept. of Health and Social Security 1975, Rozenzeig 1975), the United States (Golan and Eisdorfer 1972), and, most recently, in Italy (Gazzetta Ufficiale Della Republica Italiana 1978).

A series of laws (United States 1963, 1965; World Health Organization 1980) and several bugetary provisions transformed the ideology into an operational service delivery model. Perhaps the most ambitious and impressive undertaking was carried out in the United States, where the Community Mental Health Centers Law allocated resources for the construction of community mental health centers and for manpower development. Another impressive change took place more recently in Italy, with the passage of the most comprehensive community-oriented mental health act in the Western industrialized world (see Mosher 1982).

Although the CMH movement still lacks a well-organized theoretical base, it represents a new approach of social intervention on the community level. Its aim is to prevent mental illness and to promote mental health. The CMH movement is interested in the mental health of specified population groups, in diagnosing the level of mental health in the community, in measuring the rate and distribution of mental disorders in the community, in determining needs and resources in the community, and in finding the etiology of mental disorders and methods of preventing these disorders (Caplan 1964).

The Community Mental Health Center Movement in the United States represents one of the most advanced models based on the CMH approach applied so far. It emphasizes the principles of continuity of care, comprehensiveness of mental health services, availability and accessibility of services to the population in a specific geographically defined community. These principles have gained a wide consensus in the literature and in practice (see Levinson 1972).

Concurrent with the CMH approach, profound changes have taken place in the mental health scene, and in the pattern of services to the mentally ill. The mental hospital is no longer the hub of the mental health services delivery system. Alternative services such as day care, outpatient clinics, halfway houses, and clubs have been established in the community. The number and rate of resident patients in mental institutions have drastically declined during the last 25 years. Length of psychiatric hospitalization has been shortened a great deal. At the same time the rate of admission to mental hospitals has increased, and the use of mental health clinics and a variety of care facilities in the community has increased.

The change in the mental health service delivery system during the last 25 years is perhaps best illustrated by the drastic shift in the allocation and flow of the three most critical elements of the system: patients, manpow.er, and financial resources. In California, for example, the state's appropriations for local mental health care increased tenfold in 1 decade from 1963. In 1973 these appropriations exceeded those for state hospitals. The number of residents in state institutions declined from 37,000 in 1955 to less than 7000 in 1973 (Aviram and Segal 1973). In 1955 there were less than 1000 former mental patients residing in sheltered care facility in the community in California. Twenty years later this figure increased to more than 12,000 (Segal and Aviram 1978).

The CMH approach was also adopted in Israel. The "Reorganization Plan" of psychiatric services in Israel became an official policy of the Mental Health Services in 1972. Similar in basic approach to the American model of the Community Mental Health Center, it calls for the delivery of comprehensive mental health services in a geographically defined community (Israel Ministry of Health, Mental Health Services 1972; Tramer 1972).

Dr. A. Falik, a former head of the Mental Health Services describes the plan:

> The plan envisaged the division of the country into 20 regions for the purpose of community mental health services with a population of 150,000 in each region. Each region would have its own comprehensive mental health center and would also have a link with general medical centers in the region as well as with hospital facilities and the network of social and community services [1978, p. 9].

The first CMH centers, intended to serve as models for the rest of the country, were established in Jaffa and Ashkelon. The mental health services in Jerusalem were also organized on a geographical basis and were guided by the principles of the Reorganization Plan (Miller 1977). The policy appeared several times in the budget proposals of the Ministry of Health and Labor Federation's Sick Fund to implement the policy (Israel Comptroller General 1980).

Nine years have passed since the new policy of mental health services was announced. So far, no comprehensive evaluation of the implementation of the policy has been made. To delay such an assessment would be risky. Funds and efforts might have been invested with no adequate results; the stated policy may not have been implemented as expected.

This study is not by any means an attempt at comprehensive evaluation. As stated, its aim is to look at some of the trends and to provide information about the direction of implementation of the mental health policy. It can be regarded as a mid-course assessment of this new policy in Israel.

# Data Sources

The new mental health policy calls for a drastic change in the service delivery system. Based on its stated goals and the experience gained in other countries, one would expect changes in the three most critical elements of the mental health system: patients, manpower, and financial resources. If the implementation of the policy is successful, there will be observable changes in the flow of those critical resources in the system. Budgets will be allocated to community services, more mental health personnel will be found in the community in order to deliver community mental health services, and the flow of patients will change course—from hospitals to community. In fact, in many countries deinstitutionalization of mental patients was concurrent to their CMH programs. Decreasing the number and rates of resident patients in mental institutions has been widely accepted as one of the goals of the CMH movement (*Milbank Memorial Fund Quarterly/Health and Society* 1979).

In order to examine the flow of the three critical elements in the mental health services system, the budget proposals for the years 1972–1980 were reviewed. In addition, data about patients was gathered from the reports of the Central Bureau of Statistics and the reports of the Unit of Information and Evaluation of the Mental Health Services. Specific attention was given to the proportion of budgetary allocation to community mental health services compared to total budget of the mental health services between 1972 and 1980. The distribution of mental health personnel among the services was also examined. Also, the trends of mental hospitalization for this period were reviewed, through examination of the numbers and rates of admissions to and resident population in mental institutions between 1972 and 1979.

# Findings

## BUDGETARY ALLOCATIONS

A review of the budget proposals for the years 1972–1980 shows that the proportion of the budget allocated for psychiatric services in the community remained low throughout the period. There is only a slight difference between the amount budgeted for these services in 1972 and the allocation for 1980. The percentage allocated for psychiatric services in the community out of the total budget for mental health services was 3.2% in 1972 and 4.5% in 1980. Some slight variations do appear during the years. The proportion of psychiatric services in the community increased between the years 1972 and 1976 from 3.2 to 8%. However, the budget allocation for these services was decreased in the following year. It continued to decline, and in 1980 it reached the same level as in 1973.

**TABLE 12.1**
Percentages of Budgetary Allocations for Mental Health Services,
Israel Ministry of Health Budget Proposals, 1972–1980[a]

|  | 1972 | 1973 | 1974 | 1975 | 1976 | 1977 | 1978 | 1979 | 1980 |
|---|---|---|---|---|---|---|---|---|---|
| Mental health services | 16.1 | 12.2 | 10.3 | 9.7 | 13.0 | 18.0 | 17.0 | 16.0 | 22.0 |
| Psychiatric hospital services | 15.6 | 11.6 | 10.0 | 9.1 | 12.0 | 17.0 | 16.0 | 15.0 | 21.0 |
| Community services (part of budget of mental health services) | 3.2 | 4.3 | 4.1 | 5.7 | 8.0 | 5.7 | 5.0 | 5.0 | 4.5 |
| Capital outlays for psychiatric hospitals (part of total of capital outlays) | 14.0 | 16.9 | 21.6 | 26.3 | 10.6 | 13.4 | 16.3 | 7.0 | 10.3 |

[a]Source: See Table 12.2.

Table 12.1 shows that changes in the proportion of the mental health services in the total Ministry of Health budget were directly related to the variations in the allocations to psychiatric hospitals during the period. The allocation for mental health services dropped from 16.1% of the 1972 Ministry of Health budget to 9.7% in 1975 and then more than doubled by 1980. The same trends appear in the proportions of budgetary allocation to psychiatric hospitals out of the total budget of Ministry of Health.

Funds for development during the 8-year period were allocated almost entirely for building new hospitals or for renovating old buildings in existing mental hospitals (Israel Ministry of Finance 1972, 1974, 1978, 1980). Throughout this period the government continued to allocate considerable sums for the development of mental hospitals. The proportion of budgetary allocation for development for mental hospitals in the total development budgets of the Ministry of Health varied from 26% (in 1975) to 7% (in 1979). However, no consistent pattern is recognized. In 1980 the proportion was about the same as it was in 1976.

## MANPOWER

The total number of personnel budgeted for mental health services in the community increased almost threefold during the period 1972–1980. In 1972 the number of personnel allocated in the budget for mental health services in the community was about 100, whereas in 1980 it was close to 300 (see Table 12.2). Part of this increase was related to a general trend showing an 80% increase in the total number of personnel budgeted for the Ministry of Health

**TABLE 12.2**

**Number and Rate of Manpower of Israel Mental Health Services, by Type of Service Israel Budget Proposals, 1972–1980[a]**

| | 1972 | 1973 | 1974 | 1975 | 1976 | 1977 | 1978 | 1979 | 1980 |
|---|---|---|---|---|---|---|---|---|---|
| Total—Ministry of Health | 10,210 | 10,751 | 11,853 | 14,949 | 16,498 | 18,281 | 19,197 | 19,176 | 18,200 |
| Total—Mental Health Services[b] | 2,247 | 2,370 | 2,442 | 2,616.5 | 2,763 | 2,907 | 3,072 | 3,040 | 2,999 |
| Manpower—psychiatric hospitals | 2,148 | 2,235 | 2,304 | 2,422 | 2,482 | 2,608 | 2,775 | 2,763 | 2,738 |
| Manpower—mental health services in community | 99 | 135 | 138 | 194.5 | 281 | 298.5 | 296 | 277.5 | 271 |
| Percentage of mental health services of total manpower of Ministry of Health | 22.0 | 22.0 | 20.6 | 17.5 | 16.8 | 15.9 | 16.0 | 15.9 | 16.5 |
| Percentage of manpower in psychiatric hospitals of total manpower in Ministry of Health | 21.0 | 20.8 | 19.4 | 16.2 | 15.0 | 14.3 | 14.5 | 14.4 | 15.0 |
| Percentage of mental health services in community of total manpower in Mental Health Services | 4.4 | 5.7 | 5.7 | 7.8 | 10.2 | 10.3 | 9.6 | 9.1 | 9.0 |

[a]From Israel, Ministry of Finance. 1972, 1974, 1978, 1980. *Budget proposal for ministry of health.* Presented to the Israeli Knesset, Jerusalem.
[b]This does not include central administration main office.

during this period. The number of personnel in mental hospitals increased from 1972 to 1980 by 590 people, or by 27%.

It must be noted, however, that only 25% (172 out of 752) of personnel added for mental health services during the 8-year period were budgeted for psychiatric services in the community. This addition changed the proportion of personnel in the mental health services in the community out of the total personnel in the mental health services in the budget of the Ministry of Health from 4.4% in 1972 to 9% in 1980. Examination of the figures for each year shows that until 1978 the rate increased, but after that year the figure declined from 10.3% to 9% in 1980.

## PATIENTS

The figures on the numbers and rates of inpatients in mental hospitals and wards for the mentally ill in general hospitals show little change during the period 1972–1979 (see Table 12.3). The number of resident mental patients increased by 10%, from 8048 to 8848. The rate of people hospitalized in mental institutions per 1000 of the general population slightly decreased. (This is due to an increase in the general population in the country greater than that of mental hospitals.) In 1972 2.6 per 1000 of the Israeli population were resident mental patients, whereas in 1979 the rate was 2.4; this represents a 7.7% decrease.

A similar trend is indicated by the number and rate of admissions to mental hospitals and to psychiatric wards of general hospitals. The number of people admitted into psychiatric hospitals increased slightly between 1972 and 1979. At the end of the period, close to 13,000 people were admitted per year compared to 12,000 during 1972. The increase is less than 10%. The rate of admissions per 1000 of the general population declined during the same period by 10%, from 3.8 to 3.4. In the rates of first admissions and readmissions for this period no significant change is shown. Each year about one-third are first admissions. The average length of stay of released mental patients has increased by 30%, from 151 days in 1972 to 195 days in 1978, as indicated by the data reporting length of stay by type of hospital. In 1978 the average length of stay for patients released from psychiatric hospitalization in Israel was about 6 months.

The number of people admitted for day treatment in mental hospitals, day hospitals, and day care in psychiatric wards in general hospitals increased by more than 650 during this period reaching over 1,000 people in 1979 (see Table 12.4). The changes were minor between 1973 and 1978; the major change occurred in 1 year, from 1972 to 1973 when the number doubled. The majority of the people in day treatment received this type of service in psychiatric hospitals or psychiatric wards in general hospitals. Only 6 out of 23 units providing psychiatric day care were located in the community and affiliated

**TABLE 12.3**

**Number and Rate of Resident Patients and Admissions to Mental Hospitals and Psychiatric Wards in General Hospitals by year, 1972–1979[a]**

|  | 1972 | 1973 | 1974 | 1975 | 1976 | 1977 | 1978 | 1979 |
|---|---|---|---|---|---|---|---|---|
| *Resident patients*—end of year |  |  |  |  |  |  |  |  |
| Number of inpatients | 8,048 | 8,170 | 8,412 | 8,457 | 8,686 | 8,754 | 8,755 | 8,884 |
| Rate (per 1,000 of total population) | 2.6 | 2.6 | 2.5 | 2.5 | 2.5 | 2.4 | 2.4 | 2.4 |
| *Admissions* for inpatient care during the year |  |  |  |  |  |  |  |  |
| Total—absolute numbers | 12,010 | 12,769 | 12,800 | 12,992 | 13,724 | 12,484 | 13,205 | 12,958 |
| Rates per 1,000 population |  |  |  |  |  |  |  |  |
| Total—all admissions | 3.8 | 3.9 | 3.7 | 3.8 | 3.8 | 3.5 | 3.5 | 3.4 |
| First admissions | 1.4 | 1.4 | 1.4 | 1.4 | 1.4 | 1.3 | 1.3 | [b] |
| Readmissions | 2.4 | 2.5 | 2.4 | 2.4 | 2.3 | 2.2 | 2.2 | [b] |

[a]From Israel, Ministry of Finance. *Budget for the Ministry of Health*, 1976, 1980. Jerusalem. Israel, Central Bureau of Statistics. 1974, 1976, 1979. *Statistical Abstract of Israel* (No. 25. No. 27, No. 30) Jerusalem Israel.
[b]Not available.

TABLE 12.4
Number and Rate of People in Psychiatric Day Treatment, 1972–1979[a]

|  | 1972 | 1973 | 1974 | 1975 | 1976 | 1977 | 1978 | 1979 |
|---|---|---|---|---|---|---|---|---|
| Total number in day treatment | 406 | 790 | 780 | 807 | 887 | 841 | 896 | 1072 |
| Rate (per 100,000 of general population) | 12.5 | 23.6 | 22.7 | 23.1 | 24.8 | 23.0 | 23.9 | 27.9 |

[a]Adapted from Rahav, M. and Popper, M. 1980. Trends in the delivery of psychiatric services in Israel, 1965–1979. Ministry of Health, Mental Health Services. Information and Evaluation Unit (Hebrew,mimeo.) Jerusalem.

with a hospital (Israel Min. of Health 1972–1979). The number of units providing day treatment and located in the community did not change considerably during the period under review (Israel Ministry of Finance 1972, 1974, 1978, 1980).

# Discussion

Assessing the flow of the critical elements in the mental health system (i.e., money, manpower, and patients), we see that the implementation of the Reorganization Plan and the CMH policy fell far short of its original expectations. Eight years after the announcement of the policy there is no change in the budgetary allocation; 95% of the budget is still provided for mental hospital services. Furthermore, almost all the financial resources provided for development were for building new hospitals or renovating old ones. During this period two new governmental hospitals, one in the south and one in the north, were opened.

This trend is not congruent with trends in other countries that implemented CMH programs, where capital outlays for mental hospitals decreased and large sums of money were invested in establilshing mental health centers in the community (see Aviram and Segal 1977; Feldman 1973). Aside from some growth in the number of beds for day treatment, no major development in the establishment of alternative care facilities in the community (e.g., hostels, foster care programs, board and care programs) is found (see Israel Ministry of Finance 1972, 1974, 1978, 1980). Since the inception of the new policy, only 5 out of the 20 envisaged community mental health centers were established. Four of these centers were directly connected to mental hospitals and one to a general hospital, and their scope and efficacy is not known yet. The Israel Comptroller General in his 1980 Annual Report concludes that the process of changing the mental health clinics into community mental health centers was very slow (Israel Comptroller General 1980).

The deployment of personnel during the period under review is not, in general, congruent with the intentions of the new policy. One would expect that in order to develop community services a major effort would be made to increase the mental health personnel in the community. Although some additions are noted, especially at the beginning of the period, the increase in personnel for mental hospital services was four times higher than that for community services. This trend is in contrast to mental health manpower deployment trends in other countries which implemented the CMH policies. (See, e.g., Brown 1977; U.S. President's Commission on Mental Health 1978.)

The figures on mental hospitalization in Israel during the last 8 years also indicate that the new mental health policy was not implemented well. As mentioned, one of the goals and manifestations of the CMH policy in the Western world was a trend toward deinstitutionalization. Although the deinstitutionalization policy drew a mixed reaction from its evaluators, the fact remains that the absolute number and rates of resident patients in mental institutions have dropped drastically since the mid-1950s. Over the past 2 decades there has been a 66% decline in the resident population in mental hospitals in the United States (see Bassuk and Gerson 1978; the U.S. President's Commission on Mental Health 1978). As the data for Israel show, the absolute number of resident patients in mental hospitals actually increased. The slight decline in the rates is probably due to an increase of the general population greater than that in added hospital beds, rather than to any specific program aimed at reducing hospitalization numbers.

This conclusion is further supported by the data on admissions and length of hospitalizations. CMH programs call for crisis intervention and shorter hospitalization periods. This results in higher admissions rates and shorter lengths of stay for released mental patients. In Israel no change in the rate of admissions to mental hospitals occurred during the period reviewed, nor was there any decline in the average length of stay of released patients. On the contrary—the data show an increase in the average length of stay for discharged patients. Such a sudden increase might be the result of a large number of chronic patients being released from the hospitals; however, no such programs were undertaken in Israel during the 1970s.

The data on outpatient services is rather inconclusive. The trend of increase in the number of outpatients and the increase in the number of day-treatment patients may be a result of extending services to a population that was not served in the past (see Rahav and Popper 1980). These patients and the type of services they receive have not yet been evaluated. Even if this trend represents services to a previously unserved population in need of mental health services, the major findings regarding the stability in the trends of hospitalization during the period clearly indicate that deinstitutionalization and CMH programs in Israel fell far from their original goals.

This chapter presented an interim assessment of the new policy to reorganize the mental health services in Israel according to the principles of CMH. From the examination of the flow of the most critical elements in the mental health system, since the inception of the policy in 1972, one must conclude that at the time of the study the implementation of this policy was not going well. Establishing this fact may be important in itself. At the beginning of a process of change, some mid-course policy corrections and programs improvements might be possible. In this case, changes must be made in existing programs if the implementation of the new policy is desired (see Aviram and Segal 1973; Aviram Syme and Cohen 1976). The question of why more money and personnel have not been allocated must be answered. We must discover which conditions hindered the implementation of the policy and what might enhance its changes to succeed.

In other countries, where changes in the mental health services delivery system did take place, the development of the technological means for this change—new psychoactive drugs—was accompanied by strong economic incentives for instituting change. In the United States, the growing concern about the cost of maintaining large numbers of long-staying patients in mental hospitals, and the shift in financing mental patients from the state to the federal government created a strong economic incentive to depopulate public hospitals and develop community care programs (Aviram 1981). These incentives were further strengthened by the receptive social climate and prosperous economic conditions of the 1960s in the United States, which led to the many policies and programs of the "Great Society" (see Mechanic 1980).

As it has been shown elsewhere (Aviram 1981), an appropriate legal and organizational context is essential for the successful implementation of new policies in the mental health field. The establishment in the United States of the National Institute of Mental Health and state agencies that were independent of the mental hospital system freed the new policies from the organizational survival tendencies of the bureaucracies of the mental hospitals. The power struggle that followed the report of the U.S. Joint Commission on Mental Illness and Health (1961), between those who wanted to improve hospital treatment within the traditional medical model and those who favored a more radical approach, resulted in the success of the latter group and in legislation that gave more impetus to CMH centers which were to be independent of the old mental hospitals (see *Milbank Memorial Fund Quarterly/Health and Society* 1979).

It seems that the weak central administration of the Mental Health Services in Israel is one of the factors that hinders the policy's chances of success. A detailed report submitted by the head of the Mental Health Services in 1979 shows that organizationally the Ministry was not ready to implement the program. The Mental Health Services in Israel is actually a consultative service; budgetary and administrative responsibility remain with other sections of the Ministry of Health. Mental hospitals are controlled by the Ministry's Hospital Section and mental health clinics are controlled by its Public Health Services. Because the Mental Health Services does not control the budget, it can not translate policy principles into budgetary and personnel allocations. Lack of a comprehensive, accurate, psychiatric information system hinders any efforts to monitor and control the system and makes any effort to plan extremely difficult.

Moreover, the system is fragmented, being divided between government mental health services and the strong mental health system organized by the Labor Federation's Sick Fund, each with its own financial resources. In contrast to the federal programs in the United States, for instance, which encourage the development of alternative community programs for the mentally ill, no external financial incentives can be offered, for there is no organization in the mental health service delivery system that would have an interest, as well as the independence and capabilities, necessary to develop such resources.

The laws that govern the mental health system in Israel do not support the change envisaged in the new policy. Similar policies in the United States were assisted by laws and court decisions. The Israeli Law for Treatment of the Mentally Ill which was enacted in 1955 makes it rather simple to hospitalize people and does not encourage discharge from mental hospitals (see Aviram 1981; Segal and Aviram 1978; Aviram and Shnit 1981). In fact, the law encourages the flow of patients into mental hospitals; since the mental hospital is usually budgeted on the basis of bed capacity and occupancy, there are strong organizational incentives for the mental hospital system to discourage trends of deinstitutionalization and community mental health programs. Thus, unless the CMH policy in Israel is assisted by legislative and administrative actions and aided by budgetary and personnel allocations, it is doubtful that it has any chance of success.

## Conclusion

Despite the wide consensus among policymakers, professionals, and administrators of programs in the health and welfare field regarding the urgent necessity to evaluate policies and programs, such evaluations have been rather scarce. Many programs were initiated more on the basis of discontent with what existed than on the basis of proven effectiveness of the new procedures. Many of the policies and programs continue to operate without being assessed as to whether they actually do what they are intended to.

The scarcity of good program evaluation of mental health services has been related to the lack of incentives offered to the mental health organizations and to the threat organizations usually see in evaluative research, and to the political risks to those responsible for initiating the program involved in such evaluations.

It has been common among policymakers, mental health professionals, and administrators to refrain from much needed evaluations because of the real or imaginary conditions of complexity and the cost of such evaluations, the lack of training to carry them out, the ambiguities of the field and, at times, the vagueness of policy goals.

In the case presented in this chapter, which is similar to many cases in the health and welfare arena, it was too early to evaluate the outcome of the new policy in terms of the mental health level of the population, let alone its methodological and operational feasibility. However, information about the inputs and the direction of the most critical elements of the system may illuminate the general trend in the implementation of the policy and indicate how successful it has been.

It is believed that an interim policy assessment, which focuses on reviewing and examining inputs and on the process rather than on the outcome of the program, is desirable, feasible, and relatively inexpensive. Although it cannot prove how effective the policy will be in terms of its long-term results, it can inform us whether the implementation of the policy is in line with what it claimed it would do. This type of interim policy assessment may provide for mid-course corrections and improvements, if indeed they are necessary.

# References

Aviram, U. 1981. Facilitating deinstitutionalization: A comparative analysis. *International Journal of Social Psychiatry* 27: 23–32.

Aviram, U., and Segal, S.P. 1973. Exclusion of the mentally ill: Reflection on an old problem in a new context. *Archives of General Psychiatry* 29: 126–131.

Aviram, U., and Segal, S.P. 1977. From hospital to community care: The change in the mental health treatment system in California. *Community Mental Health Journal* 13: 158–167.

Aviram, U., and Shnit, D. 1981. *Psychiatric treatment and civil liberties: Involuntary mental hospitalization in Israel.* Tel Aviv: Zmora Bitan Modan. (in Hebrew)

Aviram, U., Syme, S.L., and Cohen, J.B. 1976. The effects of policies and programs on reduction of mental hospitalization. *Social Science and Medicine* 10: 571–577.

Bardach, E. 1977. *The implementation game: What happens after a bill becomes a law.* Cambridge, Mass.: MIT Press.

Bassuk, E.L., and Gerson, S. 1978. Deinstitutionalization and mental health services. *Scientific American* 238: 46–53.

Brown, B.S. 1977. The federal government and psychiatric education: Progress problems and prospects. In *New Dimensions in Mental Health,* Washington, D.C.: U.S. Government Printing Office, DHEW Publication No. (ADM). 77–511.

Caplan, G. 1964. *Principles of preventive psychiatry.* New York: Basic Books.

Department of Health and Social Security. 1975. *Better Services for the mentally ill.* Cmnd. 6233 HMSO, London.

Dohrenwend, B.P., and Dohrenwend, B.S. 1965. The problem of validity in field studies of psychological disorders. *Journal of Abnormal Psychology,* 70: 52–69.

Etzioni, A. 1964. *Modern organizations.* Englewood Cliffs, N.J.: Prentice Hall.

Falik, A. 1978. Mental health in Israel—General policies. In *Towards community mental health services in Israel: Activities of the Trust Fund for the Development of Mental Health Services in Israel*, ed. I. Márgules. Jerusalem: The Trust Fund. Pp. 7–11.

Feldman, S., ed. 1973. *The administration of mental health services*. Springfield, Ill.: Charles C. Thomas.

Freidson, E. 1970. *Professional dominance: The social structure of medical care*. New York: Lieber–Atherton.

Fox, P.D., and Rapport, M. 1978. Some approaches to evaluating community mental health services. *Archives of General Psychiatry* 26: 172–178.

Gazzetta Ufficiale Della Republica Italiana—N. 133 16-5-1978. Legge 13 Maggio 1978 N. 180 Accertamenti e trattamenti sanitari volontari e obbligatori. Pp. 3491–3494.

Golan, S.E., and Eisdorfer, C., eds. 1972. *Handbook of community mental health*. Englewood Cliffs, N.J.: Prentice–Hall.

Grob, G.N. 1966. *The state and the mentally ill: A history of the Worcester State Hospital in Massachusetts, 1830–1920*. Chapel Hill: University of North Carolina Press.

Hobbs, N. 1964. Mental health's third revolution. *American Journal of Orthopsychiatry* 34: 822–833.

Israel Comptroller General. 1980. Annual Report No. 30, Jerusalem.

Israel Ministry of Finance. 1972, 1974, 1978, 1980. *Budget proposal for the Ministry of Health*, Presented to the Israel Knesset, Jerusalem.

Israel Ministry of Health, Mental Health Services. 1972. *A proposal for the reorganization of mental health services: A comprehensive program*. Jeruslaem.

Israel Ministry of Health, Planning Budgeting and Medical Economics, Dept. of Medical Economics and Statistics. *Hospitals and day treatment units*, for years 1972 to 1979, Jerusalem.

Levinson, A.I. 1972. The community mental health centers program. In *Handbook of Community Mental Health*, eds. S.E. Golan and C. Eisdorfer, Englewood Cliffs, N.J.: Prentice–Hall. Pp. 687–698.

Mechanic, D. 1980. *Mental health and social policy*. 2nd ed. Englewood Cliffs, N.J.: Prentice–Hall.

*Milbank Memorial Fund Quarterly/Health and Society*. 1979. (special issue on deinstitutionalization) 57(4).

Miller, L. 1977. Community intervention and historical background of community mental health in Israel. *Israel Annals of Psychiatry* 15: 300–309.

Mosher, L.R. 1982. Italy's revolutionary mental health law: An assessment. *American Journal of Psychiatry* 139: 199–203.

Rahav, M., and Popper, M. 1980. Trends in the delivery of psychiatric services in Israel, 1965–1979. Ministry of Health, Mental Health Services, Information and Evaluation Unit. Paper presented at the Sapir International Conference on Development, Tel Aviv, 1980.

Roberts, L.M., Halleck, S.L., and Loeb, M.H. 1966. *Community psychiatry*. Madison, Wis.: The University of Wisconsin Press.

Rozenzeig, N. 1975. *Community mental health programs in England*. Detroit, Mich.: Wayne State University Press.

Rushing, W.A. 1964. *The psychiatric professions: Power, conflict and adaptation in a psychiatric hospital staff*. Chapel Hill: University of North Carolina Press.

Segal, S., and Aviram, U. 1978. *The mentally ill in community based sheltered care*. New York: Wiley.

Selznick, P. 1948. Foundations of the theory of organization. *American Sociological Review* 13: 25–35.

Sills, D.L. 1957. *The volunteers*. New York: The Free Press.

Tramer, L.A. 1972. A proposal for the reorganization of mental health service system: A comprehensive integrated plan. *Public Health* 18: 1–12. (in Hebrew)

United States. 1963. Mental retardation facilities and community mental health centers construction act. P.L.–96. *77 Stat. at, 282.* Pp. 88–164.

United States. 1965. Mental retardation and community health centers facilities Act. P.L. 89–105 Amendment, 1965, *79 Stat. at.* P. 428.

United States Joint Commission on Mental Illness and Health. 1961. *Action for mental health.* Final Report of the Joint Commission on the Mental Illness and Health. New York: The Free Press.

United States President's Commission on Mental Health. 1978. *Report to the President.* Washington, D.C.: U.S. Government Printing Office.

Weiss, C.H. 1974. Alternative models of program evaluation. *Social Work* 19: 675–681.

World Health Organization. 1980. *Changing patterns in mental health care.* Euro Reports and Studies No. 25, Regional Office for Europe WHO, Copenhagen.

# 13

## Reward Structures and the Organizational Design of Institutions for the Elderly[1]

SEYMOUR SPILERMAN AND EUGENE LITWAK

### Introduction

The configuration of rewards is one of the two mechanisms by which performance is motivated and controlled in formal organizations, the second of the mechanisms being the socialization process. By *reward structure* we mean the array of inducements and punishments associated with different levels of performance. By *socialization* we refer to the internalization of values concerning what constitutes suitable role behavior. In this chapter we use the concept of reward structure as an integrating theme; several features and problems of nursing homes are outlined in reference to this framework.

Sociologists commonly investigate how the characteristics of individuals influence performance with respect to the operation of *a particular* reward structure. For example, there have been many studies of educational achievement, the rewards in this instance being class grades. Some of the factors found to differentiate among students are IQ, race, parental SES, and parental values (Coleman 1966, Hauser 1971). There also have been numerous studies of attainment within work organizations; here the relevant rewards are occupational status and earnings. The basic finding is that family background, educational attainment, sex, and race make a substantial contribution to

[1]The research reported here was supported by a grant from the Russell Sage Foundation. Assistance was also provided by the Brookdale Institute for Gerontology and Adult Human Development, Jerusalem, Israel. The conclusions, however, are the sole responsibility of the authors.

EVALUATING THE WELFARE STATE:
SOCIAL AND POLITICAL PERSPECTIVES

explaining individual differences in occupational achievement (Blau and Duncan 1967, Jencks 1972).

Less attention has been given to the subject of *how to structure* rewards in a particular institution in order to motivate performance. We have ample evidence that features of the reward scheme are consequential for individual behavior. For example, students appear to learn more when letter grades are awarded than when a pass–fail system is used (Gage and Berliner 1975, pp. 341–342). Similarly, there have been investigations of attainment in the classroom when concrete, rather than symbolic, inducements are offered (e.g., monetary reinforcement instead of grades), and when group performance rather than individual merit is reinforced (Johnson and Johnson 1974; Michaels 1977; Slavin 1977; Slavin and Tanner 1979; Spilerman 1971). We learn from this literature, for instance, that concrete inducements are more effective than symbolic rewards at an early age and for lower class and minority youth; in short, for students who have not internalized the value of education. Where internalization has taken place, symbolic rewards appear to provide adequate motivation.

Different kinds of reward structures are also used by work organizations. Firms may remunerate employees on the basis of a piece rate, an hourly wage, or a weekly salary, the choice depending on the type of product and the style of supervision. Still different reward structures, such as the Scanlan plan (Brown 1965), provide a bonus for *group* productivity. It is recognized that these different reward structures sensitize employees to particular facets of their work roles. Piecework is the extreme case of reward for uncoordinated effort (though, as we have learned from the Bank Wiring Room study [Homans 1950, Roethlisberger and Dickson 1940], informal peer pressure may operate to reduce the variation in individual productivity that would exist among isolated workers). In contrast, group based payment plans ensure a maximum amount of cooperation and are effective schemes when coordination is required.

Where tasks are complex, an appropriately designed reward structure will be multifaceted. For example, it is not unusual for a worker's wage rate or promotion prospects to reflect individual performance while, at the same time, bonuses are offered to the work group for high productivity of completed units—a task that may require coordination. To incorporate a firm's concern about work quality, the remuneration plan might count defective units against the group's bonus.

It is also recognized that a reward structure can be ill-designed. A common example concerns the tendency in some organizations to reify "procedure" when deviations from the rules are necessary for goal attainment (Davis 1948). Individuals go by the book, in this circumstance, not because they are psychologically compulsive, but because the reward structure is more sensitive to means than to achievement. Initiative is suppressed and "ritualistic behavior" replaces "goal orientation," to use Robert Merton's (1957, pp. 131–150, 195–202) terms.

Another way in which a reward structure can be poorly designed is if it is not adequately sensitive to relevant constituencies. For instance, governmental agencies intended to serve the public sometimes are unresponsive to client needs (e.g., Blau's, 1960, analysis of welfare departments). What can be responsible is an arrangement whereby clients have little power in their dealings with staff because client satisfaction is not consequential for the careers of the workers. In contrast, in the private sector, customer treatment usually is superior. Since customers can take their affairs elsewhere, a decrease in patronization constitutes feedback to a firm that something is amiss. If the problem is correctly diagnosed, staff rewards will be adjusted to reflect perceived relations with customers. In short, the adaptive mechanism within firms in a competitive economy recognizes that customers have power, and the reward structure of employees is organized to reflect this fact.

The above examples convey the meaning of reward structure, the importance of this concept, the fact that different designs can exist for a given institution, and that a reward structure will be sensitive to certain aspects of organizational operation—or to certain constituencies—but will ignore others. To complete this discussion we point out that in a *total institution* (one in which individuals reside involuntarily and have little control over the elements of their lives) the significance of the reward structure is magnified, since there can be neither withdrawal from the facility nor appeal from its internal arrangements (Etzioni 1961, pp. 160–174). Where their preferences and dissatisfactions can be ignored, residents are effectively powerless. The pathological forms of behavior that arise in this setting (infantilism, identification with aggressors) are well documented (Bettleheim 1943, 1967, pp. 63–68).

A second integrating theme of this chapter concerns the tension between the dual goals of efficiency and responsiveness. In a nursing home, efficiency is promoted by routinization of care and by the creation of categories of patients, so that specialized mixes of services can be tailored to homogeneous groups of residents. With respect to routinization, a major difficulty is that many personal needs of patients cannot be scheduled, and attempts by a home to impose such an order tend to be burdensome for the residents. With regard to categorization, which is accomplished according to disability level, this attribute is not stable, so that the maintenance of relatively homogeneous nursing care categories entails the shifting of residents between wards and institutions. Thus, the strategies that are normally applied to obtain efficiencies in a work organization can, in a nursing home, undermine the quality of personal and social life.

In the next section we describe state reimbursement schedules for nursing home expenses and the implications of the reimbursement scheme for patient welfare. Following these comments, we turn to the matter of relations between nursing home personnel and residents, and inquire into the consequence of particular supervisory patterns for the quality of the interactions. In those two sections the underlying theoretical theme emphasizes the structure of rewards and the disfunctions of particular existing arrangements. In the third section we shift to a consideration of efficiency and responsiveness from the perspective of organizational structure and organizational design.

As a final note, we point out that a principal source of information about the daily operation of old-age and nursing homes was our own unsystematic observation over several years in four highly regarded institutions. Our presence was as relatives of patients and our attentions were directed toward their needs, not to comprehensive data gathering with pretested instruments. Yet, this sort of involvement exposes one to rather subtle aspects of decision making in the homes and to the nature of interactions between staff and patients. Our confidence in these observations is heightened by the fact that, independently, we reached many of the same conclusions.

# Reimbursement Policy and Nursing Home Adaptations

## ALTERNATIVE REIMBURSEMENT SCHEMES

Reimbursement policies for *hospitals* commonly follow a fee-for-service arrangement. Charges to a patient or a third party provider reflect the cost of diagnostic tests, treatment, drugs, and other services provided to the individual. To be precise, there usually is a fixed charge for room, food, and routine nursing care, which varies only according to the type of room accommodation (e.g., private or semiprivate). The cost of supplementary procedures is added to the basic bill.

One exception to this arrangement is that the daily rate in the intensive care ward is higher than the rate charged in other hospital units. Thus, we can view a medical facility as containing two (or more) categories of patients, with different daily rates for each. All patients within a category are billed the same fee, aside from charges for individual medical procedures. The latter, however, constitute a substantial portion of a patient's bill; indeed, this is often the larger amount.

Nursing homes for the elderly and old-age homes tend to follow different reimbursement models. The majority of *old-age homes* receive payments directly from residents or their families, not from third-party providers. Retirement homes, consequently, are able to organize their charges in a variety of ways and appear to respond to the market with regard to fees billed and services provided. Nonetheless, most operate as sheltered hotels of one sort or another and charge a fixed monthly amount which covers room, food, and ancillary services such as entertainment. Like a hospital's daily rate, the amount is usually a function only of room choice. Unlike a hospital, there is little variation among residents in the cost of their care and hence no need for supplementary charges.

*Nursing homes* operate within a more constrained reimbursement environment. For most homes, the major source of income is third-party payments, especially Medicaid, and nursing homes therefore operate in accordance with regulations that qualify them to receive these reimbursements. Although the governing provisions are state rules, because the source of the funds is federal monies the regulations vary little from state to state in many essential respects. Congress requires each state to reimburse nursing facilities on a "reasonable cost-related basis." Federal legislation is also responsible for the creation of two categories of nursing home patients, "intermediate care" and "skilled nursing care."

The logic behind establishing levels is to promote efficiency by permitting different bundles of services to be provided to each group. The distinction between the two categories involves, more or less, a consideration of whether a patient is ambulatory, alert, and needs only minor assistance in dressing and washing, or whether a higher level of care is required. In most states, like a hospital's basic room charge, the fee to a resident—or to a third-party provider—is the same for all patients in a category. Unlike hospitals, this fee is the principal charge levied by a nursing home for its services, irrespective of the needs of a particular patient.

States do differ in details of the reimbursement scheme. Some employ a system in which the fixed amount charged for each patient in a category is established prospectively, at the beginning of a billing period. Others compute payments retrospectively, on the basis of actual allowable costs. Most states have adopted "facility-related" reimbursement plans, in which state payments are based on the costs incurred by the particular home. However, a few (e.g., Illinois) use "facility independent" reimbursement schemes, in which payments are tied to patient characteristics and to the services offered by the home (Holahan, Spitz, Pollak, and Feder 1977, Pp. 106–113). A very few (e.g., California) use versions of "flat-rate" reimbursement, in which the payment is identical for all patients in a category in every nursing home in the state (Spitz and Weeks 1980a, p. 28). Nevertheless, because all states set maximums on the per diem charges they will accept, the opportunity to recover high expenses—even when properly incurred—is limited under any of the arrangements.

## NURSING HOME RESPONSES TO THE REIMBURSEMENT STRUCTURE

The reimbursement schemes under which most homes operate were designed with the objective of controlling costs, especially costs billed to third-party programs. Nursing homes have some discretion concerning how they choose to limit costs, though they must meet state licensing standards in regard to details of the physical facility, food quality, availability of registered nurses, doctors, and the like.

The criteria that homes must meet are, effectively, features of the reimbursement structure that cannot be ignored by home administrators. Existence of a minimum standard for licensing establishes threshold adaptation behavior for a profit maximizer: do enough to safely exceed the mandated minimum, but no more than necessary. Some states (e.g., Connecticut, Illinois) have complex reimbursement formulas, which depend on home quality. In Connecticut, institutions are graded A, B, C, and so forth, in accordance with a variety of physical and service characteristics, and the per-diem reimbursement rate increases with a home's quality score (Moss and Halamandoris 1977: 142). This arrangement constitutes a prescription for a nursing home administrator regarding the improvements that might be made in order to increase income. More important, schemes of this sort also designate—by omission—the features of homes and the array of potential services that will *not* enter into the reimbursement calculations.

The sort of criteria that receive weight in the evaluation of a home for licensing, or in the determination of its reimbursement rate, have characteristics of being (*a*) quantifiable; and (*b*) health related, rather than "quality of life" indices. Quantifiable standards are preferred because they usually are objective, unambiguous, and replicable. Health-related criteria are emphasized because the nursing home, as a social institution, has been viewed more as an adjunct of a hospital than of an old-age home (Kane and Kane 1978). Also, while the efficacy of health related regulations for patient well-being can be documented, this is more difficult to accomplish with "quality of life" programs. Thus, nursing homes are likely to have requirements about nutrition, room temperature, and bathing of patients, but not about the provision of social or recreational activities. Because administrators respond to the inducements of this reward structure, one often finds the physical needs of patients adequately cared for, but in an environment that is sterile—socially, intellectually, and emotionally.

The different reimbursement schemes we have discussed provide inducements for particular sorts of disfunctional adaptations. As a general statement, *facility independent* reimbursement encourages threshold mentality among administrators: On each activity covered by the state spend enough to ensure home acreditation for the activity but no more, since actual costs do not enter into the reimbursement formula. Where homes are paid on the basis of a patient's assessed level of disability (e.g., Illinois), there is little incentive for encouraging patient improvement since this would reduce income. Flat-rate reimbursement is even more pernicious from the point of view of patient welfare: Each dollar spent on a patient comes out of the home's potential profit (Vladeck 1980, pp. 83–86).

*Facility dependent* reimbursement carries little motivation to control costs because these can be passed on to the state. However, this is really a theoretical assessment, since in practice all states have a cap on the expenses they will reimburse.[2] Further, states using a facility dependent scheme have been moving toward *prospective* determination of the rate as a way to control costs. Like flat-rate reimbursement, this creates a zero-sum relationship between a home and its patients: Once the rate has been set for a year, each dollar saved can be retained by the home. Thus, an incentive is created to reduce expenditures, possibly to the detriment of patient care.

Facility dependent reimbursement with prospective determination of the rates is the most widely used arrangement. Where we do not note otherwise we will be commenting on this reimbursement structure. We wish now to describe two concrete adaptations that are rational for nursing homes to make and that, from informal discussions with staff, we believe they do make. We point out that our comments are based on observations in a few homes, though we suspect that the adaptations are fairly common (e.g., Spitz and Weeks 1980b, p. 46; Dunlop 1979, p. 89).

1. *Admission decisions.* If patients are divided into two categories— intermediate care and skilled nursing care—and if the per diem rate is the same for all patients in a category, then, on economic grounds, nursing homes should prefer the less infirm applicants from among those who qualify for a particular level of care category. Although the degree of a patient's disability affects the amount of assistance and the resources he will require from the home, the per diem billing structure is not sensitive to this consideration once the rate is set for the year. Such calculations may not be pertinent to homes with many vacant beds. However, the better institutions have waiting lists and are tempted to make cruel distinctions among the elderly, in which those with the greatest needs are disadvantaged in their quest for entrance.

2. *Who shall live.* Nursing homes for the elderly often are terminal residences for their population. The length of stay tends to be long, in comparison with hospitals; in 1973, for example, the average stay in a Medicaid-certified skilled nursing facility was 20 months (Kane and Kane 1978: 914). Among the elderly, the final years of life are accompanied by strokes and progressively incapacitating infirmities. As a result, the admissions decisions of homes usually bear relevance to the level of patient needs and patient costs only during the initial months of a stay.

In a nursing home, then, patients soon come to differ greatly in the amount of resources they require in order to be sustained. In a skilled care unit, the range of infirmity can vary from individuals who need only to be assisted from bed and dressed but are mobile with the aid of a cane or walker, to patients who are

---

[2]Norms are usually set for classes of nursing homes (e.g., in New York State, size, location, and quality affect the reimbursement rate), and homes within a category can bill no more than a certain percentage of their group average (e.g., 110%). Such payment determination tends to be insensitive to a facility's actual expenses and forces all homes in a category to have similar reimbursement rates.

paralyzed and require extensive assistance. There may also be language impairments which slow communication with a nurse or orderly, thereby requiring more staff time.

It is our view that administrators of nursing homes, at least implicitly, utilize a form of triage in allocating institutional resources. One group of patients is "profit-making" from a home's point of view, in that they require less staff time and fewer resources than the funds they bring into the home through the fixed per diem reimbursement. A second group requires resources in an amount roughly commensurate with the funds they bring to the home; the institution "breaks even" in providing for their needs. Finally, because of the range of patient infirmities within a single reimbursement category such as skilled nursing, there are individuals who require attention and resources in excess of the income they generate.

Now, the fact that, from time to time, a resident may require large expenditures by a home for brief durations—such as when one becomes ill with an infection—is unimportant with respect to the commitment of the home to maintain the resident. Rather, it is the patient who *chronically* requires a large outlay of nursing time, such as a paralyzed person, who is a threat to the economic viability of a home. Proper care may necessitate feeding, washing, turning each hour to avoid bedsores, and frequent changing of bed sheets. The high expense of nursing care for such an individual cannot be recovered under a reimbursement structure that is insensitive to patient differences in the cost of maintenance.

The adaptation that we believe occurs is that the resources required by these patients in order to survive in modest comfort and health are often denied to them. We are not alluding to the decisions of insensitive owners of profit-making homes, the scandals which have appalled us in recent years. Indeed, we suggest that in the best institutions, out of concern for the welfare of *all* residents, administrators limit the resources they permit to be spent on a chronically infirm person. The rationale is a humanitarian one: Resources expended on one patient are not available for others. At stake is not a simple moral decision of whether to meet an invalid's many needs versus maximizing the return on a financial investment, but a question of balancing the competing requirements of many elderly persons who must be maintained on a fixed budget. The result is cruel, as administrators invariably opt to care for the many, with the result that paralyzed though alert patients have to wait for assistance for intervals that exceed their endurance.[3] The psychological and physical deterioration caused by this neglect is extensive.

---

[3]Hospitals and doctors face an analogous dilemma in deciding when to discontinue the use of expensive life-sustaining equipment by a comatose patient. The situation we describe is somewhat different in that there is no question of brain death at the time support is curtailed. Further, hospital patients have legal rights in a decision to with draw support whereas the interests of nursing home patients are not represented in resource allocation decisions.

One way in which administrators implement their decisions regarding the allocation of resources among patients is by assigning a fixed number of personnel to each ward, with responsibility for all patients in the jurisdiction. Incapacitated persons may receive more staff time than other residents, but usually not an amount commensurate with their needs. Just as a home administrator must make a decision about distributing the institution's limited resources among patient wards (which is made, in part, through staff assignments), service personnel need to decide how to allot their scarce time among the assigned residents. Unlike in a hospital, the recourse of adding staff to care for patients with severe incapacities is not an option chosen by a nursing home since these expenses cannot be recovered.

A related issue concerns the provision of medical treatment in cases of acute illness. Small nursing homes do not employ a medical staff; rather, a patient's own physician visits the institution in times of sickness. A question can arise concerning when to transfer a resident to a hospital. A home's interest in this matter is that, in several states (e.g., New Jersey), reimbursement stops once a bed is vacated and it can be several days until a new resident is admitted. A physician obtaining referrals from nursing home administrators may in turn respond to the home's preference regarding transfers, except for the most serious of illnesses.

Large homes often employ full-time physicians. This ensures the ready availability of medical personnel, but it also carries a potential for conflicts of responsibility. As an employee, a staff physician must be sensitive to the home's wishes on medical-related matters. Moreover, staff physicians often are foreign nationals or immigrants, without a realistic option to enter private practice; this structural position serves to further undermine their professional autonomy.

To limit costs, homes may discourage physicians from prescribing procedures that entail intensive nursing, to the detriment of an ill resident. Also, even with physicians on staff, a nursing home has a limited capability for treating severe illness. (They may not have the facility, for example, to do IVs or monitor a heart's rhythm.) Yet, aside from a home's interest in avoiding empty beds, hospital transfers are inhibited by the fact that the justification to the state for employing physicians may involve an understanding that many illnesses which otherwise would require a hospital stay, could be treated locally. These comments pertain to the care of any acutely ill resident, but they are especially relevant to severely incapacitated patients, for whom a decision to treat

---

Yet, as N. Rango has reminded us, the case of a patient who requires intensive nursing services and has little prospect for recovery of function raises terrible ethical issues. It is a problem that we will eventually have to confront, because societal resources are limited and because the percentage of the U.S. population in the older-than-75 age group will increase substantially in the present decade.

aggressively or not carries implications for the long-term financial situation of a home.

These considerations lead to the topic of how to organize nursing homes so that they will be economically efficient *and* responsive to a patient population with a variety of needs. From what we have indicated, residents who have severe infirmities suffer acutely under the present reimbursement arrangement. One approach would be to devise entirely new reward structures. An interesting recent proposal (Kane and Kane 1978) suggests that homes be reimbursed according to the time course of a patient's level of functioning, in relation to his prognosis at the time of entry into the institution. This scheme has the advantage of eliminating the incentive to skim healthier individuals from the applicant pool. It also would associate the payments that are received by a home with patient welfare.

Yet, there are practical difficulties with a reimbursement structure of this sort. It would require that there be accurate assessments of patient functioning at the time of entry into the institution and at subsequent time points. Because of daily fluctuations in the condition of elderly persons, multiple observations would be required at each assessment to construct reliable evaluations. It also would be necessary to devise a measurement instrument that is replicatable across investigators because the same specialist might not be available to examine a patient at all times. Adding to these problems is the necessity for having the evaluations performed by specialists who are independent of the nursing home, since financial payments to the institution would be at stake. Still further difficulties involve the construction of accurate forecasts of individual functioning, and the factoring into the reimbursement model of adjustments for unpredictable events—stroke, broken hip, and the like. In short, the complications associated with managing this reward structure would be immense.

A less ambitious approach would be to tinker with existing reimbursement plans, making modifications once information has accumulated concerning specific disfunctions. For example, even with the structures currently in use, homes could be made more responsive to patient needs by creating additional resident categories, each dedicated to a particular type of infirmity or level of care, and each having a reimbursement rate appropriate to the cost of its services. A very different sort of strategy is based on the recognition that no simple reimbursement plan is likely to be devised for a complex institution, such as a nursing home, without incentives being present for some kinds of undesired adaptations. Following this reasoning, a recommended course would be to supplement the control functions of the reimbursement structure with monitoring programs and feedback channels to concerned constituencies, who might intervene to safeguard patient interests. Ombudsmen and relatives' associations can play important roles of this nature. These options are outlined and appraised in the next sections, in connection with other nursing home issues.

## Interactions between Staff and Patients

### THE STRUCTURAL CONTEXT

We are concerned with the workers who have the greatest impact on the daily affairs of residents—nurses' aides and orderlies. One must first appreciate what their work is. It consists of feeding patients, turning and washing them, inserting bed pans, cleaning bed pans, helping patients to the bathroom and wiping them. One must next understand who the workers are. Because of the nature of the task and the fact that the jobs are "dead end," the workers tend to be individuals with little education and low motivation. In large cities, they often are ethnically and racially different from the residents; in New York City, for example, the lower level staff are, predominantly, black and Spanish-speaking, whereas the residents are middle-class individuals, of Jewish, Italian, or Irish descent.

Finally, one must recognize that the conditions of most patients make interaction with staff—especially expressive interaction—exceedingly difficult. Many elderly persons have speech or hearing impairments, as a result of stroke or degenerative illness. Others are marked by some degree of senility. These maladies coupled with the fact of class, ethnic, and sometimes language differences virtually eliminate the possibility of empathy, affection, and personal consideration emerging in the relations between patients and workers.[4] This social gap is consequential because, in a context of minimum staff socialization to notions of societal responsibility for the elderly, an absence of personal bonds to moderate staff behavior means that the only mechanism available to administrators for influencing performance is the reward structure. It is our contention that the reward structures currently in effect do not adequately motivate or control staff behavior.

Lower level staff are enormously important for patient welfare. Doctors and nurses may visit patients intermittently, but they do not respond to the hourly needs of the residents. Patients are dependent upon aides and orderlies for assistance with the everyday tasks which make existence possible. How the assistance is provided determines whether or not an infirm person can live in modest comfort with some control over the immediate environment. This dependency translates into staff power. A patient who is viewed as troublesome may have to wait a long time for service. Since the degree of control over bodily functions is limited in this population, a 10 minute wait can be beyond endurance. Because there are no alternate suppliers of these services in a nursing home and

[4] In extreme cases of staff alienation, patients may be treated virtually as objects. They will be dressed without being asked which clothes they wish to wear; they will be taken to social activities or for personal services (e.g., hairdressing) without being consulted or informed about the destination. Thus, not only is control lost over the rudiments of their lives, but residents may be cut off from information concerning what is happening to them.

because patients reside there continuously, rather than for part of each day, nursing homes are effectively "total institutions" (Etzioni 1961, pp. 160–174); in an organizational sense they share important features in common with prisons and concentration camps. In each setting, residents are dependent upon staff for the essentials of their existence, powerless in their dealings with staff, and unable to withdraw from the institution.

Low-level workers have enormous power over resident comfort for several reasons. First, the staff are overworked and competing requests frequently are made for their time. As a result, failures in responding to a patient can be explained to a supervisor in terms of the concurrent needs of other residents. Second, complaints are often discounted, attributed to senility or to diffuse patient anger at their own physical incapacities, which is displaced upon staff. Third, many patients have little sense of time and do confuse a 5-minute wait with a 20 minute delay. This situation is exploited by service workers, who explain genuine complaints in terms of patient disorientation. Lower-level staff are especially powerful during the night shift, when few supervisors and no relatives are present. Finally, where the staff is unionized, it is difficult to discipline a worker in response to patient complaints unless physical abuse is evident. Disciplinary hearings involve a fact-finding procedure and, because of the mental haziness of many patients, their testimony is suspect.

Staff use their discretionary power to acquaint patients with proper behavior (from the workers' perspective), to reduce patient expectations, and thereby limit the demands for staff time. When a new resident arrives at a nursing home, relatives are discouraged by low-level workers from visiting frequently, even though the home's announced policy may encourage such visits. In a manner reminiscent of children arriving at summer camp, relatives are told that new patients resist adjusting to institutional life, that frequent visits by relatives inhibit a patient's interest in befriending other residents and slow acclimation to the home and its activities. There is merit to these remarks, but they are also self-serving: It is in the interests of staff that new patients be taught to accept long waits for service. They must be introduced to the power of workers to discipline patients, to respond to or ignore requests, and must learn that complaining to a supervisor is of no avail.

The reaction of new patients who are mentally alert is one of frustration, anger, and protest at this loss of control over the elements of their existence. In the initial weeks of stay, relatives are a problem for staff, since new patients may request concerned relatives to intervene and, unlike residents, relatives are not powerless. However, if frequent visits can be discouraged during the adjustment period, a new patient's expectations can be altered and brought into line with the facts of life in the home. In a total institution the impact of behavioral modification is enormous and few insist for long on their abstract rights.

When a patient is not severely impaired, staff socialization can make him or her self-reliant, since worker interests are not directed to limit a patient's activities but to reduce the demands made upon themselves. However, when a patient does require considerable assistance, the socialization process tends to be depressing and demoralizing, because dependence upon staff convenience and schedules is made evident. A resident who cannot control bodily functions will hear comments such as, "you just had the bedpan, you must wait a half hour," and "even though your bed is wet, I don't change linen until 2 P.M.". Socialization makes the impaired patient compliant with such directives, but the adjustment can be devastating to self-esteem. It is not uncommon for the range of interests of an alert and sophisticated individual, in this situation, to become constricted and focused on concerns about meeting toilet schedules.

## MODIFICATIONS OF THE REWARD STRUCTURE AND OTHER OPTIONS

The problem we have delineated arises from the concentration of power over patient welfare in the hands of low-level staff—hardly the most qualified of individuals—and the absence of countervailing controls to protect patients from neglect or abuse by the workers. All remedies of this situation involve a rebalancing of the power relationship, giving patients or their guardians an opportunity to evaluate staff actions and to provide effective inputs to their reward structure.

A direct approach to strengthening the hand of residents would be to have home administrators collect from them ratings of the performance of each worker. This is feasible, since the patients would not be evaluating staff in terms of technical expertise but in terms of courtesy and responsiveness. A question can be raised with respect to the interests of nonalert patients, who could not participate in an evaluation. Yet, the problem of staff performance, and their responsiveness to requests for nonroutine service, is mainly a concern of alert residents. Nonalert patients would continue to be served by the routine procedures mandated by the home. A more serious difficulty stems from the fact that residents cannot be neatly divided into alert and nonalert categories; many even vary from day to day in degree of mental clarity. For this reason, reliance could not be placed on the ratings by any single patient. However, where there is consistency in the evaluations of a worker, the result would carry greater reliability. Even more consequential than an analysis of the ratings would be the act of collecting such information. We suggest that once the staff recognize that residents will be queried periodically about worker responsiveness, this fact itself would moderate their behavior.[5]

Most homes forbid tipping. This prohibition is a testament to the effectiveness of tipping in influencing staff activity. A relative can obtain remarkably

---

[5]The evaluations would have to be collected in a manner that maintains patient confidentiality in order to protect residents from pressure or retaliation by personal care workers.

considerate service for a resident by passing a few dollars to an aide, with more forthcoming if a favorable report is provided by the resident. Tipping is forbidden because it would disrupt the home's control structure. It would distort the staff's allocation of time among patients, favoring those with external resources; it also carries a potential for extortion from patients or their relatives.[6] Yet, incentive rewards can be managed so that they do not produce these undesired consequences (e.g., Sand and Berni 1974). For example, a sum could be allocated to each worker on the basis of an average rating by the patients. Also, the allocations could be made to groups, rather than to individuals, so that the workers would be motivated to cooperate with one another in providing for patient comfort.

As an interested affiliate of a nursing home, a relatives' association can increase the sensitivity of the institution to the behavior of its staff. Home administrators recognize that many kin are concerned about patient welfare, and often collaborate with relatives' associations to the benefit of the residents. Yet, the objectives of relatives are not identical with those of home administrators; a potential for conflict exists, for example, over issues such as when to transfer ill residents to a hospital and how much conformity with a home's routine should be expected of residents. In dealing with administrators, relatives are at a disadvantage because they usually lack information about events in the home. They are not in a position to evaluate the complaints brought by patients or to challenge the explanations offered by the institution. To be effective, relatives require a source of independent information about a home's daily operation. We suggest that this could be provided by a hired representative, whose task would be to listen to complaints, observe staff behavior, and report on these matters to the relatives' association. With access to such details, the affiliate could document the insensitivities of individual workers and, generally, intervene on behalf of patient interests. For this sort of arrangement to work, it is vital that the hired observer be responsible solely to the relatives' affiliate and that his or her assessments not be diluted by the facility's view of its problems and requirements. We are therefore skeptical about the capacity of ombudsmen (who are state employees) to effect changes in a home's operation which require continuous monitoring and the focused resolve that few but concerned relatives can provide.

Each of the preceding approaches represents a different tactic for strengthening the hand of patients in their dealings with staff. In a well-governed home the administrative structure can ensure adequate delivery of routine care; what remains problematic is the performance of tasks that cannot be scheduled and that must be carried out in response to patient requests. It is our view that the schemes we have described complement one another, in that each permits staff

---

[6]Even though nursing homes are properly sensitive to the disruptive effects of tipping and bribery, administrators encourage a version of this practice. When beds are scarce a home may require a ''contribution'' from a prospective patient's family to secure admission.

behavior to be evaluated from a different perspective, though one in which the intention is to increase the influence of residents. We also favor a general strategy of redundancy in the mechanisms which protect patient interests, because their great dependency upon staff leaves patients very vulnerable.

# Organizational Design

## TYPES OF HOMES

For the purpose of understanding some of the anxieties of elderly persons in relation to nursing homes, it is useful to broaden the range of institutions under discussion. Old-age residences often are analyzed separately from nursing homes, yet in the minds of many aged individuals the two sorts of facilities are not very different; sometimes homes of each type are even linked together organizationally.

The reason why old-age homes and nursing facilities are discussed separately is that, as social institutions, they differ in a number of significant respects. Old-age residences are technically simpler; they require less capital investment, a lower level of medical skills, and utilize fewer workers. Patient needs in a nursing home are more extensive, and the complex licensing regulations of nursing facilities derive from this fact. Also, the source of income is different: old-age residences receive mainly private payments, whereas nursing homes obtain a major portion of their funds from third-party providers. For these reasons it makes sense to discuss the two institutions separately; each has its own sorts of problems and has developed a form of organization suitable to its objectives and financial environment.

What is missed by this characterization is the fact that extensive patient flows occur between these types of facilities. Old-age home residents are transferred to nursing homes if their condition deteriorates, perhaps with a hospital stay intervening. Conversely, individuals whose first residence in an institution for the elderly is a nursing facility may recover sufficiently to be moved to an old-age home, though not to a point where they can return to a private residence. One difficulty posed by these flows is that the framework of residential institutions for the aged is not arranged in a way that is sensitive to the consequence of such moves for the social and emotional well-being of elderly individuals.

According to Scanlon, Di Federico, and Stassen, et al. (1979, p. 61), in 1973, 72% of *old-age homes*[7] had fewer than 25 beds. The institutions that we observed are much larger; each has separate rooms for about 150 residents. Meals are served in a dining room, which is not unlike a comparable facility in a

---

[7]The precise category is "personal care and domiciliary care facilities."

hotel. Some recreation activities are scheduled each week by the homes; beyond this, the residents have abundant time for conversation and leisurely contact. Yet, in our observations, and according to others (e.g., Riley and Foner 1968, p. 587), the density of social interaction in an old-age home is low. To some extent, this is attributable to the impairment of mental capacities in this population. However, social distancing appears to also arise from the high rate of unscheduled departures from a home.

Sudden death is not an unfamiliar event in this age group, so one is hardly stunned to learn at breakfast that a co-resident passed away during the night. Yet, incapacitating illness is far more common, and one may hear each week about several neighbors who have been removed to a hospital or a nursing home. Although many of the departers recover, or at least stabilize at some higher level of infirmity (e.g., an inability to walk), they rarely return to the old-age home they left, especially if the institution is well regarded and has a waiting list. One reason is that full payment for room and meals is required to keep a room available, and this can be financially prohibitive if the recovery period extends over several months. An equally consequential reason is that old-age homes will not admit individuals who are even mildly incapacitated; applicants must be able to dress and care for themselves. Most homes will not accept a person who requires a wheel chair, or even permit a resident who deteriorates to this level to remain.

The old-age home is an environment in which one's friends and acquaintances are prone to disappear suddenly. The psychological adjustment made by many elderly persons to this situation is to avoid establishing close friendships since, all too frequently, the consequence of intimacy is the pain of loss. Partly for this reason, old-age homes appear to an observer to be places characterized by high levels of social isolation—although close physically, the residents are very separate emotionally.

Even more anxiety provoking than the fear of loss of friends and acquaintances is the prospect of becoming ill oneself. Because transfer to a hospital or a nursing home carries a significant probability of not returning, one's familiar surroundings and social environment are threatened. Illness not only means physical pain and mortal danger, but it can be cause for "expulsion." If one's ability to walk becomes impaired even slightly, this can generate great psychological distress. An unsteady gait is visible to staff and to other residents, and all know that further deterioration may require the individual to leave.

As a result, the organizational and physical division of institutions for the elderly into old-age homes and nursing facilities is a cause of anxiety for elderly persons as it requires moves that are disruptive of social linkages. The different costs of entry into the two markets, the different organizational arrangements and sources of payment, make the tendency to specialize in one or the other type of facility an understandable decision. Some authors (e.g., Penchansky and Taubenhaus 1965) have even recommended more extensive differentiation among homes, on the grounds that programs and resources could thereby be effectively targeted to the specific needs of residents in each facility.

One way to retain the advantages of specialization and yet reduce the trauma produced by the present organizational structure would be to promote the building of large institutions that have the scale to include both a sheltered residence and the two categories of nursing home care. An alternate approach would be to encourage vendors of smaller facilities, which provide complementary sorts of care for the aged, to locate on adjacent sites. Such arrangements (which could be promoted through tax incentives) would permit elderly individuals to continue living in the same social context as they pass through the stages of later life.

## CATEGORIES OF PATIENTS; CATEGORIES OF WORKERS

The division of patients in a nursing home into categories is an organizational arrangement intended to foster economic efficiencies (Vladeck 1980, p. 135). Categorization permits administrators to assign staff and target other resources in accordance with the diverse needs of the resident population. Within a category, services tend to be geared to the average level of disability (Penchansky and Taubenhaus 1965, pp. 593–595). The types of assistance required by only a few residents may be too rare to warrant the institution of routine care procedures; rather, such services would be provided in response to individual requests, to the extent that staff time permits. However, categorization has the potential for increasing a home's ability to respond effectively to rare needs, since, if the groupings are made homogeneous in terms of disability level, many patient requests would no longer reflect the requirements of a minority and could justify the introduction of routine procedures.[8]

Following this reasoning, the greater the number of categories the more homogeneous will be the residents in a group, and the more finely services could be tailored to their needs. Both economic efficiency and responsiveness would be served. However, elaborate categorization has costs. With respect to efficiency, the empty beds in one resident category could not be filled from an overflow of patients appropriate to another division. With regard to patient welfare, because an individual's disability level is not a stable attribute, the use

---

[8]One example relates to recreational activities. The better nursing homes have game rooms and schedule concerts and other events each week in a central auditorium. A question, however, concerns how residents get to the activities. In the homes we observed, a crucial consideration was the ability of a patient to propel a wheelchair along corridors. Where patients had this faculty, they were in a position to enjoy the recreational program of the home. However, patients who lacked the necessary arm strength were dependent upon the staff to transport them, and this was rarely done. Because most of the residents were bedridden, the routines instituted by the home were geared to patients in this condition, and the staff sought to simplify their own chores by treating all incapacitated residents as requiring, essentially, the same service routine.

of multiple categories would require considerable movement of patients, if relatively homogeneous residence groups are to be maintained. Even when such shifts occur within a single institution, they can be disruptive of the precarious social life of elderly persons. As a consequence, we would recommend against instituting more categories than the two broad ones in current use.

A different approach to categorization emphasizes the specialization of workers. The economic benefits of a division of labor are, of course, well understood, and all complex organizations utilize this principle. What is less well appreciated is the use of specialization as a tactic for administrative control over staff activities. Where workers have multiple responsibilities and where many of the tasks are nonroutine and not controlled by schedules, they have considerable discretion in deciding how to allocate their time. Indeed, as we have argued, it is precisely this discretion which creates staff power over residents and permits workers to ignore many requests for service. However, specialization can be used to ensure that each of the various responsibilities of the staff receives its proper emphasis. In particular, complex chores could be subdivided into component tasks, and each assigned a number of workers that reflects the home's view of its importance. A narrowing of responsibility would reduce worker discretion and enhance the ability of home administrators to hold staff accountable for the performance of specific jobs.

The cost of coordination is the price associated with a division of labor. The advantages of specialization, therefore, are limited to chores that either require multiple skills or that do not have to be performed at a single time with the same patient. Where this is not the case and specialization would create coordination problems, a better alternative would be to devise a complex reward structure that is sensitive to the performance of each component task, or a reward structure that incorporates the evaluations of residents. (In supplying ratings, residents would be implicitly aggregating the multiple areas of staff responsibility.) The latter approaches to control over staff were outlined in the preceding section; they are probably the preferred arrangements for providing most of the health and personal care services required by nursing home patients.

Yet, there are tasks that could be separated from the multiple responsibilities of nurses' aides and attendants and that are often neglected in the press of competing work demands. A prominent example concerns staff obligations with respect to physical rehabilitation.[9] The tasks in this area are sufficiently distinct from personal care chores that assigning them to different personnel would not create coordination problems. One advantage of separation is that, as we have

---

[9] Although many nursing homes have rehabilitation professionals on staff who work with residents a few times each week, it is also necessary that the residents exercise daily to build muscle strength. Assistance with these simple exercises is supposed to be given by personal care workers. However, the assistance often is not provided. Unlike feeding and washing patients, or changing linen, there are few overt signs that can indicate to a supervisor whether or not a patient has been properly exercised.

indicated, it would give home administrators greater control over the performance of diverse jobs. As a second benefit, it would permit a nursing home to acquaint different categories of workers with different norms, and reward them according to standards of performance appropriate to their narrow areas of responsibility. In particular, it may be unreasonable to hold personal care workers accountable for patient improvement, since the bulk of their time is occupied with patient maintenance. The situation would be different, however, for staff whose primary responsibility is to exercise residents and assist in their rehabilitation; workers with this specialization could be trained to expect patient improvement and be rewarded on the basis of patient progress.

## Implications for Policy

The better nursing homes for the aged are nonprofit institutions, often sponsored by religious associations. The physical plant may be attractive, and the administrators and senior staff are committed to providing a humane environment for elderly, infirm persons. Nonetheless, these intentions frequently are not translated successfully into practice. Although residents come to the homes to live out their lives with some modicum of pleasure and comfort, not to recover from illness, it is as social settings that nursing homes are especially problematic. The lives of residents are regimented; they are dependent upon staff schedules for assistance with personal needs and they retain little control over how the time in a day will be spent.

In this chapter our objective was to explore some of the organizational factors that are responsible for the poor quality of life in many nursing homes. We have concentrated on issues that involve the notions of *reward structure* and *categorization* (or specialization) because these considerations have received much attention in the formulation of governmental policy, and because we concur that arrangements on these matters carry great importance for patient welfare. Governmental interest in organizational issues stems from a concern about controlling the escalating costs of nursing home care and from a desire to influence the allocation of resources among patients with different levels of need. Yet, the consequences of the arrangements that have been adopted are detrimental to the quality of life of elderly persons.

It is our contention that every reward structure has built-in inducements for behaviors that are dysfunctional from the point of view of policymakers. These distortions of intent are a natural consequence of an attempt to guide behavior in a complex institution through the use of a few simple rules to determine a home's income. Analogous difficulties within a nursing home, concerning staff performance, can also be understood in terms of inadequacies of a reward structure. Here the problem was diagnosed as a situation in which personal care workers have multiple responsibilities, while residents lack the power to influence the use of time by the staff. In some institutions, supervision and the reward structure can be augmented with the control effects of socialization. However, a dependence upon value internalization requires workers who are empathetic to the needs of the elderly and, because of location, many nursing homes cannot recruit low-skilled personnel who are responsive to value training.

In line with this analysis, our inclination is *not* to conclude by proposing yet another reimbursement scheme for homes, or reward structure for staff. Improvements certainly can be devised (e.g., Kane and Kane 1978; Sand and Berni 1974) and we have suggested some innovations. However, our principal conclusion is that, because of the complexity of patient needs, no single control structure is likely to be adequate for ensuring patient welfare. Patients will fare best where a diversity of concerned groups are active, each monitoring the operation of a home from the vantage of its own perspective. In the private sector, reward structures effectively control staff performance because changes in patronization provide feedback to a firm, and the parameters of the reward structure can be adjusted accordingly. A comparable feedback mechanism does not exist in nursing homes, but we suggest that this same function could be served by the presence of multiple evaluation structures, each focusing upon patient welfare from its own special viewpoint. In this situation, the insensitivities of existing control arrangements would be moderated by the reactions of particular constituencies to behaviors that fall within their domains. State governments can play a supportive role in this endeavor, in addition to their licensing and inspection programs, by legitimizing the right of concerned groups (of relatives, elderly persons in the community, and others) to gain access to nursing homes as observers.

From a different perspective, a central problem faced by nursing homes concerns the delivery of nonroutine services in a manner that is responsive to patient wishes. Nursing homes achieve economies by routinizing the provision of care, and consequently, there is a tendency to force many patient needs into a framework of routine, even when they cannot be adequately accommodated in this way. One strategy for increasing responsiveness involves the categorization of patients or staff. This sort of solution promises to restructure the distribution of patient needs, or reorganize the delivery of services, in ways that heighten staff responsiveness as well as promote efficiency. The advantages and limitations of these approaches were discussed in the chapter. A second strategy would focus solely on arrangements to enhance responsiveness, in the view that pressures for efficiency are already powerful and one must bolster a home's commitment to meeting the idiosyncratic needs of patients. Attempts to increase patient influence in the reward structure for staff, and strategies for bringing the operation of nursing homes under the observation of concerned groups, represent solutions of the latter sort; they are not intended to contribute to efficiency. A still different approach, suggested by Litwak (1977), would make use of the special suitability of primary group members for meeting the nonroutine needs of residents. However, because primary group members often are not available, we have concentrated in this chapter on bureaucratic arrangements.

## ACKNOWLEDGMENTS

Comments by Nicholas Rango, M.D., are gratefully acknowledged.

# References

Bettleheim, B. 1943. Individual and mass behavior in extreme situations. *Journal of Abnormal and Social Psychology* 38: 417–452.

Bettleheim, B. 1967. *The empty fortress*. New York: Free Press.

Blau, P. 1960. Orientation toward clients in a public welfare agency. *Administrative Science Quarterly* 5: 341–361.

Blau, P.M., and Duncan, O.D. 1967. *The American occupational structure*. New York: Wiley.

Brown, R. 1965. *Social psychology*. New York: Free Press.

Coleman, J.S. 1966. *Equality of educational opportunity*. Washington, D.C.: U.S. Government Printing Office.

Davis, A.K. 1948. Bureaucratic patterns in the navy officer corps. *Social Forces* 27: 143–153.

Dunlop, B.D. 1979. *The growth of nursing home care*. Lexington, Mass.: D.C. Heath and Company.

Etzioni, A. 1961. *A comparative analysis of complex organizations*. New York: Free Press.

Gage, N.L., and Berliner, D.C. 1975. *Educational psychology*. Chicago: Rand McNally.

Hauser, R.M. 1971. *Socioeconomic background and educational performance*. Washington, D.C.: American Sociological Association.

Holahan, J., Spitz, B., Pollak, W., and Feder, J. 1977. *Altering Medicaid provider reimbursement methods*. Washington, D.C.: Urban Institute.

Homans, G.C. 1950. *The human group*. New York: Harcourt, Brace and World.

Jencks, C. 1972. *Inequality: A reassessment of the effect of family and schooling in America*. New York: Basic Books.

Johnson, D.W., and Johnson, R.T. 1974. Instructional goal structure: Cooperative, competitive, or individualistic. *Review of Educational Research* 44: 213–240.

Kane, R.L., and Kane, R.A. 1978. Care of the aged: Old problems in need of new solutions. *Science* 200: 913–919.

Litwak, E. 1977. Theoretical bases for practice. In *Maintenance of family ties of long-term care patients*, eds. R. Dobrof and E. Litwak. Washington, D.C.: U.S. Government Printing Office. Pp. 80–111.

Merton, R. 1957. *Social theory and social structure*. New York: Free Press.

Michaels, J.W. 1977. Classroom reward structures and academic performance. *Review of Educational Research* 47: 87–98.

Moss, F., and Halamandoris, V.J. 1977. *Too old, too sick, too bad*. Germantown, Md.: Aspen Systems.

Penchansky, R., and Taubenhaus, L.J. 1965. Institutional factors affecting the quality of care in nursing homes. *Geriatrics* 20: 591–598.

Riley, M.W., and Foner, A. 1968. *Aging and society*. Vol. 1. New York: Russell Sage Foundation.

Roethlisberger, F.J., and Dickson, W.J. 1940. *Management and the worker.* Cambridge, Mass.: Harvard University Press.

Sand, P., and Berni, R. 1974. An incentive contract for nursing home aides. *American Journal of Nursing* 74: 475–477.

Scanlon, W., DiFederico, E., and Stassen, M. 1979. *Long term care: Current experience and a framework for analysis.* Washington, D.C.: Urban Institute.

Slavin, R.E. 1977. Classroom reward structure: An analytic and practical review. *Review of Educational Research* 47: 633–650.

Slaven, R.E., and Tanner, A.M. 1979. Effects of cooperative reward structures and individual accountability on productivity and learning. *Journal of Educational Research* 72: 294–298.

Spilerman, S. 1971. Raising academic motivation in lower class adolescents: A convergence of two research traditions. *Sociology of Education* 44: 103–118.

Spitz, B., and Weeks, J. 1980a. *Medicaid nursing home reimbursement in Illinois.* Washington, D.C.: Urban Institute.

Spitz, B., and Weeks, J. 1980b. *Medicaid nursing home reimbursement in Minnesota.* Washington, D.C.: Urban Institute.

Vladeck, B.C. 1980. *Unloving care.* New York: Basic Books.

# 14

# Evaluating Slack in Public Programs by the Experience Curves Method

## GIDEON DORON AND URI ON

Most evaluative studies of public policy focus on the impact of public programs on their target population, or their ability to attain stated goals. Fewer studies examine the processes used leading to the achievement of program outputs. This latter type of study is called process evaluation (Nachmias 1979, 1980). It is in this tradition that we approach the following evaluative issue.

To evaluate processes properly, it is essential to determine the degree of efficiency with which available inputs were employed in the production of outputs. Some inputs relate to the costs of producing the goods and services the organization renders to its clients. They take the form, for instance, of raw materials, manpower, or machinery. Other inputs relate to the attempt to create conditions that are conducive to the program's execution. For that purpose, organizations invest in the "good will' of their workers and clients so as to reinforce their loyalty to a program. With employees, this usually takes the form of extra benefits; clients' loyalty is generally fostered through advertising or public relations. We define the portion of the total of resources recruited for a program or accumulated in the organization *above* the levels required to maintain the organization's internal (i.e., workers and managers) and external (i.e., clients) coalitions as slack in public program.

With one unsuccessful exception (i.e., Bourgeois 1981), we do not know of any attempt to measure the extent of slack in public programs.

This chapter suggests that by utilizing the method known as the experience curves technique it is possible to determine the extent of slack accumulation in public programs. An experience curve describes a situation in which the cost of

EVALUATING THE WELFARE STATE:
SOCIAL AND POLITICAL PERSPECTIVES

a unit of production or services decreases as a function of the learning and experience gained in the working process of the organization.

The first section of the chapter introduces the definition of slack and explains the various problems involved in producing a satisfactory definition of this concept. The second section describes the experience curves technique and demonstrates its utilization. The third section shows how to measure slack in a public program using this technique. A discussion and conclusion follow.

## The Meanings and Definition of Slack in Public Programs

The concept of organizational slack was proposed in Cyert and March's seminal work, *The Behavioral Theory of the Firm* (1963). Slack is considered there to be an important organizational condition which affects the organization's behavior in changing situations. It is important to note, however, that although Cyert and March presented a significant concept, their definition of slack did not advance organizational theory. This is because they did not define it sharply, nor did they offer any method for measuring the extent of slack within an organization. This may explain why many students of organizations, although fully aware of the importance of slack, did not confront this concept systematically.

Cyert and March offer several definitions for organizational slack. For example, slack is seen as the gap between the resources available to the organization and the payments necessary to maintain its coalition (pp. 36, 278). Since the dominant coalition of a "firm" is composed of groups and individuals who function outside the formal boundaries of the organization, slack becomes a means to induce outsiders to remain loyal to the organization. Thus, generation of slack, as a means to recruit support may become an important goal in public programs.

Elsewhere (p. 45), they describe slack as a resource that does not belong to any specific output. A pool of resources exists alongside the production process; these are uncommitted resources. Expenditure for staff (e.g., advertising, service to clients, research and development), and management expenditures (e.g., expense accounts, business related travel) are examples of this type of resources.

By defining slack as uncommitted resources we may better understand the behavior of the organization in a changing situation. For example, during a period when the organization is doing well—when demand for its products increases—the rate of profit may be absorbed as production costs. The logic is simple: During good times members of the organization may receive better payment and working conditions than are needed to keep them in the organization. Staff and management units may expand regardless of their marginal contribution to the organization.

On the other hand, when the environment becomes hostile, slack enables the firm to block shocks and survive the bad times. With slack, the organization can absorb part of the variability of the environment. Organizations with slack can adjust more easily to changing circumstances than organizations without slack. The organization can reduce operational costs by an equivalent to the amount of slack without significantly interfering with production. Slack reductions are usually expressed by such methods as cuts in personnel, changes in working conditions, and reduction of the benefits given to the employees. Slack thus stabilizes the organization in two ways: It absorbs extra resources during good times, and supplies them during bad times.

Cyert and March also consider slack as a means to resolve or avoid conflicts which among the various units and individuals in the organization, all of which operate under the dictate of scarcity of resources and functions. Slack provides greater flexibility and freedom of operation for organizations seeking solutions to internal problems. It also helps the organization cope with environmental uncertainty and is a source for financing innovation that would not be possible under ordinary conditions of scarcity (p. 116).

Thus, it is clear that slack may significantly affect organizational behavior. However, it appears that the authors confused two different meanings of slack. Slack may be a "reserve" resource ultimately consumed by the organization and thus finite, or it may be a resource invested in order to generate other resources. Or is it both? A distinction must be drawn between types of slack.

Furthermore, Cyert and March do not discuss the issue of different sources of slack. In principle, we distinguish between two factors that generate slack. One is increase in organizational efficiency, that is, the performance of the same activities at a lower cost without reducing the output. The second is successful utilization of the organization's bargaining position, enabling it to effectively mobilize the resources of its environment above the level required for production (Yuchtman and Seashore 1967).

Bourgeois (1981) understood the importance in clarifying this distinction and identified three major functions of slack in the internal maintenance of organizations. He labeled them inducement (to maintain the internal organizational coalition), conflict resolution, and workflow buffer (pp. 30–34). Giving this range of meaning, Bourgeois developed a definition that synthesizes all interpretations while permitting the measurement of slack. Bourgeois defines slack as follows: "Organizational slack is that cushion of actual or potential resources which allows an organization to adopt successfully to internal pressures for change in policy, as well as to initiate changes in strategy with respect to the external environment [p. 30]."

This definition is clearly an advance, but it is still unsatisfactory. It implicitly assumes slack to be a positive phenomenon; thus, one may infer that organizations should always try to increase the level of slack.

But slack can be negative, representing waste. To be operational, a definition should be neutral, independent of the positive or negative outcomes of the phenomenon under consideration. Bourgeois, ignoring this requirement, offers several indicators to measure slack as a positive organizational condition. However, he does not offer any method for measuring slack as a negative phenomenon. He proposes to examine an organization's public financial records in order to detect slack, using indicators such as changes in retained earnings, credit rating, and price earnings ratio (p. 38). It is clearly impossible to add these different measures together, to arrange them in order of importance and to assess their weight in terms of their relative contribution to the total amount of slack accumulated in the organization over time. A single indicator for measurement of the extent of slack in an organization without these computational problems would clearly be preferable.

This unsuccessful attempt to define and measure slack brings us back to square one. We identified three conditions necessary for a satisfactory definition of organizational slack:

1. It must be neutral. That is, the existence of slack is inherently neither positive nor negative in terms of its effect on organizational performance. Therefore, the positive or negative quality of slack depends on its utilization in the organization and should not be part of the definition.
2. It must indicate the cumulative nature of slack. Thus, it will explicitly relate the phenomenon to the time dimension. (This also implies that organizational slack is a manipulable resource: The organization may accumulate it in times of prosperity and use it in times of need).
3. It must be set on the macro-organizational level. This guarantees its objectivity and independence of the subjective evaluations of different members in the organization whose perceptions of the extent of slack in their organization may vary.

Based on this minimal set of conditions, we define slack as *the portion of total resources accumulated in the organization over time above the levels required for the maintenance of its internal and external coalitions.*

The definition of slack is an improvement over the set of definitions suggested by Cyert and March and the one offered by Bourgeois in two very important ways. First, it is inclusive, covering a wide range of forms of slack created in the organization: the negative aspect of slack (waste), as well as the positive type, which is used to generate more resources for the organization. Second, and perhaps even more important, it is simple and can be easily applied to the measurement of slack.

One aspect of the inherent problem in the measurement of slack is the many forms it takes in the organization. Slack can be a tangible and intangible resource. Yet, in Cyert and March's and Bourgeois's interpretations slack is primarily a tangible asset. According to Bourgeois it can be detected from the financial records of the organization. This approach disregards the intangible

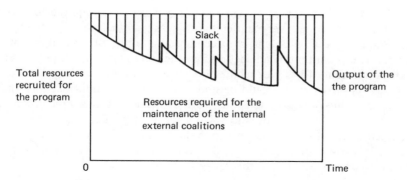

**FIGURE 14.1.** *This chart shows slack and coalition maintenance costs. The downward wavy magnitude of the line that separates coalition maintenance costs from slack reflects sensitivity to changing organizational situations and the effects of experience.*

resources of the organization, for example, the organization's reputation; the accumulated, specialized, or unique knowledge acquired in the program over time; the good will of the customers toward the program. Clearly, in order to acquire such assets the organization needs to invest tangible resources in the form of money, time, manpower, or energy.

The intangible resources should, of course, be included along with the tangible ones in any attempt to assess the extent of slack in an organization. They should be represented by a common value—money. For example, in order to expend an organization's services it is often necessary to advertise; advertising may, in turn, help to increase the clients' good will or loyalty to the program. This process can easily be translated into pecuniary values (Doron 1979).

In terms of our definition, those clients who are affected by advertising are a subset of the external coalition. Other organizations, lawmakers, media people, and similar groups are the other subsets. The organization must invest in them in order to maintain their loyalty to its programs; this investment takes many forms which could be translated into monetary value. Likewise, money can represent investments made in the internal coalition. In order to keep its workers satisfied, the organization may provide them with cultural activities, expense accounts, special uniforms, and other such benefits. Again, this expenditure can be measured in terms of dollars and cents.

All in all, the greatest advantage of using money as an indicator for organization performance is the simple means it provides to evaluate a very complicated matter. The organization's budget contains all the values necessary for the analysis, since it reflects past and present accumulation of slack in its variety of forms.

Our definition, however, does not clarify the phrase *above the level required.*

Given the possible variance of opinions on how much is required to perform successfully, it becomes very difficult to assess such a level objectively. We could approach this problem by deciding that only the members of the organizational coalitions can determine the minimally accepted level of resources necessary for their organization's successful functioning. Hence, the required level of resources could be understood as an equilibrium or a saddle point representing pressure, demands, various needs of the members. Another way to approach this problem is to solve it technically. The required level, we say, is determined by the point at which the cost of operation of a production cycle, defined by experience curve, becomes asymptotical to the $x$-axes. We turn next to an explanation of this latter approach.

## The Experience Curves Technique

When certain actions are conducted repeatedly, the experience subsequently accumulated leads to a reduction in the cost of operation. Experience curves describe improvements that occur in the process of transforming inputs to outputs as a result of experience acquired through repetition. This section discusses the conditions for the construction of the curves and then presents the function that relates the number of cycles of operation and the improvements in production to cost reductions.

The process of learning and the acquisition of experience exist at individual as well as organizational levels. The worker who repeats the same task learns, among other things, to use motoric ability more efficiently and with greater speed. Movements become simultaneous, short, and continuous. Coordination improves and the body can be used without conscious thought.

The workers learns to refrain from unnecessary actions that interfere or complicate the work. On the mental level, the worker sharpens an ability to make decisions, and quickly identifies solutions for problems that are similar to these encountered in the past. Thus, an experienced person can cope effectively with events that seem almost insoluable to the novice. The scope of "newness" is minimized for the veteran.

The individual level is customarily represented by learning curves, whereas at the organizational level we aggregate the personal learning functions and represent them by a single function known as an experience curve. Hence, the first type is a special case of the second.

What are the consequences of organizational experience? Improvements occur in the arrangement of work, by either better synchronization of actions or sequencing of operations. These improvements affect such areas as planning, production management, stock control, and spare parts supply. The quality of the product may improve with experience gained. Raw material may be saved by proper utilization of machinery and subsequent minimalization of damage. The extent of engineering and reliability changes in production of the product or the service will be lower. All such improvements may raise workers' morale, which will in turn be conducive to improved work performance.

The experience curve reflects the rate of cost reduction due to the increase in the number of operational cycles. This rate is expressed as a weighted average of the learning percentage in the areas of various organizational costs, either direct or indirect.

An operational cycle is defined as the time required for the organization to execute a specific activity, from its inception to its completion. Thus, for example, an operational cycle at the housing ministry may be the time required to complete all the operations connected with building one housing unit. An operational cycle for the courts is the time elapsed from the initiation of proceeding until the case is settled or the sentence pronounced.

From the above discussion one could infer that various ministries, departments, industries, and other types of organizations should be described by different experience curves. The variability is largely related to the human factor in the production process and to the number and length of cycles. In principle, the experience function can be described as a relationship between the number of cycles and the costs of producing them:

$$C(N) = f\, C(1) \cdot N^B \quad (-1 < B < 0). \tag{1}$$

where $C(N)$ is the cost of operation cycle $N$, $C(1)$ is the cost of the first cycle, $N$ is the number of cycles in the process, and $B$ is the coefficient of the experience rate.

The most important property of Eq. (1) is that it describes a situation whereby whenever the number of operations doubles, the cost of the cycle is reduced by a constant rate $(B)$. For example, when $N$ is the number of cycles in the process, the division of cost of the $2N$ unit by the cost of the $N$ unit be:

$$\frac{C(2N)}{C(N)} = \frac{C(1) \cdot (2N)^B}{C(1) \cdot N^B} = \frac{C(1) \cdot 2^B \cdot (N)^B}{C(1) \cdot N^B} = 2^B.$$

In order to compute the difference between $N$ and $2N$ operation cycles in cost reduction due to learning, we substitute different values for $B$. For example, if we substitute $-.40$ for $B$ then $2^B$ equals $.70$. Or, if $B = -.32$ then $2^B$ equals $.80$. In other words, the cost required to execute $2N$ cycles would be equal to 70% of the cost required to operate $N$ cycles in the first case, or 80% in the second.

Using this function Boren and Cambell (1970) constructed tables for a range of values that could be substitive for $B$. These tables supply information concerning the cost of the $N$ cycles in comparison to the cost of the first cycle at different rates. Many of these tables represent the empirical reality of actual organizations. Table 14.1 represents a computation of one such table at an experience rate of 70%.

Column 1 of Table 14.1 represents the number of cycles. The second column of the table shows computations of unit marginal cost. So that each the number of cycles doubles, the cost of production is calculated at 70% of the previous cost. Column 3 contains the figures for the average cost in this system of cycles, that is, the average between the marginal costs.

To illustrate the use of the table, assume that the cost of producing the first 10 units of a given product is $1.5 million. Since the evaluator had no historical data concerning production costs of each unit, experience curves were used to assess the nature of production. Let us assume that the rate experience in production is 70%. We would like to know how much, on the average, 10 additional units will cost.

First, the average cost of producing one unit is computed. It is $150,000 per unit. Since the experience curve is derived with regard to the cost of the first cycle, $C(1)$, we find in column 3 that each unit in a sequence of 10 cycles costs on the average .493 of the cost of the first cycle. Therefore, if $150,000 is 49%

**TABLE 14.1**
**Experience curve of 70%**

| (1) Number of cycles | (2) Marginal cycle cost as a percentage of the first unit | (3) Average cycle cost as a percentage of the first unit |
|---|---|---|
| 1 | 1.000 | 1.000 |
| 2 | 0.700 | 0.850 |
| 3 | 0.568 | 0.756 |
| 4 | 0.490 | 0.689 |
| 5 | 0.437 | 0.639 |
| 6 | 0.398 | 0.599 |
| 7 | 0.367 | 0.566 |
| 8 | 0.343 | 0.538 |
| 9 | 0.323 | 0.514 |
| 10 | 0.306 | 0.493 |
| 11 | 0.291 | 0.475 |
| 12 | 0.278 | 0.458 |
| 13 | 0.267 | 0.444 |
| 14 | 0.257 | 0.430 |
| 15 | 0.248 | 0.418 |
| 16 | 0.240 | 0.407 |
| 17 | 0.233 | 0.397 |
| 18 | 0.226 | 0.387 |
| 19 | 0.229 | 0.378 |
| 20 | 0.214 | 0.370 |

of the cost of the first unit, the cost invested in the first unit should be $304,206.

We now proceed to examine column 3. In order to find the average cost of 10 additional units, we calculate the cost of producing 20 units. The correct coefficient is .370 of the cost of the first unit. By computation, we find that the average cost of production for a unit in a sequence of 20 cycles is $112,576 (304,206 × .37). Twenty units will thus cost $2,251,520 (112,576 × 20). In order to produce 10 more units we have to invest $751.520 (2,251,520 − - 1,500,000). Hence, the average cost of production for a unit in the second sequence of 10 units is only $75,152.

Experience curves are widely used in industry. In general, the average experience rate for the industry is 80%. Since experience is a common phenomenon, curves can be fitted for every human organization, even complex ones. The phenomenon of experience is so widespread that one scholar (Hirschmann 1964) has noted that "the experience curve is the underlying natural characteristic of organized activity, just as a bellshaped curve is an accurate description of the normal random distribution of anything from human I.Q. to the size of tomatoes [p.125]."

## The Use of Experience Curves in Calculating Slack in Public Programs

The discussion thus far may be summarized as follows: Slack is a product of the working process in the organization. Learning and experience are important elements in this process; because they are inherent in many aspects of organizational activities, we may expect that resource surpluses will accumulate over time in the organization. Thus there exists a direct relationship between organizational slack and experience. All things being equal, if the organization learns to utilize its resources more efficiently, it will generate more slack. It then follows that program planners could use the information generated by the experience curves in order to achieve the amount of slack desired by their organizations. We now turn to the explanation of how to measure organizational slack with the aid of experience curves.

The estimating function Eq. (1) that describes the relationship between the number of cycles and the costs of maintaining the internal and external coalitions is presented in Figure 14.2. The costs of production are part of maintenance cost. Slack includes additional resources, accumulated in amounts greater than needed for the maintenance of the organization coalition, that is, over these maintenance costs.

The construction of function Eq. (1) is based on two assumptions. The first assumption is that an organization that starts a program and implements it during a certain time period, reaches the level of resources that guarantees the maintenance of its coalitions. The organizations must make sufficient investment in the internal and external coalitions to ensure the execution of programs. The second assumption is that with the increase in the number of production cycles, more learning and experience is acquired, so that the organization will require less resources to maintain its coalition.

From these two assumptions we deduce that we need only know the costs of maintaining the coalition for the first cycle and the rate of experience associated with these costs in order to compute the level of slack. For the purpose of our computation, we assume that the level of expenditure used to maintain the coalition will not be reduced as a result of the experience effect. Thus, slack begins to accumulate only after the initial stage of the public program or the first production cycle has been completed. Figure 14.2 describes a situation in which the costs assigned to the cycles do not change from the first cycle to the $n$th one. This assertion, manifested in the chart by budget line AA', is based on the fact that public programs are usually not financed in accordance with their marginal costs, that is, the cost of producing an additional service unit. Public programs are usually budgeted according to fixed standards, such as costs per student or hours per case. The budget line is a constant rather than a variable.

The budget represents the sum of a variety of costs such as costs of physical production (raw material, energy), overheads, wages and salaries, nonwage benefits (e.g., recreation facilities), and expenses for public relations. Experience operates on all of these costs, and the real cost for the organization is defined by the area below the experience curve. The curve is defined in turn by the coefficient $(B)$, which estimates the rate of experience. Slack is an immediate outcome of this computation, as shown in Figure 14.2. However, unless the slack is planned by the organization in order to enable its future

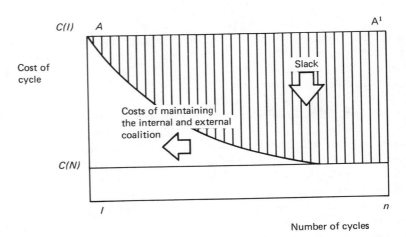

**FIGURE 14.2.** *This chart shows the relationship between the number and costs of cycles.*

flexibility and freedom of operation, management may well be unaware of its existence. In this case, organizational slack could be perceived as waste. Awareness is therefore a necessary condition for the utilization of slack, regardless of the motivation or ability of the organization to use its slack for purposive aims.

The experience curve technique has a great advantage in measuring slack: It is simple and practical. Using the previous example, we will now demonstrate how to measure slack.

The cost of the first cycle was $304,206, and the experience coefficient was .70. If the organization was budgeted in accordance with the cost of the first cycle, it should have reached $6,085,200 for the production of 20 units. The average cost of production for 20 units has already been identified as $2,251,520. The difference between the program budgeted according to the first cycle and the average production cost of 20 units (after taking experience into account) is identified as slack. Simple subtraction shows that $3,833,480 signifies the level of slack in the program.

## EVALUATION OF SLACK IN A PUBLIC HOUSING PROGRAM

The following is a practical case study of slack computation in a public program. The case selected is an hypothetical public housing program.

In order to supply welfare, education, or health services to the public, office buildings, schools, or hospitals are required. In 1977, more than one quarter of the Israeli national budget for welfare was directed toward the construction of new buildings, and the maintenance or expansion of old ones (Israeli Budget Law 1977). Table 14.2 provides information concerning investments in the construction of new and expansion of old public buildings during the years 1975–1978.

**TABLE 14.2**
**Government Investment in Public Buildings**[a]

| Years | Gross investment in public buildings in million IL | | Building area in thousands square meters | Gross investment in public building adjusted for IL per square meter | Building price index |
|-------|---------|----------|---------|---------|---------|
|       | Nominal | Adjusted |         |         |         |
| 1975  | 2700    | 2700     | 665     | 4060    | 100     |
| 1976  | 2899    | 2196     | 674     | 3260    | 132.4   |
| 1977  | 3950    | 2283     | 662     | 3450    | 173.3   |
| 1978  | 6247    | 2297     | 577     | 3980    | 272.6   |

[a]From Central Bureau of Statistics, 1979. *Israeli Statistical Abstract,* No. 30.

Notice the information in the fifth column. Although the figures in 1978 are somewhat lower than those in 1975, we cannot assign the small difference to cost saving due to experience. In reality, many different subcontractors work at the same time, building schools, hospitals, and other projects. Since the construction of one hospital constitutes only one operation cycle, experience does not accumulate. Hence the similar figures in the fifth column reflect inability to save cost, or to use resources more efficiently.

In this example, we say that it was predetermined for a subcontractor in the housing industry that the minimal cost for the production of 400 prefabricated housing units would be $1 million each. Counting the number of complete housing units and unfinished units, it was concluded that there was the equivalent of only 75 units. By now the subcontractor has received $250 million from the financing agency. Using an experience rate of 80%, the evaluators measured the extent of slack and friction and experience costs as presented here.

Based on the assertion that the cost of the 400th unit should be $1 million, an 80% experience table indicates that the cost of the 400th unit is .1453 of the cost of the first unit. Thus the cost of the first unit is $7 million. The average cost for the production of 75 units, assuming an 80% experience rate and a cost of $7 million for producing the first unit, is $2.5 million ($7 \times .3564$). The total cost of production for 75 units is $182 million ($75 \times 2.5$). The slack is the difference between the total resources recruited by the subcontractor (i.e., $250 million) and the cost of producing the 75 units ($182 million), which is $68 million.

Figure 14.3 is graphic presentation of this computation. It shows the three types of cost factors.

The cost of the 75th unit is $1.73 million ($7 \times .2491$). The experience cost accumulated until the production of the 75th unit is $182 - (1.73 \times 75)$ $52 million. The necessary cost is $130 million ($1.73 \times 75$).

Note that if the agency would have financed the subcontractor for the production of the 75 units in accordance with the cost of the first unit, line BB', then the total cost for the production of these 75 units would have been $525 million, and the slack would have been $343 million. Apparently, the agency was aware of the effect of experience on cost reduction, and financed the subcontractor accordingly.

## Conclusion and Further Policy Implications

The research issues addressed by this study are the measurement of organizational slack and utilization of the information gained by the ability to calculate its extent in public programs. The method suggested to assist in

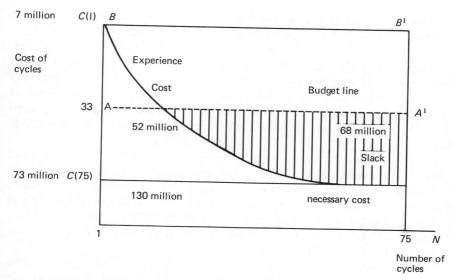

**FIGURE 14.3.** *This chart shows the costs of producing housing units.*

program evaluation is the calculation of the slack accumulated in the past and prediction of the slack that will be created in the future by the experience curve techniques. The immediate implications of the computation presented here should attract the attention of decision makers in the social policy area.

Awareness of the existence of slack and learning is a necessary condition for computing their extent and rates. Such awareness, coupled with this knowledge, could enable an organization to employ its resources in a more efficient, stable, and flexible manner. The organization could also undertake to increase certain kinds of slack so that they will contribute more to its purpose. Thus, for example, with the knowledge acquired, the organization can refrain from expending slack in areas where it will not benefit the organization in the future. In this respect irretrievable costs of workers' benefits, wages, managerial expenses, overheads, and the like could be reduced while concentrating on the creation of slack that will bring about long-term returns. Examples of the kind that contribute to the organization's expansion and to its increased ability to adapt to future environmental factors are investment in R & D, development of MIS, and better data systems. Hence the knowledge conveyed by this study could contribute directly to the improvement of programs.

Public programs are usually financed in accordance with the costs of first cycles. However, since learning takes place everywhere, the performance of the organization continuously improves, even though this may be unintentional. As a result, if programs are financed without taking these improvements into consideration, slack may take the form of hidden unemployment.

The logic of our computation is simple, and could be employed in many areas of social policy. We take the example of the planning and building of a community center to demonstrate this point. The building of a community center could serve as a turnkey project, and, with awareness of the experience gained in the first center ("first operation cycle"), the project could be organized so as to reduce relevant costs when other community centers are planned and built.

We should, then, be aware of and acquire knowledge about the experience gained in the construction work of the building, acquisition of equipment, in the training of community workers, in the drafting of activity plans, and so forth. Moreover, in other social areas we may identify equivalent programmatic factors, and apply the rates of experience computed for one area to another. Thus, for example, planning and building a school may be based on a computation similar to that of the community center.

Moreover, we suggest that the evaluation of the benefit–cost ratio of public programs should be conducted after a large number of cycles, in order to take into account the reduction of cost expected by experience. Alternatively, the same results could be attained, that is, correct assessment of the benefit–cost difference, by conducting a limited field experiment and by extrapolating the cost of future cycles based on assumptions concerning experience rates.

From the case study and the examples presented in this chapter, it is clear that friction and experience costs can be very high. Therefore, whenever possible, the adoption of an "experienced" program from other countries, states, or cities without major changes is preferable to trying to acquire this information alone. This may save all the costs involved in the process of trial and error.

Although the recommendations in this chapter were intended to assist policymakers in their decision choices among programs, the following fifth recommendation is directed to the program manager level. Commonly, the manager of a new program would attempt to gain experience in an incremental way. This is a logical attitude, taken to ensure the program's survival.

We suggest, on the other hand, a counterintuitive approach. Based on the implications of our study, the manager should rather invest a very large amount of resources (money, people) in order to produce many cycles in a short period. This will lead to faster learning and, hence, a reduction in cycle costs along with an increase in program slack.

Finally, it appears that our conclusions strongly suggest the critical importance of future empirical studies that will measure the rate of experience in various public programs.

## ACKNOWLEDGMENT

The authors wish to thank Professors Yuchtman–Yaar and Spiro for their helpful comments and suggestions.

# References

Attkisson, C.C., and Broskowski, A. 1978. Evaluation and the emerging human service concept, In *Evaluation of human service programs,* ed. C.C. Attkisson *et al.* New York: Academic Press. Pp. 3–26.

Boren, H.E. Jr., and Cambell, H.G. 1970. *Learning curve tables.* Vol. 1, 2, 3. Santa Monica, Calif: Rand Corp. RM-6191-PR(VI,V2,V3)

Bourgeois, L.I. 1981. On the measurement of organizational slack. *Academy of Management Review* 6: 29–39.

Caspari, J., Voolis Z., and Nizan, R. 1974. Learning curves: description of the phenomenon, its significance and implications. Work Study and Incentives Section, the Israel Institute of Productivity.

Cheney, W.F., LTC, USAF. 1977. *Strategic implications of the experience curve effect for avionics acquisitions by the Department of Defense.* Ph.D. dissertation, Purdue University.

Coleman, J.S. 1980. The structure of society and the nature of social research, Knowledge: Creation, Diffusion, Utilization, 1: 333–50.

Cyert, R.M., and March, J.G. 1963. *A behavioral theory of the firm.* Englewood Cliffs, N.J.: Prentice–Hall.

Doron, G. 1979. *The smoking paradox: Public regulation in the cigarette industry.* Cambridge, Mass.: Abt Books.

Eilon, S. 1979. Some useful ratios in evaluating performance. *Omega* 7: 166–168.

Fisher, G.H. 1971. *Cost considerations in systems analysis.* New York: American Elsevier.

Hirschmann, W. 1964. Profit from learning curve. *Harvard Business Review* 42: 125–139.

Nachmias, D. 1979. *Public policy evaluation: Approaches and methods.* New York: St. Martins Press.

Nachmias, D. 1980. Introduction. Public policy evaluation: An overview. In *The practice of policy evaluation,* ed. D. Nachmias. New York: St. Martins Press. Pp. 1–21.

Palumbo, D., and Sharp, E. 1980. Process versus impact evaluation of community corrections. In *The practice of policy evaluation,* ed. D. Nachmias. New York: St. Martins Press. Pp. 288–304.

Rossi, P.H., Freeman, H.E., and Wright, S.R. 1970. *Evaluation: A systematic approach.* London: SAGE Publications.

Rudwick, B.H. 1979. *Solving management problems: A system approach to planning and control.* New York: John Wiley and Sons.

Sorenson, J.E., and Grove, H.D. 1978. Using cost–outcome and cost–effectiveness analyses for improved program management and accountability. In *Evaluation of human service programs,* ed. Attkisson *et al.* New York: Academic Press. Pp. 371–410.

Suchman, E.A. 1967. *Evaluative research: Principles and practice in public service and social action programs.* New York: Russell Sage Foundation.

Yuchtman, E. and Seashore, S. 1967. A system resource approach to organizational effectiveness. *American Sociological Review:* 32: 891–903.

# IV

## Policy Evaluation in Selected Fields

*A number of different conceptual and methodological issues in the evaluation of programs and policies in education, employment, and the care of the aged are raised in this section. Coleman shows how the manipulation of data on segregation between and within school systems, along with comparative data on performance, can generate predictions as to the possible outcomes of policies that are the object of current public debates. Leinhardt and Leinhardt argue that the social outcomes of educational policies have not received the attention they deserve. They propose a methodology for assessing the impact of such policies as racial desegregation and the mainstreaming of handicapped children on social integration in the classroom.*

*Piliavin and Masters, using well-established methods of impact assessment, present findings on the effects of employment programs on ex-offenders and drug addicts, showing that the differential impacts of these programs do not conform to what common notions would lead us to expect. Litwak and Kulis propose a conceptual scheme for the study of the roles played by primary groups and formal organizations at various stages in the life of the aged. They point to the implication of their conceptual scheme for the evaluation of institutions and community service systems for the aged.*

# 15

# Predicting the Consequences of Policy Changes: The Case of Public and Private Schools

## JAMES S. COLEMAN

This chapter does two things: It shows some research results that bear directly upon an important policy issue in American education, and it uses these results to illustrate a strategy in policy research that I believe to be particularly useful. This strategy is the use of research data to explicity predict what would be the consequence of possible policy changes. The first policy change examined is reduction in the cost of private schools, relative to income, in which I ask the question, what would be the effect of that change on the racial, economic, and religious segregation in education? The second policy change is in the internal functioning of the school. There I ask what the effect on achievement in public and private schools would be if the level of discipline imposed were to be changed.

The intent of this examination is to bring policy research somewhat closer to policy itself than is ordinarily the case. Some of our usual techniques of analysis lend themselves especially well to such predictions, thus making such a task quite feasible.

In this chapter, then, I will first address the policy issue of segregation, and then the policy issue of school discipline, attempting in both cases to illustrate the general strategy I have described.

## Segregation and Private Schooling

A major policy issue in American education over a long period of time has been the role of private schooling. In the United States, as in most countries,

EVALUATING THE WELFARE STATE:
SOCIAL AND POLITICAL PERSPECTIVES

private schools existed before public schools. However, the early development of public schools, together with the use of the public school as a melting pot for the diverse cultures of immigrants, has led to a particularly strong "common school" tradition in the United States. Today, only about 10% of American children attend schools other than those of the single public school system. Unlike some countries, including Israel, religious education and schools operated by religious groups are wholly outside the public system, and unsubsidized by the state.

In the private sector, by far the largest number of schools are those sponsored by religious bodies, and of those, the largest number are Catholic, with about two-thirds of the total private school enrollment. Baptist schools are next in size, but with only about one-twentieth of the Catholic enrollment, and then Jewish schools, with about half the enrollment of the Baptist schools. However, from every religious group, including Catholic, a much larger number of children attend the public schools than attend private schools.

The 90:10 balance between public and private schools has not changed radically over the years. However, two developments have acted in recent years to affect the balance. First, the cost of education, including private education, has risen faster than the cost of living, leading to a slow decline in the proportion of students in private schools. The rise in cost has been especially great in Catholic schools, where the inexpensive services of nuns and priests as teachers have been largely replaced by the more expensive services of lay teachers. This has lead to a near-crisis in Catholic education, with the closing of many schools.

The second factor affecting the balance between public and private education has acted in the other direction. The level of dissatisfaction of parents and students with public schools has grown in recent years. This has been due to a number of factors, most prominent of which has been a general sense of lack of order, discipline, and attention to fundamentals in education, generating a "back to the basics" movement in education, as well as a shift by some parents to private schooling for their children. In addition, several recent policies in education, most at the federal level, and most prominently desegregation actions which have radically affected the organization of schools, have led to a flight from the public schools into private schools. School desegregation has led to so-called white flight which is mostly to suburban public schools, but in some part to private schools. However, there has been "black flight" as well, with black parents using the private schools to insulate their children from the general disorder and disarray of some ghetto public schools.

These two factors, one leading to lesser and the other to greater private school enrollment, have resulted in three things: first, a slight increase in the proportion of students in private schools, despite the increasing costs; second, pressures, primarily by government agencies, to send children who have fled desegregation back to public schools, and third, pressures, primarily from parents who are using or want to use private schools, for some kind of government aid or subsidy to private education. These last two pressures are in direct opposition to each other, an opposition that showed itself most strongly in an enormous public response to a recent proposed ruling from the Internal Revenue Service that would require private schools to maintain a degree of racial balance in order to continue their tax status.

The arguments opposing government barriers to private schooling have been primarily those of individual liberty to raise children without direct state intervention, supplemented by the argument that religious freedom implies an alternative to state secular education. The further argument that private education should be facilitated by some sort of state subsidy is based primarily on the issue of double taxation. That is, parents of children in private schools argue that they pay twice for education—once through taxes to provide free public education, and once through tuition for their own children's schooling. This argument is particularly strong for religious schools: If the state supports only nonreligious education, this discriminates, it is argued, against those parents who want to raise their children in a religious setting.

At different times, different issues have been central to the arguments against facilitating private schooling or for barriers to private schooling. The earliest issue was that of economic or social class segregation, with the rich seen as separating themselves from others through the use of private schools. Then was added the issue of religious segregation, with Catholic schools seen as a dividing influence, separating Catholics and non-Catholics in America. Further, any governmental encouragement, facilitation, or support of religious schools would go directly against the constitutional requirement of separation of church and state. Finally, the private schools have more recently been seen as a haven for whites fleeing desegregation, and thus making school integration more difficult to achieve.

The arguments opposing governmental barriers to private schools should, if all else were constant, be controlling, for they are based on widely held and constitutionally protected values of individual freedom. But if the charges that private schooling promotes segregation are true, then all else is not constant, since that violates other widely held or constitutionally protected values. It is here that social policy research can be of aid, because the amount of truth in these charges is at base a factual question. It is possible, by use of research data, to see just what the economic, religious, and racial differences are between the public schools and the private schools, and to see what the degree of segregation is within each of these sectors on each of these dimensions. Using such information, it is possible to go a step further—by making certain assumptions—to see how this degree of economic, religious, and racial segregation in the United States would be different if the public schools were the sole educational sector, that is, if private schools did not exist. With a slightly different set of assumptions, it is possible to take an additional step, to ask how a specific policy change would be expected to affect the degree of segregation along these dimensions. The policy change most directly addressable with the data at hand is one that would increase family income by a given amount at each income level, thus increasing their ability to afford a private school for their children. A closely related, but more likely policy change would be the reduction of the cost of a private education by providing tax credits, tuition vouchers, or something similar.

These hypothetical situations, such as elimination of the private schools or reduction of the cost of private schools, are beyond description because implicitly they ask a question of cause and effect: What would be the effect of a certain kind of policy change? As with all questions of cause and effect, they can be answered only with uncertainty, because they are questions about not what *is*, but *what would be*. Despite this uncertainty, they may still provide those who are interested in policy better information than they would otherwise have about the potential effects of policy change.

## The Current Status: Segregation between and within Public and Private Sectors

The first evidence regarding the directly factual question is shown in Tables 15.1, 15.2, and 15.3. In all three of these tables, the private school sector is broken into two groups: the Catholic schools which account for two-thirds of private school students, and the other private schools, including both schools affiliated with religious groups and those that are independent of any religious affiliation.[1]

Table 15.1, on the oldest question of private school economic segregation, shows that there is some economic difference between students in public schools and those in either Catholic or other private schools. The question is, just how great is this difference? Is it sufficiently great to be economically divisive, or not? The question is not easily answerable, but there is another step that could be carried out to get some idea about the degree of economic segregation between public and private schools. This is to compare the degree of economic segregation within the public school sector with that between the public sector and either of the private sectors, or between the public and the two private sectors taken together. However, such a comparision might be misleading. It would show a lower degree of economic segregation between any pair of sectors than between schools within any one of them; but since schools are relatively small units, whereas the sectors are very large, we would expect the heterogeneity within each sector to moderate the segregation between them.

---

[1] All data reported here are taken from a survey of high school sophomores and seniors in a random sample of 1015 high schools throughout the United States. The analyses reported are drawn from a larger report (Coleman, Hoffer, and Kilgore 1982).

**TABLE 15.1**
**Percentage of Students from Various Backgrounds in Public and Private Schools**

| Response to BB101 " . . . the amount of money your family makes in a year." | Public | Catholic | Other private | U.S. total |
|---|---|---|---|---|
| $6,999 or less | 7.7 | 2.4 | 2.9 | 7.2 |
| $7,000–11,999 | 12.5 | 6.3 | 6.3 | 11.9 |
| $12,000–15,999 | 17.2 | 12.8 | 11.5 | 16.7 |
| $16,000–19,999 | 19.0 | 17.3 | 15.2 | 18.7 |
| $20,000–24,999 | 18.0 | 20.7 | 16.3 | 18.1 |
| $25,000–37,999 | 14.6 | 20.4 | 15.0 | 15.0 |
| $38,000 or more | 11.1 | 20.1 | 32.8 | 12.4 |
| Total | 100.1 | 100.0 | 100.0 | 100.0 |

Nevertheless, it is worth noting that the between-sector economic segregation is much smaller than the between-school segregation within any sector, though this need not be true, as we shall see in the case of religious segregation.

In the case of the religious distribution of students in schools shown by Table 15.2, there is a sharp difference between the three sectors. Thus it appears that there is some basis for the argument that private schools tend to separate children of different religious groups into different schools. It is true, on the other hand, that 81% of all Catholic children in these years of school (sophomore and senior) are in public school, with only 17% in Catholic schools.

Thus, I think it is reasonable to say that as matters stand now, given the existing financial and ecological barriers to attendance of nonpublic schools, the private sector does not constitute a threat to social integration on religious grounds, and arguments to further restrict private schools on this basis are misplaced.[2]

At the same time, the religious difference between the sectors means that if the financial and ecological barriers were removed, we cannot say what fraction of parents of the 81% of Catholic children now in public schools would shift to Catholic schools nor what fraction of parents of the children from other religious groups now in the public sector would choose schools affiliated with their own religious group, rather than public schools or other private schools. There would almost certainly be an increase in religious segregation, for some parents of children now in the public schools would choose schools affiliated with their

---

[2]It may be, of course, that there are communities in which most Catholics attend Catholic schools, and non-Catholics attend public schools. If there are such communities, then the existence of a private sector may contribute to religious divisiveness in the community. This cannnot, however, be sufficiently widespread to justify further barriers to private schooling through federal policy.

TABLE 15.2
Percentage of Catholics and Non-Catholics in Public, Private and Other Private Schools

|  | Public | Catholic | Other private | U.S. total |
|---|---|---|---|---|
| Catholic | 31 | 91 | 17 | 34 |
| Non-Catholic | 69 | 9 | 83 | 66 |
| Total | 100 | 100 | 100 | 100 |

religious group. What is not known is just how many would do so. The large size of the state secular school system in Israel is clear indication that even without the financial barriers, many parents in Israel choose a secular education; and one can suppose this would also be so in the United States.

Altogether, then, the evidence undermines arguments for further restricting private schooling through federal policy on grounds of religious segregation. On the other hand, reducing the existing barriers is almost certain to increase religious segregation, but the data are silent on just how much it would do so.

Table 15.3 shows the distribution of students in each of the three sectors according to three racial and ethnic categories: students of Hispanic background (i.e., the Caribbean, Central and South America), non-Hispanic blacks, and non-Hispanic whites. Hispanics are very close to the same proportion in each sector, from a high of 7% in the public sector to a low of 5% in the other private sector. Blacks, however, are only about half as numerous in Catholic schools as in public schools, and only about half as numerous in other private schools as in Catholic schools. The non-Hispanic whites constitute the remainder in each sector, ranging from a low of 78% in the public sector to a high of 92% in the other private sector.

Again, as in the case of religious segregation, it is clear that for the country as a whole the private schools do not constitute a threat to the racial integration of schools, since a vast majority of whites attend public schools, as do most blacks. There are communities in which this is not so, particularly in some rural areas of the Deep South, where racial integration of schools led whites to set up private schools that are all white or nearly so, and where the public schools thereby became predominantly black. Existing federal policy requires such schools to be nondiscriminatory in order to maintain their tax exemption, and there are continuing arguments over whether additional federal policies can be introduced to aid racial integration without infringing on the individual freedom of parents to send their children to private schools.

Despite the contributions of private schools to racial segregation in certain localities, the small size of the private sector, together with the fact that it is not homogenously non-Hispanic white, undercuts arguments that federal (as

**TABLE 15.3**
Percentage of Hispanics, Non-Hispanic Blacks, Non-Hispanic Whites in Public, Catholic, and Other Private Schools

|  | Public | Catholic | Other private | U.S. total |
|---|---|---|---|---|
| Hispanic | 7 | 7 | 5 | 7 |
| Non-Hispanic black | 14 | 6 | 3 | 13 |
| Non-Hispanic white | 78 | 87 | 92 | 80 |

opposed to local) policies to restrict private schools are warranted on the basis of their contribution to racial segregation. This does not negate the need for federal policies targeted to those localities in which the existence of private schools clearly does contribute to segregation, so long as it does not differentially restrict the civil liberties of parents who live in those localities.[3]

All this leaves aside, of course, the question of just what degree of racial segregation there is *within* the private sector, or the Catholic and other private sector conducted separately; for if such internal segregation were pronounced, it could constitute a means by which private schooling contributed to racial segregation in education. It is to that question that I now turn, examining also the analagous question for economic and for religious differences.

## Internal Segregation in Public, Catholic, and Other Private Sectors

Until now, the examination has been confined to the differences in composition between sectors. But this is only part of the question of the possible segregating effect of private schools. The other part concerns the distribution of students with different economic, religious, racial, or ethnic backgrounds *within* each of these sectors. To compare sectors according to their internal segregation requires a measure of segregation: the measure I use is based on the proportion of whites (using the example of black–white segregation) in the average black's

---

[3]A comparison is instructive here. The existence of public schools that are nearly all white in suburban districts of central cities with large proportions of blacks clearly contributes to the segregation of black and white school children. Yet, federal policy, including court rulings, has not imposed restrictions on those districts in the absence of a finding of intent to discriminate.

TABLE 15.4

**Economic, Religious, and Racial Ethnic Segregation within the Public Sector, the Catholic Sector, and the Other Private Sector**

|  | Public | Catholic | Other private | Total private |
|---|---|---|---|---|
| Segregation between children from families with incomes over $20,000 and those from families with incomes under $12,000 | .20 | .16 | .16 | .16 |
| Segregation between Catholic and non-Catholic children | .21 | .15 | .27 | .56 |
| Segregation of Hispanics and non-Hispanic whites | .30 | .25 | .55 | .35 |
| Segregation of blacks and whites | .49 | .32 | .21 | .34 |

school, compared to the proportion in the sector as a whole.[4] The measure is 1.0 if there is complete segregation, and 0 if every school in the sector has the same proportions of the two groups in question. Values for this measure in each of the areas of potential segregation are given in Table 15.4. Values are also calculated for the private sector considered as a whole, not separated into Catholic and other private schools.

Table 15.4 shows that the internal segregation of these sectors differs considerably among areas and among sectors. Economic segregation is least of all the areas. Religious segregation is low within each of the sectors considered separately, but when the private sector is considered as a whole, it has the highest value in the table. This suggests that if all children attended private schools chosen by them and their parents, these schools would show an especially high degree of religious segregation. Racial segregation is indicated as the greatest internal segregation in the public schools. Whether the private schools are considered as two sectors or one, they are considerably less internally segregated than the public schools. The same is not true for segregation between Hispanics and non-Hispanic whites; it is lowest in the Catholic schools, but higher in the other private schools.

[4]This measure is constructed as follows: If $P$ is the proportion of whites in the sector as a whole, $P_k$ is the proportion of whites in school $k$, and $n_k$ is the number of black students in school $k$, then

$$s_{bw} = \frac{\sum_k n_k P_k}{\sum_k n_k}, \text{ and } r_{bw} = \frac{P - s_{bw}}{P},$$

where $r_{bw}$ is the index used, and $s_{bw}$ is the proportion of whites in the average black's school.

Altogether, no overall statements can be made about the relative internal segregation of the private and public sectors. The private sector considered as a whole is very religiously segregated—far more than the public sector. On the other hand, the black–white segregation is by far highest in the public sector. A marginal expansion of the private sector would mean students were moving into: (*a*) slightly less economically segregated schools; (*b*) much greater religiously segregated schools; (*c*) slightly greater Hispanic-Anglo segregation; but (*d*) considerably lower racial segregation.

## The Predicted Impact of a Policy Change Facilitating Private Schools

It is possible to go a step further. There has been much discussion of what the impact would be of making private education less burdensome financially. One proposal, nearly passed in Congress, was to provide tax credits of up to $500 for school tuition. Another widely discussed proposal is that of an educational voucher to allow all children to choose freely among private and public schools.[5]

Some have argued that such changes as this would differentially benefit the white upper middle class, who use private schools more. It would, in this view, extend still further the creaming process which leaves the poor and minorities in the public schools. Others argue that such measures would place private schooling in the reach of those who cannot now afford it, and thus differentially benefit minorities and those less well-off financially.

With these data, it is possible to predict which students would be recruited into private schools by a reduction in the financial burden (although it would be a less direct reduction than that in either of these policy proposals). In particular, we know for each income level the proportions of students from a given group (say Catholics, or blacks) in private schools. This tells us the income elasticity of private schooling for each of these groups. Thus one can predict what would be the recruitment into private schools from each group if there were a change which increased income by a fixed amount for all, or the defection from private schools if income were reduced by a fixed amount for all. I will ask the former question with respect to whites, blacks, and Hispanics: Suppose income were increased by $1000 for all, for example, by a tax rebate or by a general increase in the standard of living; would this mean that racial segregation between public and private schools would be increased, by increasing the flow of white children into the private schools? Or would it mean

[5] A Gallup poll taken in November 1980 asked a national sample about attitudes toward a voucher plan. Vouchers were favored by 47% and opposed by 42%, with 11% undecided. The support has increased from about 40% in the early 1970s. (*Cincinnati Enquirer*, December 19, 1980).

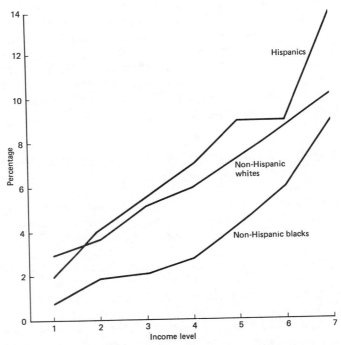

**FIGURE 15.1.** *This graph shows the percentage of students from differing income levels in Catholic schools by race and ethnicity.*

that racial segregation between these sectors would be decreased, by bringing more black and Hispanic children into the private schools?

This question can be answered by use of two items of information: the number of Hispanics, blacks, and non-Hispanic whites in the public school sector at each income level; and the increment in proportion in private schools per $1000 income increase of income level for each group. The latter is shown in Figure 15.1 for the Catholic schools, and Figure 15.2 for the other private schools.

Figure 15.1 shows that the increase in proportion of students attending Catholic schools with income increase (the slope of the curve) is greatest for Hispanics. It is greater for whites than for blacks at low income levels, but, somewhat surprisingly, greater for blacks than for whites at high income levels. Figure 15.2 shows that for all three racial and ethnic groups, the increment in proportion attending other private schools, is lower than for Catholic schools, except at the highest income levels for non-Hispanic whites. The curve is especially flat for blacks, except at the upper extreme of income.

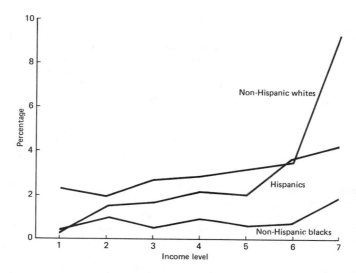

**FIGURE 15.2.** *This graph shows the percentage of students from differing income levels in other private schools by race and ethnicity.*

Using the numbers of students from each of these three groups at each income level together with the information provided in Figures 15.1 and 15.2 gives the information in Table 15.5.

The results of this hypothetical experiment are rather interesting. First, only a very small proportion of public school students—less than .5% of any of the three groups—would shift. Second, and somewhat surprising, the greatest shift would come among the Hispanics. Third, in both the private sectors, the racial and ethnic composition of those shifting (third column) includes more minorities than does the current composition of those schools. Fourth, among those shifting into the Catholic sector, there is a higher proportion of minorities (third column, $.12 + .12 = .24$) than in U.S. schools as a whole (fifth column, $.13 + .07 = .20$); but this is not true in the other private sector $(.03 + .07 = .10)$.

Altogether, what can be said in response to the question I posed is that the racial segregation between the public and the private schools as a whole would be reduced by such a change, because the proportion of minorities among those coming into the private school is somewhat greater than the proportion already in these schools—and that this comes about primarily through the shifts of minorities (especially Hispanics and higher-income blacks) into the Catholic schools. Thus the common belief that policies encouraging attendance at private schools would increase segregation is not at all supported by these data, since the data indicate that for Catholic schools, which constitute two-thirds of the

TABLE 15.5

**Predicted Numbers of Students Shifting to Catholic and Other Private Schools with $1000 Increase in Family Income[a]**

| | Predicted number | Proportion of those in public school | Proportion of those shifting | Present composition | |
|---|---|---|---|---|---|
| | | | | sector | U.S. |
| **To Catholic schools** | | | | | |
| Non-Hispanic whites | 8,221 | .0025 | .76 | .87 | .80 |
| Non-Hispanic blacks | 1,308 | .0025 | .12 | .06 | .13 |
| Hispanics | 1,281 | .0035 | .12 | .07 | .07 |
| Total | | | 1.00 | 1.00 | 1.00 |
| **To other private schools** | | | | | |
| Non-Hispanic whites | 5,595 | .0017 | .90 | .92 | .80 |
| Non-Hispanic blacks | 204 | .0004 | .03 | .03 | .13 |
| Hispanics | 401 | .0011 | .07 | .05 | .07 |
| Total | | | 1.00 | 1.00 | 1.00 |
| **Total** | | | | | |
| Non-Hispanic whites | 13,816 | .0043 | .81 | .89 | .80 |
| Non-Hispanic blacks | 1,512 | .0029 | .09 | .05 | .13 |
| Hispanics | 1,682 | .0046 | .10 | .06 | .07 |
| Total | | | 1.00 | 1.00 | 1.00 |

[a]Predicted numbers shifting to Catholic and other private schools were calculated as follows: $Nijp \times Sij$, where $Nijp$ is the number from racial or ethnic group $i$ in income level $j$ in public schools (sophomore and seniors combined) and $Sij$ is, for racial or ethnic group $i$ at income level $i$, the estimated change in proportion in Catholic or other private schools with increment of $1000 in income. $Sij$ is calculated for each income level as follows (income in thousands of dollars).

| | |
|---|---|
| level 1 (below 7) | $(P_2 - P_i)/5$ |
| level 2 (7–12) | $\frac{1}{2}[(P_2 - P_1)/5 + (P_3 - P_2)/4.5]$ |
| level 3 (12–16) | $\frac{1}{2}[(P_3 - P_2)/4.5 + (P_4 - P_3)/4.0]$ |
| level 4 (16–20) | $\frac{1}{2}[(P_4 - P_3)/4 + (P_5 - P_4)/4.5]$ |
| level 5 (20–25) | $\frac{1}{2}[(P_5 - P_4)/4.5 + (P_6 - P_5)/9]$ |
| level 6 (28–38) | $\frac{1}{2}[(P_6 - P_5)/9 + (P_7 - P_6)/12]$ |
| level 7 (above 38) | $(P_7 - P_6)/12$ |

The second column, proportion of those in public school, is obtained by taking the total number of sophomores and seniors in public school, subtracting out the number who did not report family income (and thus were not used in the above calculations), and dividing this into the predicted number shifting.

private sector, both blacks and Hispanics will respond to financial incentives to as great or greater a degree as whites will, and that both parts of the private sector would come to have higher proportions of blacks and Hispanics than they now do.

It would be preferable to predict the results of a different policy, such as a tuition tax credit, say of $500. Such a credit would have the effect of reducing the tuition for private schools by $500 divided by the number of children the family has in school. To make such a prediction, information on price elasticity of private schooling for each of these groups, rather than income elasticity, would be necessary. By making some heroic assumptions, one might be able to use these data to estimate something about the effect of such a policy. However, I will not do so here, because the assumptions appear to be rather strong.

We now turn to the second policy issue directly related to private schools. This has to do with the maintenance of discipline and order, and its effects.

## Discipline, Order, and Private Schooling

Many parents who withdraw their children from public schools to enroll them in private schools say they do so because of the greater degree of discipline and order in the private schools. This is most often stated with respect to Catholic schools, and it appears to be an especially common reason for the use of Catholic schools by black families in the ghetto.

Several questions related to policy arise. One is the descriptive fact: Are the Catholic and other private schools better disciplined and more orderly than the public schools? The second is a question of cause: If there is such a difference, what is it due to? What are the constraints under which public schools are operating, or what are the different value premises in public schools, that lead them to exercise less discipline than do private schools? The third is a question of effect: If there is greater discipline in private schools, does this affect, positively or negatively, learning?

The first question of fact can be addressed directly with the social policy research data at hand. In principle, the second question can also be answered by research data, and is important to address because it may point to some of the sources of malaise affecting the public schools. But it cannot be addressed from data at hand, and would require specially designed research.[6] The third question can be addressed with these survey data, subject always to the uncertainties about answering any question of cause and effect.

## The Current Status: Discipline and Order in Public and Private Schools

The question of whether there is greater discipline and order in private schools than in public schools can be divided in two: (*a*) Are there different

---

[6]During the design period for this research, a representative of the American Federation of Teachers recognized the importance of such information, and suggested the inclusion of questions in the school questionnaire, such as "How many days in the past month has the principal been in court?" The question was designed to show the greater constraints on public school principals for due process in student explusions, as well as other legal constraints. But such questions do not really provide the right information, for it may take only one or two such cases in a school district to change the levels of discipline imposed throughout the system.

**TABLE 15.6**

**Five Measures of Disciplinary Standards and Demands, and of Teacher Interest, in Public, Catholic, and Other Private Schools**[a]

|                                                       | Proportion responding as indicated | | |
| ----------------------------------------------------- | ------ | -------- | ------------- |
|                                                       | Public | Catholic | Other private |
| Rules about student dress                             |        |          |               |
| Sophomore report                                      | .42    | .97      | .69           |
| Administrator report                                  | .51    | 1.00     | .70           |
| Students held responsible for property damage school  |        |          |               |
| Sophomore report                                      | .64    | .77      | .71           |
| Administrator report                                  | .96    | .90      | 1.00          |
| Effectiveness of discipline "excellent" or "good"     |        |          |               |
| Students                                              | .42    | .74      | .62           |
| Fairness of discipline "excellent" or "good"          |        |          |               |
| Students                                              | .38    | .50      | .49           |
| Teachers interest in students "excellent"             |        |          |               |
| Students                                              | .11    | .25      | .38           |

[a] Student report for the last three items are averages of sophomore and senior reports. Reports by students at the two grade levels are quite consistent.

disciplinary standards and demands in the private sector?; (*b*) Are there differences in student behavior in the public and private sectors? The demands and the behavior are, of course, interdependent. But it is useful to examine them separately. Table 15.6 shows several measures of disciplinary standards, demands by the school, and teacher orientation to students. Some of the information is from reports by the schools, and some is from reports by students.

Table 15.6 shows some sharp differences, and some similarities, between the educational sectors. According to either sophomore reports or administrator reports, only about half as many (or less) public school students as those in Catholic schools are subject to rules about student dress; virtually all Catholic schools have such rules. The other private schools are about halfway between the public and Catholic schools. As for rules about accountability for property damage, administrators everywhere uniformly report that students are held accountable; but between 23% (in the Catholic sector) and 34% (in the public sector) of sophomores report otherwise. Presumably in some schools such accountability exists in name but is not practiced. Public and private sectors do not differ greatly here.

However, when students are asked how effective the discipline is, those in public schools are much less likely to report that it is excellent or good; again, as in dress rules, the other private schools are between the Catholic and public schools, though closer to the former. In fairness of discipline as reported by students, the Catholic and other private schools are alike, and better than the public schools. This is somewhat paradoxical, for the public schools are under a number of legal and administrative constraints imposed by state and federal government beyond those imposed on the private sector, to ensure fairness of discipline; yet they are regarded by their students as being less fair than the private sector schools.

Perhaps the most striking difference is in the students' belief about their teachers' interest in them: Fewer than half as many in public schools report teachers' interest as excellent, compared to students in Catholic schools, and fewer than a third as many, compared to those in other private schools.

There are, then, some rather clear differences in disciplinary standards and in teachers' relations to students in the public and private sectors, even though these measures provide only imperfect indicators of those differences. The Catholic schools have, as is popularly believed, the strongest discipline, and the other private schools appear to have teachers who show the greatest interest in students. (This last may be due to size differences: the average public high school in the United States has 758 children, the average Catholic school has 454, and the average other private school has 103.)[7] According to student reports, the public schools have the weakest and the least fair discipline, and the weakest relation between students and teachers. It is probably also true that, as in the examination of segregative tendencies of private schooling, local comparisons would show greater public–private differences than those found here, for most Catholic schools, and many if not most other private schools, are located in urban areas, where problems of discipline in the public schools are greatest.

There are some measures of student behavior that can help answer the second half of the first discipline question (that is, do the students in private schools behave better than those in public schools?) by showing how student behavior differs in the different sectors. Again, these are imperfect measures, for they address only a few selected aspects of student behavior. The results for three sectors are shown in Table 15.7.

Table 15.7 shows three different sources of information about student behavior: students' reports about themselves, reports by school administrators, and (sophomore) student reports about the behavior of the student body. By all three sources, there are considerable differences between the public schools and the two private sectors. The largest differences are in the administrators' accounts and the sophomores' reports about the student body. Again, this is possibly due to size differences, since the occurrence of some individual behavior problem, all other things constant, is twice as likely in a school that is twice as

---

[7] These sizes are based on high school students only, in those schools with grades other than high school.

TABLE 15.7

**Selected Measures of Student Behavior Related to Disciplinary Standards and Demands, in Public, Catholic, and Other Private Schools**

| | Public | Catholic | Other private |
|---|---|---|---|
| Students' reports of own behavior | | | |
| Average number of hours per week spent on homework | 3.7 | 5.3 | 5.9 |
| | *Percentage giving indicated response* | | |
| Never absent except when ill | 26 | 41 | 34 |
| Never cut classes | 58 | 82 | 65 |
| Never late to school | 39 | 45 | 32 |
| Administrators' reports | | | |
| Absenteeism is "serious or moderate problem". | 57 | 15 | 14 |
| Cutting classes is "serious or moderate problem" | 37 | 5 | 0 |
| Drug or alcohol use "serious or moderate problem" | 49 | 26 | 18 |
| Vandalism of school property "serious or moderate problem" | 25 | 14 | 12 |
| Sophomore reports on student body | | | |
| "Students often don't attend school" | 46 | 8 | 16 |
| "Students often cut classes" | 62 | 16 | 26 |
| "Students often talk back to teachers" | 43 | 23 | 22 |
| "Students often get in fights" | 27 | 9 | 6 |
| "Students don't obey teachers" | 30 | 15 | 13 |

large. But taken all together, the data are consistent and striking: Both the Catholic and other private sectors have far fewer behavior problems than do the public schools. The evidence is that a disciplined and ordered classroom is much more likely in these schools than in the public schools.

These differences make especially important the investigation of the second question posed earlier, which I indicated could not be addressed here: Which of the additional constraints imposed on public shcools or which of the value differences among public school staffs, are most responsible for the differences in discipline?

It is clear from the data examined already that the answer to the first question is strongly affirmative: The Catholic and other private schools are better disciplined and more orderly than the public schools. The disciplinary standards and demands imposed are stronger, and the students behave better; and, as suggested earlier, the differences would probably be even more striking if they were examined within local areas, since most Catholic schools and many other private schools are located in urban areas, where disciplinary standards have characteristically been hard to maintain in recent years.

But this leaves open the answer to the third question, that is, Just what difference does it make? If it makes no difference in school outcomes, then little importance can be attached to variations in discipline and order; but if it does make a difference then variations between public and private sectors are important. There have been several recent studies, mostly qualitative, which suggest that structure, discipline, and order in schools has a positive effect on achievement. It is to this question that I now turn.

## THE PREDICTED IMPACT OF CHANGING THE LEVELS OF DISCIPLINE IN THE SCHOOLS

Throughout this section, I have raised the question of what factors are responsible for the discipline differences that are found in the public and private schools. Although I have not been able to answer that question, it is possible to raise a complementary question: Suppose the public schools were able to achieve the levels of discipline and order that exist in the Catholic or other private schools. What differences would it make for the basic skills achievement of their students? Thus, as in the first half of the chapter, we can ask what is the predicted impact of a policy change. We do not know what specific policies would be affected studying the question, but we do know that there are such policies—for there are schools in the public sector that have as high, or even higher levels of discipline and order as the average Catholic school or other private school. It is exactly this fact which provides the tool for predicting what impact those policies would have.

Achievement scores in vocabulary, and mathematics were obtained for each student on subtests which were identical for sophomores and seniors. Thus it is possible to estimate a least squares regression equation, using public school students only, in which measures of the students' behavior are taken as the predictors. In estimating such an equation, background characteristics of the student are included, so that effects of differences in background do not masquerade as effects of differences in behavior (since it is only the behavior, not the backgrounds, that can be controlled by school policy). The regression coefficients for the behavior measures give an estimate of the effect of each on achievement. Then multiplying these coefficients by the differences in mean behavior levels between Catholic and public schools—or other private and public schools—will give the predicted gain in achievement that would occur by maintaining student behavior in these three areas at the level of that in the Catholic or other private schools. Table 15.8 shows the results of this analysis.

Table 15.8 shows modest but not inconsequential gains by reducing absenteeism, lateness, and cutting classes to the level of that in Catholic schools, and small gains by reducing it to the level of that in other private schools. Comparing the gains to the sophomore–senior differences in achievement shows that the gains by a change to the Catholic level are about .2 of a grade level in vocabulary, and .5 of a grade level in mathematics. The predicted

TABLE 15.8

**Predicted Achievement Gains in Public Schools if Individual's Absenteeism, Lateness and Cutting Classes Were Same as that in Private Schools[a]**

|  | Total items | Public school means | | Predicted gain from reducing absenteeism, lateness, cutting classes to the level of | |
|  |  | Sophomore | Senior | Catholic | Other private |
|---|---|---|---|---|---|
| Vocabulary | 8 | 3.7 | 4.5 | .06 | .03 |
| Mathematics | 18 | 9.4 | 10.6 | .28 | .07 |

[a] Regression equation includes student's absenteeism, lateness, cutting classes, and also father's education, mother's education, race, if Hispanic, family income, and grade level. Predicted gain is determined as the sum of products of regression coefficients of each of the three behavior measures multiplied by the difference in means between Catholic and public or other private and public schools. $r^2$ in the two equations is .191, .201.

gains by a change to the other private level are much smaller, about 8% in vocabulary, 12% in mathematics.

But this considers only gains to the student from reducing his or her *own* level of absenteeism, lateness, and cutting classes. There are also possible gains due to a reduction in the general level of disorder in the school.

The second, environmental, component of the impact of discipline on achievement may be assessed by adding to the above equation school level measures. Controlling on the student's own behavior and background it is

TABLE 15.9

**Predicted Achievement Gains in Public Schools if Discipline and Order Were Same as That in Private Schools, Holding Constant Student's Own Absenteeism, Cutting Classes, and Lateness[a]**

|  | Total items | Public school means | | Predicted gain from maintaining discipline at the level of | |
|  |  | Sophomore | Senior | Catholic | Other private |
|---|---|---|---|---|---|
| Vocabulary | 8 | 3.7 | 4.5 | −.01 | .22 |
| Mathematics | 18 | 9.4 | 10.6 | .30 | .78 |

[a] Regression equation includes four school-level measures of discipline, and school-level measures of absenteeism and cutting classes. In addition, it includes individuals absenteeism, cutting classes, lateness, father's education, mother's education, race, Hispanic, family income, and grade level. Predicted gain is determined as the sum of products of regression coefficients for school level measures multiplied by difference in means between Catholic and public or other private and public schools. $r^2$ for the two equations is .203, .217.

**TABLE 15.10**
Predicted Total Gains in Grade Levels of
Achievement in Public Schools by Maintaining
Same Discipline Levels as in Private Schools

| | Grade level gains | |
|---|---|---|
| | Catholic | Other private |
| Vocabulary | .13 | .65 |
| Mathematics | .95 | 1.39 |

possible to predict the impact on achievement if the level of discipline in the schools were maintained at the level of that in Catholic or other private schools. The results of these calculations are shown in Table 15.9.

These predictions show, except for vocabulary at the Catholic discipline level, an even stronger effect than the effect of reducing the student's own absenteeism, lateness, and cutting classes, and in general a greater effect by moving to the private school level of discipline than that of the Catholic schools. (This is because the estimated effect of those areas of behavior in which the other private schools are better than the Catholic schools is especially great.) The environmental gains predicted by moving to the Catholic levels of discipline are no gain in grade levels for vocabulary and .5 grade level for mathematics. By moving to the other private levels of discipline, the predicted gains are about .5 a grade level for vocabulary, and 1.3 grade level for mathematics.

These two components of the effect of a greater degree of discipline in the public schools are independent and can be added,[8] giving overall effects of maintaining the discipline which characterizes the average Catholic and other private school shown in Table 15.10.

These effects are substantial indeed, and give special force to the question that this research is not able to show what the factors are that prevent public schools as a whole from maintaining a higher level of discipline. The results indicate that if that discipline could be instituted (as it, of course, already is in some public schools) then students in public schools would stand to gain considerably in achievement of basic skills.

---

[8]Strictly speaking, the two effects to be added should both be calculated from the second equation, which contains both the student's own behavior measures and those of the school as a whole. This however, would make only minor differences in the predictions.

# Conclusion

I have attempted in this chapter to show both substantive results relating to social policy affecting public and private schools in the United States and to indicate a general strategy in the use of policy research. The substantive conclusions have been stated earlier so I will just summarize the general strategy illustrated in the two analyses.

In a variety of ways, a research methodology for social policy research that is distinct from the research methods in social science disciplines has slowly begun to emerge. The analysis described in this chapter is an attempt to contribute to that methodology. Many aspects of the analysis use statistical research methods designed primarily to answer social scientific questions. At one point, however, in each of the analyses carried out here, a different kind of question was asked. The general character of the question was, What would be the predicted effect if a certain policy were instituted? This question requires taking an analysis one step beyond that demanded by a social scientific question, which ordinarily asks about causes. It requires first establishing a framework in which the causal relevance of the factors controlled by a proposed policy is established, and then examining the predicted change in one or more outcome variables when values of those factors are varied.

In the first analysis, this meant first establishing the causal relevance of income for private school enrollment for Hispanics, non-Hispanic blacks, and non-Hispanic whites. In the second, it meant establishing the causal relevance of the student's own behavior (absenteeism, lateness, cutting classes) and of the level of discipline in the school. Then, in the first case, the analysis involved changing income by $1000, to examine the effect on the racial composition of public and private schools. In the second case, it involved changing the level of discipline in the school, and the levels existing in the average Catholic and other private schools were used as convenience values at which to establish the new levels. This allowed predicting the change in basic skills achievement that would occur if such a policy change were brought about.

Before concluding, it is important to recognize the uncertainty that is present in any analysis involving causal inferences and predictions. Policy research of this sort cannot give conclusive answers to questions about the effects of particular policy changes. It can express its results in a form that is particulary relevant to policy—which is what I have attempted here—but, like predictions of policy effects based on other grounds, it constitutes only an aid to reduce the uncertainties that attend policy changes.

# References

Coleman, J., Hoffer, T., and Kilgore, S. *High school achievement.* New York: Basic Books, 1982.

Coleman, J.S., Kelly, S., and Moore, J. 1975. *Trends in school segregation, 1968–1973.* Washington: The Urban Institute.
*Cincinnati Enquirer.* December 19, 1980. Gallup report. pc-16.

# 16

# The Evaluation of Social Outcomes in Education[1]

## GAEA LEINHARDT and SAMUEL LEINHARDT

## Introduction

Educational interventions are usually expected to affect the cognitive performance of individuals regardless of whether the intervention involves social or cognitive processes. As a consequence, educational evaluations tend to stress the differential impact of cognitive and social processes on cognitive outcomes. The relative neglect of social outcomes, whether purposeful or accidental, is unfortunate because it results in continuing uncertainty regarding the utility of alternative strategies for achieving the social goals of public policies. There are two basic reasons for this situation: (*a*) well-specified models that relate social processes to measurable policy-relevant outcomes are rarely proposed; and (*b*) appropriate measurement techniques and analytic tools that focus on social variables are inadequate. In this chapter we describe a conceptual framework that can aid in clarifying distinctions between social and cognitive outcomes; we explore some possible models for social interventions that follow from this framework, and we detail an analytic strategy that can improve precision in measuring social outcomes. We apply this approach to two

[1]G. Leinhardt was supported by the Learning Research and Development Center, with funds supplied in part by the National Institute of Education (NIE), United States Department of Education. S. Leinhardt was supported in part by grants from the National Science Foundation (SOC 79-08841) and the National Institute for Child Health and Human Development (1 ROI HD 12506-1). The opinions expressed do not necessarily reflect the position of policy of NIE, NSF, or NICHHD, and no official endorsement should be inferred. Authors' names appear in alphabetical order.

EVALUATING THE WELFARE STATE:
SOCIAL AND POLITICAL PERSPECTIVES

social interventions: (*a*) racial or ethnic integration; and (*b*) the mainstreaming of "special" children. Finally, we demonstrate the use of the analytic strategy through the presentation of results from an evaluation of a mainstreaming experiment.

Although this oversimplifies the situation, it is helpful to conceptualize educational interventions and their concomitant outcomes as a four-fold table consisting of academic and social interventions and outcomes. For example, academic manipulations can be designed to alter the academic behaviors of students (Case 1 in Figure 16.1), as in the introduction of a new curriculum or instructional technique (Ball 1973). Student social behavior can be manipulated with the purpose of altering academic behavior (Case 2), for example, the teams–games tournaments developed by Slavin (1978) and others. Less often, academic behavior is manipulated in order to alter student social behavior (Case 3), as, for example, in the work of Cohen, Lockheed, and Lohman (1976) on expectations in desegregation contexts. Finally, social behavior can be programmatically altered with the objective of changing the voluntary social behaviors of the students (Case 4). Desegregation and mainstreaming are examples of such interventions. Although any academic intervention can have social consequences and vice versa, we concentrate here on Case 4, social interventions designed to have social consequences.

In general, when evaluators investigate outcomes of academic interventions they usually proceed by administering a battery of achievement (academic) and attitude (social) tests (Cooley and Leinhardt 1980, Fisher, Filby, Marliave, Cahen, Dishaw, Moore, and Berliner 1978, Stebbins, St. Pierre, Proper, Anderson, and Creva 1977) but the discussion of results almost always focuses on the achievement tests alone. Clearly, education involves more than academic achievement, and loud complaints about narrowness and rigidity in evaluating programs using achievement tests alone are frequently heard. Such approaches are, however, unlikely to be abandoned (House, Glass, McLean, and Walker 1978). Indeed, when affective or noncognitive outcomes are reported, it is very frequently because nothing could be said about the academic outcomes, and we are left with the unsatisfying "happy, self-confident, but ignorant student" syndrome that plagues many evaluations (Webster 1975). Inadequate attention to the social outcomes of social interventions raises a serious problem for applied social science.

The apparent neglect of the social consequences of social interventions is surprising for several reasons. First, it is acknowledged that the educational process influences the development of social behaviors and competencies in addition to academic achievement (Cohen *et al.* 1976). Second, there is growing evidence that peer processes are an important mediator of academic learning and can, through the establishment of communication and support networks, facilitate or frustrate the acquisition of both academic and nonacademic skills (Bar–Tal 1978). Third, the phenomenon of self-imposed segrega-

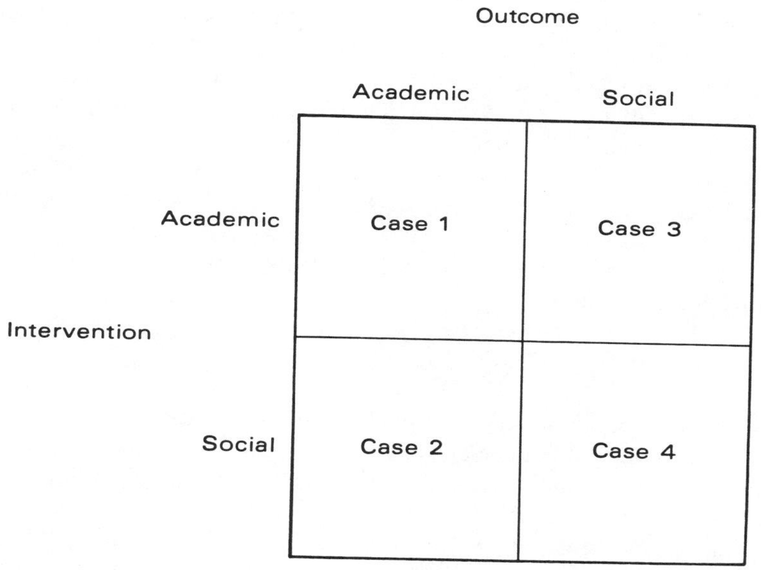

Outcome

FIGURE 16.1. *This chart relates academic and social interventions and outcomes.*

tion of minorities within programmatically desegregated schools implies that it is possible for the letter but not the intent of the law to be fulfilled (Francis and Schofield 1980), and, therefore, that procedures are needed that can assure greater compliance.

## Two Social Interventions

In the United States there are two nationwide policies that call for systematic social interventions in public education which are the focus of numerous evaluations: racial desegregation and the mainstreaming of mildly handicapped children. These policies are rooted in parallel interpretations of the constitutional requirement for equality of all before the law. Both have led to programmatic manipulations in which personal attributes of children are used as a basis for locating them in various educational facilities. In the case of desegregation, the relevant attribute is race, and by extension, ethnicity; in mainstreaming, it is a physical or mental impairment. Both programs, now established policies, have been the fruit of elaborate and costly historic trends and are still a cause of continuing public and institutional concern.

The eradication of de jure segregation following the 1954 Supreme Court decision (*Brown* v. *Board of Education*) was, relatively speaking, straightforward.[2] The eradication of de facto segregation, on the other hand, since it involves the development and implementation of new and untried social mechanisms for overcoming the natural consequences of established residential, attitudinal, occupational, and instructional patterns, is far more complicated and has led to the development of numerous intervention strategies. These strategies can be designed to achieve various legal or politically specified levels of racial balance. They also tend to have varying impacts on the targeted individuals as well as on the community. In part, different implementation strategies exist because policymakers lack adequate information on the nature of their indirect impacts.

## DESEGREGATION AND INTEGRATION

Simple desegregation, the physical presence of different categories of individuals, can and should be evaluated in a relatively straightforward manner. For the most part, such physical manipulation is a precondition to social integration and equality of opportunity, but it is not the same thing. Physical desegregation can occur at a variety of levels: the community, the school system, the school building, the grade or class type (i.e., remedial, vocational, general, academic), the classroom, or the instructional unit. It is achieved by simply placing individuals of a particular type in the presence of individuals of a different type. Legal mechanisms exist through which to obtain such mixes.[3] However, when we turn to issues of integration (the positive social interaction of the relevant groups), we face the problem of changing the voluntary behavior of individuals, a problem which is beyond the sphere of mandatory actions. The information we need to determine whether integration occurs is also signficantly more complex. It includes contextual information, the relative status of those contexts, the desegregation level in each, and the nature of the intergroup ties or contacts that occur in each situation.

Regardless of whether the objective of a desegregation attempt is simply desegregation or the more elusive integration, the evaluative model that has frequently been employed, although complex, has not been well specified. It is assumed that the simultaneous physical presence of minority and majority

---

[2]We do not mean to imply that it was simple or easy. We merely point out that, once a construct is developed in law, there are established procedures for effecting a specific outcome.

[3]A worthwhile piece of evaluative information would be the very simple documentation of this alone. For example, in 1980, the city of Pittsburgh was 22% black; the school system was 50% black. The top academic high school was 25.7% black, ninth grade was 32% black, twelfth grade was 25% black, remedial programs were 70% black, academic programs were 18% black, honors programs were 10% black, and so forth. The academically lowest high school was 99.8% black, ninth grade was 99.9% black, twelfth grade was 100% black, remedial programs were 100% black, academic programs did not exist, nor did honors programs. These nested lists of simple percentages are informative and suggest clear lines of dramatic status differentials and areas in which policy workers can and are placing their efforts.

children will, through some unspecified process, lead to an improvement in the academic performance of the minority group while leaving the academic performance of the majority group unchanged. Although there seems to be little information to support the former assumption, there is some substantial information to support the latter (Crain and Mahard 1977). Does this mean that desegregation is a failure? We would argue that the model is misguided and leads to irrelevant evaluations. The concern should focus on the social outcomes of desegregation and the mechanisms through which the social ties that permit integration to develop.

## CONCEPTUAL MODELS

Developing conceptual models of the processes that are thought to link interventions with outcomes is an important part of an evaluation. By *conceptual model* we mean simply a relational schema, or graph, in which measurable inputs are linked to observable outcomes. Such a model helps the evaluator specify the processes through which inputs are expected to affect target individuals and alter *observable* behavior. This activity forces the evaluator to be explicit about what aspects of the intervention are expected to influence the behavior of target individuals, and to what extent specific measures are acting as proxies for the elements of concern (Cooley 1978; Leinhardt 1978; Leinhardt 1980). When the evaluation focuses on academic outcomes, the use of such an approach is not novel. It does seem far less accepted, however, when social outcomes are at issue. It is quite likely that two problems are involved. One is the paucity of applicable social science theory and the other is the lack of agreement on what are observable social outcomes.

Social science theory could be a vital aid in the construction of conceptual models. Theory can suggest the components, relationships, and directionality of impacts. Further, it can help evaluators recognize when apparently different components are in fact the same. By constructing conceptual models, the evaluator, in effect, translates theory into the client's policy-relevant dimensions. Unfortunately, most relevant theoretical social science is devoid of operational implications. Consequently, the evaluator is in a position of either neglecting theory altogether and proceeding in an ad hoc fashion, or creating a theoretical framework. We choose this latter approach, but do so in a general fashion in order to establish a framework that has broad-based applicability in contexts where behavioral manipulations are designed to yield social outcomes.

In developing the models for social interventions used here, we have utilized what we call an opportunities framework as a theoretical guide. Specifically, we assume that social interventions alter individuals' opportunities for socially meaningful encounters. Successful integration of minorities and the handicapped, thus, depends in part on the opportunities for contact provided by the context. We distinguish between *passive* opportunities in which targets may observe interactions and may experience primarily cognitive alterations or confirmations, and *active* opportunities in which the targets may encounter (physically or verbally) or interact with the "others." The metric for both active and passive opportunities involves time as well as quality or significance. We are asserting that, for evaluative purposes, social interventions can best be understood in terms of the alterations in opportunities which they create for target individuals to experience passive and active social encounters which would not have occurred or would have been significantly less likely without the intervention.

Using the opportunities framework, a useful model for the impact of desegregation can be specified. The outcome of interest is the level of integration across a variety of settings, such as, athletics, subject matter, free time. The inputs of interest are the numerical levels of desegregation, the level of effort or intervention, and the repeated measures of social interactions. The point here is that desegregation is primarily a social event. The objective is to alter the social experience and behavior of individuals and promote a view of a socially moral and ethical society.

## SOCIAL OUTCOMES

Before discussing specific models of integration we need to clarify what we mean by a social outcome. We have asserted that social outcomes must be conceptualized in terms of observable social behaviors. Educational interventions involve manipulations of individuals that manifestly alter the opportunities they experience for social interaction. Such interaction or its observation is presumed to affect the development of relations between individuals. Thus, social outcomes can be measured in terms of either the actual interactive behavior of targeted individuals or the relational ties that exist between them.

Desegregation and mainstreaming create increased opportunities for interaction between members of different groups, that is, between individuals of different races or ethnicities, and between individuals who are handicapped and those who are not. Although usually described categorically, for example, as interaction between the races or between special and regular groups, each interaction involves individuals and is associated with interpersonal relations to and from them. Such interactions may have positive or negative impacts on the desire of the interacting individuals to engage in similar future interactions with the same or similar types of individuals. Observation of altered opportunities, actual interaction, and the development of interpersonal ties are straightforward. For example, we can conceptualize interventions that are designed to alter expectations, encourage interdependence, and promote physical proximity as attempts to foster interaction by making it more convenient and even necessary.

Successful integration should lead to stable patterns of relational ties that are indifferent to race or ethnicity, and the ties can serve as an observable outcome. As Cohen (1975) argues, a successfully integrated classroom within a desegregated school need not be a mass of completely affectively interconnected individuals. Successful integration occurs when contacts between members of different social groups are nearly as likely to lead to repeated contacts and lasting affective ties as are contacts between members of the same social group. In Cohen's (1975) words,

> The mechanism of desegregation is not intended to create universal love and brotherhood. The goal of the desegregation process is a *reasonable* degree of social integration and a lack of overt conflict whereby blacks and whites, given an objective important to both, can *trust each other* and *listen to each other* sufficiently well to complete the task at hand, whether it be a vocational task, an educational task, or a political task [p. 273, emphasis added].

The objective in the case of mainstreaming is analogous. No one presumes that the handicapped child will be universally admired, liked, or loved. The objective is for the child to obtain the same level of integration within the group that could be obtained by nonhandicapped children. Social indifference is the goal, that is, the probability of interaction between two dissimilar individuals should be essentially the same as the probability of interaction between two similar individuals. Integration for the handicapped child means that he or she is not universally disliked, rejected, or hated simply because of a handicap. Patterns of interpersonal ties, thus, become a metric against which to ascertain how successful integration has been.

Figure 16.2 displays a possible model for integration which possesses observable social outcomes related to programmatically manipulable opportunities. The model contains features that are important but ignored in most evaluations. Racial integration (11) is a consequence of the quantity and quality of social contacts between the members of two groups, A and B (10). The social contact can be observed directly, inferred from the structural analysis of sociometric responses, or inferred from unlinked self-reports. The quantity and quality of social contacts are a function of the temporal opportunity (6) (controlled for contexts), the physical arrangement or groupings (7), the degree to which both groups engage in similarly liked and disliked tasks and to which both groups have publicly and privately shown to have similar success (8), and finally, teacher treatment (9) of the individual members of the groups in terms of instruction, management, "fairness," and physical arrangement of the instructional setting.

Temporal opportunity and physical arrangement are in part functions of the level of desegregation (5) and the group structure immediately following

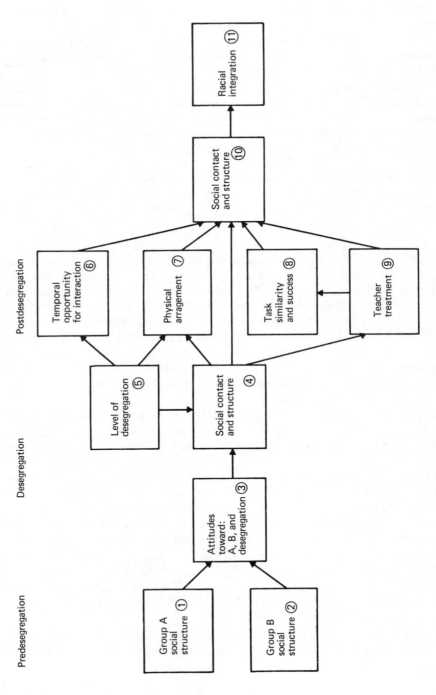

Predesegregation     Desegregation     Postdesegregation

Group A social structure ①

Group B social structure ②

Attitudes toward: A, B, and desegregation ③

Level of desegregation ⑤

Social contact and structure ④

Temporal opportunity for interaction ⑥

Physical arragement ⑦

Task similarity and success ⑧

Teacher treatment ⑨

Social contact and structure ⑩

Racial integration ⑪

**FIGURE 16.2.** *This model shows processes influencing integration.*

desegregation (4). Group structure immediately following desegregation is a function of the attitudes (3) of both groups (toward themselves, others, and desegregation) and the structures from which the individuals emerged (1 and 2). This models assumes that major interventions designed to affect integration operate through the elements we have specified. Thus, Cohen's work on expectation alteration works on opportunity for contact (6) and task skill performance (8). In the absence of such efforts, the pattern of quick resegregation and reduction of social contact—especially prosocial contact—is well documented (Cohen 1975, Rist 1979, Schoefield 1978, Schoefield and McGivern 1979).

What role does such a model play in an evaluation? The evaluation model we are proposing is designed to assess the impact of desegregation on intergroup relations. We are arguing that one must be explicit about what things influence such relationships. A useful evaluation is one that provides information relating level of impact to manipulable features of the educational environment and also indicates which elements have positive but compensating features and can be ignored. For example, if Cohen and Lockheed are right, then simply manipulating temporal opportunity and task success in the right way can have profound consequences for social contact and integration, consequences sufficient, perhaps, to overcome or alter attitudinal states or initial group structures. On the other hand, if they are not right then such appealingly simple manipulations are not sufficient and more complex mediations are required.

## MAINSTREAMING OF MILDLY HANDICAPPED CHILDREN

Mainstreaming is another educational intervention possessing a significant social outcome that has become national policy in the United States. The policy results from the passage by Congress of the "Education for All the Handicapped Children Act" in 1975 (PL 94-142). By requiring that all children be educated in the "least restrictive environment," this act, in effect, mandated the elimination of programs in which mildly handicapped children receive separate special education. Mainstreaming, like desegregation, involves physically locating one group of students, the handicapped, in the same educational context as another, the nonhandicapped. There are, however, two important differences between mainstreaming and desegregation. One involves the quite small number of children who are to be mainstreamed. The proportion of minority students who are to be integrated into United States public schools is about 30% of all children. Handicapped children make up about 12% of all children; those that are mildly handicapped and, therefore, likely to be mainstreamed, represent only about one-half of this or 6%. The density of mainstreamed children is so low that regular classrooms would contain at most two special children and rarely more than one. Thus, the dominant social system in mainstreamed classrooms is likely to remain that of the normal children.

The second difference involves the effective absence of a minority subculture of handicappedness (with the exception of the hearing-impaired). In addition, the values and attitudes of the society at large are the values and attitudes that teachers, policymakers, and parents by and large agree should be those acquired by the mainstreamed child. Indeed, proponents of mainstreaming freely admit that improved access to these values and attitudes is an important underlying rationale for mainstreaming.

The move toward mainstreaming has both academic and social components, and evaluations have evidenced these dual concerns. Evaluations of academic outcomes in mainstreaming contexts are motivated by two distinct points of view. One is the realization by special educators themselves that the use of separate facilities is *not* an effective academic mode for most children with special needs (Dunn 1968). This leads naturally to a need for evaluators to determine whether children with special needs perform at least as well in mainstream classrooms. The other point of view leads to a focus on the academic performance of normal children who share their academic experiences with a mainstreamed special child. Here the concern is that their achievement is no poorer as a consequence of the intervention.

Evaluations of the social outcomes of mainstreaming have been relatively common. Since the density of special children in mainstream classrooms is small on average, the attitudinal and behavioral reaction of the normal children to the insertion of a handicapped child into the classroom social system becomes a critical issue. If there is only one special child in a class, the archetypical situation, lack of social integration implies utter isolation. In contrast to the situation in a desegregated school where blacks and whites may voluntarily resegregate and develop parallel independent social systems, a socially isolated mainstreamed child is effectively excluded from all peer-based social activities and, as a consequence, except for the opportunity to observe normal children, has no opportunity to develop the attitudes, behavioral skills, and social expectations that immersion in the normal classroom is supposed to provide (Chaires 1966).

Because of the ease with which isolation can be observed and its evident deleterious consequences, numerous procedures have been developed to improve the chances a mainstreamed child has to develop interpersonal ties with normal classmates. The design of evaluation strategies for these procedures depends upon the conceptual model the evaluator has of the mainstreaming process.

Our model derives from the opportunities framework. As with desegregation, the point is to specify in some detail the processes that affect the level of social integration on an individual and lead to mechanisms for measuring these conditions. Our model is presented in Figure 16.3. It is very similar to that proposed for desegregation.

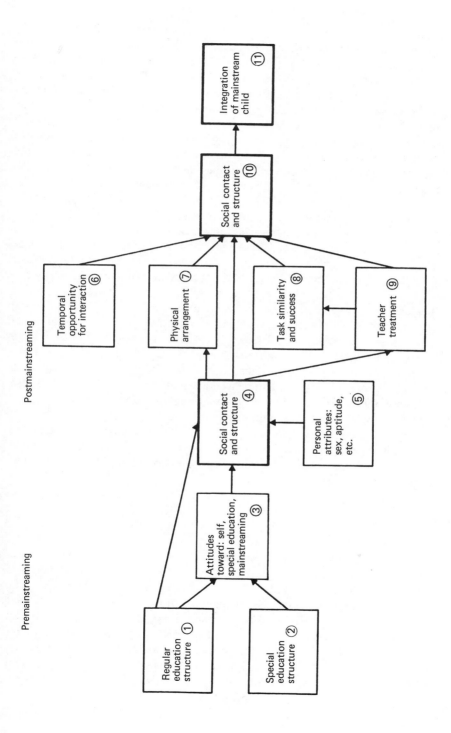

**FIGURE 16.3.** *This model shows processes influencing mainstreaming.*

In the model presented in Figure 16.3, the social integration of a target child (11) is an immediate consequence of prior social contacts, both positive and negative, and classroom social structure (10). Social structure is influenced by five aspects of classroom activity. First, the temporal opportunity for interaction between the target child and his or her peers (6) can be measured simply by using the amount of total time that they are together. (Obviously, more complex estimates can be made by setting and subgroup.) Second, the physical arrangement (7) can include an index of similarity (child has a desk, spacing is no more or less isolated, etc.) and appropriateness. Third, task similarity and performance (8) should include information on the similarity of the task, the significance of it, the visability and success of performance, and the visability and success of the product. Fourth, teacher treatment (9) should include estimates of appropriateness, frequency of contact in important dimensions such as academic versus managerial areas, compensating behaviors, and rejection or isolating behaviors. These measures most certainly should not be simple estimates of equality. Finally, initial or prior social structure (4) of the total group is expected to influence the final or posttreatment structure of the group.

Physical arrangements of space (7) and teacher treatment of all children (9) are also influenced by the initial social structure of the group (4). Initial social structure (4) is influenced by individual personal attributes (5) and by a large collection of attitudes and internalized experiences (3). These attitudes include, for example, attitudes toward handicaps, attitudes toward mainstreaming, and feelings and information about group structure and one's own role in it. These attitudes are in turn influenced by prior structure (1 and 2). One arrow, the one from regular group structure to initial structure, remains undiscussed. We feel that in many mainstreaming situations in which the special child is "dropped into" an existing group, group structure influences the effect of mainstreaming. The target child's previous experiences operate thorugh his or her attitudes, only, rather than directly on structure.

## DATA AND MEASUREMENT

The typical approach to the development of data on social outcomes involves the administration of attitude surveys or other devices designed to determine the sentiments or ideas individuals possess about various social groups. The underlying assumption is, of course, that such attitudes influence behavior. But there are several problems with this approach. First, the relationship between attitudes and behavior is poorly understood. Second, it is demonstrably difficult to change attitudes. Third, the focus of most social interventions is the modification of behavior, not attitudes. If extant interpersonal ties and interactions are the focus, then the data of interest must reflect this concern.

There are two options; one involves gathering data that represent observations of actual behavior. Unfortunately, this requires costly, time-consuming procedures possessing significant data summarization, analysis, and generalization problems. Although such procedures do yield an unmatched richness of detail and are exceptionally well-suited to providing a context-setting perspective, in most situations their defects outweigh their advantages. The second option is to focus on the network of interpersonal ties.

The procedure that seems ideally suited to the generation of data on interpersonal relations is sociometric testing. Originated by Moreno (1934), sociometric data are, relatively speaking, easily obtained, intuitively comprehensible, and possessed of a high degree of concept validity. In some respects, the sociometric instrument is simply a survey of attitudes. In contrast to a traditional attitude survey, however, it probes attitudes toward specific members of the target population, individuals who actually participate in the daily interactions that characterize integration. Further, these relational data taken together represent an observation on the social system; that is, they are the measures of interdependent ties that knit the group members together into a coherent social organization. The structural characteristics of these ties are of focal interest because they define the location of the individuals in the group's social system. Such characteristics cannot be observed in the isolated reports of the individuals because they are not properties of the individuals. They are patterns, not attributes, and can only be detected by examining the way the interpersonal relationships fit together. This is a critical point and requires some elaboration.

Clearly, the willingness of children of one category to cite children of another category as their friends can be thought of in and of itself as a relevant social outcome. But a deeper view focuses on consistent patterns of joint citation, that it, instances in which specific individuals in different categories cite one another as friends. Such outcomes are indications of the mutual trust and openness to communication regarded by Cohen and others as essential features of racial integration. Similarly, the willingness of mainstreamed children to cite normal children as friends is not relevant. Given the reality of a normal classroom, such an outcome is a foregone conclusion and, given the low density of special children in the classroom, their lack of attraction is also somewhat expected. An essential issue, however, is the establishment of mutual friendships by the mainstreamed child, that is, the development of patterns of systematic reciprocal involvement in the social network.

Sociometric data are relevant to these issues. Methods for collecting them are well known and their use in research on desegregation and mainstreaming is not novel. Most applications have, however, been methodologically constrained and are not easily generalized. Both the approach to data collection and the use of ineffective analytic procedures have been at fault (Holland and Leinhardt 1973). We propose an approach that derives from the notion of the opportunity framework and exploits some new developments in the theory of stochastic digraphs.

Our approach characterizes the educational intervention as a mechanism for manipulating opportunities for contact to occur between individuals. The interactions that take place between individuals may provide them with new information, cause them to change their attitudes and expectations, or otherwise lead to a modification in how each perceives the other. Extant ties to other members of the group may, through felt structural imperatives, also influence what is felt to be the consequence of the interaction. Regardless of the mode of operation, the interaction results in a relationship between the interacting individuals and it is the relationship, not the interaction, which persists and conditions the prospects of future interactions given the opportunities that get presented.

What we are saying, in effect, is that individuals make choices about whom to spend their time with, whom to have as friends. They cannot interact with everyone all the time. They must choose between competing options given the opportunities that the classroom schedule and management structure provide. Interaction and observation can operate to modify their priorities and can lead them to reevaluate the benefits of repetitions. Programmatic interventions can change opportunities and make interaction more or less convenient, but the relationships that develop as a consequence of the experience will be the dominant future factor influencing voluntary social behavior given consistency in context.

The next step in developing this approach requires that we link it to a statistical procedure for modeling friendship choice that relates to relevant social outcomes and can be used with sociometric data. The difficulty in accomplishing this step rests in the unique features of relational data and our desire to focus on patterns of relations, not distributions of attributes. Recent advances in the development of stochastic models for relational data have solved many of the problems associated with the analysis of reciprocation in the structure of sociometric data. The statistical development detailed in Holland and Leinhardt (1981) is quite complex and, consequently, we will not repeat it here. In essence, the theory conceptualizes sociometric data as observations on a system of affective ties which result from a "choice process," one in which individuals allocate their choices to others in a probabilistic fashion, whereas biases act to increase or decrease the probability that choices will go to specific others over time (Holland and Leinhardt 1977a, 1977b, and 1977c). These biases can be based on individual attributes such as race or ethnicity, or on structural feature of the social system such as reciprocity and even transitivity.

In this approach, reciprocity is represented as a bias that acts to increase or decrease the chance that, once a choice is made, the chosen individual will reciprocate the choice. Although deriving from a dynamic view, the approach is equally valid at the cross-sectional level. Here the reciprocity bias can be conceived of as an instantaneous force or effect. A positive reciprocity effect means that the observation of a choice of one individual by another increases the chance that, in the same data matrix, the chosen individual will be observed to reciprocate. Application to the cross-sectional case involves specifying a model that is a member of a family of exponential probability distributions defined on digraphs (square matrices containing entries that are either zeros or ones) and using an iterative algorithm to estimate the parameters of the model. (Programs for fitting these models are available from the authors.) It is important to understand that the method developed in Holland and Leinhardt (1981) is both multivariate and parametric. The multivariate feature means that the estimated effect of a bias like reciprocity is made conditional on the impact of other model-specified biases, including the attractiveness (sociometric status) or productivity (gregariousness) of each individual. The fact that the effects are estimates of the parameters of a model means that they can be compared across different samples and that the parameter values can be used as measures or data in secondary analyses.

The procedures that Holland and Leinhardt (1981) introduce permit analyses of important structural patterns in sociometric data. It is natural to ask how these statistical models can be used to evaluate the social outcomes of mainstreaming and desegregation. We pursue an application to mainstreaming in depth later, but first we discuss briefly and nontechnically how one might proceed.

The analytic framework permits the investigator to specify alternative statistical models for the sociometric data. Extensions permit disaggregating effects to suit the needs of a hypothesized social outcome. For example, an effect of desegregation might be specified in terms of altering the probability of reciprocal choice between different groups while having no impact on the chances of reciprocal choosing within each group. The situation is slightly modified in the mainstreaming situation since the groups here typically involve a single handicapped child and a large group of nonhandicapped children. If the behavior of the special child is the focus of an evaluative study, the analysis can examine whether, for example, the probability of a choice is going to the special child has increased given that there is a choice coming from the special child. It is the ability to specify the exact nature of the relational pattern and to estimate the effect that render this approach appealing.

## DETAILED APPLICATION TO MAINSTREAMING DATA

We have used this analytic framework in evaluating the social outcomes of a mainstreaming experiment. This effort is still underway and the results we have to date are preliminary and limited. Nonetheless, we present them here as an example of the way in which the opportunities framework and stochastic relational data analysis procedures can be employed in evaluative studies.

We have obtained sociometric data generated during an Office of Education-sponsored mainstreaming experiment called Project Prime which was performed in Texas, circa 1970 (Ballard, Corman, Gottlieb, Kaufman 1977). Project Prime took place over a period of 3 years and involved a series of separate studies. The particular research activity we are concerned with was designed to study the integration of mainstreamed educable mentally retarded (EMR) children. It has often been observed that mainstreamed EMR children experience deleterious social effects. Although they may have been socially integrated in their special education classrooms, within the mainstream classroom they experience affective rejection and social isolation (Corman and Gottlieb 1978). As in the case of desegregation, this voluntaristic resegregation suggests that the affected child might be academically and socially better off in a programmatically segregated classroom. Since the mainstreaming of EMR children usually involves placing only one or a small number of special children into regular classrooms, exploration of secondary interventions that would alleviate or eradicate the negative outcomes of mainstreaming would seem easily accomplished. Indeed, numerous strategies have been developed and implemented in the field. Unfortunately, there is little in reported analyses to suggest that the systematic isolation of mainstreamed EMR children by their classmates can be avoided.

The component of Project Prime with which we are concerned was designed to obtain conclusive evidence that secondary interventions could work. The research design used was that of a traditional experimental study. Approximately 40 elementary school classrooms, each containing one mainstreamed EMR child, were split into experimental and control groups. The experimental groups experienced a treatment in the form of a teacher-led group activity designed to increase the opportunities for encounters between the teacher, the special child, and the normal children, and to increase the opportunities for normal children to observe the special child successfully performing a socially important task.

It must be remembered that although the behavior of the mainstreamed child is expected to be affected by the interventions, it is the reactive behavior of the normal children that is the focus of the research. The objective is to get the normal children to accept the handicapped child, to view the handicapped child as much as possible in the same light as they view one another, and to motivate the development of reciprocity by stimulating normal children to respond to the attempts of the handicapped child to initiate interpersonal ties. In this particular context, it is explicitly recognized that the social position of the special child is a consequence of the normal children failing to accept the special child and make him or her a "regular" member of their social system.

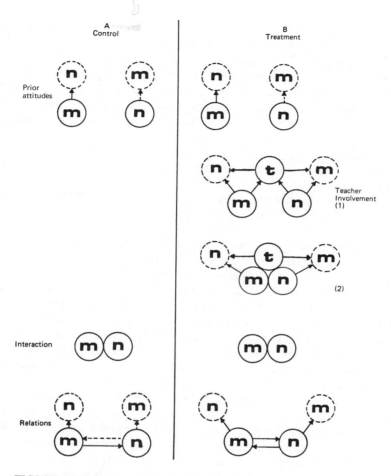

**FIGURE 16.4.** *This is a diagram of the results of the Prime experiment.*

Figure 16.4 presents the two processes diagrammatically. In the control situation, the usual social events occur. The normal child is thought to possess negative attitudes and expectations about EMR children. The mainstreamed child, on the other hand, is quite positively predisposed toward other children, handicapped or nonhandicapped. Mainstreaming creates opportunities for actual interaction. When encounters occur they confirm the children's preconceived notions. The children part, with the mainstreamed child liking the nonhandicapped child and wanting to engage in future interaction, whereas the nonhandicapped child rejects the mainstreamed child and prefers to avoid future interaction.

Under the treatment condition, the initial situation is identical. The teacher whom both like, however, steps in and, through management of a common activity, operates so as to alter the attitude of the nonhandicapped child and mediates the children's interaction. The experience is supposed to be positive. The result should be a change in attitude in the nonhandicapped child. This positive relationship is readily reciprocated and leads to future encounters which maintain the affective ties. Although not explicitly stated, the assumptions in this representation of the process seem to be those made by others who have studied the Project Prime data. The results that these investigators obtained, however, indicate that the treatment had no noticeable positive effect.

Detailed analyses of the Project Prime sociometric data will be reported elsewhere. We report here two general results. First, we investigate whether, empirically, there is any benefit accruing from the use of the multivariate stochastic procedure as opposed to a traditional univariate approach. Second, we present some results relevant to evaluating the impact of the experimental manipulation on the mainstreamed EMR children.

The traditional approach to the study of sociometric position focuses on "sociometric status" measured simply as the number of (or some normed function of) choices each group member attracts. Such measures are theoretically inadequate because they are, in effect, zero-order measurements and fail to control for the simultaneous impacts of other relevant features of the system of ties. It is, of course, one thing to have a theoretical rationale behind a complex alternative and another to demonstrate empirical differences in the measures, that is, to show that the simple measure and the complex measure give different results. For each group, we computed chi-square statistics for a hierarchy of models that included a univariate approach to the measurement of sociometric status and multivariate alternates that contained variables for group reciprocity and choice density, and individual productivity and attractiveness. First, the multivariate models that were fitted to the data were nearly always statistically significant indicating that a univariate analysis, such as is usually performed in the mainstreaming literature, was generally inadequate and would yield biased results. This finding suggests that prior reports of analyses, which found no effect for the experimental manipulation, would be erroneous.

We also contrasted the individual parameter estimates obtained under the multivariate approach with those obtained using a univariate approach. The multivariate parameter values ranged over a greater number of values than did those obtained using a univariate approach. One interpretation of this finding is that the multivariate approach makes finer, more precise distinctions between the structural features of the group members.

Finally, the individual parameter values for attractiveness (sociometric status) and productiveness (gregariousness) of ties obtained using the multivariate approach were plotted against those obtained from a univariate model.

These plots revealed that the multivariate parameters were not monotonic functions of the univariate estimates. This indicates that even simple conclusions drawn, say, on the basis of a rank ordering of the univariate effects would not necessarily be robust and should not be used to draw evaluative conclusions.

These three results taken together form a convincing argument for the use of the multivariate approach in developing measures of individual social outcomes that can be used to evaluate an intervention quantitatively. Indeed, on the basis of our admittedly limited empirical results, relying on a univariate statistic such as "sociometric status" (or any simple version of this statistic) as an indicator of social integration or interpersonal attractiveness is dangerous. In the case of the Project Prime data, it is clear that such reliance would lead to incorrect conclusions. In a recent report, in fact, researchers using univariate measures concluded that the Project Prime manipulation had no effect (Semmel, Gottlieb, and Robinson 1979). As we will show, however, an effect can be associated with the experimental manipulation. We discuss this result next.

We evaluated the effectiveness of the experimental manipulation in the following way. One of the planned objectives of the manipulation was to improve the social integration of the mainstreamed child. The opportunities framework led us to conceptualize this process as a potential influence on the attractiveness of the mainstreamed child and as an agent modifying the reciprocal nature of the social relations among mainstreamed and regular children. Here we report results that focus on attraction.

A full multivariate model was fitted to each sociomatrix. This produced parameter estimates for overall reciprocity and density, and individual production and attraction of ties. We extracted the estimates of the individual attraction parameters for each mainstreamed EMR child. We then used least-squares regression to estimate an equation in which posttreatment attraction of the EMR child was regressed on their pretreatment attraction, their gender, and the kind of treatment (experimental or control) they experienced. Thus, the estimated model was:

$$\text{attraction (post)} = \text{attraction (pre)} + \text{treatment} + \text{gender}.$$

This is, in effect, a covariance adjusted analysis in which pretreatment attraction is controlled. Gender was included because male and female EMR children are often treated differentially. We hasten to point out that the attraction measures are the parameter estimates obtained by fitting a multivariate model to each data matrix. Thus each individual EMR child's attractiveness parameter is adjusted for the structure of the group he or she was in. In terms of the evaluative model we proposed earlier, only the social structure (pre- and post-) and personal attributes were observed; whereas the indicator variable for treatment can be thought of as a surrogate for temporal opportunity and task.

The regression obtained an adjusted $r^2$ of .26 using 28 observations. The coefficients for pretreatment attraction, treatment, and gender were .78, .83, and .94, respectively, with $t$-statistics of 3.13, 1.79, and 1.86. We are concerned primarily with the results for treatment since we view pretreatment attraction and gender as nuisance parameters. The finding of a positive effect for treatment with a $t$-statistic of 1.79 lends support to the hypothesis that the treatment did have a beneficial impact on the average net attractiveness of the EMR children. Since the treatment variable appears in the analysis as a 0/1 indicator variable, when the child is in a control group, posttreatment attraction appears to depend on pretreatment attraction and gender. Being in the treatment group gives an additional boost to the child's attraction.

## Concluding Remarks

In this chapter we have proposed a conceptual framework that focuses attention on how interventions alter opportunities for interaction. We also proposed a methodology, involving the observation of social activities, which we believe can help make distinctions between social and academic outcomes of educational innovations clearer. We have argued that social relationship data is an especially useful means of obtaining information on the effects of social processes that are involved in educational interventions. Past problems in the analysis of relational data seem to have been solved and newly available techniques allow investigators to obtain empirical estimates of structural parameters in multivariate models. This results in significantly improved precision and validity of measurement. Using data from a mainstreaming experiment, we showed that this approach was essential in evaluating treatment effectiveness and demonstrated how conceptual models of programmatically altered opportunities could lead to a focus on specific outcomes that, in turn, could be associated with particular parameters of a stochastic structural model.

We have tried to capitalize on some of the advances that have been made in the area of evaluating academic outcomes and bring them to bear on the problem of evaluating social interventions. We have argued that a useful evaluation needs to have a clear focus on at least one valued outcome and that that outcome should be measureable. For the social interventions described, we offer the pattern of social relations as a reasonable outcome and sociometric data as a useful way of measuring that outcome. We have also argued that the policy analysis and evaluative dialogues are greatly enhanced by making explicit the underlying causal schema through which an intervention is presumed to operate. It is the evaluator's responsibility to develop such a schema and we suggest that evaluators can combine their knowledge of social science with an opportunities framework in order to produce such a schema.

# References

Abeson, A., and Zettel, J. 1977. The end of the quiet revolution: The Education For All Handicapped Children Act of 1975. *Exceptional Children* 2: 114–128.

Armor, D.J. 1972. School and family effects on black and white achievement: A reexamination of the USOE data. In *On equality of educational opportunity*, eds. F. Mosteller, and D.P. Moynihan. New York: Vintage Press. Pp. 168–229.

Baldwin, W.K. 1958. The social position of the educable mentally retarded child in the regular grades in public schools. *Exceptional Children* 25: 106–108, 112.

Ball, S. 1973. *A summary of the major findings from reading with TV: An evaluation of The Electric Company.* Princeton: Educational Testing Service.

Ballard, M., Corman, L., Gottlieb, J., and Kaufman, M.J. 1977. Improving the social status of mainstreamed retarded children. *Journal of Educational Psychology* 69: 605–611.

Bar–Tal, D. 1978. Social outcomes of the schooling process and their taxonomy. In *Social psychology of education: Theory and research*, eds. D. Bar–Tal and L. Saxe, Washington, D.C.: Hemisphere. Pp. 149–164.

Chaires, M.C. 1966. *Improving the social acceptance of educable mentally retarded pupils in special classes.* Unpublished Ph.D. dissertation, Indiana University.

Chennault, M. 1967. Improving the social acceptance of unpopular educable mentally retarded pupils in special classes. *American Journal of Mental Deficiency* 72: 455–458.

Cohen, E.G. 1975. The effects of desegregation on race relations. *Law and Contemporary Problems* 39: 271–299.

Cohen, E.G., Lockheed, M.E., and Lohman, M.R. 1976. The Center for Interracial Cooperation: A field experiment. *Sociology of Education* 49: 47–58.

Cooley, W.W. 1978. Explanatory observational studies. *Educational Researcher*, 7: 9–15.

Cooley, W.W., and Leinhardt, G. 1980. The instructional dimensions study. *Educational Evaluation and Policy Analysis* 2: 7–25.

Corman, L., and Gottlieb, J. 1978. Mainstreaming mentally retarded children: A review of research. In *International review of research in mental retardation*, ed. N.R. Ellis. New York: Academic Press. Pp. 251–275.

Crain, R.L., and Mahard, R.E. 1977. *Desegregation and black achievement: A review.* Paper presented at a conference of Social Science and Law in Desegregation, Amelia Island, Fl., October 1977.

Cronbach, L.J., and associates. 1980. *Toward reform of program evaluation.* San Francisco: Jossey–Bass.

Dunn, L.M. 1968. Special education for the mildly retarded—Is much of it justifiable? *Exceptional Children* 35: 5–22.

Epps, E.G. 1975. The impact of school desegregation on aspirations, self-concepts and other aspects of personality. *Law and Contemporary Problems* 39: 300–313.

Fisher, C.W., Filby, N.N., Marliave, R., Cahen, L.S., Dishaw, M.M., Moore, J.E., and Berliner, D.C. 1978. *Teacher behaviors, academic learning time and student achievement: Final report of phase III-B, beginning teacher evaluation study.* Technical Report V-1. San Francisco: Far West Laboratory for Educational Research and Development.

Francis, W.D., and Schofield, J.W. 1980. *The impact of race on interaction in a desegregated school.* Paper presented at the annual meeting of the American Sociological Association, New York, August 1980.

Goodman, H.. Gottlieb, J., and Harrison, R.H. 1972. Social acceptance of EMRs integrated into a nongraded elementary school. *American Journal of Mental Deficiency* 76: 412–417.

Gottlieb, J., and Budoff, M. 1973. Classroom behavior and social status. *Studies in Learning Potential* 3(53). (published by Research Institute for Educational Problems, Cambridge, Mass.).

Haring, N.G., and Krug, D.A. 1975. Placement in regular programs: Procedures and results. *Exceptional Children* 41: 413–417.

Hays, W. 1951. Mental level and friend selection among institutionalized, defective girls. *American Journal of Mental Deficiency* 1951: 198–203.

Holland, P.W., and Leinhardt, S. 1971. Transitivity in structural models of small groups. *Comparative Group Studies* 2: 107–124.

Holland, P.W., and Leinhardt, S. 1973. The structural implications of measurement error in sociometry. *Journal of Mathematical Sociology* 3: 85–112.

Holland, P.W., and Leinhardt, S. 1977a. A dynamic model for social networks. *Journal of Mathematical Sociology* 5: 5–20.

Holland, P.W., and Leinhardt, S. 1977b. Notes on the statistical analysis of social network data. Paper presented at the Mathematical Social Science Board Advanced Research Symposium on Stochastic Process Models of Social Structure, Pittsburgh.

Holland, P.W., and Leinhardt, S. 1977c. Social structure as a network process. *Zeitschrift fur Soziologie* 6: 386–402.

Holland, P.W., and Leinhardt, S. 1981. An exponential family of probability distributions for directed graphs. *Journal of the American Statistical Association* 76: 33–50.

House, E.R., Glass, G.V., McLean, L.D., and Walker, D.F. 1978. No simple answer: Critique of the follow through evaluation. *Harvard Educational Review* 48: 128–160.

Iano, R.P., Ayers, D., Heller, H., McGettigan, J., and Walker, V.S. 1974. Sociometric status of retarded children in an integrative program. *Exceptional Children* 40: 245–250.

Johnson, G.O. 1950. A study of the social position of mentally retarded children in the regular grades. *American Journal of Mental Deficiency* 55: 60–89.

Leinhardt, G. 1978. Applying a classroom process model to instructional evaluation. *Curriculum Inquiry* 8: 155–176.

Leinhardt, G. 1980. Modeling and measuring educational treatment in evaluation. *Review of Educational Research* 50: 393–420.

Leinhardt, S. 1972. Developmental change in the sentiment structure of children's groups. *American Sociological Review* 37: 202–212.

Levin, H.M. 1975. Education, life chances, and the courts: The role of social science evidence. *Law and Contemporary Problems* 39: 227.

Moreno, J.L. 1934. *Who shall survive.* Washington, D.C.: Nervous and Mental Diseases Publication Co.

Rist, R.C., ed. 1979. *Desegregated schools.* New York: Academic Press.

Schofield, J.W. 1978. School desegregation and intergroup relations. In *Social psychology of education: Theory and research,* eds. D. Bar-Tal and L. Saxe. Washington, D.C.: Hemisphere Press. Pp. 329–358.

Schofield, J.W., and McGivern, E.P. 1979. Creating interracial bonds in a desegregated school. In *Interracial bonds,* eds. R.G. Blumberg and W.J. Roye. Bayside, N.Y.: General Hall. Pp.106–119.

Semmel, M.I., Gottlieb, J., and Robinson, N.M. 1979. Mainstreaming: Perspectives on educating handicapped children in the public school. In *Review of research in education*, Vol. 7, ed. D.C. Berliner. Washington, D.C.: American Educational Research Association. Pp.223–282.

Slavin, R.E. 1978. Student teams and comparison among equals: Effects in academic performance and student attitudes. *Journal of Educational Psychology,* 70: 532–538.

Smith, A.W. 1980. Trends in racial tolerance as a function of group position. Paper presented at the annual meeting of the American Sociological Association, New York, August 1980.

Stebbins, L.B., St. Pierre, R.G., Proper, E.C., Anderson, R.B., and Creva, T.R. 1977. *Education as experimentation: A planned variation model. An evaluation of follow through.* Vol. IV-A. Report No. 76-196A. Cambridge: Abt Associates.

Torgeson, J. 1975. Problems and prospects in the study of learning disabilities. In *Review of child development research,* Vol. 5, ed. E.M. Hetherington, Chicago: University of Chicago Press. Pp.385–440.

Webster, W.J. 1975. *Abstracts of research and evaluation reports 1974–1975.* Dallas: Dallas Independent School District.

Weinberg, M. 1975. The relationship between school desegregation and academic achievement: A review of the research. *Law and Contemporary Problems* 39: 240–270.

# 17

# The Impact of Employment Programs on Offenders, Addicts, and Problem Youth: Implications from Supported Work

IRVING PILIAVIN and STANLEY MASTERS

## Introduction

For almost 20 years, the federal government of the United States has devoted large resources to employment and skill-training programs for disadvantaged workers, especially disadvantaged youth. Many of these programs have had as their aim the utilization of slack resources. Other programs have had more complex objectives. Their intent has been not simply to put resources into use but, through training, work experience, and other means, to help individuals become employable. Increased employability is assumed in turn to lead to reductions in the derivative problems these individuals may experience.

The concern of this chapter is with the second class of programs, particularly those that deal with individuals previously involved in crime and drug use. Our contention will be that, by concentrating on serving youth, such programs have neglected disadvantaged adults, for whom such programs often may be more effective. This assertion is based on an experimental evaluation of a major subsidized work-experience program in the United States called Supported Work. We have found this program to have little effect on delinquents' postprogram employment or on their criminal activity during or after program participation. In contrast, for adult offenders and drug addicts, particularly those over 35, we have found increased employment and reduced crime effects.

We begin this chapter by discussing the kinds of employment and training programs that have evolved in this country, including the rationale for such programs and the groups at which they have been targeted. Next we discuss the

EVALUATING THE WELFARE STATE:
SOCIAL AND POLITICAL PERSPECTIVES

Supported Work program and its evaluation. Then we compare the results for this evaluation with results for evaluations of other programs. We conclude that there is a reasonable case for redirecting our present work-experience programs to serve more adults relative to youth.

Although public efforts to improve citizens' job-related skills have a long history in the United States (i.e., public education), special programs for the disadvantaged and chronically unemployed have been a major item on the national political agenda only twice, first during the depression of the 1930s and second for an extended period beginning with the Kennedy administration in the early 1960s and continuing to the present day. The depression programs, primarily designed to put slack resources to use, were largely focused on adult workers. They were terminated in the early 1940s when the demand for manpower associated with World War II essentially eliminated involuntary unemployment.

The first factor leading to the development of employment and training programs in the early 1960s was the recession of 1958. The high unemployment resulting from the recession was often attributed to automation and the replacement of unskilled labor by machines, a diagnosis that led easily to a prescription of the need for retraining workers. An important retraining effort was the Manpower Development and Training Act (MDTA) of 1962. The initial objective of this program was to develop new skills among family heads who, although having much prior work experience, had been displaced by technological or economic changes. In most crucial respects these individuals were viewed in the same manner as the unemployed of the 1930s—motivated and otherwise ready for work but lacking job offers because of lessened demand for their skills.

A second major impetus for the employment and training programs of the 1960s was the Civil Rights Movement. One major area of concern within the movement related to job opportunities for older black workers whose unemployment problems were seen as similar to those of whites but seriously complicated by factors associated with racial discrimination. A second area of concern pertained to youth. For these individuals, unemployment was seen as being due not only to lack of marketable skills but to phenomena stemming from what was called the poverty subculture—here referring to the youth's lack of discipline necessary for sustained employment and to negative attitudes toward education and work. This thesis led many policymakers to the view that society should intervene to provide better opportunities for young people to enter the labor force and society's mainstream. The merit of such opportunities was reinforced by the hypotheses being put forth by some economists at this time that education represented an investment in human capital with a high rate of return. Denison (1962), in particular, suggested that this investment accounted for much of the economic growth of this country in the twentieth century. Similar effects were expected from training programs, especially those aimed at young people, since they have the longest working period ahead of them in which to reap the gains of better training.

The intellectual underpinnings for an emphasis on employment and training programs for youth were reinforced by events during the 1960s. First, although the overall unemployment rate fell dramatically from 6.8% in 1958 to 3.8% by 1966, the rate for those aged 16–19 only declined from 15.9 to 12.9%. This relatively mild reduction was probably caused in part by the substantial rise in the teenage population during the mid-1960s. A major consequence of this mix of circumstances is that the absolute number of unemployed youth remained constant during the 1960s, whereas that for other population segments declined.

Another critical phenomenon contributing to the developing stress on employment programs for youth at this time was the growth of urban disorder and crime, especially after the riot in the Watts area of Los Angeles in 1965. During the later years of the 1960s, political and civil rights leaders argued that providing youths with jobs to both increase income and give them "something constructive to do" would lower the incidence of crime and violence. These arguments initially provided the rationale for the development of summer job programs for teenagers and by the 1970s became the basis for the development of other programs for youth. Among others, the Neighborhood Youth Corps provided community-based work experience, and the Job Corps gave training to young people in institutional settings. Later, the Comprehensive Employment Training Act (CETA) of 1974, which was aimed to a large extent at youth, provided community-based work experiences under local government administration. Killingsworth and Killingsworth (1962) have estimated that in each year from 1965 through 1972 more than 50% of the participants in employment and training programs throughout the United States were aged 16–19, and that since then the proportion has been just under 50%.

The development of employment programs for offenders and drug addicts finds justification in a long line of studies beginning as early as 1930 with the Glueck's seminal work indicating a strong relationship between employment and crime. Although early research failed to unravel the causal linkage implied by this relationship, recent studies have provided some support for the hypotheses that unemployment increases the likelihood that individuals will commit a crime (Cook 1975; Evans 1968). These studies, and the repeated failure of alternative and less expensive efforts to stem recidivism, perhaps provided the major impetus for the manpower programs that began to appear in the early 1970s (Lipton, Martinson, and Wilks 1975).

## Impacts of Early Programs

Through the mid-1970s the achievements of employment programs for the various population groups they served could not be stated with much certainty, in part because of data problems. First, relatively few studies had been undertaken using control or comparison groups. Second, among comparison groups studies, sample-selection biases were generally not well controlled.

Third, follow-up periods were generally short. Perhaps as a result of these problems, or perhaps because some programs were run better than others, findings from various studies were not consistent. Research overviews, however, have suggested that the general conclusion of analysts on the merits of job training programs was one of cautious optimism—optimism because of measured employment gains, cautious because of the aforementioned data problems and inconsistencies (Ginzberg 1980). Conclusions concerning employment impacts on youth and known offenders were particularly mixed. A national evaluation of the summer component of the Neighborhood Youth Corp (NYC) by Somers and Stromsdorfer (1972) found that the increased post-program earnings of participants were less than the programs cost. Evaluations of the Job Corp and the Concentrated Employment Program (CEP) were also mixed, although somewhat more favorable for CEP (Kirschner 1969). However, these evaluations were based on even weaker data than were the NYC studies. The achievements of employment programs for known offenders and addicts through the mid-1970s were also poorly documented, in part because few employment programs targeted these individuals for services. One study of special interest was the experimental evaluation of Project Wildcat, a New York based work-experience program for addicts (Vera 1974). The results of this evaluation, contrary to those of other programs for offenders and addicts as well as for disadvantaged youth, indicated that for about 2 years after program entry, experimentals increased their employment and reduced their criminal activities relative to controls.

This then was the general picture with regard to employment programs for individuals of the type served by Supported Work. There were mixed results for youth. With one exception, there were generally negative results for known criminals and addicts. The exception was Project Wildcat, whose apparent success became central to the development of Supported Work. Wildcat's success was thought to be due to certain program elements not shared by other employment-training programs. These included gradual inculcation of participants to work routines, opportunity to work with peers, increasing wages accompanying increased job demands, and other features associated with precepts of learning theory. Because of Wildcat's apparent achievements and innovative character, officials of the Ford Foundation, the Department of Labor, HEW, and other major governmental agencies decided to put the program to test in a nationwide experiment. Three of the groups targeted for the program was made up of previously incarcerated offenders, known drug addicts, and youths known to be or considered by school officials as likely to become delinquent.[1] The first two of these groups clearly paralleled Project Wildcat participants. It is not clear, however, how similar the third group was to

---

[1] A fourth target group was composed of women who were long-term AFDC recipients. For this group, no crime data were collected since their criminal activity was assumed to be negligible. Consequently in this chapter we focus on the other three target groups. We shall comment further on the AFDC sample in our concluding section.

participants of other youth employment programs. The Supported Work youth sample members were selected partly because of their potential for crime. This frequently was not the case in other programs.

## Supported Work: Program and Demonstration Design

As finally implemented, Supported Work operated in 21 sites of which 10 were included in the program evaluation undertaken by Mathematica Policy Research and the Institute for Research on Poverty, University of Wisconsin. Offender participants were recruited at seven sites, whereas addict and youth participants were recruited at four and five sites, respectively. The jobs provided by Supported Work were similar to the generally unskilled or semiskilled jobs of Wildcat. Also, the Demonstration continued to emphasize the key program features that characterized Wildcat. Depending on the site, participants could remain in the program no longer than 12 or 18 months.

The evaluation of Supported Work utilized an experimental design in which participant status at each of the 10 evaluation (demonstration) sites was based on random assignments. Sample selection began in March 1975 and continued through July 1977. The evaluation sample included 2200 ex-offenders, 1400 ex-addicts, and 1200 youth. All sample members were scheduled to receive enrollment, 9-month, and 18-month interviews. Those enrolled prior to 1977 were scheduled to receive a 27-month interview, and those enrolled prior to April 1976, were scheduled to receive a 36-month interview.

The characteristics of sample members, at the time of their application to Supported Work, are presented in Table 17.1. Most are male, members of minority groups, with limited education and work experience. One-third to one-half of the sample members, depending on the target group, had not held a regular job during the 2 years preceding sample enrollment. As might be expected, ex-offenders and ex-addicts had extensive reported arrest histories.

It is important to note that the allocation of the analysis samples by target group, site, and reference period is such that the study of impacts for the various postprogram periods is based on different subgroups of enrollees, distinguished from one another by distribution across sites and by the date of program enrollment. Thus, to the extent that individual characteristics, local labor market conditions, and programs themselves varied for these sample subgroups, the long-term results based on these particular subsamples may not be representative of those that actually occurred (but were not observed) for the *full* sample. In subsequent discussions of the evaluation findings this possibility will be taken into account.

## Findings

In order to test the effectiveness of Supported Work, we estimated OLS models of two general forms. The first regressed employment and crime

TABLE 17.1

**Characteristics of the Supported Work Research Sample at Enrollment, by Target Group[a]**

| | Target group | | |
|---|---|---|---|
| Characteristics | Ex-addicts | Ex-offenders | Youth |
| Average age (years) | 27.8 | 25.3 | 18.3 |
| Percentage male | 80.1 | 94.3 | 86.4 |
| Race and ethnicity (percentage) | | | |
|   Black, non-Hispanic | 77.7 | 83.6 | 78.2 |
|   Hispanic | 8.2 | 8.8 | 15.6 |
|   White, non-Hispanic | 13.8 | 7.4 | 5.9 |
|   Other | 0.3 | 0.2 | 0.2 |
| Percentage currently married | 23.1 | 11.8 | 3.7 |
| Education | | | |
|   Average years of schooling | 10.6 | 10.4 | 9.7 |
|   Percentage with 12 or more years | 28.5 | 26.7 | 0.7 |
| Percentage receiving welfare month prior | | | |
|   to enrollment | 39.2 | 17.1 | 12.5 |
| Months since last full-time job | | | |
|   Now working or less than 2 | 11.6 | 7.4 | 12.1 |
|   2–12 | 31.1 | 20.4 | 37.7 |
|   13–24 | 20.0 | 22.3 | 19.6 |
|   25 or more | 32.4 | 38.9 | 8.6 |
|   Never worked | 4.9 | 11.0 | 21.9 |
| Average earnings during previous | | | |
|   12 months ($) | 1227 | 580 | 827 |
| Percentage reporting use of heroin | | | |
|   Regular use | 85.4 | 31.3 | 2.6 |
|   Any use | 94.3 | 44.5 | 7.8 |
| Percentage reporting use of marijuana | 90.8 | 80.6 | 60.2 |
| Percentage in drug treatment last 6 months | 88.6 | 12.2 | 1.7 |
| Arrests | | | |
|   Percentage with any | 89.6 | 99.6 | 64.2 |
|   Average number | 8.3 | 9.2 | 2.2 |
|   Percentage with any | 74.7 | 95.0 | 34.0 |
|   Average number | 2.9 | 3.0 | 0.6 |
| Average number of weeks incarcerated | 129 | 195 | 20 |
| Percentage ever incarcerated | 69.9 | 96.0 | 27.9 |

[a] From baseline interviews administered to the research sample of individuals (experimentals and controls) at 10 sites who completed the baseline, 9-month, and 18-month interviews. $N = 974$ ex-addicts, 1497 ex-offenders, 861 youths. Eligibility requirements for participation in the demonstration specify a history of drug use for ex-addicts and of incarceration for ex-offenders. However, less than 100% of the sample of ex-addicts reported drug use and less than 100% of ex-offenders reported incarceration. This could reflect either that the ineligibility of certain respondents was not detected by program operators or that the respondents inaccurately reported their histories in these areas during the research interviews.

outcomes against the experimental-status variable and a vector of site and participant characteristics assumed to be relevant to employment and criminal behavior. The second model regressed outcomes against the same independent variables as well as experimental-status interaction with selected site and participant characteristics. Average hours worked per month were used to measure employment outcomes. Crime outcomes were indexed by a dummy variable in which a score of one, indicative of failure, was given an individual after the first arrest. Interview-reported arrests rather than reported illegal activities were used to index crime because arrest data could be verified. The use of a dichotomous rather than a continuous variable to index failure was based on the assumption that multiple arrests might be misleading since arrest for a serious crime is likely to lead to incarceration and thus to no further arrests during the analysis period. Although probit or logit analyses are the appropriate techniques to use in estimating arrest equations, our approach was determined by the fact that the empirical work for this chapter was part of a very large evaluation effort for which free use of maximum-likelihood techniques were prohibitively expensive. We have, however, reestimated selection equations reported here and found the findings to be very insensitive to the estimation techniques.

## EMPLOYMENT AND ARREST RESULTS: OVERALL

For all target groups being discussed here there were strong positive employment results during the first 9 months after sample entry. This was obviously to be expected simply because experimentals (in contrast to controls) had guaranteed employment. However, the experimental–control differentials were not as great as they might have been had experimentals remained with Supported Work through their guaranteed stay. In fact, participants fell far short of this guarantee with addicts and youths remaining as active participants on average about 7 months whereas offenders remained about 6 months. Reflecting this withdrawal—the failure of many participant dropouts to obtain alternative jobs and the gradual increase in employment among controls—overall experimental control employment differences for the three target groups diminished steadily over the next 9 months, and by months 16–18 experimental–control employment differentials became statistically nonsignificant. They generally remained nonsignificant for the remainder of the follow-up analyses. These overall and not very optimistic findings do not, however, apply equally to all members of our target-group sample. Some types of participants fared substantially better than others. We will return to this point shortly.

Turning now to results concerning the percentage of sample members arrested over time, the data reveal trends that depart from those reflected in regard to employment. Among offender sample members no consistent experimental–control differences are observed over the follow-up period. By the end of the observation period, 36 months after intake, experimentals reported 8% more members remaining arrest free than did controls, but the difference was not statistically significant. Among addicts, experimentals reported more arrest-free members than controls throughout the follow-up observation period, with differences being statistically significant at the 27-month and 36-month interviews. Finally, among youths, no strong experimental–control differences appear until the 27-month observation when experimentals report almost 9% more members remaining arrest free than controls. The above findings suggest no simple consequence of Supported Work participation. Seemingly, ex-addicts benefit most consistently from the program, but even for this group, employment effects become essentially nonexistent between months 16 and 27. In contrast to the impact–decay effects that are normally anticipated following program exposure, there appear to be delayed enhancement of effects for all three target groups. Finally, no clear relationship appears between employment and crime impacts. Elaboration of these results by examination of possible mediators of program impact provides some clarification and several interesting hypotheses regarding the possible long-term effects of programs like Supported Work.

## EMPLOYMENT AND ARREST RESULTS: CONDITIONAL INFLUENCES

The possibility that different groups of participants might respond differently to Supported Work is suggested by various considerations. Thus, length of involvement in a program may be related to participants' responses to Supported Work as a result of halo effects, organization problems encountered at program start-up, quality decay problems encountered at program termination, or changes in the condition of labor markets. In addition, various individual attributes of participants may influence amenability to program intervention. Age, education, prior criminality, and previous work history have been linked elsewhere to criminality and employment. Thus it is possible these characteristics may mediate the impact of Supported Work on future criminality and employment. We now turn to these possible mediating effects.

### *Time of Sample Entry*

First, we examine data on employment responses of addicts, offenders, and youth Supported Work sample members who were early, middle, and late entrants to the Supported Work sample.[2] These are referred to respectively as

[2]Tables 17.2 through 17.7 present the results of analyses in which the dependent variables of hours worked and probability of arrest are first regressed on a vector of 31 variables including experimental status and subsequently on this same vector augmented by interactions between experimental status and those of the 31 variables that we regarded as relevant for policy purposes. Using the coefficients from these various equations and the relative proportion of the total sample that is included in each subgroup of interest, it is possible to estimate means for sample subgroups, controlling for the effects of other potentially confounding variables. These are the means supplied in our tables. We use these rather than regression coefficients because estimated means provide

the 36-month, 27-month, and 18-month follow-up cohorts. There is a general tendency, with a small exception among youths, for experimentals in the 36-month cohort to work more relative to controls than is true for experimentals in other cohorts. Better performance among the 36-month cohort experimentals is also reflected in arrest results shown in Table 17.6. The sources of this often weak but persistent phenomenon are not known. The possibility was explored that early program applicants differed from later applicants in terms of demographic characteristics relevant to program response. Although this exploration revealed some participant attributes that were marginally related to time of program application, (including participants' age, prior receipt of public assistance, and previous employment) these failed to account for the cohort effect. A plausible residual hypothesis that must be considered is that the relatively more positive response of early program entrants to Supported Work reflects a halo effect resulting from the enthusiasm and commitment often accompanying new endeavors. Unfortunately, the data here provide no opportunity to test this possibility.

### Participant Attributes

More interesting for present purposes is the degree to which certain characteristics of sample members appear to mediate the employment and arrest effects of Supported Work. The results are presented in Tables 2 through 7. First, among youth experimentals, lowered probabilities of arrest relative to controls were found to be associated with having fewer arrests at time of sample entry. Among those who reported no previous arrest histories, Supported Work experience was estimated to substantially reduce the probability of subsequent arrest. Among those with extensive prior arrest histories program experience was estimated to have no arrest-reduction effects.[3] Second, among offenders, those who were eligible to be addict target-group members—that is, those who reported they were regular heroin users at the time of enrollment—were more likely to report lower arrest probabilities and more hours of employment relative to controls. Third, among addicts and offenders there were important age effects. For experimentals in both groups, those who were older generally reported the greatest program benefits. That is, they worked more hours and had more arrest-free members relative to their controls than did younger experimentals. It is of some interest to note as well that older controls (over 35 years of age) generally had more arrest-free members than did controls who were younger. This trend was particularly strong among offenders.

---

information on the incidence of events as well as the relative effects of variables presumed to influence these events (i.e., prior criminality, age, etc.). The computation of subgroup means can be eased through use of certain computer routines as are available in SASS and Avetran. The latter, employed in this analysis, was developed by Professor Robert Avery, Department of Economics, Carnegie–Mellon University.

[3]Fewer arrests at entry had a mixed effect on the employment results for youth.

**TABLE 17.2**
**Average Hours Employed per Month by Prior Drug Use and Arrests, Youth Sample**

| | Months 1–9 | | Months 10–18 | | Months 19–27 | | Months 28–36 | |
|---|---|---|---|---|---|---|---|---|
| | Experimental-control differential | Control group mean | Experimental-control differential | Control group mean | Experimental-control differential | Control group mean | Experimental-control differential | Control group mean |
| Total sample | 80.7 | 39.7 | 11.7[a] | 58.2 | 0.6 | 68.2 | 7.2 | 81.4 |
| Prior drug use | | | | | | | | |
| Used drugs | 73.3[a] | 47.4 | 15.5 | 47.6 | 16.3 | 57.6 | 10.8 | 84.0 |
| No drug use other than marijuana | 82.5[a] | 37.4 | 10.2[b] | 61.1 | −5.8 | 72.6 | 0.4 | 85.8 |
| Prior arrests | | | | | | | | |
| 0 | 79.0[a] | 42.9 | 17.8[b] | 61.0 | −5.0 | 81.8 | 12.8 | 88.5 |
| 4 | 85.0[a] | 38.6 | 8.1 | 57.6 | 10.8 | 57.2 | 6.7 | 87.0 |
| 9 | 79.2[a] | 38.9 | 3.9 | 38.0 | 9.6 | 58.0 | 4.0 | 91.8 |

[a] Statistically significant at the 5% level.
[b] Statistically significant at the 10% level.

## TABLE 17.3
### Average Hours Employed per Month by Age, Ex-Addict Sample

| | Months 1–9 | | Months 10–18 | | Months 19–27 | | Months 28–36 | |
|---|---|---|---|---|---|---|---|---|
| | Experimental–control differential | Control group mean | Experimental–control differential | Control group mean | Experimental–control differential | Control group mean | Experimental–control differential | Control group mean |
| Total sample | 78.2[a] | 40.5 | 16.4[a] | 50.0 | 1.5 | 58.6 | 18.3[a] | 52.6 |
| Age | | | | | | | | |
| Under 21 | 69.8[a] | 49.9 | −5.7 | 68.4 | 8.6 | 69.3 | [b] | [b] |
| 21–25 | 75.8[a] | 43.2 | 12.3[c] | 51.0 | −6.4 | 60.5 | 3.8 | 57.5 |
| 26–35 | 80.1[a] | 38.7 | 21.1[a] | 49.0 | 9.4 | 58.6 | 32.8[a] | 44.0 |
| over 35 | 82.4[a] | 29.7 | 24.2 | 37.5 | −6.0 | 48.2 | −15.6 | 66.0 |

[a] Statistically significant at the 5% level
[b] Data not presented because fewer than 20 sample members appear in this category.
[c] Statistically significant at the 10% level.

329

**TABLE 17.4**

**Average Hours Employed per Month by Age and Prior Drug Use, Ex-Offender Sample**

| | Months 1–9 | | Months 10–18 | | Months 19–27 | | Months 28–36 | |
|---|---|---|---|---|---|---|---|---|
| | Experimental–control differential | Control group mean | Experimental–control differential | Control group mean | Experimental–control differential | Control group mean | Experimental–control differential | Control group mean |
| Total sample | 71.1[a] | 46.0 | 8.5[a] | 57.8 | −0.2 | 60.0 | 8.2 | 66.8 |
| Years of age | | | | | | | | |
| Under 21 | 70.7[a] | 43.6 | 3.2 | 58.4 | −4.7 | 53.0 | 33.2 | 62.5 |
| 21–25 | 73.2[a] | 46.1 | 9.2[b] | 56.2 | 0.8 | 60.2 | −2.4 | 78.0 |
| 26–35 | 69.7[a] | 44.2 | 6.5 | 60.2 | 0.3 | 61.7 | 10.7 | 50.5 |
| Over 35 | 63.5[a] | 59.7 | 28.0[b] | 51.7 | 1.2 | 65.4 | [c] | [c] |
| Prior drug use | | | | | | | | |
| Used heroin regularly | 72.3[a] | 45.3 | 12.8[b] | 52.2 | 1.1 | 45.4 | 18.5 | 59.4 |
| No regular heroin use | 70.1[a] | 46.3 | 6.5 | 60.2 | −1.0 | 66.7 | 0.5 | 70.5 |

[a] Statistically significant at the 5% level.

[b] Statistically significant at the 10% level.

[c] Data not presented because fewer than 20 sample members appear in this category.

**TABLE 17.5**
Cumulative Percentage Arrested by Prior Drug Use and Arrests, Youth Sample[a]

|  | Months 1–18 | | Months 1–27 | |
|---|---|---|---|---|
|  | Experimental–control differential | Control group mean | Experimental–control differential | Control group mean |
| Total sample | −0.3 | 27.0 | −8.8[b] | 39.3 |
| Prior drug use |  |  |  |  |
| used drugs | −7.7 | 35.3 | −10.4 | 46.0 |
| No drug use other than marijuana | 2.0 | 24.6 | −7.3 | 34.6 |
| Prior arrests |  |  |  |  |
| 0 | −1.8 | 25.6 | −13.6[c] | 37.9 |
| 4 | 1.6 | 28.3 | −4.6 | 37.9 |
| 9 | 5.9 | 31.6 | 6.8 | 37.8 |

[a] Results for the 1–36 month period are not presented because of the limited sample size (79).
[b] Statistically significant at the 10% level.
[c] Statistically significant at the 5% level.

## Conclusions

The results of the Supported Work experiment for the groups discussed here are not easily summarized. Clearly, not all participants benefited. Furthermore, crime reduction effects were not, as hypothesized, uniformly dependent on increased employment effects. An important example of this pertains to the

**TABLE 17.6**
Cumulative Percentage Arrested by Age, Ex-Addict Sample

|  | Months 1–18 | | Months 1–27 | | Months 1–36 | |
|---|---|---|---|---|---|---|
|  | Experimental–control differential | Control group mean | Experimental–control differential | Control group mean | Experimental–control differential | Control group mean |
| Total sample | −8.2[a] | 33.5 | −10.9[b] | 43.3 | −18.1[b] | 53.2 |
| Age |  |  |  |  |  |  |
| Under 21 | −3.5 | 36.6 | 14.5 | 34.7 | 39.1 | 20.7 |
| 21–25 | −12.0[b] | 37.9 | −10.9 | 46.8 | 7.7 | 64.1 |
| 26–35 | −3.9 | 31.1 | −11.1 | 43.4 | −30.8[b] | 56.6 |
| Over 35 | −14.1 | 27.1 | −26.5[b] | 36.8 | −14.6 | 23.3 |

[a] Statistically significant at the 10% level.
[b] Statistically significant at the 5% level.

## TABLE 17.7
### Cumulative Percentage Arrested by Age and Prior Drug Use, Ex-Offender Sample

| | Months 1–18 | | Months 1–27 | | Months 1–36 | |
|---|---|---|---|---|---|---|
| | Experimental–control differential | Control group mean | Experimental–control differential | Control group mean | Experimental–control differential | Control group mean |
| Total sample | 1.0 | 46.2 | 0.4 | 53.3 | −8.0 | 64.8 |
| Years of age | | | | | | |
| Under 21 | −10.4 | 55.7 | −8.9 | 68.8 | −10.5 | 54.3 |
| 21–25 | 8.5[a] | 43.2 | 11.7 | 48.6 | −0.3 | 59.6 |
| 26–35 | −0.9 | 46.1 | −8.0 | 55.0 | −5.7 | 72.2 |
| Over 35 | −7.6 | 38.5 | −14.7 | 39.4 | [b] | [b] |
| Prior drug use | | | | | | |
| Used herion regularly | −1.0 | 47.6 | −2.7 | 56.3 | −13.3 | 65.2 |
| No regular use of herion | 1.6 | 45.6 | 1.4 | 51.9 | 2.2 | 60.2 |

[a]Statistically significant at the 5% level.

group of offenders over 35 years of age. These individuals consistently reported a larger arrest-free rate than controls did, but their employment record after 18 months of observation was no better than that of the controls'. Conceivably the absence of an employment effect after 18 months could be due to employers' refusal to hire these individuals but the arrest-rate reduction in the absence of an employment effect is not explained by the theoretical models that guided Supported Work. A similar problem in interpretation is found in the failure of experimentals to uniformly report fewer arrests than controls at a time when they uniformly worked more than controls, that is, during the first year of their sample membership. At the very least, these results imply a complex and perhaps attenuated link between employment and crime.[4]

These imponderable results notwithstanding, the general pattern of the Supported Work findings suggest a few crucial attributes of participants that may mediate the impacts of employment programs for offenders, addicts, and problem youth. First, among youth, in the long run only those experimentals without prior arrests at time of intake are more likely to remain arrest free relative to comparable controls. Among experimentals with prior arrests, no arrest effects are observed. Second, as noted previously in Project Wildcat, drug addict experimentals are likely to respond favorably especially in terms of arrests. Third, this arrest-reduction effect among addicts is mediated by age of participant, with experimentals over 35 generally more likely than those who are younger to report remaining arrest free relative to controls.[5] Among ex-offenders, experimentals over 35 years of age again report higher percentages of arrest-free members relative to comparable controls; in contrast to addicts, experimentals under 21 do the same.

---

[4]This conclusion is in sharp contrast to that of Berk, Lenihan, and Rossi (1980) who state that their analysis of the data from the Transitional Aid Research Project (TARP) indicates that "for offenders, at least, unemployment and poverty do cause crime at the micro-level." TARP provided unemployment insurance or job counseling to its participants, all recent releases from prison. Although no statistically significant results were initially found across experimental treatments, the researcher did observe beneficial effects when the TARP data were analyzed using a complex structural model in which predicted TARP payment and weeks worked were both found to have a statistically negative effect on the number of arrests in the 12-month experimental period. The authors conclude that there was no simple experimental effect of the TARP payments because such payments were reduced (often dollar for dollar) as earning increased, thus leading to fewer weeks worked. Although this explanation appears plausible, we emphasize that the structural results on which this conclusion is based depend heavily on the instrumental variables developed to predict weeks worked and TARP payments. If the predicting equations include any terms that affect arrests directly, rather than just through their effects on weeks worked and payments, this interpretation of the effects of weeks worked and payment on arrests could be based on spurious relationships. The direct experimental methodology underlying our results eliminates this possibility when interpreting our results.

[5]This does not appear to be true in the 36-month follow-up but the "over 35" comparison for this period is constrained by a "floor effect" resulting from the low probability of arrest among controls.

The general pattern for the oldest group of experimentals among addicts and offenders, to experience reduced arrests relative to comparable controls is noteworthy given that these controls are consistently less likely to experience arrests relative to those who are younger. This latter phenomenon, interestingly, is not without precedent. It has long been recognized by criminologists that offenders appear to "burn out," in the sense that recidivism rates roughly decrease with age after young adulthood. A common interpretation of this decrease is that older offenders "tire" of crime, become less willing to take risks, and turn to more conventional lives. In its current general form, the "burn-out" thesis has left unanswered a variety of questions including those addressing the identity of those who burn out, the conditions that increase the probability of burn-out, and whether burn-out (reduced recidivism) may, in fact, reflect a turn to less detectable criminal activity. Despite these weaknesses, the "burn-out" thesis supplies an explanation for the finding that older Supported Work controls were less likely to incur arrests than those who were younger. The "burn-out" thesis also provides an explanation for the age-experimental-status interactions observed among the offender and addict samples. That is, it suggests that employment programs like Supported Work provide older offenders an opportunity and added incentive to move more rapidly toward an already contemplated career change. If this hypothesis is true, then the age interactions should be found among investigations of other employment-enhancing programs. Unfortunately, published findings from these studies do not in general lend themselves to such examination. An exception of sorts was found in a report of the Baltimore Life Experiment (Lenihan 1976). As noted earlier, this program provided offenders with financial assistance and employment counseling rather than jobs. However, as with subsidized employment, financial assistance can be seen as providing individuals the opportunity to make career changes; and, indeed, the results of the Baltimore Life Experiment are consistent with those of Supported Work. Among experimentals, those over 26 were found after 1 year to have an arrest rate almost 11% less than controls; for experimentals between 21 and 25 years of age the difference was 8%; for participants less than 21 it was 2.3%. Again, older controls were less likely to be rearrested than those who were younger. Obviously, the Supported Work and Life results are not definitive. They do, however, have interesting implications. Historically, programs aimed at lowering recidivism have typically been focused on juvenile and young adult criminals. Whereas the Supported Work and Life results do not flatly reject the possibility that younger offenders can benefit from these programs, the results indicate that older, more mature, offenders may be better candidates for assistance. The number of such individuals in U.S. prisons is not small. In 1977, prison population data indicated that 40% of those in penal institutions were over 30 years of age. Thus the potential benefits of targeting employment programs for older offenders are substantial

Finally, we note that the amenability of older participants to employment programs may not be limited to "burned out" criminals. We cite the following examples. Cooley, McGuire, and Prescott (1975) note that increased earnings due to training are enhanced with participants' age; a similar observation was reported by Sewell (1971). Furthermore, Supported Work itself had a fourth target group rather different than the three that are the primary concern of this chapter. This group was composed of women who had been in AFDC at least 3 years and who did not have preschool children at the time they enrolled in Supported Work. Crime data were not collected for this target group. In marked contrast to the results for the other target groups, the postprogram employment results were consistently positive, statistically significant, and sizeable. Moreover, the average age (34 years) is greater for this AFDC group than for either the ex-addicts or ex-offenders. Thus, the AFDC results are consistent with the contention that the effects of work-experience programs like Supported Work may be greater for older adults with limited employment than for seriously disadvantaged youth.

As Ginzberg indicates (1980, p. 16), employment and training programs in the United States have not given older workers much opportunity to participate in them. Presumably this is due to the assumptions that employment and training programs would have their largest payoffs for youth because youth are not yet committed to careers, legal or otherwise. Supported Work results provide some evidence that this assumption may be true for poor youth who have not yet become involved in crime, at least officially. But, more important, we believe, the evidence in this experiment and elsewhere suggests older disadvantaged workers, including those who are known offenders, may be much more responsive to the opportunity to participate in employment programs. It may well be worth the costs to provide this opportunity more fully.

# References

Berk, R., Lenihan, K., and Rossi, P. 1980. Crime and poverty: Some experimental evidence from ex-offenders. *American Sociological Review* 45: 766–786.

Cook, P.J. 1975. The Correctional carrot: Better jobs for parolees. *Policy Analysis* 1: 11–53.

Cooley T.F., McGuire T.W., and Prescott E. 1975. *The impact of manpower training on earnings: An econometric analysis*. Final Report MEL 76-01 to Office of Program Evaluation, Employment and Training Administration, U.S. Department of Labor (Pittsburgh: 1975), processed.

Denison, E.F. 1962. *The sources of economic growth in the United States and the alternatives before us*. New York: Committee for Economic Development.

Evans, R. 1968. The labor market and parole success. *Journal of Human Resources* 3: 201–212.

Ginzberg, E., ed. 1980. *Employing the unemployed*. New York: Basic Books.

Glueck S., and Glueck E. 1930. *Five hundred criminal careers*. New York: Knopf.

Killingsworth C.C., and Killingsworth M.R. 1978. Direct effects of employment policy in U.S. Department of Labor. In *Conference on Youth Employment: Its Measurement and Meaning*. Washington, D.C.: U.S. Government Printing Office.

Kirschner Associates, Inc. 1969. *Evaluation of five concentrated employment programs in regions I and II*. New York: Kirschner Associates Inc.

Lenihan K.J. 1976. *When money counts: An experimental study of providing financial aid and job placement services to released prisoners*. Washington: Bureau of Social Science Research.

Lipton, D., Martinson, R., and Wilks, J. 1975. *The effectiveness of correctional treatment*. New York: Praeger.

Sewell, D.O., 1971. *Training the poor*. Kingston, Ontario: Industrial Relations Centre, Queens University.

Somers G., and Stromsdorfer E. 1972. A cost-effectiveness analysis of in-school and summer neighborhood youth corps: A nationwide evaluation. *Journal of Human Resources* 7: 446–459.

Vera Institute of Justice. 1974. *Wildcat: The first two years*. New York: Vera Institute of Justice.

# 18

# Changes in Helping Networks with Changes in the Health of Older People: Social Policy and Social Theory[1]

EUGENE LITWAK and STEPHEN KULIS

## Introduction

A series of papers pointed out that formal organizations and primary groups were able to handle different types of tasks because of their differences in structure (Litwak and Figueira 1970). This was later elaborated to point out that the modern industrial society forces a differentiation of primary group structures and because of this, different types of primary groups handle different types of tasks (Litwak and Szelenyi 1969). This, in turn, led to an explanation of a series of findings about primary groups not easily substituting for each other (Adams 1970; Babchuck 1965; Cantor 1979; Dono, Falbe, Kail, Litwak, Sherman, and Siegel 1979; Lopata 1979; Rosow 1967). Implicit in this argument and now made explicit was the assumption that services provided by primary groups can be classified by the same dimensions of structure as that used to classify the groups. Once this is understood, there is a simple guiding principle that can be used to determine which tasks can best be managed by which groups. That principle states: *Groups can best manage those tasks that match them in structure.* In this chapter we will use this principle to show how one can predict which primary group can take over which tasks when older people move from being married and healthy, to being sick and single, to being institutionalized. The dimensions used to describe primary group structure are

---

[1]The data for this chapter were gathered under grants ROLAG00564 and RO 1MH30726 provided by the National Institute on Aging and National Institute of Mental Health. They are not responsible for the formulations therein.

those used by Cooley (1955), and are shown to relate to fundamental issues of problem solving (Litwak and Figueira 1970). It will be argued that all primary groups and all services they supply can be described in terms of the size of the group, the degree of long-term commitment required, the degree of role homogeneity or diffusion required, the degree of continuous proximity required, the degree of affection required, and the degree of duty required. In this presentation we will deal empirically with only the first four dimensions and assume that the last two exist in some form in all the primary groups discussed, whereas they are replaced by economic motivations when discussing formal organizations.

## Kinds of Helping Patterns

### UNIQUE KIN HELPING PATTERNS

Kin ties refer to ties between relatives other than ties between parents and their young children or ties between spouses. As a group, kin have the following structural features: large size contrasted with the marital dyad household or single person, long-term commitments, and both cross- and same-generation ties (e.g., children, siblings). They generally lack continuous proximity, that is, all kin do not live in the same household or next door. If our propositions are right, this structure should optimally handle tasks that have these same properties. For example, providing home nursing help for 2 or 3 weeks requires long-term commitment because it involves a large expenditure of time and energy. It requires large size because spouses alone often do not have sufficient time and energy to provide that amount of care by themselves. It does not require continuous proximity, but only ad hoc proximity, that is, people can come from across the country to stay awhile and go back. A common generation is not required but a cross-generational younger helper may be required. The reason is that age peers among the aged may have limited financial and physical resources themselves. That is why friends cannot handle this task for the aged. What must be emphasized is that a whole class of services have these same underlying dimensions although on the surface they may appear different. The following are illustrative: taking care of a widows' bills and finances when she is hospitalized, baby-sitting for grandchildren when their parents are away on trips; taking elderly parents on vacations when they are too feeble to go on their own.

### UNIQUE NEIGHBORHOOD HELPING PATTERNS

The typical neighborhood in modern industrial societies also consists of a unit larger than the marital dyad but it has continuous proximity and no long-term commitments (Fellin and Litwak 1963). A neighbor who reports an attempted burglary at an elderly person's home while he or she is out shopping is providing a form of service that matches neighborhood structure. The helping pattern requires someone who is in direct line of sight of the home, and a group sufficiently large that someone will be watching while others are performing their typical household or occupational chores. This task does not require someone with long-term commitments, since reciprocity is almost instantaneous and requires minimal individual resources. Some of the other needs of the elderly that fall within these dimensions of neighborhood are development of a neighborhood "buddy" system providing continuous visual checks, calling an ambulance when a neighbor falls, providing emergency loans of small household items, and holding extra keys in case the elderly person's are lost or stolen.

## HELPING PATTERNS UNIQUE TO FRIENDS

Friends are typically people who share homogenous statuses (Litwak and Kulis 1981; Dono *et al.* 1979). Friends do not have to be continuously proximate. They are from the same generation, and their numbers usually exceed the marital dyad. There are two types of friends, those with long-term commitments and those with short-term commitments (Jackson, Fischer and Jones 1977; Litwak and Kulis 1981). Helping patterns among the aged that are characterized by these dimensions would be: providing companionship during one's free time, providing information on everyday business such as how to report lost social security checks, how to locate doctors who are nice to older people (Horwitz 1977), or how to locate part-time jobs (Granovetter 1974). In addition, advice on how to handle daily living problems of widowhood, chronic illness, and retirement may be best provided by someone who is a friend and shares the same social status, age, marital status, and health.

## UNIQUE HELPING PATTERNS OF THE MARITAL DYAD

What characterizes the marital dyad is that it can handle all the activities defined by traditional primary groups except those requiring more than two people. The question arises as to what tasks benefit in principle from small size. Litwak and Kulis (1981) point out that there are some services where the cost of coordinating many people is much greater than the benefits that derive from large numbers (such as a detailed division of labor). The following are services where a detailed division of labor does not compensate for problems of coordination and where there is also a need for continuous proximity and long-term commitment: personal grooming such as bathing, shaving, and dressing; daily cooking; house cleaning; daily shopping; and management of household finances.

THE UNIQUE HELPING ROLE OF INSTITUTIONS

Since the last stage of the health cycle consists of older persons who are institutionalized, it is necesary to indicate which activities will be taken over from primary groups by formal organizations. The principle of matching group structure to the structure of the service would suggest that formal organizations can only take over tasks that can be routinized and for which the larger society or the older person is willing to pay (Litwak 1977). Thus, in a nursing home one person might be assigned to cook. The cook achieves economies of large scale by being able to provide one basic meal for the majority of the residents. If the cook had to prepare a different meal for each person—which the typical primary group almost does—the cook would have to prepare 80–300 different meals at each setting, depending on the size of the institution. That would be clearly impossible for one person to do. The standardization of meal choices enables the nursing home to manage.

## Sequencing of Primary Groups with Stages of Health

It is now possible to present a "theory" of a primary group sequence for the aged that parallels the stages from health to disability. The first step in the sequence consists of healthy marital household units and supporting primary groups such as kin, neighbors, and friends and the tasks they perform. The second step will show what happens when the marital household unit is disabled and can function only partially in the community. To understand which of the primary helping groups take over which tasks, one must apply the sociological principle that primary groups can best manage tasks that match their structure. The third step in the sequence consists of people that must be institutionalized because of severe disability. To find out which activities the nursing home can take over and which will be left to the helping primary groups, one must apply the same principle, in this case, the issue of which tasks can be routinized.

Given the simplification provided by our theory, we will consider five sequences for each type of primary group. First, in "primary group expansion" the helping primary group takes over tasks from the marital household at the second stage and continues through the third stage. Second, in "partial primary group expansion" the helping primary group takes over from the marital household in the second stage but the institution takes over in the third stage. In a third pattern, the "primary group continuation," the support group manages the activity in the first and continues through the next two stages as well. In a fourth pattern, the support group handles the exchange in the first and second stages, but not the third. We call this "primary group decline." The fifth pattern involves household activities which do not fit any of the typical helping groups and are consequently lost in the second and third stages. We call these "lost functions." We claim that once the services can be classified in terms of their theoretical dimensions, it is possible to predict which of the five sequences will occur for each of the helping primary groups. Although the five sequences do not exhaust all logical possibilities, they probably are the most frequent and, in any case, will enable the reader to understand the logic of the approach.

## The Analysis of Empirical Data

To show how this theory can be used we apply it to data gathered in a study of people aged 65 and older in the New York metropolitan area and the Miami Beach and Fort Lauderdale area of Florida in 1978–1979.[2] For this analysis we use only part of our data so as to highlight the theoretical issues. For the first stage we take all those who are married and who have no disabilities or only minor ones. For the second stage we take only those who are single and have major illnesses. For the third stage we take people in nursing homes who are still capable of talking intelligently. There are, of course, major dangers in treating cross-sectional data as if they were longitudinal, as we have done. For this reason the data must be considered as illustrative.

### THE USE OF PRIMARY GROUP SUPPORTS FOR HANDLING MARITAL HOUSEHOLD TASKS

To begin the analysis of sequences let us review what tasks can be theoretically handled by the marital household. The task can require only one or two people; it can be handled by either the older or a younger and older generation, but never just the younger generation. It requires continuous proximity or that distance is not a crucial factor, but it can never require long distance. It involves either long-term commitments, or that length of commitment not be relevant, but never short-term commitments only. In Table 18.1 we have taken four dimensions of primary groups, dichotomized them, and suggested eight possible combinations that describe a theoretical universe of marital dyad tasks. Ideally this universe should allow us to classify all possible marital tasks and to indicate which are consistent in principle with other primary group or formal organizational structures and therefore can be taken over by them, which cannot be taken over by any of the typical primary groups in our society, and what nature of new groups would be necessary to pick up tasks that can not be handled by present primary groups.

To understand Table 18.1, consider the two possible combinations of dimensions of tasks listed in Rows 1 and 7, which are characterized by the following dimensions: tasks that do not require a common generation or

---

[2] For a complete description of the sample see Litwak et al. (forthcoming). For a fuller but not complete description see Litwak and Kulis (1981).

## TABLE 18.1

### Sequencing of Primary Group Structures with Stages of Health Starting with Normal Functions of the Marital Household

| Rows | Dimensions of Task | | | | Primary groups at each health stage | | | Name of sequence[a] |
| --- | --- | --- | --- | --- | --- | --- | --- | --- |
| | Initial size large | Same generation required | Continuous proximity required | Long-term commitment required | First stage: Marital household intact | Second stage: Marital household broken and disabled | Third stage: Marital household broken and disabled, institution takes over | |
| *Where the institutions can handle the third stage* | | | | | | | | |
| 1 | No | No | No | Yes | Marital | Kin | Institution | Partial kin expansion[b] |
| 2 | No | Yes | No | Yes | Marital | Friend | Institution | Partial kin expansion |
| 3 | No | No | Yes | No | Marital | Neigh. Het | Institution | Partial Neighbor Expansion |
| 4 | No | Yes | Yes | No | Marital | Neigh. Hom. | Institution | Partial Neighbor Expansion |
| 5 | No | No | No | No | Marital | Acquaint. Het. | Institution | Partial Acquaint. Expansion |
| 6 | No | Yes | No | No | Marital | Acquaint. Hom. | Institution | Partial Acquaint. Expansion |
| *Where primary groups handle the third stage* | | | | | | | | |
| 7 | No | No | No | Yes | Marital | Kin | Kin | [a]Full Kin Expansion |
| 8 | No | Yes | No | Yes | Marital | Friend | Friend | Full Friend Expansion |
| 9 | No | No | Yes | No | Marital | Neigh. Het. | Neigh. Het. | Full Neighbor Expansion |
| 10 | No | Yes | Yes | No | Marital | Neigh. Hom. | Neigh. Hom. | Full Neighbor Expansion |
| 11 | No | No | No | No | Marital | Acquaint. Het. | Acquaint. Het. | Full Acquaint. Expansion |
| 12 | No | Yes | No | No | Marital | Acquaint. Hom. | Acquaint. Hom. | Full Acquaint. Expansion |

Some atypical sequences—lost functions

| | | | | | | | | |
|---|---|---|---|---|---|---|---|---|
| 13 | No | Yes | Yes | Yes | Marital | Joint household friends | Joint household with friend | Atypical—lost function[b] |
| 14 | No | No | Yes | Yes | Marital | Joint household with children | Joint household with adult child | Atypical—lost function |

[a] Some illustrations:

Partial kin expansion: help in household maintenance, like putting up pictures or curtain rods.

Partial friend expansion: planning vacation trips or recreational activities together which used to be done with spouse.

Partial neighborhood expansion: emergency first aid or calling the doctor in an emergency.

Partial acquaintanceship expansion: arranging for ad hoc occasional chauffering or purchases.

Full kin expansion: help in payment of monthly bills like rent, telephone; help in storage.

Full acquaintanceship expansion: help in writing letters to relatives.

Atypical exchanges— generally lost functions: daily grooming, dressing, cooking, clothing, housekeeping.

[b] We have empirical data for these patterns.

continuous proximity but do require long-term commitments (e.g., keeping track of monthly social security payments or storage of seasonal clothing), and small numbers of potential helpers.

What happens when one marital partner is incapacitated and cannot manage services described by these dimensions? Which primary groups have structures that overlap this combination of dimensions? We would argue that such marital tasks are logically consistent with kin structures such as children, since they typically do not live next door and yet have long-term commitments. Neighbors are ruled out because they typically do not have long-term commitments and friends are ruled out because they tend to be age peers of the incapacitated person and therefore typically lack physical and economic resources. There are four items from our survey that meet these requirements. First, individuals were asked if they had received any help in the last 6 months in monthly financial management, like keeping track of social security checks, household bills, or bank accounts. Second, they were asked if anyone helped in the last 6 months with seasonal storage of their clothes, their laundry, or cleaning. Third, we asked if anyone had helped them with fixing small things around the house, such as putting up curtain rods, fixtures for pictures, or doing similar tasks. Finally, we asked if anyone had helped them with light housekeeping like dusting rooms or making beds.

All of these services are generally handled by the martial dyad, the smallest primary group, when people are healthy. Three of the items—light housekeeping, household repairs, and storage and laundry—involve a continuous expenditure of time and energy for a nonpaid primary group member so that only someone with a long-term commitment would undertake them on a regular basis; whereas the other involves managing money, which also requires long-term commitment since one's future as well as present is affected. Therefore, they all involve long-term commitments.

What also characterizes three of the four items is that they do not require a common household or continuous proximity. Small household repairs like putting up a curtain rod is an activity requiring presence once a month or less, whereas storage of seasonal clothes, cleaning, and laundry are activities that vary between once a week to two or three times a year. All of these helping patterns can be managed by kin who live anywhere from five blocks to five hours' driving distance away. The only item that implies more continuous proximity is light housekeeping. Its wording was sufficiently ambiguous to be interpreted as either a daily activity or a weekly one (for example, making beds is daily, whereas straightening up is weekly). Thus, what seem to be three and possible four very diverse helping patterns with no relation at all, do in fact have three common underlying dimensions that match the kin structure. As such, we should be able to anticipate, by the principle of matching task and structure, that typical kin can take over these tasks if the marital household unit fails.

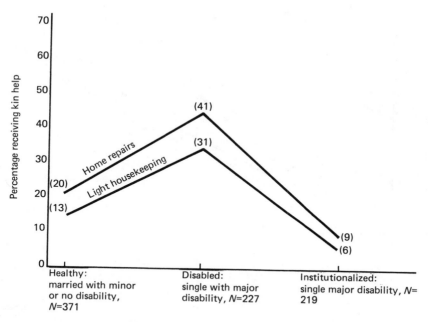

FIGURE 18.1. *This graph shows the partial kinship expansion.*

But in order to make a complete prediction of sequences, it is necessary to know how these four helping patterns differ in terms of routinizability and centrality to institutions for the aged. We would argue that two of the items involve activities that are clearly reimbursable under U.S. governmental programs such as Medicaid, and given the item wording can easily be viewed as routinizable. Thus, handling light housekeeping, such as dusting the rooms and making the beds, and doing minor fixing around the place, such as putting up curtain rods, are both considered to be central duties of staff at nursing homes as well as routinizable. Given this classification, our conceptual framework (Table 18.1, Row 7) tells us that these two exchanges (i.e., light housekeeping and small household repairs) will be handled by the household marital dyad when it is well and normal, by the kinship system when the household unit is disabled but living in the community, and by institutions when the older person moves to one. We have called this sequence partial kinship expansion. Figure 18.1 shows the anticipated curvilinear relationship between kinship aid and the stages of disability. Only 13 and 20% of our respondents had kinship aid on light housekeeping and home repairs, respectively, when they are healthy and married, but this went to 31 and 41%, respectively, when they were ill and living in the community, and then down to 6 and 9%, respectively, when they

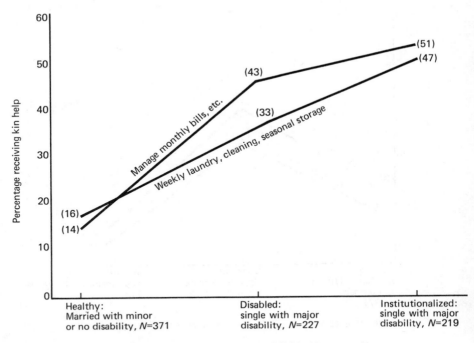

**FIGURE 18.2.** *This graph shows the full kinship expansion.*

were ill, single, and institutionalized. All predicted differences in this and other figures are significant at the .05 level or better (Litwak and Kulis 1981). The similarity of these two tasks and their distinctiveness from other patterns can be seen if we look at the pattern of "full kinship expansion."

For this purpose let us consider two more items—money management and seasonable storage of clothes and laundry. They differ from housekeeping and home repairs in that they are not handled by institutions. Handling discretionary funds for everyday purchases is too difficult to account for in a routinizable way. Therefore, staff can not be held accountable; rather, someone with an internalized commitment to the resident is required to handle such matters. Similarly, Medicaid will not reimburse nursing homes for storage of seasonal clothing and doing cleaning for residents' personal clothing. The larger society does not view this as central to nursing care.

Given these dimensions of the task, our conceptual scheme suggests a pattern of primary group sequencing called kinship expansion (Table 18.1, Row 1), that is, the move will be from the marital household unit in the first stage to kinship use in the second as well as third stages. If we examine Figure 18.2 we can see that it has a shape distinctively different from that in Figure 18.1, that is, more monotonic than curvilinear. Thus, 14% of the respondents without disability have help in money matters and 16% have help in storage and laundry, respectively. This increases to 43 and 33%, respectively, for those in the community who are sick and single. It reaches 51 and 47%, respectively, for those who live in institutions. The stereotypes of family abandonment of older people in institutions is often so great that the theoretical prediction that families may increase some services to residents (Dobrof 1976; Dobrof and Litwak, 1977) may be viewed as one of the startling predictions of this theory.

## The Sequence of Primary Groups for "Regular" Nonhousehold Functions

So far, we have examined the use of helping primary groups to substitute for a disabled spouse. Now we should like to consider tasks which are normally handled by nonhousehold primary groups even when the marital dyad is complete and well. What happens to these nonhousehold tasks when a spouse becomes permanently disabled? We think there are two possibilities. If the task was done with the elderly person (e.g., help in shopping when one spouse is sick), the larger primary group network will have to increase its help. If the task was done independently (e.g., loaning small household items in an emergency), the larger support system may not be affected by the person's disability.

Within these general considerations we can examine normal helping patterns between healthy elderly individuals and supporting primary groups. The 12 possible patterns are displayed in Table 18.2. These patterns differ from the first 12 in that they start out in the first stage with high levels of exchanges from helping networks. Therefore all patterns must involve continuation or decline, since great expansions are less likely.

There are two items that fit the kin "decline" sequences. The first asked the respondents, "Has anyone checked on you daily to see if you are all right during the last six months?" The second is a hypothetical question which asks if the respondent were sick in bed for 2 or 3 weeks, who would help by bringing food, helping them in and out of bed, and so forth. What characterizes both of these helping patterns is that they often require a primary group larger than the marital dyad, even when people are married and not chronically disabled. Both are activities that can be initiated through ad hoc contact or by a telephone call rather than through close continuous proximity. Both require sufficient expenditures of time and energy so that only a person with long-term commitments would undertake them on a nonpaid basis. In short, both activities have common dimensions that fit the structure of the kinship system. In addition, once institutionalized, both of these activities, as measured by our question, would be considered routinizable and central to the institution's staff (Table 18.2, Row 1).

**TABLE 18.2**

**Primary Group Decline and Continuation**

**Sequencing of Primary Group Structures with Stages of Health Starting with Normal Functions of Larger Primary Groups (e.g., Kin, Neighbors)**

| Rows | Dimensions of Task | | | | Primary Groups at Each Health Stage | | | Name of sequence |
|---|---|---|---|---|---|---|---|---|
| | Initial size large | Same generation required | Continuous proximity required | Long-term commitment required | First stage: marital household intact | Second stage: marital household broken and disabled | Third stage: marital household broken and disabled, institution takes over | |
| 1 | Yes | No | No | Yes | Kin | Kin | Institution | Kin decline[a] |
| 2 | Yes | Yes | No | Yes | Friend | Friend | Institution | Friend decline |
| 3 | Yes | No | Yes | No | Neigh. Het. | Neigh. Het. | Institution | Neighborhood[a] |
| 4 | Yes | Yes | Yes | No | Neigh. Hom. | Heigh. Hom. | Institution | Neighborhood[a] |
| 5 | Yes | No | No | No | Acquaint. Het. | Acquaint. Het. | Institution | Acquaintance |
| 6 | Yes | Yes | No | No | Acquaint. Hom. | Acquaint. Hom. | Institution | Acquaintance |
| Where primary groups handle third stage | | | | | | | | |
| 7 | Yes | No | No | Yes | Kin | Kin | Kin | Kinship continuation[a] |
| 8 | Yes | Yes | No | Yes | Friend | Friend | Friend | Friend continuation |
| 9 | Yes | No | Yes | No | Neigh. Het. | Neigh. Het. | Neigh. Het. | Neigh. continuation |
| 10 | Yes | Yes | Yes | No | Neigh. Hom. | Neigh. Hom. | Neigh. Hom. | Neigh. continuation |
| 11 | Yes | No | No | No | Acquaintance | Acquaintance | Acquaintance | Acquaint. continuation[a] |
| 12 | Yes | Yes | No | No | Acquaintance | Acquaintance | Acquaintance | Acquaint. continuation |
| Some atypical sequences—lost functions | | | | | | | | |
| 13 | Yes | Yes | Yes | Yes | Joint household friends | Joint household friends | | Atypical–lost function |
| 14 | Yes | No | Yes | Yes | Joint household with children | Joint household with children | | Atypical–lost function |

Figure 18.3 shows that of the married couples in the first stage of health, 33% said they would use kin for home nursing and 42% said that kin had checked on them daily over the last 6 months. In the second stage of disability these figures go to 48 and 57%, respectively. But in the third stage, where institutions take over, these figures drop to 9 and 23%, respectively. Figures 18.3 and 18.1 resemble each other in shape. That is, in both cases the kinship system is used by a smaller percentage in the first and third stages, producing a curvilinear effect. They differ in the absolute height of the curve; that is, in Figure 18.1, the elderly in the first stage use kinship help from 13 to 20%, whereas in Figure 18.3 people in the first stage use kin between 33 and 47%. In both cases the third stage leads to a very low percentage saying kin would or do help.

Let us now turn our attention to the sequence of network supports we called kinship continuation (Table 18.2, Row 7). The respondents here use kinship in all three stages of disability. This resembles kinship decline in all respects but one—the institutions do not see the tasks as central or routinizable. We have four tasks that fit this pattern. Respondents were asked if in the last 6 months anyone talked to them when they were feeling low and made them feel better. They were also asked if in the last 6 months anyone helped them keep in touch with their relatives, took them out to dinner or brought them special food, or bought them small items to make their place more homey, like pillows and bedspreads or a television set. The way our questions were worded, two of the items are clearly nonroutine tasks that the institution cannot manage, providing residents with special furnishings and food. The institutions provide only standardized foods except to those on special medical diets. Similarly, they provide standardized room furnishings; the residents are expected to bring their own things if they want to indulge personal preferences.

Our other two items are not as obviously noncentral or nonroutinizable for nursing homes. Although some states provide money for social work functions in institutions, the usual ratio of one social worker to scores of residents means that they simply do not have time to provide the kind of everyday cheering up that our item implies (Litwak and Kulis 1981). We would make the same analysis of keeping in touch with relatives. If this is correct, these four seemingly diverse helping patterns share in common the fact that they are supplementary services to the healthy marital dyad, that most of them can be carried out through telephone or ad hoc contact and that, in general, they take enough time and energy to require some long-term commitment by a nonpaid primary group member. Figure 18.4 shows that this pattern of kinship continuation starts like the prior one with physically robust marital households having a high percentage of their populations using these kin services. The range goes from 40% providing household gifts to 68% using kin to talk to when they are feeling low. In the second stage of disability, when the respondent is sick and single, the figures range from 47% using kin for household gifts to 79% who use them to talk to when they are feeling low. In the third stage the range sinks

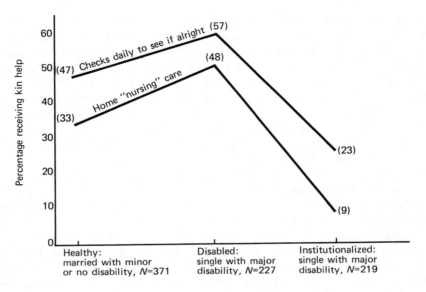

**FIGURE 18.3.** *This graph shows the kinship decline.*

slightly, going from 44% who received household gifts to 71% who talk with relatives when feeling low. However, there are more people in the third stage using kin than in the first stage, even though the respondents in the middle stage are the highest users of all. Therefore, we refer to it as primary group continuation.

Thus far our analysis has concentrated on marital households and kin. However, our theory tells us that other supporting primary groups have different structures and therefore different services to supply. We had two items that we thought would illustrate neighborhood services. The first asked respondents, if they went out on their daily chores like shopping, who would spot a burglary attempt in the home and report it to the police? The second question asked from whom they could borrow a small household item, such as sugar or a bandaid, in an emergency. These seemingly diverse tasks were classified as having the following theoretical dimensions in common: (*a*) they require close continuous proximity; (*b*) they extend to a larger group than the one- or two-person household; (*c*) they could be handled by either the same or a different generation; and (*d*) they do not require long-term commitments. What further characterizes these activities is that they are not likely to be accepted by the institutions for the aged as central and partially routinizable (Table 18.2, Row 4). Given these dimensions we would expect the primary group sequence we have called neighborhood decline. It resembles the pattern in Figure 18.3 which we called kinship decline in two respects. In the first stage—the robust marital

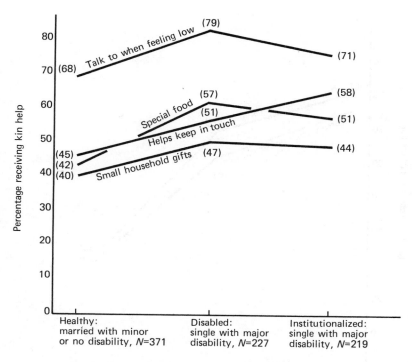

**FIGURE 18.4** *This graph shows the kinship continuation.*

household—there is a heavy use of a supporting primary group, neighbors. This remains relatively constant in the second stage, and in the last stage there is a very substantial decline in the use of supporting primary groups. As shown in Figure 18.5, at the first stage 80% say neighbors will spot and report a "break-in" and 74% say neighbors will loan them small household items in an emergency. This drops slightly to 67 and 61%, respectively, for each task when the elderly person is disabled, and then there is a large drop to 34 and 36% when the older person is institutionalized. This same analysis has been extended to friendship groups (Litwak and Kulis 1981).

In summary the empirical data is related to the theoretical expectations, while having some unanticipated bulges and squiggles. This suggests that our items may reflect some mixed pattern (which we will not present in this deliberately simplified statement, but is developed in Litwak and Kulis 1981). Nor has it taken into account the influence of factors such as income and ethnic, racial, or religious differences that can affect exchanges. Such factors do add to the complexity of the analysis but do not change the basic trends presented (Litwak and Kulis 1981).

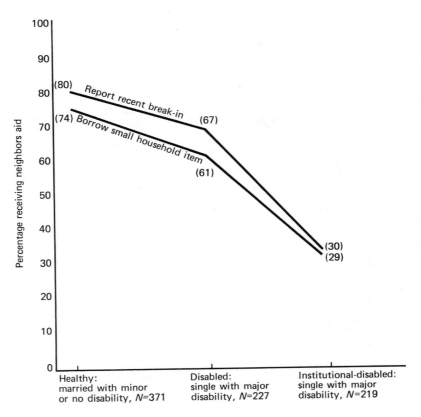

**FIGURE 18.5.** *This graph shows the neighborhood decline.*

## Research and Social Policy

Before considering general policy implications, let us consider the implications for research design. Past investigators have had no general theoretical framework for defining the universe of exchanges or services. As a result they selected services for study under the assumption that they all had the same dimensions or they based their selection on immediate pragmatic considerations which led to biased conclusions as to which group was most important to older people. For instance, Rix and Romashko (1980) concluded that the only important primary group was the marital dyad. However, the exchanges they studied all came from one limited domain of the universe of possible services. They looked specifically at cooking, financial management, everyday house cleaning, and shopping, which are all characterized by the need for continuous proximity, long-term commitments, and small size. If they had a theoretical definition of the universe of exchanges they would have immediately known that there are many other domains, for example, one characterized by large size, continuous proximity, and short-term commitments, encompassing services such as emergency borrowing or small household items, reporting break-ins, or holding emergency spare keys for elderly neighbors. Using this set of exchanges they would have come to the conclusion that neighbors were the most important primary group. In short, depending on the domain from which the investigator selects items for study, different primary groups will emerge as the most important providers of services. This has important implication for survey design, and helps explain much confusion in past studies (see Dono *et al.* 1979).

One of the chief aims of the present theoretical effort is to provide policymakers with a general framework that will enable them to locate all programs in terms of which natural support groups are likely to use them and which are not, which class of exchanges are likely to be encouraged and which ignored. For instance, if a policymaker is presented with a program to support centralized senior-citizen centers that would develop recreational and social programs and be the location for inexpensive hot meals, the policymaker who understands the framework presented in this study should immediately note that such centralized senior-citizen centers do not address themselves to tasks or groups that require immediate neighborhood proximity (e.g., emergency medical help, household protection, holding "safe" keys, providing information on local shopping). Nor does such a program address itself to tasks that require kin aid—long-term commitment without continuous proximity such as taking care of rent and household bills when the older person is hospitalized, providing postoperative home care for several weeks, helping in planning new residences for chronically disabled persons, providing continuous emotional support for the chronically ill.

This theory also has some interesting implications for housing and migration policy. One current solution that takes into account the stage of disability is a retirement community that has separate dwellings for older persons who are robust, similar to a hotel with maid service for those who are too ill to handle everyday tasks but who could still be maintained in the community, and a nursing home arrangement for those who are too ill to live by themselves. The theory would suggest that such a solution will fail at the second and third stages. At the second stage it assumes that everyday care can be handled by paid staff (hotel service) and neighbors since retirement communities tend to rule out the proximity of children. This theory suggests that paid staff cannot be relied on to handle nonuniform aspects of personal grooming and household functions. At best they will routinize them to avoid the strong incentives for exploitation in nonroutine tasks based in economic ties. Neighbors do not have the long-term commitment to perform such tasks. For these reasons we argue that only younger kin can supply the nonuniform services necessitated by the seriously disabled living in the community.

Given this analysis policymakers should not encourage the development of retirement communities with this three-tier housing unless they can find some means to locate them near children. One possible alternative would be to develop specialized housing for older persons at each stage of disability. The theory would suggest that people who are healthy and married would benefit from large, age-homogenous housing projects. They provide the aged with economies of large scale as well as suitable companions. For the second stage of disability, where people are living alone and are chronically ill, the optimal housing would be small age-homogenous projects scattered throughout the city, or subsidies for children to fix up housing quarters for older people in their own homes. These housing policies locate older people close to children and younger relatives who can provide home care. In the third stage, when older people must be institutionalized, the same considerations suggest moderate-sized nursing homes scattered throughout the city. The assumption is that they must be small in order to ensure reasonable proximity to community kin of the residents and at the same time they must be sufficiently large to take advantage of economies of large scale (Litwak 1977). The assumption is that older persons cannot receive optimal care in a nursing home without community primary group participation.

The idea of specialized housing for different stages of the life-cycle is only a continuation of earlier patterns in which people change their residence with changes in their life-cycles from single, to married without children, to married with children, to children leaving the home, and so forth. However, if specialized housing cannot be developed, the social policy should be one that makes clear to older persons that they may have to confront three different problems which require different housing solutions. This will permit them to decide upon their priorities. As things now stand, many people move to retirement communities or special housing for the aged without fully realizing its implications for later stages of disability.

So far we have spoken about primary group ties as being nonpaid. One major policy question is whether one could pay neighbors, friends, or kin to take care of the ill older person. In that case the older person would not have to worry as much about routinization or exploitation, and might not have to move with shifts from stages of health to disability. There are several questions which can be raised with this solution. If one pays a helper to take full-time care of an older person, who will take care of the helper's family? This, of course, is a problem for helpers who are at home taking care of children or spouses who are disabled. For helpers who are currently working, the question arises as to how the society can compete financially and otherwise with those holding well-paying and interesting jobs. In the latter case a possibility is to provide money to kin to hire others as caretakers with the proviso that kin will supervise. Either of these solutions would be ideal for the older person who does not require 24-hour care and still retains sufficient capacity to observe the caretaker. For those requiring

24-hour care, the economies of scale would probably demand an institutional setting.

The policy of paying kin presents another problem which must be addressed. If one introduces an economic incentive, will it destroy the primary group relationship which is based on affection and duty? There is good reason to believe that introducing moderate economic incentives, such as social security benefits, increases solidarity between parents and children (Anderson 1977). However, if one is talking about paying kin as full-time housekeepers, then the relationship between employer and employee might erode kinship ties.

The idea of paying primary group members raises yet another problem. Will such full-time pay open the flood gates for requests for payments from all kin for all services they provide? That could eventually bankrupt the society. Such matters require further study before definitive answers can be given.

Yet another policy—that children and relatives should be forced to take care of older persons—violates a basic tenet of industrial democratic societies, that people should be free to move geographically and socially according to their abilities. To insist that parents and children are tied together in old age would put enormous pressure on parents to intervene in the occupational life of their children if they are to ensure care in their old age. It is this fundamental clash between the needs of an open class system with laws of filial responsibility that has made the latter impossible to enforce when they have been tried (Schorr 1960).

In this section we have tried to show how a theoretical orientation can provide a basis for the policymaker to evaluate key policies in the field of aging. We have not tried to cover all the policy implications (Litwak and Kulis 1981). It would be naive to assume that such a framework would always be decisive. The fact is that the policymaker is confronted with existing groups with contending vested interests. These interests may be more powerful than any theoretical statement as to what is most effective. Nevertheless, there are times when the policymaker has some options. It is for such circumstances that the above analysis might be used.

For fellow social scientists we have suggested that primary groups and exchanges can be classified by the same limited set of dimensions. There is a simple principle of "matching" that permits one to say which groups can handle which tasks most effectively. That principle can be applied to problems of disability in aging so as to predict which groups will substitute for the marital dyad when it becomes disrupted by ill health and death. We would hope that the theories and data are sufficiently intriguing that others will pick them up and seek to document them. Many social scientists might well question the use of theories that are not as yet completely verified as a basis for making policy. It is unfortunately the case that policymakers must make decisions before all the facts are available. The obligation of the social scientist, is to point out the limits of verification and with this qualification to present the theories which they think are most promising. It is with this spirit that we present our formulations for the consideration of policymakers.

## ACKNOWLEDGMENTS

We would like to thank the following people for their advice and help on various parts of this chapter, though they cannot be held responsible for our formulations: John Dono, Cecilia Falbe, Seymour Spilerman, and Joe Schwartz.

# References

Adams, B.N. 1970. Isolation, function and beyond: American kinship in the 1960's. *Journal of Marriage and the Family* 32: 575–597.

Anderson, M. 1977. The impact on the family relationships of the elderly of changes since Victorian times in governmental income-maintenance provision. In *Family, bureaucracy and the elderly*, eds. E. Shanas and M.B. Sussman Durham: Duke University Press. Pp. 36–59.

Babchuk, N. 1965. Primary friends and kin: A study of the associations of middle class couples. *Social Forces* 43: 484–493.

Cantor, M.H. Neighbors and friends: An overlooked resource in the informal support system. *Research on Aging* 1: 434–463.

Cooley, C.H. 1955. Primary groups. In *Small Groups*, (eds.) P. Hare and E. Borgotta. New York: Alfred Knopf, Pp.15–17.

Dobrof, R. 1976. The case of the aged: A shared function. D.S.W. dissertation. School of Social Work, Columbia University.

Dobrof, R., and Litwak, E. 1977. *Maintenance of family ties of long-term care patients* DHEW Publication No. (ADM) 77-400. Washington, D.C.: U.S. Government Printing Office Pp.80–111.

Dono, J., Falbe, C., Kail, B., Litwak, E., Sherman, R., Siegel, D. 1979. Primary groups in old age. *Research on Aging* 1: 403–433.

Fellin, P., and Litwak, E. 1963. Neighborhood cohesion under conditions of mobility. *American Sociological Review* 28: 364–376.

Gordon, M. 1977. Primary group differentiation in urban Ireland. *Social Forces* 55: 743–752.

Granovetter, M. 1974. *Getting a job: A study of contacts and careers.* Cambridge: Harvard University Press.

Horwitz, A. 1977. Social networks and pathways into psychiatric treatment. *Social Forces* 56: 86–103.

Jackson, M.S., Fischer, C.F., and Jones, L.M. 1977. The dimensions of social networks. In *Networks and places.* eds. C.S. Fischer New York: The Free Press. Pp. 39–58.

Litwak, E. 1977. Theoretical bases for practice. In *Maintenance of family ties of long-term care patients.* DHEW publication no. (ADM) 77-400 eds. R. Dobrof and E. Litwak Washington, D.C.: Superintendent of Documents, U.S. Government Printing Office, Pp. 80-11.

Litwak, E., and Figueira, J. 1970. Technological innovation and ideal forms of family structure in an industrial society. In *Families in east and west: Socialization process and kinship ties.* eds. R. Hill and R. Konig. The Hague: Mouton. Pp. 348–396.

Litwak, E., and Kulis, S. 1981. *The dynamics of network change for older people: Social policy and social theory.* Preprint Series # 74. New York: Center for the Social Sciences at Columbia University.

Litwak, E., and Szelenyi, I. 1969. Primary group structures and their functions: Kin, neighbors and friends. *American Sociological Review* 34: 465–481.

Lopata, H.Z. 1979. *Women as widows.* New York: Elsevier North Holland.

Rix, S, and Romanshko, T. 1980. With a little help from my friends. Final Report Submitted to the Administration on Aging, Department of Health, Education and Welfare. Washington, D.C., Grant No. 90-A-1320.

Rosow, I. 1967. *The social integration of the aged.* New York: The Free Press. Pp.194–245.

Schorr, JA. 1960. *Filial responsibility in the modern American family.* Social Security Administration, Washington, D.C.: Superintendent of Documents, U.S. Government Printing Office.

# V

# Debate, Choices, and the Impact of Evaluation

*Does policy evaluation contribute to the improvement of social policy? Weiss offers a cautious affirmative answer in line with current research on the utilization of evaluation. She suggests a process of "enlightenment," whereby the accumulated findings of evaluation research feed into a diffuse, incremental process of decision-making. The results of policy evaluation serve to inform policymakers and to reduce the degree of uncertainty under which they operate.*

*The three other chapters in this section alert us to more specific aspects of policy debates relevant to the utilization of evaluation research. Tarschys argues that the receptivity of policymakers to the outcome of policy analyses is related to the "stage in the life cycle" of a policy issue. At some stages, policymakers and the public are actively seeking more information and new ideas. At others, they are inclined to reject them.*

*Gamson and Lasch, while not addressing themselves specifically to issues of research utilization, offer a conceptual framework for the analysis of the context of policy debates. Policy debates and policy decisions occur within the context of a political culture, which determines values evoked, frames of reference, and symbols used. Cohen addresses himself to the choices involved in policy decisions. He argues that some choices are "harder" than others. "Hardness of choice" can be seen as a variable explaining receptivity to new information, and the choice itself can become the subject of evaluation.*

# 19

# Policy Evaluation as Societal Learning

## CAROL H. WEISS

A distinctive characteristic of human service policies in the United States in the past 10–15 years has been the mandate for evaluation that has accompanied such policies. Almost every major policy initiative in health, social services, and education has been attended by formal, systematic evaluation of the effects of the policy for its intended beneficiaries. Hundreds of millions of dollars are being spent annually by the federal government to learn how well human service policies are achieving the ends for which they were designed.

The upsurge in evaluation activity and expenditures has a rational cast. The presumed purpose of all this analysis is to improve the effectiveness of policy. Evaluation, the rhetoric goes, will identify the programs and policies that are working well so that they can be expanded, and locate the programs and policies that are working poorly so that they can be terminated or modified. Evaluations that give fine-grained detail about strategies of intervention—that indicate which components of policies are successful for which types of clientele under which conditions—will provide the basis for modifying policies and attuning them to the needs and life conditions of the participants. The enterprise, in short, is to use the methods and techniques of social science in the service of rational allocation of resources and the improvement of welfare policy.

American social scientists by the thousands have been attracted to evaluation and associated policy studies. Not only do they find research funds available for the study of important and interesting social and economic phenomena, but the social consequences of the work also look attractive: evaluation results will be put to work to improve the lot of the needy. Despite reservations among a few

EVALUATING THE WELFARE STATE:
SOCIAL AND POLITICAL PERSPECTIVES

social scientists about becoming technicians for the bureaucratic welfare state, policy studies look like an ideal opportunity to combine research practice with social conscience. Researchers are able to do good while they are doing well.

Yet by the early 1970s, after about 5 or 6 years of relatively large-scale evaluation and policy studies, it was becoming obvious that study results were not having visible impacts on policy decisions. Programs that evaluators had found relatively ineffective, like the Head Start preschool program, were continued—and even expanded. Programs that evaluators had found effective, like direct federal loans to low-income college students, were cut back; and much of the detailed advice contained in the recommendations sections of policy study reports simply went unheeded. Social scientists who had expected their work to shape future government policy became disillusioned. Not only were they not counselors to the prince, they were not even influential advisers to the bureau of vocational education. Given their general tendency to turn their experience into "findings," they began to contribute articles to the scholarly journals about the nonuse and abuse of policy studies. During the 1970s there was a persistent recitation of the nonutilization tale—the resistance of self-serving government agencies to the lessons from research, the ignorance or inattention of legislators, the waste of social science wisdom, the triumph of bureaucratic routine and special-interest politics.

Recent investigations, however, provide a different interpretation of events. True, cases of immediate and direct influence of research findings on specific policy decisions are not frequent. Examples can be found, and may even be increasing, but they remain relatively uncommon. But to acknowledge this is not the same as saying that research findings have little influence on policy. On the contrary, evidence suggests that evaluation and policy studies have had significant consequences, but not necessarily on discrete provisions nor in the linear sequence that social scientists expected (Weiss 1980b).

Rarely does research supply an "answer" that policy actors employ to solve a policy problem. Rather, research provides a background of data, empirical generalizations, and ideas that affect the way that policymakers think about problems. It influences their conceptualization of the issues with which they deal; it affects the facets of the issue that they consider inevitable and unchangeable or amenable to policy action; it widens the range of options that they consider; it challenges some taken for granted assumptions about appropriate goals and appropriate activities. Often, it helps them make sense of what they have been doing after the fact, so that they come to understand which courses of action they have followed and which courses of actions have gone by default. In sum, policy studies—and social science research more generally—have made highly significant contributions by altering the terms of policy discussion.

This kind of indirect conceptual contribution is not easy to see, not visible to the naked eye. Sometimes it is manifested only over lengthy periods of time and after numbers of studies have yielded convergent results. For example, scores of evaluations were done of counseling programs for prison inmates, most of which concluded that counseling had little effect in reducing subsequent recidivism. Correctional authorities paid little attention, and efforts at in-prison rehabilitation went on relatively unchanged for a long while. However, the research results percolated through relevant bureaus, agencies, and legislative chambers, and in the past few years, significant changes have been made. Not only correctional practice but also sentencing codes and judicial acts have been affected.

The state of California, for example, used to view correctional institutions as agencies of rehabilitation. Judges sentenced convicted offenders to indeterminate terms of imprisonment, letting prison authorities decide the date of a prisoner's release on the basis of the prisoner's progress toward rehabilitation. A few years ago, the California legislature officially gave up on rehabilitation. It changed the indeterminate sentencing law, and provided instead for relatively fixed terms of sentence. Further, the new law begins with a statement of change of goals. The preamble, in a marked shift, states that the purpose of imprisonment is punishment. Prison programs aiming at rehabilitation continue, although more and more on a voluntary rather than compulsory basis, but the state has absorbed the lessons of evaluation: It has scaled down its expectations of rehabilitation and shifted to a different rationale for incarceration. Research results played a large part in the change.[1]

In similar ways, social science results and social science concepts have had an effect in many fields. It is not usually a single finding or the recommendation derived from a single study that is adopted in executive or legislative action (although this occasionally happens). More often, it is the ideas and general notions coming from research that have an impact. Nor is it usually the particular decisionmaker for whom the study was done that uses the findings. Since few decisions in government, and almost no decisions of sufficient scope to qualify for the category of policy, are made by a single decisionmaker or even by a small group of decisionmakers, this is not the usual route to influence. Instead, what seems to happen is that generalizations and ideas from numbers of studies come into currency indirectly—through articles in academic journals and journals of opinion, stories in the media, the advice of consultants, lobbying by special interest groups, conversation of colleagues, attendance at conferences or training programs, and other uncataloged sources. Ideas from research are picked up in diverse ways and percolate through to officials in many offices who deal with the issues.

As the ideas from research filter through, officials test them against the

---

[1] Social scientists continue to debate whether the evaluation studies that provided much of the impetus for the change were valid enough to support the conclusion that in prison programs "nothing works."

standards of their own knowledge and judgment. They do not uncritically accept every set of conclusions they hear about, even if the conclusions bear the imprimatur of social science. They have many sources of information other then social science, ranging from their own firsthand experience to systematic and unsystematic reports from the field. The extent to which they accept a research idea, or give it at least provisional hearing, depends on the degree to which it resonates with their prior knowledge. If it helps to organize and make sense of their earlier knowledge and impressions, they tend to incorporate it into their stock of knowledge (Weiss and Bucuvalas 1980).

This prevalent process of merging research results with other sources of information and ideas has two curious consequences. First, the merger often gives research results extra leverage as they shape officials' understanding of issues. Because research provides powerful labels for previously inchoate and unorganized experience, it helps to mold officials' thinking into categories derived from social science. Think of the policy effects of such category labels as *externalities, achievement scores, deinstitutionalization, reindustrialization, white flight, intergenerational dependency.*

Second, because social science is merged with other knowledge, officials are largely unaware of when and how they use research. An investigator going out to study the uses of policy research quickly finds out that respondents have great difficulty disentangling the lessons they have learned from research from their whole configuration of knowledge. They do not catalog research separately; they do not remember sources and citations. With the best will in the world, all they can usually say is that in the course of their work they hear about a great deal of research and they are sure it affects what they think and do. They cannot give specific illustrations of their use of a specific study, because that is not how they work (Weiss 1980a).

So, if recent investigations of the consequences of research for policy leave us with greater respect for the influence of research, the influence appears to lie in affecting the shape and content of policy discourse rather than concrete choices. The nature of the effect has been called "enlightenment": Research modifies the definition of problems that policymakers address, how they think about them, which options they discard and which they pursue, and how they conceptualize their purposes. For those who had hoped for greater direct influence on policy, it is a limited victory.

Elsewhere I have noted that even in the provisionally optimistic imagery of enlightenment, there lurk some dangers. For one thing, the research that policy actors hear about and come to accept is not necessarily the best, most comprehensive, or most current research. Sometimes they become aware of shoddy studies, outmoded ideas, and biased findings. No quality control mechanisms screen the good and relevant from the partial and sensational. The phenomenon that has been discussed as enlightenment may turn out to be, in fact, endarkenment.

Another limitation is that for all the potential power of shifts in policymakers' awareness and attention, thinking differently is not the same as acting differently. Although changed discourse is likely to result—eventually—in new modes of action, the process may be agonizingly slow and inexact. The policy action that finally emerges cannot be expected to correspond closely with the preferred state envisioned by the social scientist.

The discussion thus far has been prologue. The question to which I now turn is why the use of evaluation and other social science research goes through such tortuous process. Why is there not more immediate and direct use of research results in the making of policy? Given the fact that government agencies responsible for particular policies sponsor studies with the avowed intent of improving those policies, why do they not put the results to use directly?

Obviously the answers to this question are multiple and complex. Some of them have to do with the inconclusiveness of the research. Many, probably most, studies are fragile guides to action, either because of limitations in the research, or the ambiguous nature of the findings, or—often most serious—the problematic relationship between the findings and any clear-cut policy recommendations. (Researchers who have done a painfully careful evaluation study often throw caution to the winds when they come to drawing implications for action and leap to unanalyzed, untested, and perhaps unworkable recommendations.) Other reasons for the lack of immediate adoption have to do with the nature of government agencies (e.g., their limited repertoire of available policy responses), and the imperatives of policy decisions (e.g., the overriding need to reconcile diverse interests as well as reach "right" decisions). But one important reason has received little attention, and it is this reason that I want to talk about—the nature of political decision making processes.

## The Nature of Policy Decision Making

Both the popular and the academic literature pictures decision making as an event: A group of authorized decision makers assemble at a particular time and place; they review a problem (or opportunity); they consider a number of alternative courses of action with more or less explicit calculation of the advantages and disadvantages of each option; they weigh the alternatives against their goals or preferences; and then select the alternative best suited for achieving their purposes. The result is a decision.[2]

---

[2]There was a time when the characterization of decision making was considerably crisper than this. In what is commonly referred to as the rational model, several additional assumptions were made, for example, explicit goals consensually weighted, generation of all possible alternatives, explicit calculation of all costs and benefits for each option, selection of the optimal option. Scholars from the several disciplines engaged with decision making have been chipping away at the formulation for over a generation in the light of actual organizational behavior. The statement here is what generally remains.

There are five major constructs in this imagery of decision making. The first is *boundedness*. Decision making is, in effect, set off from the ongoing stream of organizational activity. It involves a discrete set of *actors* who occupy authoritative positions; they are people who are officially responsible for, and empowered to make, decisions for the organization. Decision making is bounded in *time*, taking place over a relatively short period. It is usually also bounded in *location*, with the relevant actors in contact with each other, or able to be in contact with each other, to negotiate the decision. The customary conceptualization of decision making thus has much in common with the three unities of Greek drama.

A second construct is *purposiveness*. It is commonly assumed that decision makers have relatively clear goals in view: They want to bring about a desired end state or avoid an undesired state. Since Simon's seminal work (1947), it has become accepted that decision makers do not try to optimize decisions but rather satisfice, that is, settle for something "good enough." Nevertheless, they are expected to have overt criteria for what is good enough, and to seek a decision that promises progress toward attaining their purposes.

The third construct is *calculation*. Decision makers are expected to generate (or have generated for them) a set of alternatives. In the past decades, scholars have recognized that no comprehensive set of alternatives is developed; limits on human abilities of cognitive processing preclude a complete canvass of options. But in the going imagery, decision makers consider the costs and benefits of a variety of responses. Their calculation will often be informal and intuitive rather than systematic, as they proceed on the basis of experience, informed judgment, customary practice, or gut feeling. Their goals need not represent only properly respectable public objectives, but will usually include such unexpressed aims as bureaucratic advantage, career interests, and the furtherance of electoral chances. But however mixed the objectives and however informal the assessment procedures may be, it is assumed that decision makers weigh the relative advantages of several alternatives against their goals and their formulation of desired end states. The alternative that registers an acceptable balance of costs and benefits will be selected. Scholars have lowered their expectations for the rationality of the calculus employed, and they have tempered their assumptions of systematic and methodical assessment of trade-offs, but they retain belief that a process of calculation takes place.

Fourth, implicit in the concept of decision making is a construct of *perceived significance*. A decision marks a step of some moment. People who make the decision perceive the act as consequential (i.e., having consequences). When the decision involves "policy," whichever of the many meanings are invested in the term *policy* (Heclo 1972), the connotations of far-reaching importance are underscored, and a "policy decision" is doubly endowed with intimations of significance. People who make a policy decision are viewed as being self-consciously aware of registering a decisive commitment to an important course of action. Scholars have noted that some decisions involve a choice to do nothing, to leave the situation unchanged. Yet even when this is the case, the choice is expected to represent a matter of consequence to those who make the decision.

Finally, there is an assumption of *sequential order*. The sequence is regarded as beginning with recognition of a problem. It proceeds to the development and consideration of alternative means for coping with the problem, goes next to assessment of the relative advantages of the alternatives, and ends with selection of a decision.[3]

These five constructs—boundedness, purposiveness, calculation, perceived significance, and sequential order—underlie most images of decision making. They capture essential elements of much of the decision making that goes on at bureau, division, and department levels, in executive agencies and legislatures, in private and public organizations. Allison's (1971) account of the "essence of decision" by President Kennedy and his small group of advisers considering the American response to the Cuban missile crisis is an archetypical decision of this kind. Similarly, a corporation deciding whether or not to construct a new plant, the Congress debating passage of tax cutting legislation, an executive agency developing proposals for change in highway speed-limit regulations—all go through a process that may be well represented by these constructs.

Yet many policy decisions emerge through processes that bear little relationship to these descriptors. Much decision making differs from the traditional model because one or more of the five characteristics is low, or even absent. Policies, even policies of fateful magnitude, often take shape by jumbled and diffuse processes that differ in vital ways from the conventional imagery.

Government is a continuous bustle of activity, with people in many offices bumping up against problems, new conditions, discrepant rules, unprecedented requests for service, and the promulgations of other offices. In coping with their daily work, people in many places take small steps, without conscious awareness that their actions are pushing policy down certain paths and foreclosing other responses. They do not necessarily perceive themselves as making—or even influencing—policy, but their many small steps (writing position papers, drafting regulations, answering inquiries, making plans, releasing news bulletins) may fuse, coalesce, and harden. Over time, the congeries of small acts can set the direction, and the limits, of government policy. Only in retrospect do people become aware that policy was made.

---

[3]Despite the ubiquity of the term *problem solving*, most people understand that present government problems are rarely "solved" once and for all, or even for long periods of time. Any solution is temporary, and is as likely to generate new problems as it is to remove the condition that it is intended to solve. Many problems, such as poverty or insufficient oil resources, are so deeprooted and intractable that government action can at best make modest inroads. Therefore, I have selected the word *coping* rather than *solving* to characterize the kinds of alternatives that officials consider.

Although the people who engage in incremental adaptations are not conscious of participating in policymaking, officials at the top echelon may be equally convinced that they are not making decisions. From the top, it often looks as though they are presented with a fait accompli. Accommodations have been reached and a decision negotiated by people in the warren of offices below, and they have little option but to accept it. Only rarely, and with the expenditure of a considerable amount of their political capital, can they change or reject the advice they are offered. To them, the job often seems to be rubber-stamping of decisions already made.

Even in legislatures, the quintessential locus of decision making, individual legislators have limited options. In the United States, committees receive drafts of complex legislative bills from the executive agencies. Committee staffs may identify controversial points in the light of legislators' general preferences and work out accommodations with agency staffs. Once in a while, a particularly interested and influential legislator can get particular provisions amended. But when the lengthy bills come up for vote, no individual legislator can be familiar with more than a handful of provisions. By and large, he or she must either vote against the entire bill or accept it. To the participants, their own influence on policy often looks marginal.

Given the fragmentation of authority across multiple bureaus, departments, and legislative committees, and the disjointed stages by which actions coalesce into decisions, the traditional model of decision making is a highly stylized rendition of reality. Identification of any clear-cut group of decision makers can be difficult. (Sometimes, for example, a middle-level bureaucrat has taken the key action, although he or she may be unaware that the action was going to be—or was—decisive.) The goals of policy are often equally diffuse, except in terms of "taking care of" some undesirable situation. Which options are considered, and what sets of advantages and disadvantages are assessed, may be impossible to tell in the iterative, multiparticipative, diffuse processes of formulating policy. The complexity of government policymaking defies neat compartmentalization.

## Alternative Routes to Policy

Yet policies do get made. If government often proceeds to decisions without bounded, purposeful, sequential acts of perceived significance, how do decisions emerge? Some of the undirected strategies appear to be these:

1. *Reliance on custom and implicit rules.* Officials do what the agency has traditionally done. Even if a situation is unprecedented, officials may interpret it to fall within customary procedures. In so doing, they in effect make new policy by subsuming the novel contingency within a familiar rubric.

2. *Improvisation.* Another tactic is to improvise. Confronted with an unanticipated situation, officials may exercise their ingenuity, stretching a point here, combining a few tried-and-true procedures there, adding a dash of novelty, much like a chef concocting a new recipe. Through impromptu accommodation, an agency may begin to fashion new policy.

3. *Mutual adjustment.* As Lindblom (1965) has indicated, "partisans" (office holders who lack any sense of common purpose) may reach decisions by simply adapting to decisions made around them. If one office has invoked convention or made improvisations, other offices can adjust their actions to accommodate the situation.

4. *Accretion.* Once officials have extemporized under the press of events, or adapted to actions taken in other offices, they may repeat the procedures when similar—or even not so similar—situations recur. The first responses provide a precedent, and if they seem to work, they will be followed again. Over time, when numbers of cases have been handled in like fashion, or when several different contingencies have been adopted to deal with an array of exceptional circumstances, they may coalesce and rigidify. Like skeletons of millions of tiny sea creatures building up into giant coral reefs, the result can become fixed.

5. *Negotiation.* When authority is fragmented and agencies have overlapping and discrepant mandates, overt conflicts may arise. Many are settled by direct negotiation among the interested units. Threats and promises, discussion and debate on the issues, trade-offs of advantage and obligation—these are the currency of bargaining. The aim is less to reach a rational decision in the usual sense than to work out an arrangement that will at least minimally satisfy the key interests of each of the parties. Through processes long familiar in the Congress (log rolling, horse trading), a bargain is arranged.

6. *Move and countermove ("chicken").* If bargaining breaks down, an agency may take a unilateral move to advance its position. Other affected agencies counter with moves of their own. This kind of antagonistic adjustment is particularly likely when present policies leave some new policy territory unclaimed (e.g., the agencies' scramble to move into the turf of "children's policy"). The series of competitive moves may continue until mutual adjustment reaches stalemate, or until resolution is shifted up to higher levels. Move and countermove is an accustomed mode of decision in international relations.

7. *A window for solutions.* Not infrequently, the solution precedes the identification of a problem. Officials have pet remedies that they seek to implement. One group may want to install a computer system, and they engage in a search for places and occasions that would justify its introduction. Another group may be wedded to the idea of deregulation as an all-purpose panacea and scour the federal system for areas amenable to regulatory rollback. This is a case where the solution is in hand, and partisans actively seek a "window" that will provide an opening for their ready-made nostrum.

8. *Indirection.* Another route by which policy emerges is as a by-product of other decisions. In this case, policy outcomes are unintended, but because of decisions made to achieve other desired ends, they nevertheless come about. Federal guarantees of home mortgages, undertaken after World War II to help families purchase their own homes, led to an exodus from central cities and the massive growth of suburbs. Federal aid to education, designed to improve the quality of education particularly for disadvantaged and low-achieving students, is leading to a shift of authority over educational practice from local to state and federal education agencies. No decisions were consciously made to create such shifts, but they emerged by indirection.

This list of nondecisional processes that produce policy outcomes is probably not exhaustive. Nevertheless, it indicates a variety of ways in which major outputs can issue from government without considered review or rational assessment. In time, ad hoc agency actions may have to be formalized by legislation. But often the early response is decisive, and legislative action merely ratifies the decisions that have already emerged. In some areas, it is only a slight exaggeration to say that ratification of the status quo, and allocation of funds to support it, is a main function of legislation.

## The Place of Research

If government policy can "happen " without the set piece of formal decision making, how does policy research get a hearing? When decisions take shape over long periods of time, through the incremental actions of multiple actors, and often without participants' awareness that they are shaping decisions, the opportunity for formal consideration of research information looks distinctly limited. In such situations, research data on constituents' needs, the benefits and costs of policies, and the effectiveness and shortcomings of programs seem to have little chance for impact.

Yet one of the interesting facets of the situation, verified repeatedly in empirical investigation and borne out by the record, is that U.S. officials value social science research. They say that it is important and useful, and they sponsor large numbers of studies. If opportunities to use research results as a guide for policymaking are as limited as I think they are, there must be other purposes that research serves. It seems important to identify them.

One possible reason for officials' allegiance may be that research serves as a device of control. In a federal system, federal agencies set policy and allocate resources but local agencies deliver direct services. With daily control of education, health services, and welfare in local hands, there can be a wide gap between federal intent and local performance. Only when the federal agency has good information about what local services are doing—their structure, the processes of service delivery, and the outcomes for clients—can it begin to exercise the authority that rule making and resource allocation allow. Evaluation and policy studies can become the mechanism by which federal agencies keep informed.

Federal education officials, intent on ensuring compliance with federal purpose, can find out whether local school districts are actually spending funds provided under Title I of the Elementary and Secondary Education Act to enrich educational opportunities for low-income and low-achieving students. Federal health officials can find out the extent to which neighborhood health centers improve the health status of low-income clientele. If local agencies are found to be performing poorly, the federal agency can institute stricter controls over recipient agencies—tightening up rules, and even terminating particular local grants. Research results may become the basis for control—and the mere decision to undertake research can serve as an implicit threat that firmer control is possible. Congress sometimes seems to write evaluation provisions into legislation for just this kind of purpose—to serve notice on agencies that it will have the capability to review the effectiveness of their operations—even if it never does.

Another purpose that policy research can serve is to provide support and vindication for current policies. Federal officials often expect research to justify at least some of their claims—that large numbers of people are in need of their services, that programs do some good, that constituents like the attention and want services to continue. Even an evaluation showing little direct benefit to clients will often yield some positive evidence of this kind. They can use findings selectively to buttress the agency's case for legislative reauthorization and additional funding.

If these reasons for continued sponsorship of policy research seem unduly skeptical, a third basis can be advanced. It is possible that federal officials support research because they recognize the conceptual contributions that it makes. They may have come to realize that every agency, even the most progressive, tends to grow musty and stale. It settles into a rut, taking old assumptions for granted, substituting routine for thought, tinkering at best with policy minutia rather than venturing in new directions. To overcome hardening of organizational arteries, they may welcome the fresh insights and critical perspectives that good research brings. By subjecting conventional practice to evaluation, they may seek to help the agency renew its sense of mission and adapt to changing conditions.

One may hope that some part of the reason for high levels of research support comes from motives of this latter sort. But even if the thrust for evaluation and policy studies springs from less high-minded sources, even if it is the resultant of adversarial forces (department heads checking on the performance of bureaus, Congress checking up on departments, agencies seeking legitimation for their programs), even if it represents only rhetorical commitment to the norms of accountability and rational procedure, even then it has consequences. The regularized practice of evaluation and analysis has become embedded in government structures. Offices of research and evaluation exist at the bureau, division, and department level in many federal agencies. Their professional staffs do what evaluation and analysis staffs know how to do—continue and expand the flow of research information to the agency. Even the General Accounting Office, which used to serve Congress only as financial auditor, now has its Institute of Program Evaluation. As procedures develop to transmit the results of policy studies routinely to officials throughout the government, an important mechanism for learning becomes institutionalized.

Nor is communication of research restricted to officialdom. The mass media are increasingly reporting the results of social science research, including evaluation and policy studies. Coverage by major national and regional newspapers and the weekly news magazines is bringing news of research to attentive publics. When the public reads evidence of failures in current policies, the demonstrated promise of alternative policies, or new concepts of programming, pressure increases on government to take account of the evidence.

A final collateral development is worth noting. In the United States, public policy discussion is becoming permeated with social science concepts and data. Policies are proposed, defended, and criticized in terms that the social sciences have brought into fashion—client outcomes, implementability, inflationary consequences. Data are marshaled by all sides in the debate to strengthen their cause. Even the Congress, rarely renowned as a champion of research, now routinely expects the case for policy to be supported with systematic and objective evidence. Social science is becoming a prevalent language of discourse in the policy arena. Partisans speak the language to make their arguments convincing. But once they adopt its symbols and use its grammar, they find their positions subtly influenced by the structure of its rules.

The point of these remarks is that policy research is no longer a trivial and transient appendage to the policymaking process. It is being built into the system. In the last few paragraphs, discussion of its place in the system has moved from its relatively concrete manifestations in research, evaluation, and planning offices in federal agencies, to media reporting of its results, to its infiltration of policy discourse. This shift toward progressively more diffuse influences is not accidental. It is an attempt to indicate the variety of indirect and circuitous ways in which research exercises its influence on policy.

## Conclusion

One of the significant features of the policy process, at least on certain issues at certain times, is the diffuse manner in which decisions accrete. When policy happens without synoptic review and "rational" choice, there seems to be little opportunity for careful consideration of relevant policy research. Officials respond to situations by hunch and experience, drawing on whatever mix of knowledge—and, of course, much else besides knowledge—they have at hand.

None of the traditional advice to policy researchers on how to get their conclusions heeded seems to apply. The familiar admonitions are: Locate the potential user of research in advance, understand which policy variables he or she has the authority to change, concentrate the study on the feasible (manipulable) variables, involve the potential user in the research process, establish a relationship of trust, demonstrate awareness of the constraints that limit options, provide practical recommendations, write results clearly and simply, communicate results in person. All these prescriptions are directed at influencing one decision maker, or a small group of decision makers, to use research in making a direct, concrete, immediate choice. In that context the advice makes notable sense. None fits the world of diffuse policy decisions.

But there are other ways that research gets a hearing. Officials absorb a great deal of research knowledge through informal routes. They read widely, go to meetings, listen to people, discuss with colleagues, all without necessarily having a particular decision in mind. Research information and ideas filter into their awareness, whether or not they label it research as they absorb it. This diffuse process of "enlightenment" contributes to their stock of knowledge. When they engage in the stream of activities that aggregate into policy, they draw upon the knowledge that they have gathered from a variety of sources, including research, and apply it to their work.

The diffuse process of research use that we are calling "enlightenment" is highly compatible with the diffuse processes of policymaking. It informs the work of many policy actors in many locations as they perform their bits and pieces of policy work. Unlike the usual notion of a single research sponsor who acquires a directed set of findings for a particular decisional purpose, it does not suggest a monopoly on research knowledge by the bureaucrat who funds the study. Many different people, with different interests and ideologies, inside and outside government, can be enlightened by research, and they can exercise their knowledge at many points, cooperatively or adversarially, as policy takes shape.

Of course, the enlightenment image represents no ideal model. When research comes to people's attention haphazardly, the process is unorganized, slow, wasteful, and sloppy. Some policy actors may fail to hear about relevant research; others may fail to take the research they hear about seriously. Some people may become enchanted with catchy, faddish, irrelevant, obsolete, partial, or invalid findings, or latch onto only the subset of findings that supports their predispositions and policy interests. The whole process reeks of oversimplification. People tend to forget the complexities and qualifications and remember the slogans ("the poverty program failed," "a guaranteed income leads to little reduction in work effort"). Diffuse enlightenment is no substitute for careful, directed analysis of the policy implications of research. Ways have to be found to improve targeted applications of targeted research as well.

Nevertheless, the fit between the diffuse processes of policymaking and officials' diffuse absorption of research is noteworthy. It seems to represent one of the most important contributions that social science research makes to public policy. The ideas derived from research provide organizing perspectives that help people make sense of experience. These ideas offer frameworks within which problems are interpreted and policy actions considered. Retrospectively, they help people understand what government has been doing and what the consequences have been. Prospectively, they help raise the possibility of alternative courses of action.

Perhaps most valuable of all, research can be a medium of criticism. Subjecting old assumptions to empirical test and introducing alternative perspectives are vital contributions. Even if officials have themselves suspected policy shortcomings or negative side effects, research crystallizes the suspicions and provides an occasion for mapping new responses. Of course, research may not prevail, but at least it offers officials a conceptual language with which to rethink accustomed practice.

To the extent that such contributions to the public arena are important, they suggest different lessons to policy researchers from those associated with direct research application. Concern about pleasing—or at least, satisfying—the client is secondary. Being practical and timely and keeping the study within feasible boundaries may be unimportant, or even counterproductive. If the research is not completed in time for this year's budget cycle, it is no great loss. The same issues, if they are important, will come up again and again. In the enlightenment tradition, the researcher is well advised to broaden the scope of the question and take time to do first-quality research.

The critical ingredients will be independence of thought, conceptual sophistication, and methodological rigor—and when the research has produced something worth saying—serious efforts through many channels to get its message heard.

# References

Allison, G.T. 1971. *Essence of decision: Explaining the Cuban missile crisis.* Boston: Little Brown.

Heclo, H.H. 1972. Review article: Policy analysis. *British Journal of Political Science.* 2: 83–108.

Lindblom, C.E. 1965. *The intelligence of democracy.* New York: Free Press.

Simon, H.A. 1947. *Administrative behavior.* New York: Free Press.

Weiss, C.H. 1980a. Knowledge creep and decision accretion. *Knowledge: Creation, Diffusion, Utilization.* 1: 381–404.

Weiss, C.H. 1980b. *Social science research and decision-making.* New York: Columbia University Press. With M.J. Bucuvalas.

Weiss, C.H., and Bucuvalas, M.J. 1980. Truth tests and utility tests: Decision makers' frames of reference for social science research. *American Sociological Review* 45: 302–313.

# 20

# Fluctuations in the Political Demand for Policy Analysis

## DANIEL TARSCHYS

The relationship between the profession of policy analysts and that of policymaker is not an altogether happy one. Grumbles and snide remarks vis-à-vis "those people" are heard in both camps. Policy analysts, the politicians complain, are far too often ivory tower academics, myopic theoreticians, and "quantomaniacs" making too much of their endless regressions and standard deviations; in short, impractical people. In addition, they are frequently ax-grinding advocates or politicos in disguise who, under the facade of immaculate objectivity, hold strong convictions that infallibly color their findings. The policy analysts' view of the policymakers will often be about as flattering. Herbert Simon may have given a reasonable explanation for the limited attention capacity of decision makers, and of their volatile agenda, but in the eyes of the analyst that will hardly excuse the glaring irrationalism, anti-intellectualism, and obsession with ripples in public support found in most politicians, and their corresponding indifference to most fruits of serious policy analysis. The evaluator who finds his or her results neglected by the relevant policymaking community is probably a more typical member of the profession than the successful contributor to the policy process.

The interface between politicans and policy analysts and the related problem of utilization versus nonutilization of policy analysis have become important topics in the rapidly growing literature on policy evaluation and other aids to policymaking (Rich 1977; Weinberg 1979; Weiss 1975; also recent years of *Policy Analysis* and *Policy Studies Journal*). In the 1970s, much of the early optimism about the role of scientific analysis in the real world of decision

EVALUATING THE WELFARE STATE:
SOCIAL AND POLITICAL PERSPECTIVES

making has been succeeded by growing doubts about the penetrability of
political thickets. "Producing data is one thing! Getting it used is quite another"
(House 1972). Nonutilization or underutilization have been identified as salient
features of the policy analysis industry, and a number of authors have observed
that only a small fraction of all studies in the field appear to have had any
impact whatsoever (Cohen and Garet 1975; Deitchman 1976; Sharpe 1977;
Wholey 1970). And "while the utilization crisis concerned all types of applied
social science, nonutilization seemed to be particularly characteristic of
evaluation studies [Patton 1978]."

A crucial factor discussed in these contributions is that of "timing," and
many case stories confirm its importance. The reason why report $X$ was brushed
aside, it is asserted, is that it came at the wrong moment when nobody was
interested in that particular message. Report $Y$, on the other hand, happened to
arrive at a more fortunate time, when everybody was frantically looking for just
that piece of information. When the $Z$ study started, there was a great deal of
enthusiasm about it, but upon its conclusion, it was immediately filed and never
heard of again. Etcetera. The demand for policy information would thus appear
to be liable to great changes over time, and ad hoc explanations for such
changes are frequently proffered. But are there patterns in these variations? I
think so, and in this brief chapter I wish to present some observations of two
such regularities. In the first place, I argue that the political demand for different
types of policy analysis varies over the policy cycle. Second, I suggest that there
are fluctuations in the orientation of analytical knowledge required that are
related to differences in the growth rate of the economy.

In the mind of the policymaker, analytical information competes with and
supplements other kinds of knowledge about established or proposed programs.
The politician's judgment of a policy may be influenced by systematic
evaluation, but it is also the product of personal observations, gossip,
customers' or clients' complaints, newspaper stories, and the like. Projections or
predictions about the expected results of a new policy will be similarly
supplemented with hunches based on the decision maker's experience and
knowledge of similar undertakings. Few formal reports are strong enough to
make an impact unless they "make sense,"—that is, unless they are in
fundamental harmony with the deep-seated beliefs of the audience. Policy
evaluation, in other words, is one particular kind of formalized feedback, and its
influence is shaped in combination with other kinds of formalized feedback
(e.g., accounts, official reports), and above all the massive flow of informal
feedback reaching the decision makers.

The relative weight accorded to formalized feedback in comparison with
informal feedback appears to differ a great deal between personality types
(intellectuals vs. nonintellectuals, readers vs. nonreaders, open vs. closed
minds), but the argument of this chapter is that there are also interesting
intrapersonal variations to reckon with. The same policymaker may be open to

a particular kind of information at one time but not at another, and these changes in receptivity are at least partially predictable.

Receptivity to results—that is, preparedness to take notice of the findings of policy studies, to consider the evidence and recommendations presented, and to utilize such information in the policy formulation process—may be regarded as the most significant indicator of the political demand for policy analysis. Yet there are also other stages in the course of an analytical undertaking at which politicians may demonstrate their interest. Much analytical work is in one way or the other commissioned by politicians, either ad hoc or in the framework of a broad mandate for a certain kind of studies to be carried out by a certain institution (universities, auditing bodies, think tanks, etc.). Some analytical work, furthermore, requires the participation of politicians in various capacities (committee members, respondents, etc.). Without further specification, we may take "political demand" to mean the interest shown in policy analysis by elected politicians and their close associates.

## Fluctuations in the Political Demand for Analysis over the Policy Cycle

Bringing bad news to the king was always a risky undertaking. Though capital punishment is seldom meted out today, more subtle sanctions are still applied for the transmission of unpleasant information. This has some well-known repercussions on the quality of organizational information systems. As Kaufman and others have pointed out, negative facts often fail to reach the top, with the result that the supreme leadership tends to take a more optimistic view of the organization's performance than do the rank and file (Kaufman 1973).

From the pinnacle of the hierarchy, many organizations appear to be semitransparent: You see the light spots but not the dark ones. In the literature on management information systems (MIS), a good deal of thought has been given to the problem of reequilibrating the stream of data flowing from the bottom up by a variety of controls, information requirements, auditing procedures, and the like (Churchman 1971).

Yet, of course, there are kings and kings. Some leaders appear to be fundamentally hostile to negative information; however, others will be more open, curious, and appreciative. Such interpersonal differences aside, there also appear to be great intrapersonal differences in receptivity to unpleasant facts. As all courtiers know, kings have their "moods." People who are close to them usually find a time and a way of breaking the bad news and of eliciting a positive response to negative reports. But when do these golden opportunities occur? Supplicants without intimate knowledge of royal moods and habits spend much time pondering and asking others about the proper timing and tuning of their messages to the king. Given the weight actually attributed to this problem, surprisingly little has been written on the general problem of "speaking truth to power" (Wildavsky). Is it felt to be too much of an art to allow for valid generalizations? Or is it simply that we lack the empirical underpinnings for theory construction? Whatever the explanation, the topic must certainly deserve more attention than it has thus far received. Many efforts in policy analysis, including evaluation, are now wasted not because they are intrinsically poor in method and performance, but because of weaknesses in marketing and delivery. The most accurate and sophisticated prescriptions may needlessly be filed or shelved because of weak timing, packaging, or targeting. Hence, several investments in the field of policy studies would probably be far more profitable if we knew more about the volatile receptivity of the strategic decision makers.

One contingency worth considering in this context is the common changes in attitude over the "policy cycle." Recent scholarship on "agenda setting" or "agenda building" has sharpened our understanding of how social and natural conditions are translated into political issues. At one stage, a given state of affairs (e.g., air pollution) is accepted as fatally inevitable and incurable. In this phase it is not a problem but a predicament; there is no hope for change. Yet, when new information is infused, a different outlook develops and there ensues a process of "problematization," followed in many cases by "politicization." Some progress has been made in measuring the entry of new problems on the political agenda and devising criteria of "issueness" (Cobb and Elder 1972; Crenson 1971; Enloe 1975; Funkhouser 1973; Tarschys 1979). At some intersection in the policy cycle, a major political decision is taken, and the rest is implementation. On many occasions, the pattern may of course be much more intricate; but for the sake of simplicity, we shall assume a pure policy process with a major decision in its center. How, in this case, do attitudes shift over the cycle?

The normal tendency seems to be that certainty about "the right option" increases with proximity to the major decision point. At the early stage of the process, politicians tend to be uncertain and to be groping for solutions. After some exposure to information, they make up their minds, and when the decision is made at least a very large number of decision makers seem to be convinced that they are taking the right position. This conviction remains for some time, but it often erodes in the latter part of the policy cycle. When the decision is implemented, some negative sides of "the right option" will often become visible, and there will be growing doubts about the wisdom of the chosen path. Thus, initial uncertainty reappears as terminal uncertainty which may set off a new policy cycle.

The effect of certainty on the demand for policy analysis is not difficult to divine. The catholic thirst for all kinds of information, regardless of its tendency, will be at its height neither in the first stage of the policy cycle, when the issue has not yet climbed to the upper part of the agenda, nor at the late predecision stage when the positions have already become crystallized. Instead, this interest will be at its peak in the phase between these two stages, and it will recur in the latter part of the policy cycle only when doubts have developed about the soundness of the decision, and only if the issue is hot enough to attract continuing attention.

Between these two stages of relative openness to all kinds of knowledge, there will be a period when the demand for policy analysis is likely to be much more selective. In the midst of a heated controversy of the wisdom of positions already taken, politicians generally constrict their intake of information to facts that support their own standpoint or undermine that of their opponents. One may moralize a bit over this narrow field of vision, but in the midst of a struggle, there is certainly an undeniable economy in the absorption of information that is one-sided and one-sided only. When the shooting is heavy, what you need is good ammunition; a lot of other things you do not need at all, at least not there, not then, and not in that form.

In the early postdecision phase, the lingering taste for selective information is perhaps best explained as a psychological need for reassurance. Communications experts tell us that car buyers tend to read advertisements for the car they have just bought, not so much to gather more information, but to dispel any remaining doubts and to reassure themselves that they made the right decision. There is a similar penchant in many politicians; good news about a measure you recently worked for or bad news about one you recently opposed is likely to receive a favorable reception. Yet after some time, both car buyer and policymaker will probably exhibit a more relaxed attitude to the matter. The process of internal and external justification does not last forever, and most judgments that turn out to be erroneous appear ever more pardonable as time wears on.

We have thus identified three different attitudes to policy-relevant information: the lack of interest displayed when an issue is not on the agenda, the catholic interest for all shades of information shown when the issue is on the agenda but no favored option has yet been chosen, and the selective interest for information pointing in one particular direction typical of the stages immediately preceding and succeeding the decision point. It might be added that the latter condition ("selective interest") prevails not only around such formal decision points as parliamentary rollcalls, but also before and after elections in which particular issues dominate the campaign, or in connection with referenda. When positions crystallize in a fierce political battle, it is quite clear that the different sides lose much of their interest in nonbiased or nonpartisan information.

Polarization appears to affect the amplitude of the attitudinal fluctuations in at least two different ways. In the first place, it tends to increase their depth by reinforcing the preference for supportive over neutral information. When there is a strong clash of views and the fighting camps are locked in fierce struggle, the demand for policy analysis will probably be high but distinct. Second, the length of this selective period will also be extended. By pleading a case very strongly, you may or may not convince your audience, but you are at least likely to convince yourself; views expressed in public have a far better chance of becoming long-lasting convictions than views held silently or presented in a limited company only. Many years after the conclusion of a major discussion, some veterans of the battle remain passionately eager to vindicate their positions. Polarization prolongs the cooling-off period needed to restore the climate in which policy questions can be discussed and considered without undue bias.

In the argument thus far I have assumed the existence of an omnivorous consumer of policy information turning more fastidious but eventually returning to an original indiscriminate voracity. It may be objected that this reasoning makes too much of the intellectual mobility in political life while underrating the strong elements of stability and continuity in the political outlook of policy-makers. Regardless of any policy cycle, an advocate of a particular social, economic, or regional interest will be keen to study findings that are useful to that special segment of society. The old adage, "where you stand depends on where you sit," holds true not only for positions on policy but also for positions on the desirability of policy analysis. Some evaluation shops have firm relationships with institutional constituencies that take an abiding interest in their efforts. Thus, we must note that there are many degrees in the vulnerability of policy studies to the jerks of the political market. Yet even in organizations permanently devoted to the promotion of a particular cause, there are policy cycles of sorts; and some ups and downs in the attention to analysis can often be observed in this setting as well. It seems clear, however, that the policy-cycle fluctuations in the demand for policy analysis discussed in this chapter are more typical of political than of administrative organizations and, among the former, more typical of broad and comprehensive bodies (i.e., governments, parliaments, parties) than of narrow and specialized units.

To summarize this section, the "ideal type" sequence of attitudinal changes among policymakers to policy studies can be said to consist of five stages. In the first stage ("the empty mind") the politician pays no interest to the message because there is little awareness of the issue; the processes of "problematization" and "politicization" have not gone far enough to place the matter on the political agenda. In the second stage ("the open mind") the question has surfaced as a problem and there is concern but no certitude yet about a preferred option. At this point, different strategies are scanned in the search for promising solutions. When such a solution has been found—and in politics they tend to be found quickly, whether doubts can be set at rest or not—there follows a stage ("the closed mind") in which the demand for analytical information narrows down to data supportive of the chosen position. This penchant will be particularly strong if the issue is highly controversial, in which case the third stage may also become protracted. At any rate, it will last from some time before to some time after the major decision point in the policy cycle. In the fourth stage ("back to the open mind") the continuing concern about the issue is mixed with unfavorable impressions of the chosen policy, and a renewed search for solutions is set in motion. A new cycle can start from here, or the old one can close with a fifth stage ("back to the empty mind") in which the matter is no longer considered to be a political issue or even a social problem.

## Fluctuations in the Political Demand for Analysis over the Economic Cycle

The concept of "policy analysis" covers a wide range of intellectual enterprises. In the many typologies that have been proposed in recent years we find such distinctions as (*a*) analysis for policy versus analysis of policy, (*b*) summative versus formative analysis, (*c*) ex ante analysis versus ex post analysis, (*d*) normative versus empirical analysis, (*e*) comparative versus one-shot analysis, and (*f*) external versus internal analysis. Several of these distinctions are also applied to the major subsets of the concept, such as policy evaluation, policy audit, policy review, and policy proposals.

Looking at the geographical dispersion of policy studies, we notice significant national differences not only in their total volume but also in the "mix" of the various species. In the United States, there is a great emphasis on policy evaluation studies, whereas countries like Sweden have concentrated more analytical resources on effectiveness auditing and on prospective policy studies undertaken by government commissions. The difference can be partially explained in cultural and structural terms. The deeper mistrust of government in the United States and the common practice of contracting out the production of public goods and services to private corporations makes it imperative for American legislators to require a substantial amount of reporting on the use of government expenditures. Sweden, on the other hand, is a "fiduciary" democracy where the close cooperation between government and bureaucracy and the openness of all public records tend to reduce the need for control and legitimation through evaluation. Instead, there is a firmly entrenched tradition of looking very carefully at policy innovations through investigative teams composed of the major social interests affected, including the political parties. Western Germany appears to take financial auditing more seriously than many other countries, and has also developed a particular type of experts' reports (*Gutachten*) that play some part in policy formulation. The list could easily be extended; each country has its own institutional pattern of policy analysis, although the phenomena frequently appear under other labels.

Turning from the geographical to the chronological distribution of policy studies, there is a clear increase over time. The last decade in particular has seen the multiplication of projects and the maturation of analytical techniques in many countries. This development can very well be looked upon as an intellectual dispersion process with its center in the Anglo-Saxon countries, but it can also be linked to new needs emerging from the rapid expansion of the public sector. Throughout the Western world, government has been the most successful growing industry of the postwar period. The significant change in its quantitative scope is overshadowed only by the even more impressive qualitative shifts contained in the same process. Through far-going specialization, the modern government has become ever more complex and ramified, and the approaches employed to deal with social, technological, and economic problems have become exceedingly sophisticated. The need for intellectual inputs into the policymaking and policy-implementing processes has grown more than one would expect from looking at the expansion in terms of sheer volume.

Yet, what will happen now as the growth of government appears to be grinding to a halt in the OECD countries? The recurring oil shocks of the last decade and other disturbances in the world economy have, at least temporarily, removed some of the fundamental preconditions for continued policy development along earlier lines. The prevailing moods have shifted significantly as conservative or nonsocialist governments have been established in a large number of countries, and austerity measures have been signaled and carried through by virtually all governments regardless of political color. My conjecture is that this development is likely to produce a shift in the demand for policy analysis toward types of study other than those hitherto favored. Some support for this hypothesis has been presented in a recent report by a Swedish government commission on public policy planning (SOU 1979, p. 61).

A principal contention in this Swedish report is that a widening rift is appearing between the supply and demand for policy analysis. It is not a question of too little or too much being analyzed, or of analysis being applied to the wrong policy areas. Rather, the problem is a growing disparity between the objectives and orientation of the policy studies produced and those required, and this mismatch is linked both to the permanence of certain "standard operating procedures" in the analytical industry and to the sectoral interests involved in the analytical process (Allison 1971). Over several decades of rapid social reform, the main aim of policy analysis has been to develop and refine the tools of government intervention in the economy, and to produce master plans for new fields of public services. A subsidiary task has been to enhance the efficiency and effectiveness of government operations, a function carried out largely through computerization.

Whereas the expansive tendency in this intellectual activity was in good harmony with the political ambitions of the 1960s and the 1970s, it is no longer in tune with the needs of a government participating in the international movement of cutting down on public expenditures. Hence, there exists a gap

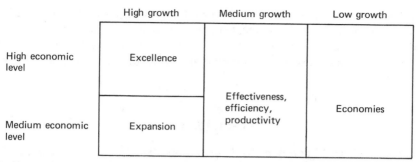

**FIGURE 20.1.** *The shifting goals in the political demand for policy analysis under different economic conditions.*

between demand and supply: while the analytical apparatus goes on grinding out proposals for quantitative or qualitative reforms which cannot be utilized because the funds are missing, the government is in dire need of well-prepared proposals for savings that are simply not coming forth. Why aren't they coming forth? The apparent reasons range from lack of training to lack of incentives to lack of encouragement and positive orders from the government.

A tentative generalization derived from this observation would be that the demand for policy analysis is linked to the growth rate of the economy in such a way that a particular economic situation will produce a need for a particular kind of policy information. Under conditions of stable and lasting growth, the main orientation of public policymaking is the extension and improvement of public services and benefits, and the knowledge required will have to correspond to these objectives. Policy development under growth frequently assumes the form of planning, and the plans typically outline the expansion of certain measures over a certain period of time. Second, under conditions of weaker and unstable growth, more attention is given to the rational use of resources; policy analysis is accordingly expected to provide information promoting efficiency, effectiveness, and productivity. Under a third condition—zero-growth or a weak decline in national output—even such endeavors prove insufficient, and politicians become increasingly interested in the spotting and examination of potential cuts in public expenditures.

These suggestions are summarized in Figure 20.1. What is depicted is, of course, merely the shifting emphases in the political demand for policy information, and there is no intention of saying that only one type of information is desired in a given economic situation. There are at least three reasons why the structure of demand is much fuzzier in the real world than it is in this figure. First, there are many policy studies where the goals are less explicit or less clearly defined than here; second, there will always be residual interests pressing for qualitative and quantitative growth in certain policy areas, even under stagnation or decline in the total economy; and third, there will often be lags in the attitudes of policymakers toward political goals. For the same reasons—and this is a second tentative generalization derived from the current mismatch—similar lags and distortions are likely to appear in the supply of policy analysis.

## Conclusion

The emergence of policy analysis is an important element in the qualitative growth of government activities. Rational collective action requires knowledge about the costs and benefits of various policy options. Yet, what is the outlook for policy analysis in an age of tax revolts, expenditure cuts, and austerity packages? The suggestion in this chapter is that evaluators and other analysts might increase the effectiveness of their efforts by paying more attention to fluctuations in the political demands for analysis. In the first place, there are oscillations related to the policy cycle: as issues mount in importance on the political agenda and views become polarized, the receptivity of politicians to analytical information frequently becomes more selective. In the second place, there are variations linked to the long-term growth rate in the economy. With expectations for the 1980s running low, we can look forward to a surging demand for knowledge about cutback management, policy termination, priority setting, decremental budgeting, value-for-money auditing, and similar sinister topics and approaches. Will the supply side be able to adjust to these needs? If not, the outlook for policy analysis in the next decade may not be much brighter than the outlook for policymaking.

## References

Allison, G.T. 1971. *Essence of decision: Explaining the Cuban missile crisis.* Boston: Little, Brown and Company.

Churchman, C.W. 1971. *The design of inquiring systems.* New York: Basic Books.

Cobb, R.W., and Elder, C.D. 1972. *Participation in American politics: The dynamics of agenda-building.* Boston: Allen and Bacon.

Cohen D.K., and Garet M.S. 1975. Reforming educational policy with applied social research. *Harvard Educational Review* 45: 17–41.

Crenson, M.A. 1971. *The un-politics of air pollution: A study of non-decisionmaking in the cities.* Baltimore: The Johns Hopkins Press.

Deitchman, S. 1976. *The best-laid schemes: A tale of social research and bureaucracy.* Cambridge, Mass.: The MIT Press.

Enloe, C.H. 1975. *The politics of pollution in a comparative perspective: Ecology and power in four nations.* New York: David McKay Company.

Funkhouser, R.G. 1973. The issues of the sixties: An exploratory study in the dynamics of public opinion. *Public Opinion Quarterly* 37: 62–75.

House, E. 1972. The conscience of educational evaluation. *Teachers College Record* 73: 405–414.

Kaufman, H. 1973. *Administrative feedback: Monitoring subordinates behavior.* Washington: The Brookings Institution.

Patton, M.Q. 1978. *Utilization—focused evaluation.* London and Beverly Hills: Sage.

Rich, R.F. 1977. Uses of social science information by federal bureaucrats: Knowledge for action vs. knowledge for understanding. In *Using social research in public policy making,* ed. C.H. Weiss. Lexington: Lexington Books. Pp. 199–211.

Sharpe, L.J. 1977. The social scientist and policymaking: Some cautionary thoughts and transatlantic reflections. In *Using social research in public policy making,* ed. C.H. Weiss. Lexington: Lexington Books. Pp. 37–54.

SOU 1974. *Förnyelse genom omprövning.* Kungälv: Liber. An English summary of this report *(Policy innovation through policy reappraisal)* is available from the Swedish Ministry of Finance.

Tarschys, D. 1979. *The Soviet political agenda: Problems and priorities 1950–1970.* London and Basingstoke: Macmillan.

Weinberg, H. 1979. Using policy analysis in congressional budgeting. In *Evaluation in Legislation,* ed. F.M. Zweig, Beverly Hills and London: Sage. Pp. 28–44.

Weiss, C.H. 1975. Evaluation research in the political context. In *Handbook of Evaluation Research,* eds. E.L. Struening and M. Guttentag, Beverly Hills: Sage.

Wholey, J.S. 1970. *Federal evaluation policy.* Washington DC: Urban Institute.

Wildavsky, A. 1980. *The art and craft of policy analysis.* London and Basingstoke: Macmillan.

# 21

# Hardness of Choice[1]

## ERIK COHEN

## Introduction

All human conduct involves choice, but some choices are harder to make than others. This chapter examines this usually neglected aspect of decision making, and relates it to some fundamental problems in the structure of pluralistic value systems. It discusses one facet of the wider problem of value incommensurability: The problem of decisions between values in the absence of a common standard of comparison, such as utility or pleasure, by the help of which such values could be traded-off rationally. I am currently engaged in a wider study of this topic, which has been seldom explicitly addressed in sociology (Cohen and Ben Ari, forthcoming). Though the present chapter, an offshoot of the wider study, deals with one facet of the problem on an abstract, theoretical level, my concern with the problem itself grew out of a variety of more concrete topics of research, such as work on the Israeli kibbutz (Cohen 1966) and social ecology (Cohen 1976), all of which pointed, in different ways, to the importance of value incommensurability in various social or cultural systems. Since it relates to some of the basic premises on which evaluation rests, the problem is of relevance to evaluation, and hence to the conditions under which evaluation of decisions is, or is not, possible.

Earlier decision-making theory assumed, at least tacitly, a single master criterion (value or standard of comparison) which a rational decision maker

[1] This chapter is a further step in the sociological analysis of the problem of value incommensurability, begun in Cohen and Ben Ari (forthcoming).

EVALUATING THE WELFARE STATE:
SOCIAL AND POLITICAL PERSPECTIVES

should maximize. Recent decision-making theory, increasingly plagued by the complexities of concrete situations of choice, eventually gave up the simple single-criterion models in favor of multicriteria ones, such as multiattribute or multicriteria evaluation, multiple criteria problem solving or decision making, or nontransitive multiple preference theory (e.g., Fishburn 1978; Huber 1979; Keen 1977; Keeney and Raiffa 1976; Yilmaz 1978). Though some authors talk of optimization in multicriteria decision making (e.g., Keen 1977), their models are in fact not fully calculable; rather, by clarifying the structure of the decision-making process, they help to pinpoint the kind of subjective decisions (i.e., "hard choices") that the decision maker has to make. Evaluation of such subjective decisions may follow two principal tracks. One is to take the hard choice (the basic subjective decision) for granted, and merely evaluate the manner in which its implications were worked out. The calculus is based on the basic hard choice, which yields a gamut of technical or professional decisions— "soft choices" in our terminology (Cohen and Ben Ari, forthcoming). For example, after a hard choice was made to prefer economic development to environmental protection in a given situation, the various soft choices concerning the realization of the goal of economic development can still be evaluated in terms of their respective environmental impacts. Alternatively, however, evaluation may attempt to question or criticize the basic subjective decision, the hard choice itself. To return to our example, it may relate to the question, given the potential costs of economic development in terms of environmental degradation, in a given situation, which of the two goals should have been preferred? Although evaluation mostly takes the first track, we shall discuss here some fundamental problems inherent in the second track—the evaluation of hard choices.

## The Hardness of Hard Choices

Hard choices are faced in situations of value incommensurability. They are "hard," because they are not rationally calculable. However, it is a commonplace observation that, although incommensurable ultimate values clash in many situations of social life, not all hard choices appear to be equally hard. What, then, determines the hardness of hard choices?[2] The hardness is obviously influenced by the "momentousness" of the choice, which again will depend on such factors as the social saliency of the values involved and the concrete exigencies of the choice situation—whether the choice involves

[2] In what follows, I am not interested in psychological questions like what personality traits cause one person to find the making of choices harder than another, or why for one person a given kind of choice is harder than another, but the opposite holds for another person. Rather, my intent is to deal with "structurally derived hardness, that is, hardness produced by the structure of the value system on the one hand and of the social consensus on the other.

indivisibles, or has irreversible consequences, and so on. However, not all equally momentous choices are equally hard. There is something in the nature of the decision-making situation which makes for different degrees of hardness of choice. This has to do with the structure of social consensus concerning the choice, and hence with the extent to which the decision maker may merely "reproduce" a socially accepted decision, or whether he is called upon to "produce" a new decision without social guidance (Giddens 1976, pp. 358–359). Such situations exist when new problems of choice arise, or when no socially agreed precepts exist concerning the acceptable rates of trade-off between values, even where the choice itself is not new.

In the following we shall deal only with the latter case, which will be stated in a formal model and represented graphically. Assume the existence of an intransitive (Huber 1979; Tversky 1969) system of values ($A$, $B$, $C$, etc.), arranged in a lexigraphic semiorder (Luce 1978; Tversky 1969, p. 32).[3] That is, consider a system of values in which there is no common standard of comparison by which the trade-offs between values (the cost in values $B$, $C$, etc., of an increase of benefit in $A$) could be unequivocally determined; still, the decision maker is not fully commited to the maximization of the highest-ranking value ($A$), and is willing to forego some of it to realize the lower-ranking values ($B$, $C$, $D$, etc). He or she is then faced by a hard choice, since there are no rules in such a system by which to determine rationally the trade-offs between the values. Our problem is: What determines the hardness of the decision maker's choice in such indeterminate situations?

Let me illustrate the model with a concrete example. Suppose the values in the system are security, freedom, equality (in that order). When a decision maker faces the need to trade off security and freedom, what determines the hardness of choice? I argue that, other things being equal, the hardness of choice will be related to the range of possible rates of trade-off between the two values, and will be different for different rates of trade-off. The theoretical relationship between the range of all possible trade-offs of values $A$ and $B$ (e.g., security and freedom) and hardness of choice is graphically represented in Figure 21.1.

On the abscissa in Figure 21.1 appear all possible rates of trade-off between the values $A$ and $B$: They range from an immense gain in $A$ for a negligible cost in $B$ at the left, to a negligible gain in $A$ for an immense cost in $B$ at the right. On the ordinate appears the hardness of choice inherent in each possible rate of trade-off between $A$ and $B$.[4]

---

[3] Although I formulated my argument for a system of values in a lexigraphic semiorder, the same would hold a fortiori for the extreme case of apparently ultimate values in no order whatsoever; however, the assumption of a lexigraphic semiorder is a fairly realistic one, whereas that of an unordered group of values is not.

[4] The choice of a normal curve in Figure 21.1 to illustrate my argument is arbitrary; to the best of my knowledge, no empirical evidence exists as yet concerning the actual shape of such curves. For the main parameters along which the curve may vary, see Figure 21.2.

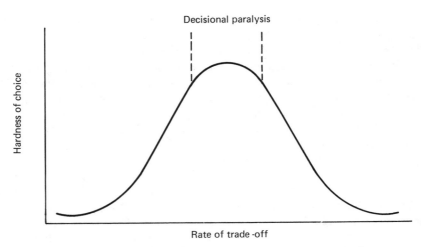

**FIGURE 21.1** *This graph shows the relationship between "hardness of choice" and rates of trade-off between incommensurable values A and B.*

The hardness of choice is low at the extremes of the figure: When the benefits in terms of *A* are socially agreed to be very high relative to the costs in *B*, it is relatively "easy" to decide on *A*; and when the opposite is the case, it is relatively easy to decide on *B*. The hardness of choice increases as the rates of trade-off diminish in either direction and culminates toward the center of the diagram, when the situation of choice presents the decision maker with an acute dilemma. Indeed, in situations involving indivisibilities and irreversibilities (e.g., life and death situations, such as the decision to go to war), the hardness of choice may be so overwhelming that the decision maker becomes incapable of choosing, and enters a state of "decisional paralysis" (dotted line in Figure 21.1). The dilemma appears to be the logical opposite of the illusory "donkey's dilemma": Whereas the donkey is presumably unable to decide between two equally attractive, completely *alike* heaps of fodder, the decision maker is genuinely unable to decide between two crucial, but completely *different* outcomes. Nevertheless, like the donkey, the decision maker, if and when he overcomes his decisional paralysis, "picks" rather than "chooses" one of the alternatives—though it is a "hard" or "existential" rather than trivial picking. (Ullman–Margalit and Morgenbesser, 1977).[5] I shall return to the problem of evaluation of such picking in the concluding section of this chapter.

[5]This kind of picking is called deeper-level picking by Ullman–Margalit and Morgenbesser (1977, pp. 783). In words "this is different from [trivial] picking...in that it is not because of *symmetry* of preferences that one picks but because of the *absence* in principle of preferences that one picks [p. 783m]." Such an absence is due to lack of a common standard of comparison between values.

Our analysis makes it possible to pinpoint situations in which even a conformist decision maker will have to "produce" decisions, rather than to "reproduce" socially prescribed ones. The low degree of hardness of choice at both extremes of the curve in Figure 21.1 signifies that a conformist decision maker takes it for granted that the costs, in terms of one value, of realizing the other, are reasonably acceptable; such acceptability does not, however, reflect any universal absolutes, but only the value structure of the decision maker's culture.[6] In this portion of the range the decision maker, in fact, merely "reproduces" socially agreed decisions rather than "produces" new ones. Toward the middle of the range, however, consensus on the acceptability of trade-offs weakens, and no clear guidelines for a decision exist: The growing hardness of choices here indicates the absence of social consensus and hence the need for the decision maker to "produce" a decision. The shape of the curve for any pair of incommensurable values thus reflects the structure of social consensus regarding the acceptability of the different rates of trade-off between them. Three parameters of that structure should be noted, as shown in Figure 21.2.

1. The inclination of the curve reflects the sharpness of the boundaries of social consensus (i.e., of the points on the range of rates of trade-off) at which there ceases to be consensus that either of the two values controls the decision— *without there being agreement that the other value takes over control*. This point resembles what Kaplan (1978, pp. 61–66) calls thresholds. Beyond the threshold the choice becomes socially "wide open"; this is, to use Kaplan's term (p. 61), a "gray area" on the range of rates of trade-off, in which the hardness of choice steeply increases until the opposite threshold is met—the point at which consensus exists, that control passes to the other value.[7] This can be illustrated with out previous example of security and freedom: Consensus may exist that the freedom of citizens should not include the right to disclose "secrets of state" that could impair "national security" (lower threshold); also, the first point notwithstanding, their freedom should not be curtailed in the name of securing those "secrets of state" by unwarranted house searches, listening devices, and the like (upper threshold). Between these thresholds lies the gray area, in respect to which opinions differ: Decisions concerning measures to safeguard security "sufficiently" without impairing "too much" individual freedom are much harder to make than decisions beyond the thresholds. The crisper the definition of the threshold (e.g., by law, religious custom, or

---

[6]Cf. Kaplan (1978): "Clearly, we shall not start a nuclear war to rescue one person [p.60]." Although the decision between "rescuing persons" and starting a nuclear war is, generally speaking, a hard one in Kaplan's view, this is not really the case at the extremes, since he assumes it to be a matter of consensus that the rescue of one person is not worth a nuclear war.

[7]Cf. Kaplan (1978): "Events [decision in our context] that occur in the gray areas—those not clearly above or below one or the other threshold—are a source of human tragedy and often become the subject of great drama...[p.61]."

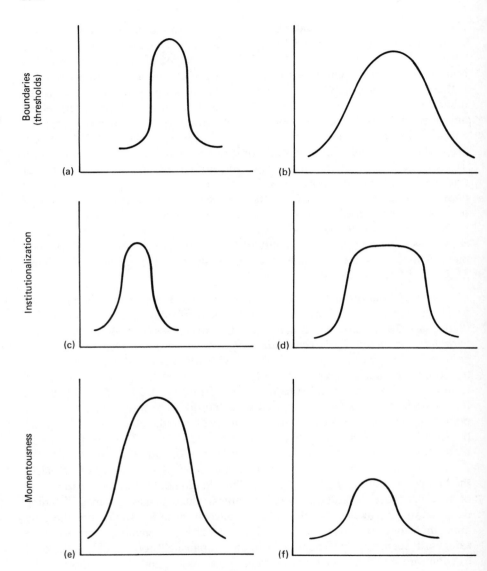

**FIGURE 21.2** *These graphs show parameters of hardness of choice, through differently shaped curves.*

convention) the steeper the inclination of the curve (Figure 21.1*a*); the fuzzier the definition, the flatter the curve and there is no recognizable threshold (Figure 21.1*b*).

2. The width of the curve reflects the degree to which the trade-off between the values is institutionalized—that is, the extent to which the mutual implications of any pair of values are socially agreed upon. In conventional sociological theory such agreement is often tacitly assumed—for example, that the socially accepted restrictions on freedom implied in a social definition of security dovetail with the restrictions on security implied in the social definition of freedom. In actual fact, however, such definitions are often discrepant and not integrated—thereby creating the gray area of hard choices between the thresholds. The smaller the discrepancy, the narrower that area (Figure 21.2*c*). The greater the discrepancy, the wider that area (Figure 21.2*d*).

3. Finally, the height of the curve reflects the socially felt momentousness of the choices within the gray area between the thresholds, that is, the area where no social consensus exists concerning the acceptable rates of trade-off. It is, then, only in this section of the curve that the momentousness of the choice determines its hardness: The more momentous the choice, the greater the hardness experienced by the decision maker (Figure 21.2*e*); the less momentous the choice, the less the hardness (Figure 21.2*f*). Thus, other things being equal, problems of trade-off between security and freedom—two highly salient values in many modern, industrialized, and democratic societies—will probably, in the gray area, pose harder choices than, for example, problems of trade-off between such less salient values as public welfare and natural beauty (in cases where the provision of public amenities conflicts with preservation of natural sites). In postmodern societies, however, the saliency of the latter choice, in comparison with the former, may well increase, posing more momentous, and hence harder, choices. Exceptionally momentous choices in the gray area may heighten the decision maker's dilemma to such a degree that he or she is caught in a state of decisional paralysis.

So far we have assumed a conforming decision maker. If we drop the assumption of conformity, the hardness of choice facing the decision maker will no longer reflect the structure of social consensus regarding the range of rates of trade-off between the values. Will the decision maker's hardness of choice thereby be augmented or diminished? The answer depends on the structure of the decision maker's value system. Insofar as his or her value system—like the society's—is also intransitive and values are ordered in a lexigraphic semiorder, this person will face harder choices than the conformist throughout the range of rates of trade-off, since all decisions will, in principle, be of the nature of "productions" and not merely "reproductions" of socially agreed decisions. Insofar, however, as the structure of his or her value system differs from that of society's, the hardness of choices will decline in direct proportion to its internal consistency: The more transitive it is, or the more the values tend to be ordered in a full lexigraphic order, the easier choices will become—even in those cases where they deviate markedly from the existing social consensus (i.e., from the extremes of the curve in Figure 21.1). To take only the extreme case of "value rational" (*wertrational*) decision makers: their value system consists of only a single, paramount value which they will maximize, whatever the society's perception of the cost incurred in terms of other values salient for society. In theory, such decision makers face no hard choices at all, even where their decisions are the opposite of the socially preferred ones—as when they decide in favor of their paramount value $A$ in Figure 21.1 in the righthand section of the curve, an area for which there is social consensus that $B$ should be chosen, owing to the (socially perceived) prohibitive costs of even a slight increment in $A$. Looking at "value rationality" from this angle enables us to transform it into a continuous variable, instead of the qualitatively different discrete ideal type that it is usually viewed as. One can define a person as more value rational the more he or she is prepared to stick to his or her paramount value $A$, even in face of a social consensus that, owing to prohibitive costs, the opposite value $B$ should be chosen. The advantage of this definition is that, empirically, only few if any individuals would be prepared to stick to their paramount values *whatever* the costs, as socially perceived. But there certainly are individuals who would go to various lengths, in disregard of such costs, in pursuit of their paramount value. Our formulation thus provides a way to measure the degree to which an individual is value rational.

## The Evaluation and Judgment of Hard Choices

It follows from the preceding analysis that choices can be evaluated, in a strict sense, only if one or both of the following conditions exist:

1. There exists a general standard of comparison, such as "efficiency" or "utility," which makes an unequivocal ranking of choices possible (evaluation of rationality)
2. in the absence of such a standard (i.e., where the application of a standard of efficiency, utility, etc., is not possible or sufficient to assess the choice), there exists a high degree of consensus on the preference of one choice owing to the prohibitive costs (as socially perceived) of the other (evaluation of optimality).

When, however, neither a general standard is applicable nor consensus exists—namely, where the hardness of choice is particularly severe—the choice cannot be evaluated, either in terms of rationality or of optimality. The evaluator's criticism will in such a case represent nothing but his or her own hard choice in a socially "open" situation, that is, a choice devoid of consensus concerning the relative weight of the costs and benefits to be traded-off in the decision.

I illustrate this conclusion by an example from the general area of welfare policy. Suppose the goal of a given welfare program is to "help people to help themselves." Given that goal, a fairly crisp criterion for the determination of success of any specific project within that program would be its "multiplier effect," that is, how much self-help has been generated by a given amount of initial help. The relative merits of a prospective project could thus be evaluated in terms of the ratio between self-help and initial help (evaluation of rationality). The propensity for self-help, however, is not equally distributed among the various categories of people receiving initial help; thus, such a program could increase inequalities between various welfare populations. Consensus may exist, however, that a "small" increase in inequalities is a price well worth paying for a "considerable" increase in self-help; hence, the evaluator may find a proposed project A, with a large multiplier effect preferable to project B which has a much lower multiplier effect, even if the latter generates somewhat fewer inequalities than the former (evaluation of optimality). If, however, project A creates significantly higher inequalities than project B, no general consensus may exist concerning their relative merits. The decision maker faces a situation of considerable hardness of choice, and whichever project is eventually decided upon, the choice cannot be evaluated either in terms of rationality or of optimalilty. Asked to profer an opinion as to which choice is "better," evaluators in such situations—provided that they comprehend the difficulties and act honestly—are reduced to the lame response that this is a matter of subjective "value preferences."

In the absence of the possibility for a rational evaluation of hard choices, is there indeed nothing else one can say about them except that they are "subjective"? Does this preclude any further discussion or criticism of the decisions? This is a difficult question, and I can, in conclusion, only indicate a possible way out of the subjectivist impasse. It seems useful to distinguish here between the "evaluation," strictly speaking, of hard choices, and their "judgment." Even if they cannot be evaluated, hard choices can possibly be judged, in a sense analogous to that in which the merits of works of art or of new scientific theories can be judged. Crucial for such a judgment are the reasons or justifications forwarded by the decision maker to explain or justify the decision. Such judgments would involve not specific criteria of evaluation, but such diffuse notions as the perceived wisdom of a decision, or its boldness, attractiveness, or potential creativity. Judgment of hard choices in these terms would be similar to the judgment of new artistic productions. But the matter is not thereby necessarily relegated into the realm of mere aesthetics: A particularly creative decision, taken in a situation of hard choice, may represent an important new social "production," offering a novel solution to a critical situation, and opening up new avenues to deal with fundamental social dilemmas. If such a decision is also retrospectively perceived as having been wise, it may become an exemplary or prototypical one, to be "reproduced" by later decision makers in similar situations. It could thus become a historical turning point for an emergent social consensus on the issue at hand. The artfulness of judgment, in contrast to the calculativeness of evaluation, consists precisely in the ability to assess the wisdom and creativeness, or any other diffuse quality, of hard choices. Although one cannot evaluate precisely the outcomes of such choices, one can probably rank them in terms of their diffuse excellence and thus select those worth of further consideration, and, possibly, emulation.

ACKNOWLEDGMENT

Thanks are due to M. Inbar for his useful comments.

# References

Cohen, E. 1966. Progress and communality: Value dilemmas in the collective movement. *International Review of Community Development* 15–16: 3–18.

Cohen, E. 1976. Environmental orientations: A multidimensional approach to social ecology. *Current Anthropology* 17: 49–70.

Cohen E., and Ben Ari E. Forthcoming. "Hard choices": A sociological analysis of value incommensurability.

Fishburn, P.C. 1978. A survey of multiattribute multicriterion evaluation theories. In *Multiple criteria problem solving*, ed. S. Zionts, New York: Springer.

Giddens, A. 1976. Functionalism: *Après la lutte. Social Research* 43:325–366.

Huber, O. 1979. Nontransitive multidimensional preferences: Theoretical analysis of a model. *Theory and Decision* 10: 147–165.

Kaplan, M.A. 1978. What is a life worth? *Ethics*, 89: 58–65.

Keen, P.G.W. 1977. The evolving concept of optimality. *TIMS Studies in the Management Sciences* 6: 31–57.

Keeney, R.L., and Raiffa, H. 1976. *Decision with multiple objectives: Preferences and value trade-off.* New York: Wiley.

Luce, R.D. 1978. Lexicographic trade-off structures. *Theory and Decision* 9: 187–193.

Tversky, A. 1969. Intransitivity of preference. *Psychological Review* 76: 31–48.

Ullman–Margalit, E., and Morgenbesser, S. 1977. Picking and choosing. *Social Research* 44: 757–785.

Yilmaz, M.R. 1978. Multiattribute utility theory: A survey. *Theory and Decision* 9: 317–347.

# 22

# The Political Culture of Social Welfare Policy

WILLIAM A. GAMSON AND KATHRYN E. LASCH

By 1969, welfare had become a major issue in American politics. The number of welfare recipients had doubled during the decade and welfare roles were rising at the rate of 1 million persons annually. Existing programs were under attack from those of many different political tendencies—each, of course, emphasizing different interpretations of what was going on and why.

In the summer of 1969, the fledgling Nixon administration, amidst great fanfare, announced a plan for sweeping welfare reform. This Family Assistance Plan (FAP) represented a classic Nixon ploy. Critics to the left were confounded by the inclusion of a guaranteed minimum income provision; conservative critics were lured by the promise of putting welfare recipients to work and dismantling welfare bureaucracy. Indeed, the initial reaction suggested that the Family Assistance Plan had found a broad consensus and would lead to the most sweeping welfare reform since the early New Deal.

In the next 2 years, this ball unraveled. The apparent consensus proved illusory, the FAP's chief backers within the administration lost influence, and, ultimately, Nixon turned his attention elsewhere, letting welfare reform languish. This interesting story continues, but it is not the story that concerns us and it has been told elsewhere (see Bowler 1974, Heffernan 1974, and Marmor and Rein 1972).

The story of this aborted effort at welfare reform unfolded in a particular symbolic environment. Political discourse surrounding the welfare issue draws on a catalogue of available idea elements, and makes use of a variety of symbolic devices to express these ideas. This set of idea elements, organized and clustered in various ways, comprises the culture of an issue.

EVALUATING THE WELFARE STATE:
SOCIAL AND POLITICAL PERSPECTIVES

Events such as the introduction and defeat of the Family Assistance Plan provide an occasion for display of the culture of social welfare policy. Public officials and their political opponents display it in their speeches and presentations, journalists display it in their commentary on these events. Hence, the set of events concerning the Family Assistance Plan makes this culture visible and provides us with an opportunity to analyze it.

Clearly, an issue culture is rooted in time and space. We would not expect the issue culture surrounding social welfare in the United States to be the same in 1970 as in 1935. Nor would we expect the culture of the welfare issue to be the same in different countries. On the contrary, we would assume that differences in political and religious traditions would produce a different political culture for discourse about social welfare.

## The Nature of Issue Cultures

The idea elements in a culture do not exist in isolation but are grouped into more or less harmonious clusters or interpretive packages. The different idea elements in a given package mutually support and reinforce each other. Frequently, it is possible to suggest the package as a whole by the use of a single prominent element.

We begin our analysis of political culture by dividing these packages into two parts. The framing half deals with the gestalt or pattern-organizing nature of the political culture. A number of writers have employed similar concepts to analyze this framing process. Edelman (1964, 1971, 1977), for example, has "sensitized" us to the importance of political symbolism in providing meaning to political events. Bennett (1975) attempts to capture this idea with the concept of political scenario, inspired by the work of Burke (1969). He suggests that political scenarios provide a "lay theoretical framework in which to organize the sense data of politics [p.65]." He points to the use of paradigmatic or compelling examples to provide a highly abstract, symbolic container to deal with an unfolding reality.

The second half of the package deals with reasoning and justifications for positions. Where framing devices suggest integration and synthesis into wholes, reasoning devices emphasize analysis and differentiation into parts. A complex whole is broken down into discrete causes and consequences in temporal sequence. These devices are pieces of a potential argument that one might make in justifying or arguing for a particular position on an issue.

An interpretive package has a core consisting of an overall frame and position that defines it. The frame suggests a central organizing idea for understanding events related to the issue in question. For example, the Johnson administration's package on Vietnam offered a core frame in which the Vietnam struggle was to be understood as the United States' attempt to meet the challenge of indirect aggression by a worldwide, Soviet-led communist adversary. This framework allows for some differences on the best way to meet this challenge—through counterinsurgent special forces, airpower, or other means—but the common position endorsed the necessity of making an effective military response in resisting the challenge.

One can display a package other than through directly invoking its core. Through political usage, we come to recognize the package as a whole by the use of a variety of symbolic devices (also termed *tropes* or *figures of speech*) that display its characteristic elements. Every package has a *signature*—a set of elements that suggest its core frame and position in a shorthand fashion. The falling-domino metaphor is a good example for the Vietnam package.

These signature elements of a package are the condensing symbols by which it is displayed. As Willett (1980) suggests, in discussing art in the Third Reich, "Style is crucial, just as language is crucial; the Nazis so put their mark on them that a few words in a speech or article, a quick look at a building, statue or picture, could imply all the rest of the ideological package, and with it the measures to which that package led [p. 6]."

We divide our signature elements into framing and reasoning devices. The devices that suggest a framework within which to view the issue are metaphors, exemplars, catchphrases, depictions, and visual images. The devices that provide justifications or reasons for a general position are roots, consequences, and appeals to principle. Each of these requires a brief comment and example.

1. *Metaphors.* A metaphor always has two parts—the principal subject that the metaphor is intended to illuminate and the associated subject that the metaphor evokes to enhance our understanding. The associated subject contains what Lakoff and Johnson (1979) call entailments. These entailments are characteristics of the associated subject that, by implication, attach to the principal subject.

We distinguish two kinds of entailments—attributes and relationships—and this distinction suggests two kinds of metaphors. In *dynamic* metaphors, there are two or more entities in the associated subject, acting in relation to each other. In *single-valued* metaphors, the focus is simply on the attributes of a single associated subject. Political cartoons are a rich source of dynamic metaphors and we will use them in illustrating packages on the welfare issue.

2. *Exemplars.* Real events of the past or present are frequently used to frame the principal subject. As with metaphors, exemplars may be dynamic or single-valued. The Korean War was probably the most important exemplar for the Vietnam example, with Munich receiving some play as well.

3. *Catchphrases.* Commentators on events frequently try to capture their essence in a single theme statement, tagline, title, or slogan that is intended to suggest a general frame. Catchphrases are attempted summary statements about

the principal subject. "Invasion from the North" was the title of the State Department paper produced just prior to the Johnson administration escalation of the Vietnam War in 1965. "If we don't stop them in Vietnam, we'll be fighting them on the beaches of Malibu" is another memorable catchphrase for this package.

4. *Depictions.* Packages have certain principal subjects that they characterize in a particular fashion. They may do this through single-valued metaphors or exemplars or simply through some colorful string of modifiers. Lyndon Johnson depicted the critics of his Vietnam policy as "nervous nellies" and a later administration gave us "nattering nabobs of negativism."

5. *Visual images.* We include here icons and other visual images that suggest the core of a package. The American flag is the most obvious icon associated with this Vietnam package but there are a number of visual images that suggest its frame—for example, imagery underlining the communist nature of the adversary in Vietnam.

6. *Roots.* A given package has a characteristic analysis of the causal dynamics underlying the set of events. The packages may differ in the locus of this root—that is, in the particular place in a funnel of causality to which the root calls attention. The root provided in the Vietnam package is that of a military attack by a Soviet proxy against a United States ally that is an independent country.

7. *Consequences.* A given package has a characteristic analysis of the consequences that will flow from different policies. Again, there may be differences in whether short- or long-term consequences are the focus. The signature consequences emphasized in the Vietnam illustration are the negative effects on American national security of a communist takeover of South Vietnam.

8. *Appeals to principle.* Packages rely on characteristic moral appeals and uphold certain general precepts. In the Vietnam example, the principles appealed to included the defense of the weak and innocent against unprovoked aggression and the honoring of one's word and commitment to friends.

One can summarize the culture of an issue in a *signature matrix* in which the rows represent the cores of different packages and the columns represent the eight different types of symbolic device. The cell entries in this matrix are the signature elements of the different packages—for example, a characteristic exemplar of a given package.

Interpretive packages are produced in a complex process involving an interaction between sources and journalists. Although this social process is not a direct focus of our research, our examination of cultural elements is organized in part on some assumptions about the social and political system.

Our view of the political system utilizes distinctions made by students of collective action (Gamson 1975, McCarthy and Zald 1977, Tilly 1978). There is a bounded polity consisting of authorities and members who have vested interests and routine, low-cost access to authorities. Beyond the boundary, there are challengers or social movement organizations attempting to mobilize some constituency for collective action, directed toward influencing outcomes produced through the polity.

These actors—authorities, members, and challengers—utilize the cultural system in their efforts to achieve their goals. More specifically, they attempt to further the careers of particular interpretive packages and act as sponsor or organizational carriers for some of these packages. It is useful to identify packages with particular sponsors. For example, we expect to identify one or more *official* packages on an issue—packages that reflect the frames and positions of public officials who are protagonists in the set of events. The opposition political party, or established interest groups, may be identified with other packages. Finally, there may be packages associated with challengers and, perhaps, found only in the publications that they control and direct to their own constituency.

Frequently, these various actors in the symbolic arena are organizations with media or public relations specialists. Such professionals maintain continuing relationships with journalists who cover their organization. Many have previously worked as journalists. To be effective, their present role requires that they become attuned to the news needs of the mass media representatives with whom they routinely must deal. In meeting these needs, they supply, with varying degrees of skill, the elements of interpetive packages about the issues that engage their interests. An apt metaphor or catchphrase will be picked up and amplified through the media—serving the interest of both sources and journalists in presenting events in a context of meaning. Sources, then, are one major fount of cultural elements.

But journalists are themselves highly active in organizing such elements. Indeed, there are journalistic roles that emphasize precisely this task. Political cartoonists, political columnists, and editorial writers, for example, are evaluated by their fellow journalists and readers for their talent in this regard. Halberstam (1979) describes the admiration that his colleagues feel for Peter Lisagor of the *Chicago Daily News* as a coiner of succinct catchphrases: "It was Lisagor—smart, quick, verbal—who always seemed to be able to define an event in a few words. Other reporters were always quoting Lisagor [p.669]." Columnists with a light touch—Art Buchwald and Russell Baker, for example—are especially creative in generating extended, dynamic metaphors.

Constructing a signature matrix is only the first step in analyzing the culture of an issue. This culture can then be measured systematically through a content analysis of media materials. The signature matrix provides the categories used in this analysis. The study employs two measures of issue culture: (a) *prominence of display* is based on a sample that includes television network coverage, the three major newsmagazines, and the metropolitan newspapers available in a particular locale, and each of these sources is weighted by circulation or audience figures; (b) *media usage* is based on a sample of nationally syndicated columnists and cartoonists. Ultimately, we plan to integrate this analysis with a study of popular discourse about the same set of issues. Hence, we will be able to explore the complex relationship between media usage and prominence and popular usage and support.

This chapter, then, is a first step in the analysis of the issue culture of social welfare policy. We suggest a signature matrix for the issue and, briefly, some of the resonances of these packages with cultural themes or counter themes.

## The Culture of Welfare Policy

We will describe four packages on welfare by using their signature elements. We have gleaned these elements from sponsor materials (that is, speeches, testimony, newsletters, pamphlets, and the like), books, journal articles, and commentary on the welfare issue, supplemented by exemplars from our sample of media materials. These packages address the question of what provisions, if any, should be made for the welfare of the poor.

### WELFARE FREELOADERS

A political cartoon is a compelling device and we will use one to introduce each package. A cartoon can draw on several different framing devices simultaneously—it presents a dynamic metaphor, particular visual imagery, and its caption can employ a catchphrase.

Consider the first cartoon, "Welfare—On the House," (Figure 22.1). The cartoonist shows a welfare bureaucrat and a bum, living it up on public funds. Note that the principal subject, "welfare recipient," is depicted here as a rather piggy-looking but robust and able-bodied male in the genteel hobo tradition. "On the house" and "welfare handouts" appear as catchphrases.

The signature exemplars for this package include celebrated cases of welfare fraud or welfare recipients driving Cadillacs. The lesson in either case is "Welfare recipients are playing us for suckers." "Workfare, not welfare" is a signature catchphrase and its depictions include welfare recipients as freeloaders or chiselers who could work at regular jobs if they chose to.

What is the frame being suggested by these various elements? The core issue in the social welfare controversy is "how to keep the country from going broke supporting a huge welfare bureaucracy and a lot of blacks and other minorities who are too lazy to work."

The root cause of the rapid rise of welfare roles lies in the personal failures of the welfare recipients who were either too profligate to acquire the necessary skills when they had a chance and/or too lazy to take available jobs when they can live on the dole. As for the consequences of the Family Assistance Plan, this package emphasizes the dangerous precedent of a guaranteed income, the

FIGURE 22.1 *Cartoon by Kevin Wachs (WOX).*

level of which will inevitably be raised, and the likelihood of vigorous political attacks on the work incentive portion of the plan. As Henry Hazlitt (1969) puts it, writing in the National Review, "Most certain of all, the whole program of trying to force people to work for their benefit payments will soon be denounced as a sort of slavery." The moral principle appealed to in this package is that of just deserts: People should not be rewarded unless they have earned it through honest, hard work.

The core policy position suggested by these justifications is one in which healthy adults should receive no form of welfare at all and the burden of proof is on the applicant. The less mean-spirited sponsors might exempt some marginal categories such as mothers of preschool children from the general work requirements. Specifying a more detailed position, one uncovers minor variations of these ideal-types.

## WORKING POOR

This package shifts attention somewhat from the personal failures of the poor. The poor are assumed to be rational in the sense that they will welcome the

"No, keep the dime. But Brother,
could you spare a job?"

**FIGURE 22.2**   *Cartoon by Kevin Wachs (WOX).*

ability to earn more through work but are discouraged in doing so by disincentives. As Milton Friedman puts it, "When you pay people to be poor, there are going to be plenty of poor people."

The second cartoon, (Figure 22.2), expresses it in the caption, "Brother, could you spare a job?" The poor person is represented as a man who prefers work to a handout. Its signature exemplars relate sad stories of people who have sought work, but who find that by working, they are worse off financially than they would be on welfare.

This package provides the official frame and justification for the Family Assistance Plan and it is not surprising that many of the key phrases are provided in Nixon's speech introducing the FAP. He speaks of "A way to independence through the dignity of work" and "The government's willingness to help the needy is linked to the willingness of the needy to help themselves." Its signature depictions focus less on the personal failures of the poor and more on the inadequacies of a welfare system that encourages dependency and penalizes those who would prefer to work.

The core issue in the welfare controversy is how to provide recipients with an incentive to work while providing adequate coverage for their basic needs. The root of this package recognizes the need for providing the poor with better job training and the discouraging effects of living in a culture of poverty, but assumes an underlying motivational structure in which individuals will choose work if they can receive significant financial gain for doing so.

Its fundamental appeal to principle goes back to the Poor Laws: "No one should receive more for being idle than for working." Or, as Nixon puts it, "It is morally wrong for a family that is working to try to make ends meet to receive less than the nonworking family across the street."

Within this basic package, there are a range of equally consistent positions on the value of the FAP. Administration officials argued that it achieved an appropriate balance by providing the poor with adequate minimum support while at the same time including requirements and incentives to work. Some critics of FAP challenged the balance on the grounds that the minimum support was not adequate and should be higher; other critics challenged that the work incentive portion was too weak and ineffective. But within these variations, the core position provides a policy in which no one starves but there are clear advantages for those who work.


POVERTY TRAP

Although the previous package contains some blame for the system, the poverty trap is more resolutely opposed to blaming the poor for their poverty. Ryan's (1976) catchphrase "blaming the victim" is one of its signature elements. As Figure 22.3 shows, the victim carriers the burdens of the system—lack of available jobs, poor schools, inflation, racial prejudice. On top of this, there is merely a false promise of prosperity if he should somehow make it up the steep cliff to the Employment Hilton.

To put welfare recipients through the humiliation of a means test is, in this view, a bit like knocking someone down and then demanding he produce a doctor's certificate of injury before he can be treated. Its signature exemplars include the kind of universal family allowance program found in European welfare states and in Israel. The lesson of these exemplars is that universal payment protects the dignity of the poor and makes sure that all can live adequately. Means-tests merely add insult to injury.

Poverty is depicted as a trap or a treadmill and the view of welfare recipients as able-bodied is dismissed as self-serving myth. Poverty is fundamentally a lack of money and power. As Ryan (1976) puts it, "The overwhelming majority of the poor are poor because they have, first, insufficient income; and second, no access to methods of increasing that income—that is, no power [p.140]." All of these devices suggest a core frame in which the issue is how to help the victims of poverty out of a trap that is not of their own making.

The root cause of poverty in this view is the failure of the economic system to provide full employment. George Meany said, "It does not serve the nation or its people to train the unemployed for jobs that don't exist." The FAP is clearly inadequate in this view since (*a*) most welfare recipients are unable to work; and (*b*) it does nothing to provide jobs for that portion of the poor who can work. The

**FIGURE 22.3** *Cartoon by Kevin Wachs (WOX).*

moral principle to which appeal is made focuses on the right of all citizens to a life of dignity free of the despair wrought by poverty.

The core policy position in this package rests on income maintenance and universal family allowances combined with economic programs aimed at creating a full employment economy.

**FIGURE 22.4** *Cartoon by Kevin Wachs (WOX).*

## REGULATING THE POOR

Our fourth cartoon (Figure 22.4) suggests the frame for this package. It is the only package in which the welfare system is viewed as working as it is supposed to. In this package, welfare serves a dual function. On the one hand, it regulates and maintains a labor reserve or, to use one of the catchphrases, "a reserve army of the unemployed." At the same time, relief functions to ameliorate discontent and assure quiescence and dependency in the "surplus population." In the cartoon, the business partner points out to his workers that there are unemployed waiting to take their jobs while the government partner provides a few welfare peanuts to the unemployed to keep them in line.

There is no clear exemplar for this package, but "regulating the poor" is its signature catchphrase. This phrase has the virtue of including both forms of regulation, each of which takes precedence at different stages. Piven and Cloward (1971) say that welfare reform, in this view, "signals a shift in emphasis between the major functions of relief arrangements—a shift from regulating disorder to regulating labor [p.342]. the poor in this package are depicted as a "surplus population" needed for capitalist accumulation (cf. Braverman 1974, and O'Connor 1973).

The core issue suggested by these framing devices is how to change an economic system in which poverty is a permanent feature and relief is provided to regulate the poor both through maintaining a labor reserve and through cooling out rebellious collective action.

The root cause of poverty in this package is the capitalist organization of production. The FAP would serve the purpose of increasing the capacity for social control of the poor without moving them out of poverty. "The work requirement" as a New York Times editorial (August 15, 1969) put it, "will become an instrument for herding the needy into dead-end jobs at rock-bottom wages." (It is interesting that this display of radicalism should come from such a good, gray paper.) The appeal to principle in this package is the familiar one, "From each according to his ability, to each according to his needs."

The core position of this package rejects welfare reform within a capitalist framework. The only solution to poverty and welfare is to institute a socialist economy in which there is work for everyone who is able-bodied and adequate support for those who are not.

Table 22.1 summarizes these packages in a signature matrix.

## Resonances with Cultural Themes

Beyond the issue culture, there is a larger political culture containing what are usually called ideologies or belief systems. These metapackages contain more general idea elements with potential applicability to a range of issues.

We deal with this level of analysis through the concept of cultural themes. These themes may be though of in a manner similar to packages—that is, they contain a core frame and a set of signature elements that provide this frame in shorthand.

We view themes as existing in a dialectic relationship with counterthemes. Expression of a countertheme has an adversarial quality; it is more common in the belief systems sponsored by challenging groups than in those of members. Themes, in contrast, have the status of pieties; one can safely intone them on ceremonial occasions with the assumption of general social approval, albeit some private cynicism.

The themes we focus on provide core frameworks for viewing politics in American society. They are analytically independent of one another but not mutually exclusive. Each of the themes and counterthemes has, elsewhere, a rich literature in which it is expressed or discussed.

A. *The technocratic theme.* "American emphasis upon efficiency has consistently impressed outside observers," Williams (1960, p.428) comments in his discussion of American values. " 'Efficient' is a word of high praise in a society that has long emphasized adaptability, technological innovation, economic expansion, up-to-dateness, practicality, expediency, 'getting things done.' [p.428]"' The inventor as cultural hero: Benjamin Franklin; Thomas Edison; mastery over nature is the way to progress; know-how; problem-solving.

This theme can be reflected in a view of politics. How can we solve the problem, how much is it going to cost, and is it worth it? As an organizing framework for an issue, the question resonates with this theme. Overtly nonideological, it presents itself as pragmatic, willing to try whatever is needed to do the job. Issues present technical problems to be solved and one ought to get the best expertise available to help overcome the problems that the country faces.

(a) *The soft-path countertheme.* American culture also contains a counter-theme, more skeptical of, or even hostile to, technology. Harmony with nature, rather than mastery over nature. We live on a "small planet." Our technology must be appropriate and in proper scale. There is an ecological balance to maintain. The more we try to control nature through our technology, the more we disrupt its natural order and threaten the quality of our lives.

Things are in the saddle, riding human beings. Chaplin's *Modern Times.* Huxley's *Brave New World.* Kubrick's *2001.* Runaway technology, out of control, carried on in the name of progress. In the words of the Joni Mitchell song, "Paved paradise, put up a parking lot."

B. *The pluralism theme.* We draw again on Williams's (1960) discussion of American values: "The theme of democracy was, concretely, an agreement upon procedure in distributing power in settling conflicts. Liberal democracy, American model, arose in reaction to an epoch in which the great threats to security and freedom were seen in strong, autocratic central government [p.461]."

As a view of politics, it is reflected in what Lowi (1967) called "interest group liberalism." "The most important difference between liberals and conserv-atives, Republicans and Democrats—however they define themselves—is to be found in the interest groups they identify with. Congressmen are guided in their votes, presidents in their programs, and administrators in their discretion, by whatever organized interests they have taken for themselves as the most legitimate; and that is the measure of the legitimacy of demands."

There are a lot of competing political groups in the United States and each group gets some of what it wants some of the time. If people do not like what is happening in the country, a majority can always change things by electing different officials. A political group that thinks it is not getting its fair share has plenty of opportunity to fight for a better share without breaking any rules.

America as a nation of minorities. The Federalist Papers. DeTocqueville's *Democracy in America.* Politics as the art of compromise. Half-a-loaf is better than none.

(b) *The egalitarian counter theme.* There is an antipluralist tradition that

**TABLE 22.1**
**Signature Matrix for Social Welfare Issue**

| Package | Core frame | Core position | Metaphor | Exemplars |
|---|---|---|---|---|
| Welfare freeloaders | The issue is how to keep the country from going broke supporting a huge welfare bureaucracy and a lot of blacks and other minorities who are too lazy to work. | Able-bodied people should not be given any money without requiring that they work for it. | A cartoon showing a gluttonous bureaucrat sharing a generous meal with a well-fed welfare bum at public expense | Stories of welfare fraud; welfare recipients driving Cadillacs<br><br>Lesson: Undeserving people are taking advantage of welfare. |
| Working poor | The issue is how to provide recipients with an incentive to work while providing adequate coverage for their basic needs. | A minimum support level should be provided so that no one starves while at the same time, manpower training and extra rewards should be offered to encourage the able and willing to work. | A cartoon showing a poor person disdaining a handout while eagerly accepting an offer of honest work. | Stories of deserving poor who choose work over the dole but find that they lose money by doing so<br><br>Lesson: Many on welfare would prefer to work given adequate incentives and skills. |
| Poverty trap | The issue is how to help the victims of poverty out of a trap that is not of their own making. | Welfare measures such as a universal family allowance, income maintenance, and unemployment insurance for the long-term unemployed should be provided along with programs aimed at creating more jobs. | Requiring a dehumanizing means test is like knocking someone down and then demanding that he produce a doctor's certificate before he can be treated. | Family allowance programs in European welfare states<br><br>Lesson: A universal payment system protects the dignity the poor and makes sure that all can live adequately. |
| Regulating the poor | The issue is how to change an economic system in which poverty is a permanent feature, and relief giving serves to regulate the poor by maintaining a labor reserve and cooling out rebellious collective action. | Poverty cannot be eliminated within a capitalist framework. The only solution is to institute a socialist economy in which there is work for everyone who is able-bodied and adequate support for those who are not. | A cartoon showing two fat capitalists, one facing a group of poor people, the other a group of factory workers; the workers are warned that others would like their jobs and the poor are given a few crumbs and a vague promise of future work to keep them in line | |

**TABLE 22.1** *Continued*

| Catchphrases | Depictions | Roots | Consequences of FAP | Appeals to principle |
|---|---|---|---|---|
| Workfare, not welfare. | Welfare recipients as "freeloaders," "bums," "chiselers" Welfare payments as "handouts" | Welfare rolls are inflated because of individual laziness and personal failure to acquire adequate work skills on the part of the recipient. | FAP would set a bad precedent since the support floor will inevitably be raised and the work incentive portion attacked as some sort of slavery or forced labor. | Rewards should be commensurate with effort. People should not be rewarded unless they have earned it through honest, hard work. |
| A way to independence through the dignity of work. The government's willingness to help the needy is linked to the willingness of the needy to help themselves. When you pay people to be poor, there are going to be plenty of poor people. | Present welfare system as offering disincentives to work and degrading recipient by encouraging dependency. | Welfare roles are inflated because the poor lack adequate job skills, have poor motivation, and have been socialized into a self-perpetuating culture of poverty, and because the welfare system provides disincentives to work. | ProFAP: FAP achieves an appropriate balance by providing the poor with adequate minimum support plus the incentive to work. AntiFAP$_1$: The floor for minimum support is not high enough. AntiFAP$_2$: The work incentive is too weak and ineffective. | No one should receive more for being idle than for working. It is morally wrong for a family that is working to try to make ends meet, to receive less than the nonworking family across the street. |
| Blaming the victim. Guaranteed income. The disillusioned poor, trapped in a prison of poverty and dispair. It does not serve the nation or its people to train the unemployed for jobs that don't exist. | Poverty as a trap; the welfare system as a treadmill; means tests as an affront to dignity or humiliating; the idea of welfare recipients as being able bodied is false and a myth. | Economic policies that fail to provide full employment. | FAP is inadequate because most welfare recipients are unable to work and it fails to address the economic roots of poverty. | Every citizen has the right to a life of dignity, free of the despair wrought by poverty. |
| Regulating the poor. Surplus population. Reserve army of the unemployed. | Poverty as serving the interest of the rich and powerful; welfare and relief giving as means of social control | The root cause of poverty is the capitalist mode of production. | FAP would increase the capacity for social control of the poor but not move them out of poverty. The work requirement will become an instrument for herding the needy into dead-end jobs at rock-bottom wages. | From each according to his ability, to each according to his needs. |

emphasizes the elitist nature of the American political system and its departure from a more egalitarian ideal. The contemporary version is reflected in Wolin's (1981) editorial in the opening issue of the new journal, *Democracy: A Journal of Political Renewal and Radical Change*. "Every one of the country's primary institutions—the business corporation, the government bureaucracy, the trade union, the research and education industries, the mass propaganda and entertainment media, and the health and welfare system—is antidemocratic in spirit, design, and operation. Each is hierarchical in structure, authority oriented, opposed in principle to equal participation, unaccountable to the citizenry, elitist and managerial, and disposed to concentrate increasing power in the hands of the few and to reduce political life to administration [p. 2]."

Elections do not change anything since the people being elected do not have the real power. The rules of American politics favor the rich and powerful few at the expense of the many. Political groups that are not getting their fair share will never get anywhere unless they're willing to break some rules.

The people versus the interests. Mills' *The Power Elite*. The ruling class. The military-industrial complex. In earlier eras, "share the wealth," "every man a king." The robber barons. Citizen Paine.

C. *The civic duty theme.* "Ask not what your country can do for you, but what you can do for your country," President Kennedy told a responsive audience. Ordinary people have a duty to participate in the affairs of their local community—at the very least, to vote. As Gans (1979) puts it, in describing values in the news, "Citizens should participate and 'grassroots activity' is one of the most complimentary terms in the vocabulary of the news."

In peacetime, the role of the citizen remains a relatively passive one—to pay taxes, obey the law, keep informed, and vote intelligently at election time. In times of war, disaster, or other crisis, the obligations of a citizen may expand and sacrifices may be required. At such times, the president has a special role in defining civic duty and what is expected of citizens.

"The news upholds the legitimacy of holders of formal authority," Gans (1979, p. 44) suggests, "as long as they abide by the relevant enduring values, both in public and private realms [p. 60]." Let them depart from it, and they are fair game. Political machines, corruption, and bureaucratic malfunctioning are departures from an unstated ideal. Politics should "follow a course based on the public interest and public service [p. 43].

Everyone has a responsibility to vote even if he does not care much about the outcome. It is the duty of every citizen to obey the law no matter how much he or she may disagree with it. Every American traveling abroad is an ambassador for the United States.

(c) *The rebellion countertheme.* The countertheme emphasizes rebellion and the duty to disobey unjust authority. To quote Jefferson, "The tree of liberty must be refreshed from time to time with the blood of patriots and tyrants. It is its natural manure." It is the use of power to destroy liberty that is the primary problem, not the abuse of power for personal gain. The countertheme is distrustful of the claims of authority. "Don't tread on me."

*The rebel as hero.* It is the duty of every citizen to follow his conscience even if it means breaking the law. Obedience may lead to evil. Witness the good German carrying out his duty in the Third Reich. Witness My Lai. The hero resists, survives attack, triumphs in the end. Muhammad Ali. Jane Fonda.

D. *The self-reliance theme.* Striving, risk taking, achieving, independence. To try hard against difficult obstacles is creditable. To fail because of lack of effort when success is possible is reprehensible. Calculated risk taking is frequently necessary to overcome obstacles and, indeed, is part of striving. One cannot expect everything to fall one's way and bad luck is simply an obstacle that one must overcome—not something to whine about.

Starting out poor is a special case of bad luck. The truly admirable are those who, by striving, were able to overcome the obstacles of humble birth and go on to fame and fortune. The self-made man embodies all of these ideals—a person who has pluck and resourcefulness, tries hard, makes use of the opportunities that come his way and is not thrown off or demoralized by the bad luck he encounters, learns by his mistakes and improves, until he makes it. Horatio Alger.

"The 'success story' and the respect accorded to the self-made man are distinctly American, if anything is," writes Williams (1960). "The ideal individual struggles successfully against adversity and overcomes more powerful forces . . . .'Self-made' men and women remain attractive, as do people who overcome poverty or bureaucracy," writes Gans (1979, p. 50).

The best thing that we can teach children is how to stand on their own two feet. The people to admire are those who start at the bottom and work hard to get ahead, relying on their own judgment and resources rather than on others.

(d) *The mutuality countertheme.* The countertheme emphasizes emotional bonding over self-reliance, and selflessness over individualism. The ideal is one of a community of intimates who are caring and sensitive and place the needs of others ahead of their own. Striving for success is an ego trip.

The best thing we can teach children is to need and care about other people. The people to admire are those who are more concerned about being true to their friends than about getting ahead. One should try to understand and respect others' point of view even if it means reconsidering what one thinks.

# Welfare Resonances

The various packages that comprise the culture of the welfare issue resonate in different ways with these broader themes and counterthemes. These resonances, we argue, give the packages special appeal, amplifying them and increasing their media usage, prominence of display, and popular usage.

Resonance with themes is more helpful, of course, than with counterthemes. But even resonance with counterthemes gives a package special appeal in various adversarial subcultures.

The four pairs of theme and countertheme define a four-dimensional space into which we can map the different welfare packages. A package may resonate with more than one theme or countertheme. To determine resonance, one compares the signature elements of each package with corresponding elements in the theme. A metaphor in one package, for example, may be similar to or identical with a characteristic metaphor of some theme or countertheme.

Applied to the welfare packages, we argue that both the welfare-free-loaders and working-poor packages—particularly the former—have a strong resonance with the self-reliance theme. Rewards should be commensurate with effort. No one should receive more for being idle than for working. Welfare encourages dependence and laziness. One should help the needy to help themselves. Workfare, not welfare.

Although it has a weaker resonance with the self-reliance theme, the working poor package also has a strong resonance with the technology theme. The core problem to be solved is simultaneously providing a minimum support level and a work incentive, a trade-off between two functions. Technical evaluations by economists and other professionals are required in executing the policies called for by this package. Here is the package that comes closest to calling for a technofix.

Both the poverty trap and regulating the poor packages resonate with the egalitarian counter theme. Poverty is a reflection on the unfulfilled democratic promise of equality of outcome, of a fair share for everyone. From each according to his ability, to each according to his need. Inequality of power lies behind inequality of income. Poverty serves the interests of the rich and powerful, and welfare functions as a means of social control.

In addition, the poverty trap package has some resonance with the mutuality countertheme. A fair share is an entitlement of citizenship. Family allowance and minimum income programs reflect a social responsibility for the needy that should be present in a decent society.

## Conclusion

This chapter has presented a general strategy for analysing the political culture of an issue. We have applied the first step to the social welfare issue. Ultimately, studies that present taxonomies and analytic schemes leave one up in the air. The question inevitably arises as to what one can do with them.

We have indicated our intention of measuring media usage and prominence of display of the different packages using a systematic sample of mass media materials. Although this alone can enhance our understanding of political culture, charting the ebb and flow of prominence and media usage over time provides a more dynamic view. Thanks to such modern conveniences as video tape and microfilm, we are able to follow a cartoon strip over a period of 20 or 30 years, charting the changes in our measures.

This analysis becomes more interesting still when we consider it jointly with popular usage and support. In the next phase of our research, we will assemble groups in which selected issues will be discussed among peers, using cartoons and other material from our signature matrix as the stimulus material for such discussions. From such discourse, we can explore the complex relationship between media usage and display, and popular usage and support.

# References

Bennett, W. 1975. *The political mind in the political environment.* Lexington, Mass.: D.C. Heath & Co.

Bowler, M.K. 1974. *The Nixon guaranteed income proposal.* Cambridge, Mass.: Ballinger Publishing Co.

Braverman, H. 1974. *Labor and monopoly capital.* New York: Monthly Review Press.

Burke, K. 1969. *A grammar of motives.* Berkeley: University of California Press.

Edelman, M. 1964. *The symbolic uses of politics.* Urbana, Ill.: University of Illinois Press.

Edelman, M. 1971. *Politics as symbolic action.* Chicago: Markham Publishing Co.

Edelman, M. 1977. *Political language: Words that succeed and policies that fail.* New York: Academic Press.

Gamson, W.A. 1975. *The strategy of social protest.* Homewood, Ill.: Dorsey Press.

Gans, H. 1979. *Deciding what's news.* New York: Pantheon Books.

Halberstam, D. 1979. *The powers that be.* New York: Knopf.

Hazlitt, H. 1969. Welfarism out of control. *National Review* 21: 903.

Heffernan, W.J. 1974. The failure of welfare reform: A political farce in two acts. Institute for Research on Poverty: Discussion Papers. Madison: University of Wisconsin.

Lakoff, G., and Johnson, M. 1979. Toward an experimentalist philosophy: The case from literal metaphor. Working Paper. University of California, Berkeley.

Lowi, T. 1967. The public philosophy: Interest group liberalism. *American Political Science Review* 61: 5–24.

Marmor, T., and Rein, M., 1972. Flim, flam, flop in welfare. *Society* 9: 38–41.

McCarthy, J.D., and Zald, M.N. 1977. Resource mobilization and social movements. *American Journal of Sociology* 82: 1212–1241.

O'Connor, J. 1973. *The fiscal crisis of the state.* New York: St. Martin's Press.

Piven, F.F., and Cloward, R. 1971. *Regulating the poor.* New York: Random House.

Ryan, W. 1976. *Blaming the victim.* New York: Random House.

Tilly, C. 1978. *From mobilization to revolution.* Reading, Mass.: Addison–Wesley.

Willet, J. 1980. Art in the Third Reich. *New York Review of Books,* June 26, 6.

Williams, R.M. Jr. 1960. *American society.* New York: Alfred A. Knopf.

Wolin, S. 1981. Editorial statement. *Democracy: A Journal of Political Renewal and Radical Change* 1:2–4.

# Index